Book-keeping

Made Simple

The Made Simple series
has been created
especially for self-education
but can equally well
be used as
an aid to group study.
However complex the subject,
the reader is taken
step by step,
clearly and methodically,
through the course. Each volume
has been prepared by experts,
taking account of
modern educational requirements,
to ensure the most
effective way of
acquiring knowledge.

In the same series

Accounting
Advertising
Auditing
Biology
Book-keeping
British Constitution
Business Calculations
Business and Enterprise
  Studies
Business Law
Calculus
Chemistry
Child Development
Commerce
Computer Electronics
Computer Programming
Computer Typing
Cost and Management Accounting
Economic and Social Geography
Economics
Education
Electricity
Electronics
Elements of Banking
English
Financial Management
First Aid
French
German

Graphic Communication
Italian
Latin
Law
Management
Marketing
Mathematics
Modern European History
Modern World History
MSX
Music
Office Practice
Personnel Management
Philosophy
Photography
Physical Geography
Physics
Politics
Psychiatry
Psychology
Russian
Salesmanship
Secretarial Practice
Social Services
Sociology
Spanish
Statistics
Teeline Shorthand
Typing

Preface

This revised edition of what has become a very popular textbook all over the world, covers all the basic principles of elementary book-keeping and provides the student with numerous practice exercises of graded difficulty. Worked examples and test pages help the student to arrive at a complete understanding of one topic before another is introduced.

Although principally designed for self-study, the book is of equal value to schools and colleges. Teachers will find that it meets their requirements for examinations up to the General Certificate of Secondary Education and covers the syllabuses of all elementary examinations.

The Answer section which appears at the back of the book gives the answers to all the exercises and at least one exercise in each set has been fully worked in examination form so that students studying alone can see a typical answer in good style as it should be presented in examinations.

In writing books today authors must constantly face criticisms about the use of pronouns such as he and she, which appear to give a sexist bias to the description of business events. The law on this point is quite clear – the Interpretation Act 1978 makes it clear that whenever a male word is used the female word is also intended and vice-versa. Therefore, where attempts to 'write out' the use of a sexist pronoun would result in a dull, less-lively text, the male word has been used.

One word of advice to the student working alone: Work at your own pace. If you find you have assimilated all the important points of a chapter and have satisfactorily answered some of the questions, go on to the next chapter; don't feel you have to work laboriously through all the questions in a section simply because they are there. On the other hand, if you still feel a little doubtful about some aspects of a topic, continue to work at the questions, referring back where necessary, until you have a full grasp of the subject.

In preparing this book I have received much helpful assistance from a number of business firms and individuals. Whilst expressing my grateful thanks for their assistance I must take full responsibility for all statements, calculations, etc., made in the book.

Teachers of book-keeping often have to invent their own questions, especially the easier ones, which introduce the student gradually to difficulties likely to be met in the final examination. In inventing such questions the names of former students fly into the brain much more easily than the names of imaginary people; if any former students of mine recognize themselves in an exercise I hope they will take it as a sign of my affectionate regard.

Geoffrey Whitehead

This book is jointly dedicated to my wife, Joan, and to the tutorial and administrative staff of the Commerce Degree Bureau, London University.

Contents

Contents xiii

1
Starting a business – a capital idea

1.1 Starting a business

When we consider setting up in business we do so because we feel
that we have some useful product, or service, to offer to our fellow
men. We live in a world where people want things from the day
they are born to the day that they die. Some of these 'wants' are
physical wants, a need for goods of various sorts, food, clothing,
shelter, and so on. Some of them are emotional 'wants', a need for
education, entertainment, or recreation. In satisfying such wants
business people perform useful services to their fellow humans. In
return they expect to earn a reasonable reward for their efforts in
the form of profits on the enterprise.

Before such profits can be earned we must establish the
enterprise. This involves three things: (a) a location (premises of
some kind), (b) other assets (furniture, equipment, etc.) and (c)
an organization. Having determined where and how we will
conduct our affairs we may offer our goods and services to the
public. The provision of these three things requires a fund of
money, called the proprietor's capital. Capital is essential to the
start of any enterprise, and while many businesses start off in a
small way, growth is only possible if further capital is accumulated
as the years go by. The provision of the initial capital is the first
transaction that takes place.

1.2 Business transactions

The noun 'transaction' implies a transfer of goods or services from
one person to another. Any type of business deal, however simple
or complicated, is a transaction. Millions of transactions take place
every day. Where the transaction involves the provision of goods
or services in return for immediate payment it is called a **cash
transaction.** Where payment is delayed until a later date it is called

a **credit transaction**. The provision of the goods or the provision of services is really a separate activity from the payment. The two activities are:

(a) The good, or service is supplied.
(b) Payment is made for it.

The time interval between the happening of event (a) and event (b) is termed the period of credit, and varies from no time at all in the case of a cash transaction to years in the case of such transactions as hire purchase, or mortgage arrangements.

1.3 Keeping a record of transactions – the Ledger Accounts

The primary purpose of keeping a record of transactions is to record the debts of other people to the business and the debts of the business to other firms. In order to control expenses it is useful to keep a record of payments made even if they were cash transactions, and no actual debt was involved. Finally, in most countries today the government is interested in securing a share of the profits of a business, so that accurate records are required for taxation purposes. These records also enable proprietors to decide whether the profits earned make the business worth while, or whether the trouble is too great for the reward earned.

These records are kept in a book called a **Ledger**. It takes its name from a Saxon word meaning 'the one that lies' on a merchant's counters. The word here means 'lies down', it has nothing to do with telling lies. A ledge is a level shelf. In the early counting houses the ledger lay on a ledge, usually under a window where the light was good. Each page in the Ledger is called an **Account,** and bears at the top the name of the person, or good, or thing which is being accounted for. Figure 1.1 shows a page in the Ledger. You should note the following points:

(a) The page is divided down the middle
(b) The left-hand side is called the **debit** side, or **debtor** side, and often has the abbreviation Dr. printed at the top.

Dr.							Cr.
Debit Side				Credit Side			
Date	Details	Folio	Cash	Date	Details	Folio	Cash

Figure 1.1 The Ledger page

(c) The right-hand side is called the **credit** side, or **creditor** side, and often has the abbreviation Cr. printed at the top.

(d) Columns are drawn on *each* side for the date, details, folio numbers (to be explained later), and cash.

The student should purchase a supply of ledger paper, or a small ledger booklet, from a stationer.

1.4   The first transaction – the contribution of the assets by the proprietor

When starting a business the very first transaction that takes place is the transfer to the firm of the owner's accumulated capital. These valuables may be money, stock, equipment, or vehicles which will in future be regarded as the property of the firm. Such valuables are called **Assets,** and the proprieter is called a **sole trader.**

1.5   Classifying the assets – current and fixed

The assets may be divided into two main groups. The first group consists of assets which are intended in the course of events to be changed into cash. These are called **Circulating**, or **Current, Assets** (French *courrant* = running). Figure 1.2 illustrates this class of assets.

Figure 1.2   Circulating Assets, or Current Assets

The commonest current assets are:

Cash in Hand
Cash at Bank
Debtors
Stock
Investments

Note: If investments are held as a useful way of earning money with idle cash not at present required in the business they are current assets.

Other assets are used to carry on the business. They are called **Fixed Assets** because they cannot be sold without seriously interfering with the conduct of the business. They will be used to manufacture, warehouse, or sell the goods offered by the proprietor, or to provide the services he makes available to the general public.

The commonest fixed assets are:

Land and Buildings
Plant and Machinery
Furniture and Fittings
Motor Vehicles

1.6   Opening the Ledger

Let us imagine that a businessman, John Brown, is about to start a firm in the clothing trade. He is a qualified craftsman and has been saving up hard, that is, he has been accumulating capital. He hears of suitable premises to rent, and decides to take them. To begin his book-keeping he buys a small Ledger.

He takes the first page and records his cash on it, say £3 000.00. This is the amount of **Capital** he is contributing to the business. He puts the cash on the debit side of the Cash Account, as shown in Figure 1.3. He enters the same amount of capital on his Capital Account, as shown in Figure 1.4 on the credit side. A full explanation of the use of debit and credit columns is given on page 16.

Dr.		CASH ACCOUNT					L1 Cr.
19. . Jan. 1	Capital	L2	£ 3 000.00				

Figure 1.3   The Cash Account

The Ledger is now in full working order as the opening entries have been made. We shall see later that a more formal way of opening the books is used in real life, through an entry called an **Opening Journal Entry.** For the present our two accounts will illustrate the opening of the books adequately.

The proprietor has contributed £3 000.00 of assets, which appears on the debit side of the Cash Account. To balance this, £3 000.00 appears on the credit side of the Capital Account. Another name for the Capital is the **Net Worth** of the business to the owner. The sole trader's capital account will always show the net worth, that is the clear worth of the business to the owner, and this will be, in a simple case like this, equal to the assets of the business. This equality is clearly shown if we draw up a Balance Sheet.

Dr.				CAPITAL ACCOUNT – JOHN BROWN			L2 Cr.
				19. . Jan. 1	Cash	L1	£ 3 000.00

Figure 1.4   The Capital Account

1.7   The Balance Sheet – and an oddity of history

A Balance Sheet is a list of the accounts in the Ledger. On one side it shows the accounts that have a debit balance, and on the other side the accounts that have a credit balance.

It would be extremely sensible if these were listed in the same way that they appear in the Ledger, with the assets on the left-hand side and the **liabilities** on the right-hand side, as shown in Figure 1.5(*a*):

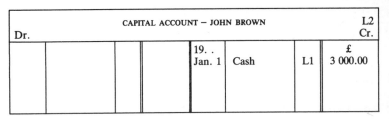

JOHN BROWN
BALANCE SHEET
as at January 1, 19. .

CURRENT ASSETS	£	CAPITAL	£
Cash	3 000.00	At Start	3 000.00
	£3 000.00		£3 000.00

Figure 1.5(*a*)   A simple Balance Sheet in logical form

But they are not listed this way at all. By a peculiar quirk of history the countries associated with Britain including South Africa, Australia, New Zealand, India, and Malaya have developed the habit of presenting the Balance Sheet the wrong way round. It is illogical that we do so. (A full explanation is given on page 252). John Brown's Balance Sheet would therefore appear as follows (Figure 1.5(*b*)).

We can see that a Balance Sheet is what its name says, a sheet on which we make a list of balances that already exist on the accounts. *Nothing can appear on a Balance Sheet unless it actually appears as a balance on one of the pages of the Ledger already.*

JOHN BROWN
BALANCE SHEET
as at January 1, 19. .

CAPITAL		£	CURRENT ASSETS		£
At Start		3 000.00	Cash		3 000.00
		£3 000.00			£3 000.00

Figure 1.5(*b*)   A simple Balance Sheet in traditional British style

1.8   Buying assets for use in the business

Let us continue for a little while with Mr Brown's affairs. He will have to pay out some rent for those premises, and buy sewing machines, work benches, and other assets.

The money spent will be recorded on the credit side of the Cash Account, and on the debit side of the Rent Account, Furniture Account, and Machinery Account. To save drawing a Ledger Account each time we will use accounts without column rulings to show quickly what these entries look like.

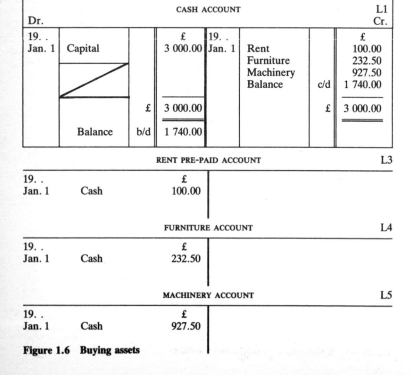

Figure 1.6   Buying assets

Brown's Balance Sheet will now have altered as shown in Figure 1.7. The capital still remains at £3 000.00, but the asset cash has been partly changed into other assets, some of which are Current Assets and some are Fixed Assets.

JOHN BROWN
BALANCE SHEET
as at January 1, 19. .

CAPITAL	£	CURRENT ASSETS		£
At Start	3 000.00	Cash	1 740.00	
		Rent Pre-paid	100.00	
				1 840.00
		FIXED ASSETS		
		Furniture	232.50	
		Machinery	927.50	
				1 160.00
	£3 000.00			£3 000.00

Figure 1.7   A more advanced Balance Sheet

1.9   Transactions involving liabilities

When a cash transaction takes place the goods are transferred at the same time as the payment is made, and neither party is in debt to the other. When the proprietor of a business purchases assets on credit, he incurs a liability to pay. Usually this liability will be discharged at the end of the month, when the seller renders a **Statement of Account,** which the purchaser pays. A credit transaction therefore involves a liability to pay in due course. It is the normal business procedure between businessmen who are known to one another as reliable.

The person supplying the goods becomes a **Creditor** *of the person receiving the goods. The person receiving the goods becomes a* **Debtor** *of the person supplying the goods.*

The following illustrations shows such a transaction. John Brown has ordered a second-hand motor vehicle from Rex Garages Ltd for £800.00. The payment will be made one month later. In the meantime Motor Vehicles Account will be debited with the value of the vehicle received and Rex Garages Limited will become a creditor for £800.00.

MOTOR VEHICLES ACCOUNT   L6

19. .		£	
Jan. 1	Rex Garages Ltd	800.00	

REX GARAGES LTD ACCOUNT   L7

		19. .		£
		Jan. 1	Motor Vehicles	800.00

Figure 1.8   A transaction which incurs a liability

1.10 Classification of liabilities – Current Liabilities, Long-term Liabilities, and Capital

The type of liability referred to in the last paragraph will be settled at the end of the month, usually by cheque. It is therefore of a current nature, it will be wholly settled within the next few weeks. Such liabilities are called **Current Liabilities.** Any liability which will be settled in less than a year is called by this name, but the usual length of time will be much less, accounts being settled monthly.

The commonest types of Current Liability are:

Creditors (Accounts Payable)
Wages Due
Salaries Due
Commission Due
Bank Overdrafts (these are very short-term loans which the bank can require us to repay at short notice)

A second type of liability is called a **Long-term Liability.** This is usually a formal loan of money either from a bank or a building society or some other institutional investor like a finance company. These liabilities are evidenced by a formal agreement stating the amount of the loan, the terms of repayment, the rate of interest, and the **Collateral Security** provided. Collateral means 'lying alongside' and the security provided may be a mortgage on the deeds of the proprietor's property or a life assurance policy on his life.

The commonest types of long-term liability are:

Bank Loans
Private Loans
Finance House Loans
Mortgages

The third type of liability is the Capital itself. It is what the business owes back to the owner of the business. It is helpful if the student acquires early in his studies the habit of regarding the proprietor as someone separate from the business. In the final analysis he/she is *the last creditor* of the firm.

1.11 Buying assets on credit and borrowing money

To continue our study of John Brown's affairs. He has furniture and machinery, and he has rented premises, but he still has no material to make the suits and other garments he hopes to produce. He will also need to pay wages and is therefore anxious to keep some of his capital in cash form. He sees his local bank manager who agrees to make him a loan of £5 000.00 repayable over three years, provided that Brown deposits £1 500.00 in his current account and also takes out a life assurance policy as collateral. This Brown does, paying a premium of £100.00 for the first year. He also buys on credit (payable at the end of January) £1 500.00 worth of material, cottons, etc. These assets will mean further items on the assets side of the Balance Sheet, but these are not balanced by increased capital, but by the new types of liability, Current Liabilities and Long-term Liabilities.

His Balance Sheet now reads:

JOHN BROWN
BALANCE SHEET
as at January 1, 19. .

	£		£	£
CURRENT LIABILITIES		CURRENT ASSETS		
Creditors	2 300.00	Cash in Hand	240.00	
		Cash in Bank	6 400.00	
		Stock	1 500.00	
		Rent Pre-paid	100.00	
		Assurance Pre-paid	100.00	
LONG-TERM LIABILITIES				
Bank Loan	5 000.00			8 340.00
CAPITAL		FIXED ASSETS	£	
At Start	3 000.00	Furniture	232.50	
		Machinery	927.50	
		Motor Vehicle	800.00	
				1 960.00
	£10 300.00			£10 300.00

Figure 1.9   A complete Balance Sheet

NOTE:

(a) The date of the Balance Sheet has been given at the top.
(b) The separate classes of assets have been sub-totalled. This is very useful in bringing out certain statistical control figures required later.
(c) The separate classes of liabilities have been similarly displayed.
(d) The Net Worth (Capital Fund) is no longer equal to the assets, because other liabilities have entered the equation.

1.12   A page to test you on capital, assets, and liabilities

Cover the page with a sheet of paper, then read a question at a time.

Answers	Questions
	1 What is business?
1 Business is the conduct of commercial activities to produce goods and services in return for profit.	2 What word is used to describe each business deal?
2 Each deal is called a transaction.	3 What is the function of book-keeping?
3 It is to record transactions.	4 What twofold process is involved in transactions?
4(a) The provision of a good or a service to the customer; (b) the payment by the customer.	5 What is a cash transaction?
5 It is one where the goods are supplied and the money paid at precisely the same moment.	6 What is a credit transaction?
6 It is a transaction where the goods or services are supplied, but payment is delayed until a later time.	7 What is the most usual credit period?
7 Cash 30 days.	8 What are assets?
8 They are goods bought for use in the conduct of the business.	9 What are fixed assets?
9 Assets of a durable nature for long-term use in the business.	10 Name four fixed assets.
10 Land and Buildings; Plant and Machinery; Furniture and Fittings; Motor Vehicles.	11 What are current assets?
11 Assets which change into cash as business continues.	12 Name four current assets.
12 Stock in Trade; Debtors; Cash at Bank; Cash in Hand.	13 What are liabilities?
13 They are the debts for which a business is liable.	14 What are the chief classes of liabilities?
14 Current Liabilities; Long-term Liabilities; Capital.	15 Name three current liabilities.
15 Creditors; Wages Due; Rent Due.	16 Name three Long-term Liabilities.
16 Bank Loans; Private Loans; and Mortgages.	17 What is Capital?
17 It is the sum contributed by the owner to the business, or accumulated by him out of profits ploughed back into the firm.	18 What is collateral security?
18 It is a security lying alongside a debt – often the deeds to a property or a life assurance policy.	19 How many did you answer correctly? Go over the list again.

1.13 Answers to exercises in *Book-keeping Made Simple*

Success in book-keeping can only be achieved if students work a comprehensive set of questions, and answer them in good style as required in examinations and in the real world of accountancy. For this reason the book contains a large number of graded exercises and a full set of answers, one of each set showing exactly how each answer should appear, in good style.

The best method of using these answers is as follows:

(a) Make up your mind at the very start to work every question in this textbook, in correct sequence. They are carefully graded – difficulties increase as you do each question in the set.

(b) Try the first question in any set. If you get hopelessly bogged down, turn to the question which is answered fully in the answer book and see where every item in the question goes. Work it through carefully with the answer.

(c) Now try another question unaided. You will do better this time. Compare your result with the answer book.

(d) Buy a lever arch file and make sections in it for each chapter of the book. File away your completed answers in this file. Don't take any notice of other students who say 'Why do you work so hard – you don't have to do everything'. On examination day they will realize why you did it!

(e) Don't expect your teacher/lecturer to mark all your work – they simply could not do it. It is part of your training to appraise your own work – that's what you have to do in real life. The book-keeper keeps a set of books, does his/her best with them, proves as much as possible that everything is all right and argues with the auditor, the accountant or the Inland Revenue authorities if they claim something is not correct. There is no teacher or lecturer to hold your hand in the real world of employment. The answers we have provided are all the help you need.

1.14 Opening Balance Sheets

The usual time for preparing a Balance Sheet is at the end of the financial year when we are trying to determine the profitability of the business. This is explained fully later (see page 251) but here it is important to mention that a Balance Sheet should be prepared on the very first day of a business.

This *opening Balance Sheet* tells us the opening position, what assets we have, what liabilities we have incurred and how much capital the proprietor has contributed. From this opening Balance

Sheet the accounts can be opened, and we are off on our book-keeping activities for the years and years that lie ahead of us.

1.15   Exercises set 1.1 – Opening Balance Sheets

1. Prepare a Balance Sheet from the following information, as at January 1, 19. ., of Alice Spring's affairs:

Cash in Hand	1 000.00
Cash at Bank	49 000.00
Stock-in-Trade	62 500.00
Land and Buildings	40 000.00
Office Equipment	32 500.00
Prepaid Rent	2 500.00
Capital (at Start)	187 500.00

2. Prepare a Balance Sheet of A. Londoner's affairs from the following information, as at January 1, 19. .:

Cash in Hand	8 000.00
Cash at Bank	27 000.00
Stock	52 500.00
Office Equipment	2 500.00
Land and Buildings	75 000.00
Advertising Prepaid	1 250.00
Capital (at Start)	166 250.00

3 and 4. Prepare Balance Sheets from the figures given. On these two you will have to find out the capital for yourself. Date, January 1, 19. .:

Sole Traders	John Smith	Peter Green
Cash in Hand	127.50	213.00
Cash at Bank	6 352.50	8 027.00
Trade Debtors	5 226.00	8 631.50
Stock	12 356.50	13 126.50
Prepaid Expenses	42.50	32.00
Motor Vehicles	9 375.00	2 750.00
Furniture	5 900.00	2 475.00
Plant and Machinery	14 825.00	9 375.00
Land and Buildings	36 300.00	13 200.00

5 and 6. On the last two Balance Sheets you will have to work out the Capital, but do not forget that as there are some Current Liabilities and Long-Term Liabilities the Net Worth equation now reads:

$$Assets = Current\ Liabilities \\ +\ Long\text{-}term\ Liabilities \\ +\ Capital$$

Proprietor	No. 5 Jan. 1, 19. . Mark Jones	No. 6 Jan. 1, 19. . Peter Clemens
Cash in Hand	122.50	162.50
Cash at Bank	5 302.50	3 632.50
Trade Debtors	6 182.50	7 921.25
Stock	4 725.00	7 600.00
Prepaid Expenses	87.50	86.25
Motor Vehicles	8 752.50	8 277.50
Furniture	1 329.00	1 627.50
Plant and Machinery	6 736.00	36 200.00
Land and Buildings	15 000.00	20 000.00
Creditors	5 250.00	5 260.00
Wages Due	487.50	247.50
Mortgage	10 000.00	15 000.00
Bank Loan	7 500.00	5 000.00

2
The Ledger –
the main book of account

2.1 Introduction

From the earliest days of book-keeping until the last century the
Ledger was a bound book which was left in the counting house on
a ledge fitted against the wall. The clerk would record all the
transactions in date order in a daily record (a Day Book or Journal
– which will be dealt with shortly). He then 'posted' these daily
transactions into the Ledger Accounts.

Businesses are much larger today, and it is impracticable to keep
the Ledger as a bound book. Loose-leaf books, card indexes, and
computer records may now take the place of the bound book, but
the Ledger is still the main book of account and must be posted
daily with all the transactions that take place. In this chapter we
attempt to develop a real understanding of Ledger Accounts.

The Ledger, then, is the main book of account. It has pages
which are numbered, and each page is called 'an account'. The
numbers are written in the top right-hand corner and are called
folio numbers (Latin *folium*, leaf).

2.2 Use of the accounts

Transactions take place every day. Each transaction involves a
change in the assets or liabilities of the business. We may spend
cash and buy postage stamps, or sell stock and receive cash. To
record these changes the Ledger is used. The record, or account,
of each change in the value of an asset is to be found somewhere in
the Ledger. An expenditure of cash will be recorded in the Cash
Account. The purchase of furniture will be recorded in the
Furniture Account. The loss of wealth that occurs when a debtor
goes bankrupt will be recorded in the Bad Debts Account.

An account may therefore be defined as a record of the changes
occurring under a particular heading.

2.3   The three types of account

There are three kinds of account: personal accounts, real accounts, and nominal accounts.

Figure 2.1   Bob Cratchet at work on the Ledger in Scrooge's office (Charles Dickens, *A Christmas Carol*)

Personal accounts
Every personal account has the name of a person with whom the business deals at the top. These may be sole traders (Tom Jones, for instance) or partnerships (Brown and Green) or private limited

companies (R. Brownjohn Ltd), or public limited companies (Thompson PLC). Limited companies have had legal personality bestowed on them either by Royal Charter or by Act of Parliament. Whichever kind of 'person' they are the account will keep a record of our dealings with this person. Capital Account is a special case of a personal account. The value of the proprietor's investment in the business is recorded there; the real assets he/she brought in are recorded in the real accounts.

Real accounts
Every real account has the name of an asset *the business owns* at the top. These assets are real things; we can sit on the chairs, type with the typewriters, spend the cash, etc. We have already seen that some assets are current assets and some are fixed assets. All asset accounts are real accounts.

Nominal accounts
Every nominal account has the name of a loss or profit of the business at the top of the page, e.g. Light and Heat Account, Wages Account, Rent Received Account, etc. We keep track of these losses and profits during the year and at the end of the year use them to work out the final Profit and Loss Account of the business.

The word 'nominal' means 'in name only'. We may have £2 500.00 on the Wages Account but it is not really there, the workers have taken the wages home and used them to support their families.

2.4   How to keep a Ledger Account –
Rules for making entries in the three classes of accounts

A Ledger page is divided down the middle and the two sides are called the debit side and the credit side. As there are three classes of account it is best to learn three separate rules for making entries in the accounts, but in fact a general rule covering all entries in accounts does apply. The beginner in book-keeping may be puzzled to see how it fits all cases because some experience is necessary in dealing with accounts before it becomes really clear.

The general rule
Debit the account that has received value (goods, services, or money).
Credit the account that has given value (goods, services, or money).

We may abbreviate this rule to read

Debit the receiver, credit the giver

If we now apply this rule to the three classes of account already mentioned we have the following special applications of the general rule:

Rule for entering up the personal accounts
Debit the person who receives goods, services, or money from the business.
Credit the person who gives goods, services, or money to the business.

Rule for entering up the real accounts
Debit increases in value of the asset (the asset concerned has received a larger share of the resources of the business).
Credit decreases in value of the asset (the asset concerned has given up some of its value in the service of the business – we call this 'depreciation').

PERSONAL ACCOUNTS TOM JONES	L1
Debit Jones when he receives goods, value, or money from the business.	Credit Jones when he gives goods, value, or money to the business.

REAL ACCOUNTS LAND AND BUILDINGS ACCOUNT	L2
Debit increases in value of assets.	Credit decreases in value of assets.

NOMINAL ACCOUNTS POSTAGE ACCOUNT	L3
Debit expenses in 'Loss' Accounts.	

COMMISSION RECEIVED ACCOUNT	L4
	Credit gains in 'Profit' accounts.

Figure 2.2   Rules for keeping Ledger Accounts

Rule for entering up nominal accounts
Debit expenses, i.e. *losses*, in the appropriate nominal account (the expenses account named has received money 'in name only' from the business).
Credit gains, i.e. *profits*, in the appropriate nominal account (the account named has given money 'in name only' to the business).

These rules are illustrated in Figure 2.2.

2.5   Personal Accounts – debtors

When a merchant sells goods on credit, payable in the usual course of events at the end of the month, he is taking part in a transaction that involves a debtor. The person to whom he sells the goods will be debited with the goods received. The merchant will usually not enter into this type of transaction unless a course of business dealing has convinced him of the reliability of the customer. A new customer might be asked for a reference from his banker, or to give the names of businessmen with whom he had conducted business over a considerable time. If these references are satisfactory the transactions will be allowed to proceed.

In very large firms these accounts might be so numerous that they would be kept, not in a book, but in a card index system – we would call this card index the **Debtors' Ledger.**

As we saw in the last section, the rule for keeping Personal Accounts is to debit the persons who receive goods, services, or money, and to credit them when they give goods, services, or money.

Dr.				Tom Brown, 27 Hill Rd., Newton, Essex			DL 27 Cr.
19. .			£	19. .			£
Jan.	1	Balance	637.50	Jan.	7	Cheque	602.50
	3	Sales	126.00		7	Discount	35.00
	4	Sales	231.50		18	Returns	62.50
	4	Carriage	21.00		31	Balance	863.00
	17	Sales	379.50				
	20	Sales	136.25				
	20	Carriage	31.25				
			£ 1 563.00				£ 1 563.00
19. .			£				
Feb.	1	Balance	863.00				

Figure 2.3   A Personal Account – a debtor

When the rule above is used to record the transactions of our firm with a debtor, Tom Brown, an account like the one in Figure 2.3 results. The following points should be carefully noted:

(a)   Tom Brown was a debtor on January 1 for £637.50. This was the balance on the debit side of his account, showing that he received goods of that value during December, and has not given us anything for them.

(b)   On January 3 Brown bought more goods from us. This time he received £126.00 worth of goods. This was our sales figure to him on that date.

(c) On January 4 Brown bought more goods valued at £231.50 and in addition we charged him £21.00 for transport charges, carriage on the goods to be received.

(d) On January 7 Brown paid us a cheque for £602.50 which was in full settlement of his debt owed at January 1. This means that we must have allowed him discount of £35.00 which appears on the next line below.

(e) On January 17 Brown bought more goods valued at £379.50.

(f) On January 18 he returned some of the goods, which must have been unsatisfactory for some reason. £62.50 was the value of the goods given back.

(g) On January 20 he once again purchased goods from us for £136.25 and was charged carriage £31.25.

(h) The outstanding balance of £863.00 was carried down to the debit side of the account. Tom Brown is a debtor once again on February 1 for this balance. A debtor is a person who owes us money, because he has received goods or services for which he has not yet paid.

(i) The small column which has not yet been used is called the Folio Column. Its use will be explained later.

We can see from a careful study of this Ledger Account that a complete rule for entering a Debtor's Account would be:

Rule for entering a Debtor's Account
Debit the debtor when he *receives* goods or services.
Credit him when he *gives* money or goods, or *when he is excused from payment* by being given discount.

The student should now try to record on a piece of Ledger paper each of the four accounts named below. In a real Ledger every leaf in the book is an account, and must be kept for the particular person, or thing, named at the top of the page. It would be very expensive to use a whole page for each exercise, but to make it clear that you are really keeping separate accounts it is usual to rule off right across the page when you start another account, and put a new folio number in the 'corner' as if you really had begun a new page.

2.6   Exercises set 2.1 – simple Debtors' Accounts

1. R. Brown has an account with us. It is folio number DL27. On April 1, 19. ., there is a debit balance of £830.65 on the account. Head the account properly, and then make the opening balance entry, followed by the entries below:

Apr. 2 R. Brown sends us a cheque for £500.00 on account. (This means he is unable to pay the full amount at present.)
    3 We send Brown goods valued at £73.15.
    4 We send Brown further goods valued at £875.50.
    7 Brown sends us a cheque for the balance of the money that he owed us on April 1.
    9 Brown returns us goods valued at £127.50 (wrong colour).
    19 We send Brown goods valued at £312.50 and we also charge him carriage £7.25.
    27 We send Brown goods valued at £136.75.
    30 The account is balanced off and the balance brought down ready for the new month.

2 J. Brown has a Ledger Account with us. Its folio number is DL24. On January 1 it had a debit balance of £1 253.00. Open the account and make these further entries:

Jan. 2 We send Brown further goods valued at £236.30.
    3 Brown pays the amount owing on January 1 by cheque and is given £31.32 discount.
    4 He buys further goods valued at £137.50.
    5 He returns some of the goods bought on January 2 valued at £26.50.
    26 He buys further goods valued at £223.25. We charge delivery charges £10.00.
    31 Balance off the account and bring down the balance.

3 One of our customers is called M. Petersen. He is a debtor with an account DL95. Enter the following entries in his account:

Jan. 1 Balance owing by M. Petersen £135.80.
    2 Petersen buys more goods valued at £127.50.
    3 Petersen buys more goods valued at £86.25.
    4 Petersen returns goods valued at £60.00.
    7 Petersen pays balance owing on January 1, less discount £6.79, by cheque.
    9 Petersen buys goods valued at £900.00.
    10 We charge Petersen £23.00 carriage and £7.50 insurance.
    11 We sell Petersen goods valued at £70.00.
    18 We sell Petersen more goods valued at £132.50.
    28 Petersen returns goods valued at £21.40.
    31 Balance off the account and bring down the balance.

4 R. Thomas is a debtor of ours with an account DL37. Enter the following items in his Ledger Account:

Jan. 1 Balance owing by R. Thomas £1 235.80.
    2 R. Thomas buys more goods valued at £275.00.
    3 R. Thomas sends us a cheque for £1 174.01 *in full settlement* of the amount outstanding on January 1.
    14 R. Thomas buys more goods valued at £240.00. He is charged £12.50 delivery charges.

19 He returns goods valued at £70.00.
29 He buys further goods valued at £226.25.
31 Balance off his Ledger Account and bring the balance down.

2.7 Personal Accounts – creditors

When a merchant buys goods on credit he undertakes to pay the supplier of the goods in due course, usually at the end of the month. The supplier's account will be credited with the goods supplied, and with any charges like carriage or insurance on the goods. The supplier will thus become a creditor – a person to whom we owe money.

Once again these accounts may be so numerous that we remove them from the Ledger and have a loose-leaf – or card index – system. This would be called the **Creditors' Ledger.**

Example:
Apr. 1 Henry Wills was a creditor of ours for goods worth £252.50 supplied during March. His account is CL197.
2 Bought goods from Wills valued at £4 502.50.
3 Returned goods valued at £377.50 to Wills (not up to specification).
5 Sent Wills a cheque for £242.50 *in full settlement* of the balance owing on April 1.
30 Balanced off the account.

Wills's account is seen below:

Dr.		HENRY WILLS						CL197 Cr.
19. .			£	19. .				£
Apr. 3	Returns		377.50	Apr. 1	Balance			252.50
5	Bank		242.50	2	Purchases			4 502.50
5	Discount		10.00					
30	Balance		4 125.00					
		£	4 755.00				£	4 755.00
				19. .				£
				May 1	Balance			4 125.00

Figure 2.4   A Creditor's Account

If you compare Figure 2.3 and Figure 2.4 you will notice that they are the opposite of each other. Instead of selling to a debtor we are purchasing from a creditor; the goods returned in Figure 2.4 to Wills are received by him on the debit side. Brown was credited with the returns in Figure 2.3 because he gave them back.

Rule for entries on a Creditor's Account
Debit the creditor when he *receives* payment from us, or goods that
  we return, or when he excuses us from payment.
Credit the creditor when he *gives* goods or services of any sort.

The student should now try to record the following matters in the
Creditors' Accounts Exercises 2.2.

2.8   Exercises set 2.2 – simple Creditors' Accounts

1. One of our suppliers is called P. Peters. His account in our Ledger is
CL121.
  On July 1st it has a balance of £1 203.75 on the credit side. Open the
account and then continue with these entries:

July   2 P. Peters supplies goods valued at £565.75.
        3 We pay Peters by cheque the amount owing on July 1, less
          discount £30.09.
        4 Peters supplied more goods valued at £128.80. He also charges
          us £11.70 transport charges.
        5 We return goods valued at £60.50 (not up to specification).
       16 Peters supplies goods valued at £123.75.
       29 Peters supplies goods valued at £1 060.85.
       31 The account is ruled off ready for the next month's business.

2. Tom Brown is a creditor of ours, with an account CL28. On January 1
it had a credit balance of £1 825.00. Open the account and make the
following further entries:

Jan.   2 We pay Brown the amount owing, £1 825.00 by cheque.
        3 Brown sells us more goods valued at £210.50.
       14 Brown sends us more goods valued at £1 235.60.
       15 We return to Brown goods valued at £35.60.
       15 Brown sends us further goods valued at £5 400.00 and charges
          £125.80 for delivery charges.
       29 We purchase more goods from Brown valued at £128.75.
       31 Balance off the account.

3. M. Pierson is a creditor of ours with an account CL129. He has a credit
balance of £1 253.25 on June 1. Open the account and make the following
entries:

June   5 We buy goods valued at £23.25.
        6 We buy goods valued at £364.80.
       16 We return goods valued at £27.70.
       18 We pay by cheque for the goods bought during May, less £31.33
          cash discount.
       19 We buy goods valued at £378.00.
       29 We buy goods valued at £375.50 and are charged insurance
          £12.50.
       30 Balance off the account and bring down the balance.

4. Copy out the Creditor's Account in Figure 2.5. Balance it off on the last day of the month, and bring the balance down. Now answer these questions:

(a) What took place on October 27?
(b) Who owes the balance to whom?
(c) Now complete this sentence. 'In this example we have a creditor who was on October 31 temporarily a...'

			£	19. .			£
19. .				Oct. 1	Balance		3 602.50
Oct. 2	Bank		3 512.44	11	Purchases		2 132.50
2	Discount		90.06	19	Purchases		1 122.50
14	Returns		132.50	20	Carriage In		125.50
27	Motor Vehicles		3 750.00				

G. M. WHITESIDE — CL59

Figure 2.5 An exercise for the Creditors' Ledger

2.9 Real Accounts – accounts that record assets

When a proprietor sets out in business, the assets that he contributes will be recorded in separate Asset Accounts. The usual method of doing this this is to draw up an opening Journal Entry, but we will deal with this a little later in our studies. For the moment let us just consider what these 'real' accounts look like. The busiest of them are the Cash Account and the Bank Account, because receipts and payments, either in cash or by cheque are extremely common. Most of the other real accounts change very little, because the assets recorded there are used over a very long time and therefore the 'account' of what happens to them has little to record. It may tell us that we depreciated the asset by a certain amount at the end of each year, and that eventually we sold it as it was obsolete or worn out. We might buy a new machine and sell off an old one, but these events will be quite rare items. Apart from the Cash Account and the Bank Account you might expect the Stock Account to be a busy one, but in fact it is the least busy of all, for the purchases of new stock are recorded in the Purchases Account – a nominal account – and the sales of stock are recorded in the Sales Account – another nominal account. The Stock Account only records the balance of stock in hand on the last day of the financial year, and therefore it only has to be entered once a year.

Here are illustrations of one or two Real Accounts; the Cash Account and Bank Account will be dealt with in more detail on page 25.

Dr.	LAND AND BUILDINGS ACCOUNT						**L1** **Cr.**
19. . Jan. 1 May 31	Capital Bank		£ 28 500.00 9 250.00				

Figure 2.6   A 'Real' Account

Notice that the page is headed with the name of the asset concerned.

The premises owned when business commenced were worth £28 500.00. Later we built on a small extension for £9 250.00.

Businessmen do not usually depreciate land and buildings; indeed land and buildings often get more valuable as the years go by. An account like this would not even be balanced off to make it look tidy – but it would be added up neatly in pencil so that we could read off the total figure of £37 750.00 if we really wanted to know it.

The student should develop the habit of picturing events from the Asset Account. What happened in Figure 2.7 on June 30? What happened on October 1? Clearly on that date we bought a new vehicle for £4 500.00 and traded in the old one, removing it from the books. Its book value must have been £2 700.00. It does not follow that we were given an allowance of £2 700.00 for it. Possibly we receive more, possibly less; but we must remove the book value of the asset from the account.

Dr.	MOTOR VEHICLES ACCOUNT							**L2** **Cr.**
19. . Jan. 1 June 30	Capital New Vehicle		£ 3 750.00 4 250.00	19. . Dec. 31 31	Depreciation Balance	c/d	£ 800.00 7 200.00
		£	8 000.00			£	8 000.00
19. . Jan. 1 Oct. 1	Balance New Vehicle	b/d	£ 7 200.00 4 500.00	19. . Oct. 1 Dec. 31 31	Rex Garages Depreciation Balance	c/d	£ 2 700.00 900.00 8 100.00
		£	11 700.00			£	11 700.00
19. . Jan. 1	Balance	b/d	£ 8 100.00				

Figure 2.7   Another 'Real' Account

We do not want an asset that has been disposed of still recorded on our books. *Note:* In this example depreciation has been deducted at 10 per cent of the book value on December 31 each year.

Rule for entering up Asset Accounts
Debit the Asset Account whenever the asset increases in value, because the Asset Account has received the benefit of expenditure by the firm.
Credit the Asset Account whenever it decreases in value, either by depreciation or by actual sale. In these cases the asset has given service to the firm, either in use or by being turned into cash.

2.10 Folio Numbers

In Figure 2.7 you will notice that the letters c/d for 'carried down' have been inserted where the balancing figure was put on the credit side and the letters b/d for 'brought down' have been inserted on the balance line below on the debit side. These are the first 'folio numbers' we have met, and they are not numbers, but letters. Every single line in the Ledger should be cross-referenced with a folio number which tells you where the other half of the double entry is. We shall learn more about double entry as we go on, but at least here you can see the double entry for the balancing items, and it is possible to fill in the folio numbers c/d and b/d whenever we balance off an account.

2.11 The busiest Real Accounts – the Cash Account and the Bank Account

Later we shall see that in most businesses these accounts are treated in a special way, by being written in a special book called the **Three-column Cash Book.** Before this book was 'invented', and in small firms or clubs and societies where the number of entries is too small to justify the expense of a Three-column Cash Book, the Cash Account and Bank Account are ordinary Real Accounts on separate pages in the Ledger. They are exactly alike, but in the Cash Account it is money that is being paid and received, while in the Bank Account it is cheques that are being paid in and out.

The Cash Account shown on page 26 illustrates the keeping of these two accounts.

Dr.			CASH ACCOUNT					GL25 Cr.
19. . Mar. 1	Balance	b/d	£ 637.50	19. . Mar. 1	Postage	GL 29	12.50
1	Cash Sales	GL 37	430.50	1	Fares	GL 14	7.00
1	R. Jones	DL 36	137.75	1	R. Peters	CL 72	76.00
1	Staff Telephone	GL 40	0.50	1	P. Lamb	CL 42	81.25
				1	C. Avion	CL 1	51.25
				1	Cash Purchases	GL 73	56.25
				1	Sales Returned	GL 81	12.50
				1	Bank Account	GL 26	500.00
				1	Balance	c/d	409.50
		£	1 206.25			£	1 206.25
19. . Mar. 2	Balance	b/d	£ 409.50				

Figure 2.8   A simple Cash Account

Notes:

Debit Side

(a) As you would expect, because it is an asset, the 'cash £637.50' appears on the debit side at the start of the day. This is the balance received from yesterday. The folio column says b/d, brought down.

(b) Cash Account receives £430.50 from the sale of goods. This would be the day's takings from the tills, and some firms actually use the words **Daily Takings.** The double entry for this is in Sales Account which is in the General Ledger on page 37.

(c) R. Jones pays us cash, which is received in the Cash Account. Clearly he must have been a debtor, and the double entry for this would appear on the credit side of the R. Jones Account. This is DL36, so that this number is shown in the folio column.

(d) A small sum has been received from a member of staff for a private telephone call. This will be received in the Cash Account and credited in the Telephone Account, which is GL40 (account number 40 in the General Ledger).

Credit Side

(e) We have expenditure on postage, fares, and cash purchases. In each case the Cash Account gave away money for these reasons and the double entry for the cash entry will be in these Nominal Accounts in the General Ledger.

(f) We have also paid three suppliers, Peters, Lamb, and Avion, sums of money. They must have been creditors, and the corresponding entries will appear in the Creditor's Ledger.

(g) The Sales Returns item is an unusual one. Shops do not usually like to return money, and will give a credit note instead which entitles the holder to spend that amount of money at a later date. However it is now quite clear in law that cusomers do not have to accept a credit note, and shops must now return cash if the customer insists. This is what has happened here. The folio number GL81 is the folio number of the Sales Returns Account in the General Ledger.

2.12   Double Entry Book-keeping

The student should note carefully at this stage that every transaction that takes place has a twofold nature. If we pay out cash £100.00 for a filing cabinet we shall have spent a real sum of money which we shall credit in the cash account. Cash has given £100.00. The filing cabinet will be recorded in the Furniture and Fittings Account as an increase in value, on the debit side.

We therefore have a debit entry exactly equal and opposite to a credit entry. This kind of double entry gives book-keeping its proper name **Double Entry Book-keeping.**

A full explanation of the system will be found in Chapter 3.

2.13   Folio numbers and Double Entry Book-keeping

You should, in the entries you do from now on, invent sensible folio numbers to fill in the folio column. *They are usually the numbers of the account where the double entry will be found.* Folio numbers are the signposts which tell us where to look for more information about an entry. They tell us where to find the other half of the double entry, or which subsidiary book to look at for fuller information. These subsidiary books will be dealt with later.

Rule for keeping the Cash Account
Debit the Cash Account whenever cash is received.
Credit the Cash Account whenever cash is given in exchange for goods or services.

2.14   Exercises set 2.3 – simple Cash Accounts

Using ordinary Ledger paper, draw up simple Cash Accounts for the
following four exercises.

1. Enter the following items in a simple Ledger Account – the Cash
Account GL27.

19. .
Dec.   1 Balance of cash in hand £85.50 paid wages £63.00; drew from
        bank for office use £100.00; paid postage £5.75.
       2 Bought coffee (Sundry Expenses A/c) £1.50; bought stationery
        £15.50; bought new Ledger £11.25.
       3 R. Jones sent £10.50 to us in cash; P. Brown sent cash £19.00 to
        us; we sent £5.75 to R. Lewis in cash.
       4 Paid sundries £11.25; tip to dustmen (Gratuities Account) £1.00;
        cash sales from till £920.50. Paid to bank £750.00.

  Balance off the account and bring down the Cash Balance.

2. Enter the following item in a Cash Account, GL56, balance off at the
end, and bring down the balance:

19. .
Jan.   1 Balance of cash in hand £185.50.
       2 Paid for repairs to lock on front door £16.25.
       3 Paid garage expenses (Motor Vehicle Expenses Account)
        £38.60.
       4 Cash sales £706.50. Paid to Bank £550.00.
       5 Paid wages £65.50.
       6 Paid to R. Hero £12.25.
       7 Paid to P. Jacobs £71.25.
       8 Paid office expenses £7.50.
       9 Paid to R. Hero £15.75; cash sales £707.80.
      10 R. Jones paid us the sum of £123.25. Paid to bank £600.00.
      11 Received from R. Lucas £76.30.
      12 Paid to R. Heilbrane £123.15.
      13 Paid for office expenses £2.75.
      14 Cash sales £976.50. Paid to Bank £500.00.

3. Enter these items in a Cash Account. Balance the account and bring
down the balance at the end of the fortnight ready for next day.

19. .
Jan.   1 Balance of cash in hand £160.50.
       2 Paid for postage £10.00.
       3 Paid office expenses £8.25.
       4 Cash sales £734.50. Paid to bank £600.00.
       5 Paid wages £83.00.
       6 Paid to A. Askham £16.25.
       7 Paid to M. Bryan £63.25.
       8 Paid repairs £6.25.

9 Cash sales £757.50.
10 R. Jones paid us the sum of £85.80. Paid to bank £700.00.
11 Received from M. O'Connor £23.75.
12 Paid to M. Haly £73.25.
13 Paid for office expenses £3.25.
14 Cash sales £886.75. Paid to bank £650.00.

4. Enter the following in a simple Cash Account, GL55.

19. .
Oct. 1 Balance of cash in hand £128.50.
      2 Bought stamps £3.40; bought teas for visitors £7.50 (Sundry Expenses A/c).
      3 Cash sales £806.50. Paid to bank £700.00.
      4 Paid R. Jones in cash the sum of £27.50.
      5 Paid R. Peters in cash £20.50.
      6 T. Brown paid us £26.25.
      7 M. Wilmot paid us £19.25.
      8 Paid wages £123.00.
      9 Paid M. Jones £8.00.
     10 Paid R. Brown £21.25.
     11 Cash sales £793.25.
     12 Paid into bank £650.00.
     13 R. Lomax paid us £5.75 in cash.
     14 Paid for cleaning materials £2.25; balanced off the Cash Account ready for the next fortnight.

2.15 The Bank Account

This is kept in exactly the same way as the Cash Account. It may seem tedious to practise the same work over again, but in a later chapter we shall be dealing with the Three-column Cash Book, in which these two accounts, Cash Account and Bank Account, are combined in a rather special way. It is therefore worth while being very sure of these two accounts separately, before we learn how to combine them.

Rule for keeping the Bank Account
Debit the Bank Account whenever cheques are received, or cash takings paid in.
Credit the Bank Account whenever cheques are paid out, or are presented for the withdrawal of cash.

2.16 Exercises set 2.4 – simple Bank Accounts

1. Open a simple Ledger Bank Account GL21 and enter the following items:

19. .
Jan. 1 Began business with a capital of £2 500.00 in the bank; withdrew £100.00 for office cash box.
2 R. Jones paid us £25.50 by cheque.
3 T. Smith paid us £863.25 by cheque.
4 Paid R. Miller £927.50 for goods supplied by cheque.
5 Paid by cheque rent £200.00.
6 Paid by cheque rates £75.00.
7 M. Blenkiron paid us £20.50 by cheque.
8 Paid by cheque for electric fire £30.50 (Furniture and Fittings a/c).
9 Balanced off Bank Account and brought down the balance.

2. Enter the following items in a Bank Account, GL40, balance off at the end and bring down the balance:

19. .
Jan. 1 Balance of cash at bank £760.50.
2 Paid for repairs to lock on front door £16.25 by cheque.
3 Paid motor expenses £8.75 by cheque.
4 R. Brown paid us by cheque £70.50.
5 Paid wages £85.50 by cheque.
6 Paid to R. Hero £12.25 by cheque.
7 Paid to M. Palmer £71.25 by cheque.
8 Paid office expenses £31.25 by cheque.
9 R. Silver paid us £70.80 by cheque.
10 R. Jones paid us the sum of £123.25 by cheque.
11 Received from Inspector of Taxes, a tax rebate of £76.25 by cheque.
12 Paid to R. Hebron £123.25 by cheque.
13 Paid for office expenses £31.50 by cheque.
14 M. Thomas paid us £68.75 by cheque.

3. Enter the following items in a Bank Account, L14, and balance off the account at the end of the week:

19. .
Jan. 14 Balance in bank £5 255.85; paid R. Jones £107.25 by cheque; paid M. Thoms £213.50 by cheque.
15 M. Chuzzlewit gave a cheque for £275.00 to our Sales Manager for goods to be delivered that day.
16 Paid rates by cheque £210.50 paid water rate by cheque £87.50.
18 Mrs. M. Lupin paid by cheque £120.50 for account rendered on January 1.
18 T. Jolly paid his Account, value £243.80 by cheque.
19 Paid wages by cheque £220.50.
20 Received cheque from Transportation Ltd, insurance money on goods damaged £23.75.

4. Enter the following items in a simple Bank Account, L24:

19. .
Dec.   1 Balance of cash in bank £1 085.50; paid wages by cheque £63.25;
        drew from bank for office use £100.00; paid R. Johnson by
        cheque £5.75.
       2 Bought coffee for canteen by cheque £31.75; bought stationery
        £15.50 by cheque; bought new Ledger £11.25 by cheque.
       3 R. Jones sent us £10.75 cheque; P. Brown sent us a cheque for
        £19.25; sent £30.75 to R. Joiner by cheque.
       4 R. Howard paid us by cheque £170.45; cash sales from till
        £620.50 banked.

Balance off the Bank Account and bring down the balance.

2.17 Nominal Accounts – accounts that record losses and profits

These accounts, as mentioned earlier, are accounts which record
the use of money which has been spent, not in buying assets but in
buying goods or services which are necessary to the conduct of the
business, but give us nothing real to show for our money. If we
send a parcel to Zanzibar the postage is necessary, but its benefit is
lost with the delivery of the parcel; there is no enduring asset to
show for the expense. Such sums of money are expenses, or losses
of the business. We keep a nominal record of them, and at the end
of the year write them off the profits of the business. Here is such
an account, the Rent Paid Account. The Cash Account has also
been shown to bring out the double entry nature of the work.

Dr.				£					£
		RENT PAID ACCOUNT							GL7 Cr.
19. . Jan. 1	Cash	GL 1	300.00		19. . Dec. 31	Transfer to Profit and Loss Account	GL 121	1 200.00	
Apr. 1	Cash	GL 1	300.00						
July 1	Cash	GL 1	300.00						
Oct. 1	Cash	GL 1	300.00						
		£	1 200.00				£	1 200.00	

| CASH ACCOUNT | | | | | | | | GL1 |
Dr.								Cr.
19. . Jan. 1	Balance	b/d	£ 2 500.00	19. . Jan. 1 Apr. 1 July. 1 Oct. 1	Rent Rent Rent Rent	GL7 GL7 GL7 GL7	£ 300.00 300.00 300.00 300.00	

| PROFIT AND LOSS ACCOUNT | | | | | | | | GL121 |
Dr.								Cr.
19. . Dec. 31	Rent Paid	GL7	£ 1 200.00					

Figure 2.9   A 'Loss' Account – Rent Paid Account

There are many such Loss Accounts: Wages, Salaries, Postage, Telephone, Motor Vehicle Expenses, Light and Heat, Rent and Rates, etc. There are also some which are the result of the receipt of sums of money. These are profits, because the money has been received and is put in the cash-box, or the bank. The double entry is recorded in a profit account, for instance the Rent Received Account, Discount Received Account, Commission Received Account, or Professional Fees Received Account.

Rule for keeping Nominal Accounts
Debit all losses in a loss account because that account has received the benefit of expenditure by the firm.
Credit all gains in a profit account because that account has given some benefit in cash to the firm.

2.18   'Continuous Balance' Ledger Accounts

The Ledger Account below (see Figure 2.10) shows an alternative type of Ledger Account called the 'continuous balance' or 'running balance' type of account. This is most useful in a simple computerized system where the machine can do the calculations almost instantaneously. If a book-keeper kept the accounts in this way a great deal of time would be wasted doing the calculations involved. The computer is very quick and cannot make mistakes.

NAME Pearson & Co.				A/C NO. 127	
ADDRESS 1274 High St., London, SW26				SHEET NO. 1	
Date	Particulars	F	Debit	Credit	Balance
19. .			£	£	£
1 Mar.	Balance	b/d	175.84		175.84
13 Mar.	Sales		38.56		214.40
17 Mar.	Sales		327.83		542.23
19 Mar.	Cheque			167.05	375.18
19 Mar.	Discount			8.79	366.39
24 Mar.	Returns			24.50	341.89

Figure 2.10 A 'continuous balance' ledger account

Notes:

(a) The balance on March 1 is a debit balance, Pearson and Co. are debtors.
(b) On March 13 and again on March 17 they purchased goods from us, and their debt consequently increased.
(c) The debt was reduced on March 19 when the balance owing on March 1 was settled by cheque (less 5% discount).
(d) Finally, some returns on March 24 reduce the balance payable still further.

Although you are not recommended to keep all accounts in this way, which is really only appropriate for computerized accounts, the following exercises in continuous balance accounts will help you understand how the accounts are presented by a computer print-out.

2.19   Exercises set 2.5 – Continuous Balance Accounts

Prepare the following Ledger Accounts in 'continuous balance' style. Rule up paper similar to Figure 2.10 and make the entries on this special paper.

1. From the following information prepare R. Bird's account as it would appear in your computerized ledger:

19. .
Jan. 1 Balances due from Bird £160.00.
     14 Bird paid £28.50 by cheque and was allowed £1.50 discount.
     16 Sold Bird goods for £120.00 less 25% trade discount.
     18 Purchased furniture from Bird for £200.00.
     21 Bird returns goods sold to him on the 16th instant, the catalogue price being £20.00.

29 Received a credit note from Bird in respect of defective furniture £30.00.

From your running balance state whether you owe Bird, or Bird owes you, money.

2. From the particulars given below show the account of M. Bagret on Sheet 1 in the Ledger of George & Co. for the month of March.

19. .
Mar. 1 Balance due from Bagret £150.00.
   10 Sold to Bagret 5 dozen table lamps at £12.00 each, less 20% trade discount.
   11 Bagret paid the balance due from him on March 1 by cheque deducting 5% for cash discount.
   18 Bagret reported that six of the table lamps sold to him on March 10 were badly finished, and an allowance of one-half of their price was agreed.
   19 Sold to Bagret two tables at £87.50 each, less 20% trade discount.
   20 Paid carriage on tables £4.00; to be charged to Bagret.
   29 Bought from Bagret a second-hand lorry for £250.00.

State whether the balance should be inserted in the debit or credit column of Sheet 2 when carried down and whether Bagret or George & Co. should pay the amount of the balance.

3. (a) From the information given below prepare the account of J. Mace as it would appear in the Purchases Ledger of B. Barnes; balance the account and bring down the balance on January 1.

19. .
Dec. 1 Balance owed to Mace £200.95.
   4 Barnes bought goods from Mace, value £290.00; Mace charged Barnes carriage, £12.00.
   6 Barnes sent Mace a cheque for £190.90, taking discount £10.05.
   7 Barnes returned goods to Mace, £9.00.
   11 Mace sent Barnes goods for £65.85.
   30 Mace accepted a machine in part payment from Barnes, £100.00.

(b) Who owes whom, and how much on 30 December.

(RSA – *Adapted*)

2.20 A page to test you on the Ledger

Cover the page with a sheet of paper, then read one question at a time.

Answers	Questions
—	1 What is the Ledger?
1 The Ledger is the main book of account.	1 What is an account?
2 An account is a page in the Ledger which records the transactions relevant to the person, asset, expense or profit named in the heading.	3 Are the accounts numbered?
3 Yes – with folio numbers.	4 What does 'folio' mean?
4 It comes from the Latin word for 'leaf'.	5 Where do we write these folio numbers?
5 In the top right-hand corner.	6 What are the three classes of accounts?
6 Personal a/cs, nominal a/cs, and real a/cs.	7 What are personal accounts?
7 They are the accounts of persons with whom we deal, i.e. our Debtors and our Creditors.	8 What is a debtor?
8 A person who owes us money.	9 What is a creditor?
9 A person to whom we owe money.	10 What are real accounts?
10 They are accounts in which we record the real things we own, i.e. the assets of the business.	11 Name five business assets recorded in real accounts.
11 Land and Buildings; Plant and Machinery; Furniture and Fittings; Motor Vehicles; Office Machinery.	12 What is a nominal account?
12 An account which records a profit or loss of the business.	13 What does 'nominal' mean?
13 'In name only.'	14 Why is the money recorded in name only?
14 Because really it has been spent (or gained)	15 What do we use these nominal accounts for?
15 To work out the profits of the business at the end of the financial year.	16 What are the two sides of an account called?
16 The debit side and the credit side.	17 What is the rule for entering in the Ledger?
17 (a) Debit an account that has received goods, services, or money; (b) credit an account that has given goods, services, or money.	18 Put briefly this rule says:
18 Debit the receiver. Credit the giver.	Go over this page again until you know it all.

3
How Double Entry
Book-keeping works

3.1 The double entry system

The chart which is the chief feature of this chapter shows clearly
how the double entry system of book-keeping works. This method
of keeping books so that the businessman knows his exact financial
position at any given time is explained in the diagram, and the
student should return to it regularly to discover how each section
of his studies fits into the pattern of double entry.

At this stage let us take a very quick look at Figure 3.1 on pages
38–9 to pick up the general framework of book-keeping. The
numbers 1 to 5 are guideways through the diagram.

3.2 The Original Documents (1)

Every transaction that takes place, whether it is a purchase, a sale,
a return, a payment, or some other type of transaction has an
original document. These documents are called Invoices, Credit
Notes, Statements, Receipts, Petty Cash Vouchers, or they may
be formal agreements like a Hire Purchase Document or a Legal
Contract. Even mere letters of complaint require some action to
be taken.

3.3 The Books of Original Entry (2)

When you have a document you first record it in a Book of
Original Entry. These books may be Journals, that is Day Books,
or Cash Books like the Three-column Cash Book or the Petty
Cash Book. We may also have Bill Books to record Bills of
Exchange, Consignment Books to record Consignments and other
specialized books. These Day Books keep a record of the
documents received in *chronological order*.

3.4 Posting the Day Books to the Ledger (3)

When we have entered our Original Documents in the Day Books we then post the transactions into the Ledger, which is the main book of account. Every transaction will appear twice, because one account will be receiving value and another giving it. For this reason the entries will be a debit entry in one account and a credit entry in some other account. Hundreds, even thousands, of accounts may be involved, but if we do our double entry carefully the total entries on the debit side will exactly balance the total entries on the credit side. This is the way we check the books, by taking out a Trial Balance.

3.5 The Trial Balance (4)

This is what its name implies, an attempt to discover whether the books really do balance. If they do not we know that someone has made a mistake somewhere, and we must discover it.

To take out a Trial Balance we must look at every account in our Ledger, and there may be thousands of them. Each account will be in one of three positions:
(a) It may have a debit balance outstanding.
(b) It may be clear – having no outstanding balance.
(c) It may have a credit balance outstanding.

We usually do a Trial Balance at least once a month, taking the opportunity to 'tidy up' accounts where we can, and bringing all the debit balances into a list of debit balances, and all the credit balances into a list of credit balances. These two columns of balances should come exactly equal, and we may conclude that if they do, it is fairly certain we have done our book-keeping well. The idea of the Trial Balance is the most important idea in book-keeping by the double entry system, and the whole of Chapter 16 is given to this idea.

Book-keeping to the Trial Balance level is the first stage of accounting knowledge, which most people can learn very easily in about 15–20 hours of instruction or self-study. One often sees advertisements reading 'Book-keeper to Trial Balance level required'. Once you have reached Chapter 10 in this book you should be quite capable of taking employment at this level. The second, and rather more difficult, stage of book-keeping is called 'Final Accounts level'. This is explained below.

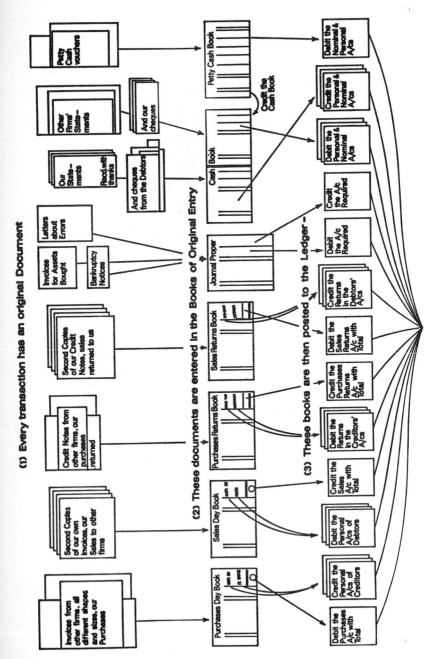

(1) Every transaction has an original Document

(2) These documents are entered in the Books of Original Entry

(3) These books are then posted to the Ledger—

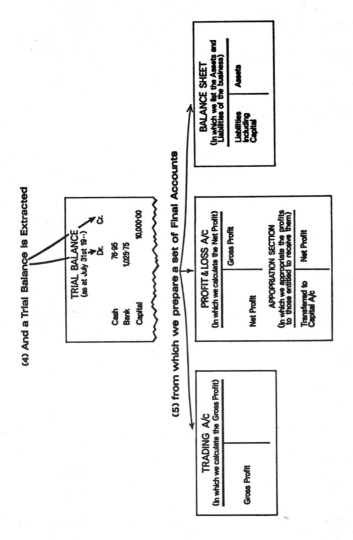

(4) And a Trial Balance is Extracted

TRIAL BALANCE
(as at July 31st 19-·)

	Dr.	Cr.
Cash	76·95	
Bank	1,025·75	
Capital		10,000·00

(5) from which we prepare a set of Final Accounts

TRADING A/c
(In which we calculate the Gross Profit)

Gross Profit

PROFIT & LOSS A/c
(In which we calculate the Net Profit)

Gross Profit

Net Profit

APPROPRIATION SECTION
(In which we appropriate the profits to those entitled to receive them)

Transferred to Capital A/c	Net Profit

BALANCE SHEET
(In which we list the Assets and Liabilities of the business)

Liabilities including Capital	Assets

Figure 3.1 Double Entry Book-keeping

3.6 Final Accounts – the Trading Account (5a)

We are now ready to find out whether our business is profitable or running at a loss. To discover this we first do a simple Trading Account. This shows whether we are selling at a profit. We find our sales figure from the Sales Account; we find our purchases figure from our Purchase Account. After one or two adjustments, chiefly connected with opening and closing stocks, we discover the cost of the goods sold. A few more little matters help us discover the Cost of Sales, which is not quite the same as the Cost of Goods Sold, since, it includes a few expenses. Then Sales minus Cost of Sales gives us our overall profit – called in book-keeping the **Gross Profit.**

3.7 Final Accounts – the Profit and Loss Account (5b)

In this second half of our Final Accounts we start with the Gross Profit and deduct from it all overhead expenses. We add items of profit which are not part of normal trading, such as commissions or rents received. This leads us to the clear profit or clean profit – called in book-keeping **Net Profit.** This Net Profit is the reward of the businessman for his efforts, and is added to his Capital Account.

With partnership enterprises, and with limited companies, the Net Profit has to be shared among the partners, or shareholders. This is done in a section of the Profit and Loss Account, called the **Appropriation Account.** We give the profit to the appropriate persons in the appropriate proportions according to the **partnership agreement,** or the resolution passed at the **annual general meeting** of the company.

3.8 The Balance Sheet (5c)

When we have prepared the Final Accounts and added the profit to the owner's Capital Account (or perhaps deducted the loss from the owner's Capital Account) we have established what degree of success the business has achieved, and all we need to do now is summarize the final position of the business by drawing up a Balance Sheet which shows the assets and liabilities of the firm.

This is the general pattern of double entry book-keeping. **As the student learns about each document and how to keep each book of original entry he should study its position in the general picture by looking again at the chart on pages 38–9.**

3.9   Computerization of Book-keeping

Computers are electronic machines which can be programmed to do many routine activities. Since book-keeping to the Trial Balance level is a routine and repetitive process it is relatively easy to instruct the computer how to keep book-keeping records to the Trial Balance. The more difficult level of work is the work to Final Accounts level. It is not usual to program a computer to do this as the cost of writing the programs is much greater. Some awkward decisions have to be made at this level which a human being can do much more easily than the computer programmer can prepare a program. Some people do go to the extra expense involved, but it is hardly necessary.

As we proceed through this book reference will be made at convenient points to the methods used when computerized accounting systems are employed (see Sections 5.5, 6.4 and 12.4).

4
Subsidiary books and original documents

4.1 Introduction

We already know that the Ledger is the main book of account. The other books we use are called subsidiary books, because they give additional help to the main book. It is in these books that the original documents are recorded, so that they are the books of original entry, already referred to. The most important subsidiary book is the Journal. This is an old French word meaning 'Daily Record', and it was so called because everything that happened every day was entered into the book at once, before the businessman could forget the exact details of the transaction. It therefore gives us a **chronological** record of the transactions into which the businessman enters.

The dividing-up of the Journal
If you have only one Journal it is possible for only one book-keeper to use it at a time. In a past age it was found that when a business grew one person could not do all the work. The Journal was therefore divided into parts so that several clerks could work at once. It was also found that the work could be divided into two main sections:

(a) Transactions that happened repeatedly, because they dealt with 'goods' that the firm could call its 'normal line of business'.
(b) Transactions that happened much more rarely, say once or twice a year.

Section (a) was found to consist of the purchase of goods, the sale of goods, returns outwards (i.e. purchases returned) or returns inwards (sales returned by dissatisfied customers).

Transactions of this sort took place every day, sometimes many times a day.

Section (b) was found to consist of much rarer items, such as the purchasing of assets like furniture, which might last twenty years, or writing off bad debts which might only happen a few times a year.

Larger firms therefore began to divide the Journal, or Day Book, into five parts:

The five subsidiary books
The **Purchases Day Book,** in which purchases were recorded.
The **Sales Day Book,** in which sales were recorded.
The **Purchases Returns Book,** in which returns outwards were recorded.
The **Sales Returns Book,** in which returns inwards were recorded.
The **Journal Proper,** containing all the items not to do with 'goods' that are the firm's 'normal line of business', i.e. the rarer items of section (b).

4.2 The pattern of business in an established trading firm

Once a trading business has been successfully launched the profit-yielding activities are repeated endlessly. The businessman buys goods, which he calls **purchases** and records in his Purchases Day Book. Eventually he sells them, recording the **sales** in his Sales Day Book. Now and then an unsatisfactory purchase will be returned and its return will be recorded in the Purchases Returns Book, while occasionally the customer who bought goods will be dissatisfied and return them as sales returns. The endless succession of these activities is called **turnover.** The turnover of any business is a very important figure.

Each of these transactions begins with an original document. Purchases and sales begin with **invoices.** Purchases returns and sales returns are acknowledged by a **credit note.** In every case it is the seller who makes out the document, sending one copy to the other party in the transaction. You should study carefully the documents shown in this chapter and follow the copies as they move to the departments where they are required, and where they will be recorded in the Day Books.

4.3 Documents for sales and purchases – the invoice

Definition: An invoice is a business document which is made out whenever one person sells goods to another. It can be used in the courts of law as evidence of a contract for the sale of goods. It is made out by the person selling the goods, and in large businesses it may have as many as five copies, of different colours.

Figure 4.1 on page 45 shows the usual form of invoices in use in large firms. It must have the following information:

(a) Names and addresses of both the interested parties to the sale.

(b) The date of the sale.

(c) An exact description of the goods, with quantity and unit price, and details of the trade discount (if any) given.

(d) In the United Kingdom it must give details of the VAT charged as it becomes a tax invoice for VAT purposes.

(e) It may give the terms on which goods are sold, i.e. discount and credit period. The words 'Terms Net' mean no discount is allowed. The words 'Prompt Settlement' mean no credit period is allowed.

Lastly, many firms write 'E & O E' on the bottom of the invoice. These letters mean 'Errors and Omissions Excepted'. If an error or omission has been made, the firm selling the goods may put it right. In English law written evidence may not be varied by oral evidence so that if an invoice were presented in the courts it could not be said orally, 'But my Lord, that was a mistake'. But the words 'E & O E' written on the invoice would permit this to be done. In fact this has been tested in the Courts. In the case of Webster *versus* Cecil (1861) it was held that a genuine slip of the pen could be corrected so that the phrase 'E & O E' is not really necessary.

What happens to the four copies?

Top Copy: This is sent by post or by hand to the person buying the goods, and he uses it to enter in his Purchases Day Book. He then keeps the invoice as his copy of the contract of sale.

Second Copy: This is usually the Sales Day Book copy, which is kept by the seller, entered in his Sales Day Book, and then filed to be kept as his copy of the contract of sale.

Third and Fourth Copies: These are sent together to the Stores Department of the seller, where the storekeeper takes the goods out of store. The third copy, often called the **Delivery Note,** is given to the carman to take with him to the buyer's warehouse, where he presents it with the parcel of goods and gets a signature on it to prove that the goods arrived safely. This copy is then taken back by the carman to the storekeeper and is filed in the store after being entered in the Stores Record Book. The fourth copy is wrapped up in the parcel before it is given to the carman. It is often called the **Advice Note** and it enables the buyer's storekeeper to check the contents of the parcel and record the stores that have just arrived in his Stores Record Book.

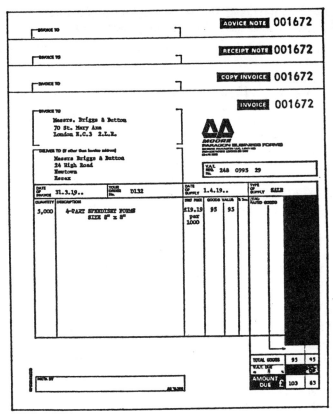

Figure 4.1 A four-copy invoice system ...

Sometimes there is a **Representative's Copy** which is sent to the commercial traveller who took the order. He is then able to prove to the buyer that his firm has handled the sale in a proper manner and can remind the customer what he ordered. This may save a great deal of time because the buyer may say 'All right, repeat that order will you?'.

How long do we keep an invoice?
Usually for six years. Under the Limitation Act of 1980 an action in the courts on a simple contract cannot begin more than six years after the contract was made. If we keep our invoices for six years the chance of the invoice being needed as legal evidence disappears. Many firms get rid of their old invoices by shredding them into packing material.

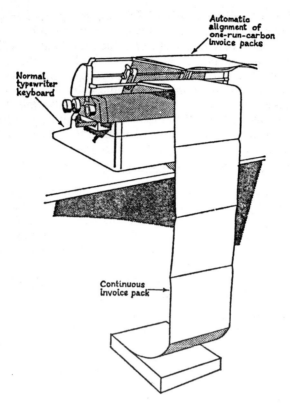

Figure 4.2   A continuous-pack invoice typewriter

4.4   Cash Discounts, Settlement Discounts and Trade Discounts

Cash Discounts and **Settlement Discounts** are very similar. Cash Discount *is given to customers who pay 'prompt cash'*. Settlement Discount *is given to debtors who pay promptly for their goods when the time for payment arrives*. It is a great inconvenience to businesses to have debtors who are slow in settling their accounts, because it means that their capital is being used by somebody else. To encourage prompt payment a cash discount is offered. Naturally this means a smaller total profit than would otherwise be earned, but it may be cheaper to give this discount than to allow debts to accumulate and perhaps suffer bad debts.

In the specimen Ledger Account in Chapter 2 we saw how these types of discount appear in the account.

Trade Discount is quite different. *It is a reduction in the* *catalogue price of an article, given by the wholesaler or manufac-turer to the retailer, to enable the retailer to make a profit.*

Take the example of a manufacturer of bicycles. Leaflets will be produced about a particular brand of bicycle explaining the merits of the machine. The price will either be printed on this literature or on a separate price list supplied on request, but the important point is that the manufacturer, and everyone else, will think of this particular machine as the £78.50 model. When invoicing a supply of machines the simple way to invoice them is to list them at the catalogue price. The invoice might therefore read:

6 'Mercury' bicycles, 26-inch frame at £78.50 = £471.00

Clearly the retailer canot sell these at the catalogue price if they have been purchased at the catalogue price. The manufacturer therefore deducts Trade Discount at an agreed rate, usually somewhere between 10 per cent and 45 per cent of the catalogue price. If these figures seem high the student must remember that durable goods of this sort may remain in stock for some considerable time before being sold, and the profit margin must be fairly large on such slow-moving items.

6 'Mercury' bicycles 26-inch frame at £78.50 = 471.00
Less Trade Discount 25% = 117.75
_____
£353.25
\=\=\=\=\=\=\=

Important note:
Trade Discount never enters an account of any sort at any time. It is deducted on the Purchases Day Book or Sales Day Book when the Invoice is recorded but it is not part of the debtor's debt. The retailer owes only the net figure of £353.25 and there is *no such thing as a Trade Discount Account.*

4.5 The Debit Note – a document very like an invoice

Definition: A Debit Note is a document which is made out by the seller whenever the purchaser has been undercharged on an invoice, or when he wishes to make some charge on a debtor which increases the debtor's debt. It may also be made out whenever a purchaser returns goods. It then advises the creditor what goods are being returned, and invites him to send a credit note (see page 66).

Suppose that an invoice has been sent to a purchaser of a typewriter valued at £300.00, but by mistake the typist had typed

£30.00 as the purchase price. Clearly the seller will want to correct this undercharge, but another invoice would not be appropriate since no 'goods' are being delivered. A debit note for £270.00 treated exactly like an invoice and put through the Day Books in exactly the same way as an invoice will put this matter right. In the same way charges for carriage, or insurance, which were not known at the time the invoice was made out, could be charged to the debtor by means of a Debit Note.

4.6   Value Added Tax and invoices

Value Added Tax is a tax which is added whenever goods or services are supplied by one person to another. At present (April 1986) there is only one rate of tax, a **standard rate** of 15 per cent, the higher rate having been abandoned. Since it is added at every stage of production, everyone who buys goods for resale, or for use in a business, pays tax on the goods purchased.

This is called **Input Tax.** Later, when selling the goods, or charging people for services, the appropriate rate of tax is charged to the customer. The business thus collects tax from customers every time it supplies an output of goods or services, and this is called **Output Tax.** Of course this Output Tax has to be paid over to the collecting authority, which is HM Customs and Excise Department (VAT), but before doing so the businessman is allowed to deduct the amount of Input Tax which he paid when he bought the goods, raw materials, etc. He therefore only pays over the *extra* tax which he has collected from his customers, since the Output Tax will usually be bigger than the Input Tax. The formula is:

Output Tax − Input Tax = Tax payable to HM Customs

A few classes of goods, notably food and children's clothes, are not taxed, and are said to be zero-rated. It follows that a grocer does not charge his customers VAT on the food they buy from him, but he will pay VAT on many things he buys for use in his shop, like cash registers, paper bags, etc. For such a trader the Input Tax he pays will always be greater than the Output Tax, which is zero. He will therefore be entitled to a refund of Tax from HM Customs and Excise.

Tax due to HM Customs is paid every three months. Refunds to zero-rated traders are paid back every month, to avoid hardship to retailers paying VAT which they cannot collect back from their customers.

As far as invoices are concerned in the United Kingdom the VAT must be shown on the invoice, which becomes a **tax invoice** for VAT purposes. A tax invoice must be recorded in the accounting system and be available for inspection by HM Customs for a period of six years. The tax on it, whether Output Tax or Input Tax will be posted to a special account (the VAT Account) which is the ledger account for HM Customs in the books of the trader concerned. It will usually be a creditor account in the Creditor's Ledger, since the trader will normally owe money to HM Customs (the Output Tax being larger than the Input Tax). However, traders who sell zero-rated items may prefer to keep the account in the Debtors' Ledger, since HM Customs will usually owe them money.

The VAT Account fits very easily into the double-entry system, it is just one more account that we have to deal with. However, the work of capturing the figures for VAT requires us to use an extra column in the day books, as shown in Section 4.7 below. For the sake of simplicity, since VAT rates are liable to change at any time at the whim of the Chancellor of the Exchequer (usually on Budget Day), the VAT calculations throughout this book have been made at 10 per cent.

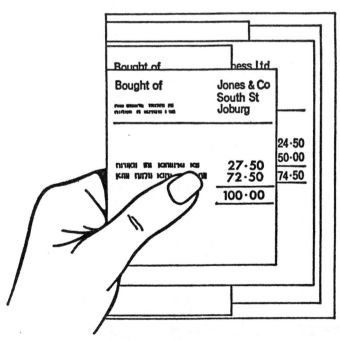

Figure 4.3 This morning's collection of Purchases Invoices
(*Note:* They are of assorted shapes, sizes, and colours – can you say why?)

4.7   The Purchases Day Book

When a businessman places an order for goods that he needs, the seller of the goods makes out an invoice. The top copy of this invoice is received by the purchaser and is recorded in the Purchases Day Book. There may be several of these invoices arriving every day, possibly as many as a hundred. They will all be the top copies of other firm's invoices, and since they may have come from a hundred different firms the bundle of invoices will look like that shown in Figure 4.3.

These invoices would now be recorded in the Purchases Day Book. The ruling of the Purchases Day Book is basically as shown in Figure 4.4, but many firms use larger paper with additional columns for collecting statistical data. These rulings will be discussed later under 'Analytical Purchases and Sales Day Books'.

19. .		F	Details	VAT	PDB1
Jan. 1	R. Brown & Co.				
	2 dozen sheets at £4.50 each	CL1	108.00	10.80	118.80
17	Peter Young Ltd.				
	4 dozen counterpanes at £8.50		408.00		
	2 dozen pillowcases at £1.20		28.80		
		CL2	436.80	43.68	480.48
21	Ambrose Smith Ltd.		36.00		
	6 dozen ounces wool at £0.50		23.40		
	3 dozen ounces wool at £0.65				
		CL3	59.40	5.94	65.34
31	Major & Co. Ltd.				
	12 'Bettawear' machines at £47.10		565.20		
			188.40		
	Less Trade Discount at 33⅓%				
		CL4	376.80	37.68	414.48
		£	981.00	98.10	1 079.10
			GL27	GL28	

Figure 4.4   The Purchases Day Book

Explanation of Figure 4.4. In fact there will be many invoices each day, filling several pages of the book by the end of the month. The four invoices shown are supposed to represent the hundreds of invoices dealt with in a month. The following points should be noted:

(a) The name of the supplier is written, or typed, on to the next clean line of the paper, next to the date. It is underlined.

(b) The details of the transaction are recorded on the next line down, giving a separate line to each item of goods supplied.

(c) The first money column is used to record the value of each group of items invoiced. If there are two or more they are added. If trade discount is deductible it is done in this first column. *Note: The Trade Discount is never entered in the books apart from the Day Books. It does not (like Cash Discount) appear on the Ledger Accounts.*

(d) The second column is used to record the VAT, which is calculated at 10 per cent in this book. This is Input Tax, which we can reclaim from HM Customs.

(e) The last column is used to record the total amount owing to each creditor for goods and VAT.

(f) The columns are then totalled (be careful as you total the first column) and the totals are cross-totalled to make sure they are correct.

(g) Folio numbers are explained in the next section.

4.8 Posting the Purchases Day Book to the Ledger

Posting is the name given to the action of entering into the Ledger accounts the figures recorded in the books of original entry. It is at this time that the transactions come into the Ledger – the main book of account.

Each supplier has given us goods as stated on the invoice. Probably these have been supplied on monthly credit terms, so that at present we have not paid for them. Since the suppliers have given value their accounts will be credited with the value of the goods supplied, including VAT. Since we have received goods our account will be debited. Our account in this case will be the Purchases Account, a nominal account in which we record the goods received. The total VAT will be debited in the VAT Account, since HM Customs are our debtors for this tax, which is Input Tax, and therefore reclaimable by us.

It is at this point that we can achieve a great saving of labour in the posting of these entries into the Ledger. Each of the Creditors, the people to whom we owe money because they have given us goods, must be credited with the value of the goods supplied and the VAT. The double entry for each of these items will be a debit to Purchases Account, and a debit to VAT Account, but we need not debit them individually. It will be enough if the *Total* of the first column of the *Purchases Day Book* only is debited to Purchases Account, and the total of the VAT column is posted to VAT Account. The entire month's credit entries in hundreds of accounts will be balanced by a single entry in each of these accounts. Figure 4.5 illustrates these postings. To save space, a ledger account without ruled columns is shown instead of ruling up proper Ledger pages.

Rule for posting the Purchases Day Book
Credit each creditor's personal account because he has given goods to us.

Debit the Purchases Account with the total purchases for the month since this is our account and we have received the goods. Debit the total VAT to VAT Account.

R. BROWN & CO. LTD		CL1
	19. . Jan. 1 Purchases PDB1	£ 118.80

PETER YOUNG LTD		CL2
	19. . Jan. 17 Purchases PDB1	£ 480.48

AMBROSE SMITH LTD		CL3
	19. . Jan. 21 Purchases PDB1	£ 65.34

MAJOR & CO. LTD		CL4
	19. . Jan. 31 Purchases PDB1	£ 414.48

PURCHASES ACCOUNT		GL27
19. . Jan. 31 Sundry Creditors PDB1	£ 981.00	

VAT ACCOUNT		GL28
19. . Jan. 31 Sundry Creditors PDB1	£ 98.10	

Figure 4.5   Ledger Accounts to Figure 4.4

4.9   Exercises set 4.1 – the Purchases Day Book

1. You are the book-keeper who keeps the Purchases Day Book. Enter the following invoices in the Purchases Day Book and then post them to the Ledger:

19. .
Apr. 1 Bought of G. Emerson 24 pictures at £2.65 each = 63.60 + VAT
£6.36.
3 R. Longfellow sold us stationery as follows:
200 boxes envelopes at £1.25 box = £250.00 and
100 writing pads at £0.65 each = £65.00 + VAT £31.50.
14 M. Twain supplies goods:
48 prints at £3.20 each = £153.60 and
36 files at £1.50 each = £54.00 + VAT £20.76.
25 S. Clemens sells us goods – boxes of paints and paint brushes 24
sets at £2.35 each set = £56.40 + VAT £5.64.
30 H. Melville sends us goods:
240 boxes sticky tape at £0.55 each = £132 and
60 boxes paper clips at £0.18 = £10.80 + VAT £14.28.

2. Enter the following invoices in the Purchases Day Book and then post
them to the Ledger. Do not forget to post the total of the book to the
Purchases Account and the VAT Account.

19. .
May 2 Bought from M. Ortega the following goods:
24 boxes grapes at £12.25 a box, = £294.00 and
72 cases oranges at £16.50 a case = £1 188.00. No VAT.
13 Received goods from C. Del Sol as follows:
30 Spanish leather handbags at £8.50 each = £255.00 + VAT
£25.50.
14 Bought of M. Lorenza:
20 cases grapefruit at £8.75 per case = £175.00, and
5 cases mandarin oranges at £9.50 per case = £47.50. No
VAT.
25 Bought from C. Del Sol 24 pairs 'Estancia' boots at £17.50 per
pair = £420.00 + VAT £42.00.
26 Bought of R. Mendoza 7 cases grapes at £12.50 per case =
£87.50. No VAT.
31 Bought of M. Ortega a repeat order of goods supplied on May 2.

3. Enter the following items in the Purchases Day Book of C. Allen, and
then post to the appropriate Ledger Accounts. You will need to do some
simple calculations.

19. .
May 1 S. Allen sold us 2 white damask table cloths at £8.80 each +
VAT £0.88
12 H. Bartlett sold us goods as follows:
24 linen tablecloths at £7.50 each + VAT £0.75.
24 tea towels at £0.90 each + VAT £0.09.
23 J. Broomfield sold to us as follows – 4 only pale blue
counterpanes at £13.50 each + VAT £1.35.
31 S. Burch sold to us as follows:
20 metres roller towelling at £37.50 + VAT £3.75 the 20 m
length.

> 40 metres roller towelling at £45.00 + VAT £4.50 the 20 m length.

4. Enter the following items in the Purchases Day Book of Janet Butcher, milliner, and post to the Ledger. You will need to do some simple calculations.

19. .

Aug. 1 Bought of R. Carr floral decorations assorted types at £35.50 + VAT £3.55 the collection.
12 Bought of M. Darwood felt for trimmings – 24 sheets 30 × 20 inches at £36.00 + VAT £3.60 per dozen sheets.
23 J. Fielding sold us the following items:
24 flowered hats at £4.50 + VAT £0.45 each.
36 straw boaters at £8.60 + VAT £0.86 each.
24 berets at £2.20 + VAT £0.22 each.
31 F. Ford sold us the following items:
12 riding hats at £6.50 + VAT £0.65 each.
12 reinforced 'Military Style' peaked hats at £13.60 + VAT £1.36 each.

4.10 Invoices for services – the Expenses Journal or Expenses Day Book

Very similar to the invoices described in the last section which are issued whenever one person sells goods to another are invoices for services supplied, sometimes called **Expense Invoices.** These are sent out by gas companies, water boards, electric power authorities, local councils, and government departments of various sorts. Garages send invoices for fuel supplied and repairs carried out to vehicles. All such invoices must be recorded in a day book very similar to the Purchases Day Book. The personal account of the suppliers will be credited since that person is now a creditor to whom our firm owes money for services rendered. The other half of this double entry will be in the nominal account, i.e. loss account, for instance Light and Heat Account, Motor Vehicle Expenses Account, and so on.

Where a firm is only in business in a small way and the volume of work would not merit the trouble of having a separate Expenses Day Book such invoices would be dealt with through the Journal Proper, which is discussed later, in Chapter 7.

4.11 The Sales Day Book

When a business supplies goods to a customer an invoice of the type described earlier is made out. The top copy is sent to the purchaser who records it in his Purchases Day Book. The delivery of the goods will now take place, but meanwhile the supplier who made out the invoice has to record the transaction in his books. The book of original entry is now the *Sales Day Book* and the second copy of the invoice, which is retained by the supplier, will be entered into this book of original entry.

Imagine you are going down the corridor at your office and you meet Charlie, the office boy, carrying the bunch of invoice second copies to the young lady who keeps the Sales Day Book. He is holding this bunch of invoices tightly because he doesn't want to lose any. Scattering sales invoices like confetti is a great nuisance; they have to be picked up and put in order, and there is always the chance that one will fly down the back of a radiator and be lost. Compare this illustration with the one in the Purchases Day Book section (Figure 4.3).

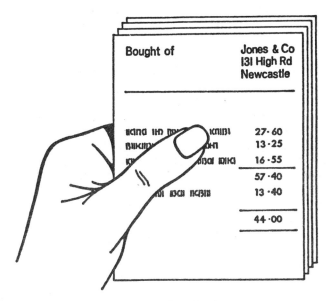

Figure 4.6 This morning's collection of Sales Invoices

You will notice at once that this time we have a collection of invoices that look alike; they are the same size, shape, and colour. This is clearly because they have all come from the same firm, our firm, and if we were to look through them we would find they were all about the same type of goods, the goods that we sell to our customers. Every day the bundle of Day Book copies of the invoices typed yesterday by the invoice department, whose top copies have already been sent through the post to the purchasers,

will be taken to the Sales Day Book clerk, who will enter them in
the Sales Day Book.

The ruling of the Sales Day Book is exactly the same as the
Purchases Day Book, and is illustrated below.

19. .			Details	VAT	SDB1
July 1	R. Smith & Co. Ltd				
	1 set Roll-over Doors	L27	37.50	3.75	41.25
4	M. Brown				
	6 sets Roll-over Doors		225.00		
	6 sets Keys		18.00		
			243.00		
	Less 20% Trade Discount		48.60		
		L3	194.40	19.44	213.84
11	R. Jones				
	1 set Lift Doors 10′ wide	L15	236.00	23.60	259.60
19	M. Luce				
	3 sets Roll-over Doors	L17	112.50	11.25	123.75
		£	580.40	58.04	638.44
			L46	L28	

Figure 4.7   The Sales Day Book

Explanation: There is no real difference between the layout of
this book and the layout of the Purchases Day Book shown earlier.

The student may like to note the following points:

(a)   A common mistake made by book-keepers is to write the folio
numbers on the wrong line. The correct line is opposite the
final money figure going to the personal account of the
debtor. This is £213.84 on July 4. Do *not* write it on the line
that says M. Brown, nor against any of the inset figures.

(b)   The folio number for the total sales is written under the
ruling-off lines. This gives us a monthly total figure which is
clear and has obviously been posted into L46, the 46th page in
the Ledger.

(c)   The total VAT which is carried to the VAT Account is £58.04
and the folio number of this account, L28, is entered at the
foot of the VAT column.

(d)   Not all invoices would have Trade Discounts, since many
goods are not supplied direct to the trade. In this case, garage
doors may be supplied in quantities to builders developing a
site, or in single items to private persons. The latter would be
charged the full catalogue price.

4.12   Posting the Sales Day Book into the Ledger

	R. SMITH & CO. LTD	L27
19. .	£	
July 1 Sales SDB1	41.25	

	M. BROWN	L3
19. .	£	
July 4 Sales SDB1	213.84	

	R. JONES	L15
19. .	£	
July 11 Sales SDB1	259.60	

	M. LUCE	L17
19. .	£	
July 19 Sales SDB1	123.75	

	SALES ACCOUNT	L46
	19. .	£
	July 31 Sundry	
	Debtors SDB1	580.40

	VAT ACCOUNT	L28
	19. .	£
	July 31 Sundry	
	Debtors SDB1	58.04

Figure 4.8   How sales appear when posted to the Ledger Accounts

The postings from the Sales Day Book are shown in Figure 4.8. Each of the debtors is debited with the value of the goods received (including the VAT) – *debit the receiver*. The Sales Account is credited with the full sales value for the month, since it has given these goods to the debtors – *credit the giver*. The VAT Account is also credited, because HM Customs has become a creditor of ours for this amount which we have collected from our debtors – or at least we will collect it when they settle their accounts.

Once again the student should note that the double entry is perfect. We have on the debit side, scattered through four accounts, amounts which total £638.44, the exact amount credited in the Sales Account and the VAT Account. The debit entries therefore equal the credit entries.

4.13   How to 'carry forward' from one page to the next

Whichever book we use in book-keeping, we are bound to come sooner or later to the bottom of the page. If we are to keep the book tidy and arithmetically correct we have to 'carry forward' from one page to the next. This is illustrated in Figure 4.9 (note *c/f* means 'carried forward' and *b/f* means 'brought forward'):

		L12			171.50
	R. Smith				
	1 set passe-pictures		45.68		
	2 gross hinges		3.41		
	1 gross packets of braces		17.50		
		L7	66.59	6.66	73.25
		c/f	1 624.50	162.45	1 786.95

					SDB56
		b/f	1 624.50	162.45	1 786.95
	M. Jones				
	2 dozen plastic frames	L11	11.59	1.16	12.75
	P. Loiter				
	1 dozen passe-pictures		45.68		
	1 gross hinges		1.71		
		L29	47.39	4.74	52.13

Figure 4.9   Carrying forward from one page to the next page

Notice that the page that is nearly filled is ruled off with a single line and added up, but the adding up is not closed off with two ruled lines as it would be in an ordinary addition sum. The figures to be carried forward are open, and the letters c/f are written in the folio column. This open figure is then carried forward to the start of the next page, where it is labelled b/f in the folio column.

4.14   Exercises set 4.2 – the Sales Day Book

The student should now try the following Sales Day Book exercises. In each case you have to enter the invoices in the Sales Day Book, total the book at the end of the month and post it to the Ledger Accounts not forgetting the:

Rule for posting the Sales Day Book
Debit the personal accounts of the debtors.
Credit the total sales for the month in the Sales Account, and the

total VAT for the month in the VAT Account. To help you carry forward you should particularly try Question 3.

1. 19. .
   Mar. 1 R. Gordon purchases from us a presentation pencil case at £12.30 + VAT £1.23.
   2 D. Symons purchases a pen and pencil set at £12.50 and six cigarette lighters at £4.40 each. Total VAT £3.89.
   3 R. Gordon purchases 6 presentation pencil cases at £12.30 each + VAT £7.38.
   4 W. Archer purchases from us 2 cigarette lighters at £4.40 each, a silver pencil at £8.85, and 24 ball-point pens at £0.20 each. Total VAT £2.24.
   5 R. Driver purchases 24 silver pencils at a special price of £5.60 each. VAT £13.44.
   6 D. Symons purchases 3 cigarette lighters at £4.40 each. VAT £1.32.

2. 19. .
   May 1 R. Parker purchases goods as follows:
       24 boxes dominoes at £1.15 each = £27.60.
       36 boxes draughts at £1.20 each = £43.20.
       24 boxes ludo at £1.25 each = £30.00. Total VAT £10.08.
   2 A. Grace purchased goods as follows:
       36 dartboards at £7.45 each = £268.20 + VAT £26.82.
   23 M. Peacock bought goods as follows:
       1 grand piano (model size) £35.80 + VAT £3.58.

3. 19. .
   Jan. 1 S. Marner buys goods as follows:
       24 articles of clothing at £3.45 each = £82.80.
       36 pairs shoes at £8.25 per pair = £297.00.
       48 pairs socks at £1.14 per pair = £54.72. Total VAT = £43.45.
   2 Sold to G. Eliot goods as follows:
       12 suits at £23.50 each = £282.00.
       24 pairs of socks at £1.14 per pair = £27.36.
       36 pairs of shoes at £7.25 per pair = £261.00. Total VAT = £57.04.
   3 G. Cass purchases as follows:
       36 pairs shoes at £8.25 per pair = £297.00.
       24 pairs shoes at £7.95 per pair = £190.80. Total VAT £48.78.
   4 D. Calthorpe purchased goods below
       84 pairs of socks at £1.15 per pair = £96.60.
       36 pairs stockings at £1.28 per pair = £46.08. Total VAT = £14.27.
   8 Sold goods to D. Varden as follows:
       48 sets nylon underwear at £9.35 per set = £448.80.
       24 sets night negligée at £8.65 per set = £207.60. Total VAT = £65.64.

11 Sold to M. Archer goods as follows:
   36 pairs of stockings at £1.28 per pair = £46.08.
   48 sets nylon underwear at £9.35 per set = £448.80. Total VAT = £49.49.

17 M. Brown buys goods as follows:
   24 pairs stockings at £1.28 per pair = £30.72.
   24 pairs shoes at £8.95 per pair = £214.80.
   36 pairs shoes at £7.25 per pair = £261.00. Total VAT = £50.65.

18 R. Ebenezer buys goods as follows:
   36 pairs shoes at £8.95 per pair = £322.20 + VAT £32.22.

23 Sold to G. Eliot goods as follows:
   24 suits at £23.50 each = £564.00 + VAT £56.40.

27 G. Cass purchased goods as follows:
   36 pairs shoes at £7.25 per pair = £261.00 + VAT £26.10.

4. This exercise has Trade Discount in it. You will find some information about Trade Discount in Section 4.4. Read it before you do this exercise.

Enter the following items in your Sales Day Book. As your goods are nationally known articles like 'Scrumptious – the biscuits your dog will really enjoy' you quote the price to the public on your invoices and give the retailer Trade Discount of 25 per cent. You will need to calculate this discount.

19. .
Jan.   1 R. Harper buys goods as follows:
          24 dozen tins of Scrumptious Biscuit Meal at £0.65 per tin = £187.20.
          12 dozen packets Scrumptious Dog Biscuits at £0.50 per packet = £72.00.
          Trade Discount of 25% given on the total value of the invoice. VAT on invoice = £19.44.

        3 We sell T. Birchin goods as follows:
          30 dozen tins of Scrumptious Biscuit Meal (large size) at £2.50 per tin = £900.00.
          Less 25% Trade Discount. VAT on invoice £67.50.

       14 We sell R. Harper goods as follows:
          24 dozen tins of Scrumptious Biscuit Meal at £0.65 per tin = £187.20.
          6 dozen packets Scrumptious Dog Biscuits at £0.50 per packet = £36.00.
          Trade Discount of 25% given on total value. VAT on invoice = £16.74.

       25 We sell M. Jones goods as follows:
          3 dozen tins Scrumptious Biscuit Meal (large size) at £2.50 per tin = £90.00.
          6 dozen packets Scrumptious Biscuit Meal at £0.65 per packet = £46.80.
          Trade Discount of 25% on total value of invoice. VAT on invoice = £10.26.

4.15 Documents for returns – the credit note

Introduction
We must expect in the course of business that some of our
customers will return goods for valid reasons. A purchaser is not
entitled to return something just because he has changed his mind
about having it; but occasionally we may oblige a client by
accepting this type of return. The usual reasons for returning
goods are:

(a) The purchaser holds that the goods are unsatisfactory for
    some reason, e.g. wrong colour; wrong size; not up to sample;
    not up to specification; imperfectly finished; damaged in
    transit, etc.
(b) The purchaser is entitled by contract to return goods, for
    instance goods sent on approval.

   In these circumstances the document used is the credit note.

Definition
A credit note is a business document made out whenever one
person returns goods to another. It is usually printed in red, to
distinguish it from an invoice, and like an invoice, is made out by
the seller of the goods, who is now receiving them back again.
Usually there are only two copies.
   The credit note should show:

(a) The names and addresses of both parties to the transaction.
(b) An exact description of the goods being returned.
(c) The unit price, the number and the total value of the goods
    returned.

Other reasons for sending a credit note

(a) Sometimes goods that are unsatisfactory for some reason are
    not returned because of the incovenience and cost. A piece of
    furniture that has been damaged by rain in transport may only
    need repolishing. The purchaser may be perfectly prepared to
    have this repolishing carried out by one of his own employees,
    provided the seller will make him an allowance to cover the
    cost. This will be done by sending a credit note for the agreed
    amount. This is called an **Allowance.**
(b) We saw in Section 4.5 above that when an undercharge is
    made on an invoice a document called a debit note was sent to
    increase the original invoice to the proper figure. Invoice
    typists can make errors which result in overcharges instead of
    undercharges. Supposing the typewriter valued at £300.00 was

invoiced at £3 000.00. Clearly a credit note for £2 700.00 will be required to correct the overcharge.

Credit notes may therefore be sent for three reasons:

(a) To credit a debtor with returns.
(b) To credit a debtor with an allowance.
(c) To credit a debtor to correct an overcharge.

Figures 4.10 and 4.11 illustrate some points about credit notes.

CREDIT NOTE

Messrs Brewis and Jeffrey,	No. 7864
Cherrydown,	RIDER & Co. Ltd.
Newtown,	High Street
Essex.	London, W.C.2.

DATE	20th May	19..		REP.	M. TYLER.

No.	Description	Cat. Price (£)	Value (£)	VAT (£)	Total value £
3	Dining Chairs (damaged in transit)	£21.50	64.50	6.45	70.95

Fig. 4.10 A credit note: the Original Document for returns
(*Note:* Credit notes are always printed in red.)

A pitfall for students – 'catalogue price'
Students using this book to prepare for examinations should beware of a common pitfall set for them in written papers: there may be an entry which reads as follows:

July 10 Jones returns goods sent to him on July 3, Catalogue price £70.00.

If students refer to July 3 they will almost certainly find that these goods were sold at a Trade Discount in the original order. It would be quite wrong to give the customer a credit note for the full catalogue price when the trade discount price only was charged on the original invoice. This would be as good as giving him his profit. For instance, if the Trade Discount were 25 per cent the customer

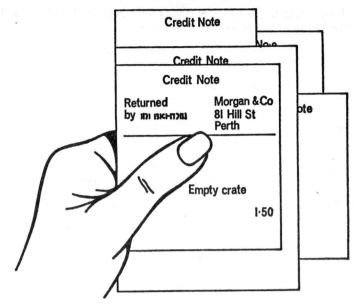

Figure 4.11   **This morning's postbag of credit notes for purchases we have returned.**
(*Can you explain why they are all shapes and sizes?*)

would have been invoiced for the goods at £52.50. If we made a refund of £70.00 the customer would finish up £17.50 better off. Clearly this is wrong.

The credit note will only be made out for £52.50 to cancel out the original invoice.

What happens to the two copies?
Usually credit notes are made out in duplicate. The top copy is sent to the purchaser who has returned the goods, and is recorded in his Purchases Returns Book. The duplicate is kept by the seller and is recorded in his Sales Returns Book.

4.16   The Purchases Returns Book

This is the third subsidiary book. It is kept in exactly the same way as the other books, and is illustrated in Figure 4.12.

PURCHASES RETURNS BOOK					PRB1
19. .			Details	VAT	
Jan. 7	R. Miles				
	1 packing crate	L5	5.00	0.50	5.50
11	M. Joynson				
	2 boxes address cards				
	(incorrectly displayed)	L7	8.90	0.89	9.79
29	R. Brown				
	1 dozen boxes invitation cards				
	on approval – (not required)	L11	8.50	0.85	9.35
		£	22.40	2.24	24.64
			L3	L35	

Figure 4.12   The Purchases Returns Book

4.17   Posting the Purchases Returns Book into the Ledger

If Figure 4.12 was posted into the Ledger accounts the entries would be as in Figure 4.13.

The balances on the credit side were put in to make the accounts look more realistic. Clearly if we are returning goods to a creditor we must have had some goods to return. It would be possible to have no balance on the accounts and still return goods, if they were goods for which we had already paid in full. In that case our creditor would owe us money for the goods returned, and would temporarily turn into a debtor. At present it is best to disregard this type of complication. Notice that the creditor has been debited with the return since he has received the goods back again. Our account, the Purchases Returns Account, has been credited because we have given the goods back again. The VAT Account has been credited, since we can no longer claim the Input Tax on the items returned. Note that once again the debit items (totalling £24.64) exactly balance the credit entries in the Purchases Returns Acc̶ ̶ ̶t and the VAT Account.

̶ ̶ing the Purchases Returns Book
̶ ̶onal account of the creditor who is receiving the
̶ ̶e returned.
̶ ̶ases Returns Account with the total returns for

R. MILES ACCOUNT   L5

19. .		£	19. .			£
Jan. 7	Purchases Returned PRB1	5.50	Jan. 1	Balance	b/d	400.00

M. JOYNSON ACCOUNT   L7

19. .		£	19. .			£
Jan. 11	Purchases Returned PRB1	9.79	Jan. 1	Balance	b/d	280.00

R. BROWN ACCOUNT   L11

19. .		£	19. .			£
Jan. 29	Purchases Returned PRB1	9.35	Jan. 1	Balance	b/d	260.00

PURCHASES RETURNS ACCOUNT   L3

			19. .		£
			Jan. 31	Sundry Creditors PRB1	22.40

VAT ACCOUNT   L35

			19. .		£
			Jan. 31	Sundry Creditors PRB1	2.24

Figure 4.13 How Purchase Returns appear in the Ledger Accounts

the month, since we have given them back. Credit the VAT
Account with any VAT which can no longer be reclaimed from
HM Customs.

4.18 Exercises set 4.3 – the Purchases Returns Book

1. Enter the following items in Thomas Brown's Purchases Returns Book
and post to the Ledger:

19. .
Apr. 5 Returned to H. White & Co. containers valued at £7.50 + VAT
£0.75.
    12 Returned to R. Robertson containers valued at £12.00 + VAT
£1.20.
    17 Returned to M. Smith 24 posters (damaged) £4.25 per copy =
£102 + VAT £10.20.
    24 Returned to R. Jones 1 picture (definition poor) at £15.00 +
VAT £1.50.

2. Enter the following items in Roger Freedom's Purchases Returns Book
and post to the Ledger.

19. .
July   3 Returned to H. Jones & Co. crates valued at £9.60 + VAT
£0.96.
       15 Received a credit note from M. Lomax for goods returned to
him as follows:
          1 white leather-covered dining suite and table at £265.00 +
VAT £26.50.
       17 Returned to M. Norrish goods as follows:
          1 whitewood kitchen set at £78.00.
          1 rosewood suite at £350.00. VAT added £42.80.

3. Enter the following credit notes in P. Palmer's Purchases Returns
Book and post to the Ledger.

19. .
Sept.   4 Returned to M. Haddow
          1 white bedspread at £7.25.
          1 set sheets and pillowcases at £12.35. VAT added £1.96.
          Damaged in transit (rainwater).
       14 Returned to R. Playle 1 packing case charged at £8 + VAT £0.80.
       27 Returned to B. Harlow 2 mattresses £38.00 each (not up to
sample). VAT added £7.60.

4. Enter the following credit notes in T. Harman's Purchases Returns
Book. Total the book and post to the Ledger.

19. .
Oct.   3 Returned to M. Venables 1 woollen jumper (seams not sewn
properly) at £8.40 + VAT £0.84.
       14 Returned to M. Spurgeon 2 tablecloths, best linen (faded) at
£12.25 each. VAT added £2.45.
       17 Received a credit note from H. Morton as follows:
          2 white woollen scarves (marked) at £3.60 each.
          1 'Orlon' jumper (wrong colour) at £15.95. VAT added £2.32.

4.19.   The Sales Returns Book

When the seller makes out a credit note in duplicate, he sends the
top copy to the purchaser who has returned the goods. The second
copy is taken to the clerks in the Accounts Department, who
proceed to enter it into the Sales Returns Book. This is the last of
the four subsidiary books which deal with the movement of goods
into and out of our business.

Once again it is interesting to visualize this morning's collection
of credit notes on its way to the Accounts Department (see Figure
4.14). This time it is a bundle of second copies of our own credit
notes, the top copies having been sent off yesterday to the
creditors who returned the goods. Unlike the untidy collection in
Figure 4.11 they form a neat bundle, since they were all made out
by the same firm – our firm.

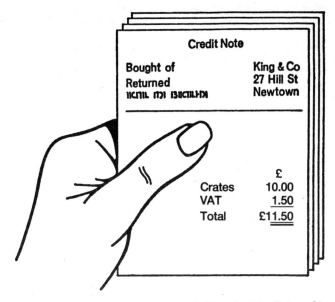

Figure 4.14 This morning's collection of Credit Notes for Sales Returned to us; the second copies go from the typist to the Accounts Department

When entered in the Sales Returns Book these credit notes will appear as shown in Figure 4.15. Again the ruling of this book is exactly the same as the other day books.

19. .		F	Details	VAT	SRB27
July 3	Brown & Co.				
	2 crates at 3.50 each	L1	7.00	0.70	7.70
7	Smith & Jones				
	4 chairs (wrong pattern)	L2	60.00	6.00	66.00
19	Hook & Co.				
	1 bedroom suite		185.00		
	1 mirror		27.00		
		L3	212.00	21.20	233.20
		£	279.00	27.90	306.90
			L4	L5	

Figure 4.15 The Sales Returns Book

4.20   Posting the Sales Returns book into the Ledger

Once again when we post the Sales Returns Book into the Ledger
we have to ask ourselves the question 'Who is the receiver in this
case, and who is the giver?' Since we are dealing with Sales that
have been returned the 'person' receiving the goods is our own
firm, the persons giving the goods are the debtors who are
dissatisfied with them. The rule for posting Sales Returns is
therefore:

Debit the Sales Returns Account with the total returns for the
month, and the VAT Account with the tax we no longer need to
pay, since we will not be collecting it from the debtors.
Credit the individual amounts in the debtors' accounts to reduce
their debts to us.

When posted into the Ledger Accounts the entries now appear
as in Figure 4.16.

BROWN & CO.				L1
19. .	£	19. .		£
July 1 Balance	b/d 120.00	July 3 Sales Returns	SRB27	7.70

SMITH & JONES				L2
19. .	£	19. .		£
July 1 Balance	b/d 65.50	July 7 Sales Returns	SRB27	66.00

HOOK & CO.				L3
19. .	£	19. .		£
July 1 Balance	b/d 72.80	July 19 Sales Returns		
			SRB27	233.20

SALES RETURNS ACCOUNT			L4
19. .	£		
July 31 Sundry Debtors			
SRB27	279.00		

VAT ACCOUNT			L5
19. .	£		
July 31 Sundry Debtors			
SRB27	27.90		

Figure 4.16 How Sales Returns appear in the Ledger Accounts

Notes: Once again it makes the accounts more realistic if we invent
some balances of goods unpaid for on the Ledger Accounts of our
debtors. They will be most likely to return goods in the first few

days after delivery, before they have actually paid for them. In this respect the period of credit given before payment is needed is an advantage. It acts as a safeguard to the debtor. He has the chance of rejecting the goods before he has paid for them.

4.21 Exercises set 4.4 – the Sales Returns Book

1. Enter the following credit notes in R. Jones's Sales Returns Book and post to the Ledger:

19. .
Jan.   4 Sent M. Smith a credit note for 2 steam irons at £12.85 each (heating element faulty). VAT added £2.57.
    15 Sent R. Thompson a credit note for 3 electric fires at £23.30 each (switches faulty). VAT added £6.99.
    17 Sent R. Leighton a credit note for a 'Washette' dishwasher (faulty motor) at £237.50. VAT added £23.75.
    18 Sent M. Kehu a credit note for an overcharge on an invoice (typing error), £10.00 + VAT £1.00.

2. Enter the following credit notes in R. Johnson's Sales Returns Book and post to the Ledger:

19. .
July 12 Sent R. Day a credit note for goods returned as follows:
        1 table (leg broken) at £42.75.
        2 containers for Zahl polish valued at £2.50 each. VAT total £4.78.
    17 Sent M. Grossmith credit note for goods returned as follows:
        2 dozen tiles (broken) valued at £7.20 altogether
        1 chair (not glued in manufacture) at £34.80, VAT total £4.20.
    29 Sent R. Thorpe credit note for goods as follows:
        1 imitation Chesterfield suite (not up to quality of sample) at £348.00 + VAT £34.80.

3. Enter the following credit notes in R. Larkin's Sales Returns Book and post to the Ledger:

19. .
Aug.   4 M. Seager returned to us goods valued at £24.50 + VAT £2.45 (picnic outfit crushed in transit).
    11 R. Lester returned to us goods as follows:
        1 camp bed (joints insecurely riveted) at £25.25.
        2 camp tables (painting inferior) at £13.25 each. VAT total £5.18.
    17 M. Shoreditch returns goods valued at £37.25 + VAT £3.72 (tent damaged in proofing process).
    29 M. Lower sent back goods as follows:
        1 kit bag (eyelets torn) at £4.25.
        2 sleeping bags (mildewed due to bad storage) at £12.50 each. VAT added £2.92.

4. Enter the following credit notes in R. Lowry's Sales Returns Book:

19. .

Aug. 7 Sent M. Team a credit note value £6.45 + VAT £0.64 for containers returned empty.

   13 Sent R. Jorgensen a credit note value £87.75 + VAT £8.78 (for a damaged central heating unit).

   27 Sent M. Stevens a credit note as follows:

   1 wrought-iron gate (hinges defective) at £62.50.

   1 wrought-iron lampholder (insecure welding) at £25.00. VAT total £8.75.

4.22 Recapitulation

We have now considered in this chapter the four subsidiary books that deal with the movement of goods into and out of our business. Remember 'goods' are the items that we normally buy and sell in our type of business. Flour is 'goods' to a baker, and so are cakes and bread, but a filing cabinet is not 'goods' to a baker even though it is a useful commodity and most large-scale bakeries would buy many of them. A filing cabinet is an asset, and would be recorded in the Journal Proper, which is dealt with in Chapter 7.

A really sound understanding of these four Day Books, and of the postings to the ledger from them, is vital to any book-keeper. Any businessman who wants to keep his own accounts, and any student, is strongly advised to work through at least some of the exercises in order to acquire real experience in the handling of these entries. Even if the simpler systems explained in the next chapter are to be used they can only be fully understood if book-keepers are familiar with the traditional daybook entries.

4.23 A page to test you on the journals

Cover the page with a sheet of paper, then read one question at a time.

Answers	Questions
—	1 What is the main book of account?
1 The Ledger.	2 What do we call all other books?
2 Subsidiary Books.	3 What does 'subsidiary' mean?
3 'Giving additional help to.'	4 Which is the most important subsidiary book?
4 The Journal.	5 What does 'journal' mean?
5 Daily Record.	6 Is the Journal still in existence in its original form as a day book in which everything that happens every day is written down?
6 No. It is split up into five parts.	7 What are the names of five 'Day Books' or Journals now?
7 The Purchases Day Book; The Sales Day Book; The Purchases Returns Book; The Sales Returns Book; and the Journal Proper.	8 What are the first four of these books concerned with?
8 The Purchase, Sales, and Returns of goods.	9 What are 'goods'?
9 They are the commodities that form our normal line of business.	10 Is bread 'goods' to a baker?
10 Yes.	11 Is a delivery van 'goods' to a baker?
11 No. He doesn't buy and sell delivery vans.	12 Would a garage call 'delivery vans' goods?
12 Yes, because garages buy and sell vans.	13 Where do we enter it when we buy something that is not our normal line of business, i.e. typewriters for use in the office?
13 We enter it in the Journal Proper.	14 Where would we put a Bad Debt entry?
15 In the Journal Proper.	15 How many questions did you get right out of 14?

Do the test again and again until you get *all* the answers right.

4.24   A page to test you on invoices and debit notes

Answers	Questions
—	1 What is an invoice?
1 An invoice is a business document which is made out whenever one person sells goods to another.	2 Is it a legal document?
2 No, but it may be used as evidence of a contract of sale.	3 How many copies are there?
3 Usually three, four, or five.	4 Name the five possible copies, and the places they go to.
4 Top Copy, sent to purchaser, who puts it in his Purchases Day Book; Day Book Copy, goes to Accounts Dept. to go in Sales Day Book; Delivery Note, goes to stores and is taken by carman for signature on delivery; Advice Note, goes to stores to be wrapped with goods so that purchaser can check them; Representative's Copy, goes to commercial traveller who took the order.	5 How long do we keep invoices?
5 Six years.	6 Why six years?
6 Because the Statute of Limitations says if six years expire from the time an ordinary contract is made, then legal action cannot be taken.	7 What must an invoice have on it?
7 (a) Names and Addresses of both parties; (b) exact description of goods; (c) value of goods; (d) terms and conditions of sale; (e) it often has E & O E (f) VAT details	8 What does E & O E mean?
8 Errors and Omissions Excepted.	9 Why is this put on the invoice?
9 Because otherwise a genuine mistake or omission would perhaps not be able to be corrected.	10 What is a debit note?
10 It is a business document which is made out whenever an invoice has an undercharge on it, to correct the undercharge.	11 What else could it be used for?
11 To charge carriage or insurance.	

4.25 A page to test you on credit notes

Answers	Questions
—	1 What is a Credit Note?
1 It is a business document made out whenever a buyer returns goods to a seller.	2 Who makes it out, and when?
2 The seller makes it out when the goods return to his premises.	3 What safety device prevents anyone mistaking a Credit Note for an invoice?
3 A Credit Note is always made out in red and may be printed with the red ribbon on the typewriter.	4 How many copies are made out?
4 Two copies.	5 Where do they go?
5 One copy is sent to the debtor who returned the goods; he enters it in his Purchases Returns Book. The other copy is kept by the seller and entered in his Sales Returns Book.	6 Why might a debtor return goods?
6 (a) Because they were damaged on arrival; (b) because they were the wrong size, colour, or type; (c) not up to sample; (d) not up to specification; (e) goods sent 'on approval' and not required.	7 Can the buyer return the goods because he has decided after all he doesn't want them?
7 No. This would be a breach of contract.	8 Why else do we send someone a Credit Note (two reasons)?
8 (a) If an invoice is incorrect, having been overstated, a Credit Note will put it right; (b) if goods are not satisfactory, the buyer may agree to have them at a cheaper price instead of returning them. This is called 'an allowance' and it is made by sending him a Credit Note.	9 How many questions did you get right out of 8? Go over the page several times till you get it all correct.

5
Reducing the work
on Day Book entries

5.1 Saving work on the Day Books

As firms have grown bigger and have had to deal with more and
more suppliers and customers the work of keeping day books has
become very time consuming and accountants have looked for
ways of saving work in this area. The point is really that at the end
of all the work all you have to show for your efforts is a permanent
record of the documents – which can really be discarded now – and
an indication of where they have been posted. This is a great deal
of effort for a rather limited result.

There are three ways of saving work in this connection:

(a) Use the documents themselves as day books.
(b) Slip systems of book-keeping.
(c) Use a three in one system of simultaneous records.
(d) Computerize the accounting.

5.2 Using the documents themselves as Day Books

If documents such as invoices can be securely kept in binders or
lever arch files so that they are quite safe, they can themselves
become the permanent record that we require. It is usual to 'batch
them up' into groups of about ten or twenty, which can be dealt
with at the same time. Thus ten sales invoices would be debited in
the accounts of the ten debtors, and then the totals of the invoices
(and if necessary the VAT) are added up on an adding-listing
machine, or an electronic printing calculator. Both these machines
give us a printed list of the amounts added and a total for the
batch. The individual items have already been posted to the
debtor's accounts but the total of them must now be posted to the
credit side of Sales Account. In the United Kingdom where Value
Added Tax also enters into the picture the VAT on the invoices
would also be totalled to give the entry in the VAT Account. We

Example No. 1—Bank in Credit — Week No. **14** — Commencing: **6TH APRIL 1986**

RECEIPTS

Day	Date	Gross Daily Takings (cash) Col 1		Gross Daily Takings (cheques) Col 2		Other Receipts Col 3		Particulars
Sunday	: 6/4	196	27					
Monday	: 7/4	232	44	28	80	35	60	TAX REFUND
Tuesday	: 8/4	256	26			5	48	DEBTOR P. SMITH
Wednesday	: 9/4	112	27	12	64			
Thursday	: 10/4	299	85	19	74			
Friday	: 11/4	364	24	26	34			
Saturday	: 12/4	382	72	62	50			
	Totals	1824	05	147	02	41	08	

PAID TO BANK

	CASH Col 4		CHEQUES Col 5		TOTAL Col 6	
	420	00	66	88	486	88
	520	00	58	72	578	72
Totals	940	00	125	60	1065	60

PAYMENTS FOR BUSINESS STOCK

Date or Chq. No.	To Whom Paid	By Cash Col 7		By Cheque Col 8	
7/4	J. CONLAN & SONS	48	50		
7/4	J. BREWER & CO. LTD.			36	50
8/4	A. J. GOOD LTD.			136	85
8/4	J. BROWN & CO. LTD.	33	80		
11/4	F. LINGSEY & CO.	26	70		
11/4	A. NEWCOMBE			86	25
	Totals	109	00	259	60

PAYMENTS OTHER THAN FOR STOCK

Nature of Payment		By Cash Col 9		By Cheque Col 10	
Rent		35	00		
Rates					
Light and Heat				63	50
Carriage		9	45		
Postages £1·70 24p. £2·38		4	32		
Paper				27	46
Motor Expenses	PETROL	16	12		
—do—	REPAIRS			86	50
Travelling		7	32		
Cleaning		5	00		
Printing & Stationery				23	20
Repairs & Renewals				15	78
Insurance (Business)					
Advertising					
Telephone					
Wages (Wife)					
Wages (Employees)		65	76		
Sundries		1	05		
Private Pension Contributions					
Inland Revenue (PAYE + NI)				27	96
Drawings for Self (see Note. 10)		85	00		
—do—					
—do—					
Capital Items (see note 7)					
	Totals	229	01	244	40

WEEKLY CASH REPORT

	Cash in Hand (as counted) brought forward	6	46
	Gross Weekly Takings (Col 1 + Col 2)	1971	07
Add	Other Receipts (Col 3)	41	08
	Cash Drawn from Bank	–	–
	Total	2018	61
	Stock Payments (cash)(Col 7)	109	00
Deduct	Other Payments (cash)(Col 9)	229	01
	Amount paid to Bank	1065	60
	Total	1403	61
	Cash Balance on books	615	00
	Cash in hand (as counted)	614	73
	Difference on books (+ or –)	–	27

WEEKLY BANK REPORT

	Opening Balance brought forward			1543	56
Add	Total Paid to Bank during week (Col 6)			1065	60
	Total			2409	16
	Cash drawn from bank	–	–		
Deduct	Stock Payments (Col 8)	259	60		
	Other Payments (Col 10)	244	40		
	Bank Standing Orders	–	–		
	Bank and Interest Charges	–	–		
	Total			504	00
	Closing Balance carried forward			1905	16

Figure 5.1 The Simplex weekly page

should thus have done a proper double entry for all the invoices in the batch, without keeping any day books. The batches of invoices would be filed away in their binders and any query could always be settled by turning up the actual invoice.

In this way the Purchases Day Book, Sales Day Book, Purchases Returns Book and Sales Returns Book can be dispensed with.

The most ingenious method of avoiding keeping day books, which is most appropriate for small businesses, is the Simplex system. This is marketed by George Vyner Ltd., Simplex House, Mytholmbridge Mills, Holmfirth, Huddersfield, HD7 1BR. A single book, the Simplex D Account Book contains a whole year's records. There are 53 weekly pages (every few years there are 53 weeks in a year). Each weekly page, as shown in Figure 5.1, has room for 'Receipts' (a cash book for sales), 'Payments for Business Stock' (a Purchases Day Book), 'Payments other than for stock' (for recording expense invoices), etc. The invoices are simply recorded on the weekly pages, and are then carried to summaries at the back of the book. It is a very straightforward system which takes short cuts on the double entry system. Anyone who knows double entry will easily follow the system and find it very convenient, while those without this knowledge can simply follow the detailed instructions in the front of the book.

5.3   Slip systems of book-keeping

In some businesses, particularly banks, day books are avoided because the customer puts in documents in slip form which can be entered directly into the ledger accounts (or more likely these days into the computer). If a customer makes out a paying-in slip to pay money into his account, or makes out a cheque to draw money out of the account, these slips can be used as the basic document from which to make entries.

5.4   Simultaneous records

The second method of saving work on the keeping of day books is the type of system called 'Three in One' systems, or simultaneous records. They are one of the most time-saving and ingenious ways of keeping records. Many firms now produce this type of system, which is particularly useful for the medium-size business, but the most celebrated name in this field is probably 'Kalamazoo'. The system described and illustrated in Figure 5.2 by kind permission of Kalamazoo Ltd, is called the 'Compact System'. An even more

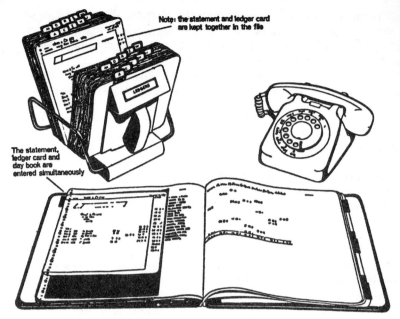

Figure 5.2 Records made simultaneously

compact Kalamazoo 'Small Business Pack' provides the entire records of a business in one small case, the size of a brief case.

The basic idea of the system is the simultaneous entry of invoices in the Day Book, the Ledger, and also on the statement. The Day Book takes the form of loose-leaf sheets housed in a binder. The same binder can hold both the Purchases and Sales Journals, and the Returns Journals

The interesting feature of the system is the line of holes punched down the edge of the Day Book pages, which enable a flat board called a Collator to be secured under the Day Book page by the studs which stick up through the holes down the edge. The page is raised a little, the collator slipped underneath so that its studs stick up through the holes, and a sheet of carbon paper is placed on top.

The ledger card and the statement, which are always kept together in a mini-tray are now positioned over the Day Book page so that what is written will occupy the next clean line on all three records. The invoice details are then written, and simultaneously bring the statement, the ledger card, and the Day Book up to date. The ledger card and statement are replaced in the tray, the next account due to be entered is selected and positioned, and a further entry is made from the next invoice. Checks are built into the system to ensure that the total value of invoices received or dispatched that day equals the total value entered in the Day Books. Our Day Book pages then provide the figures for the postings to the nominal accounts, and also any analysis figures required about particular departments.

The ledger cards, or accounts, have already been posted, and no errors in posting can have occurred, while the statements are kept up to date and are ready for dispatch on the last day of the month.

It is difficult to imagine a more simple or efficient system.

A further example of these methods is given in Chapter 15, pages 214–19, which deal with Wages Books.

5.5 How book-keeping records are computerized

In the last quarter of a century the development of computers has revolutionized office practices. A program of instructions is fed into the computer which enables it to process any data supplied. Thus the entire debtors' ledger can be stored on a fast computer medium such as disc or magnetic tape, each debtor being given a unique code number which identifies him in the system. The average computer works at a speed of a million operations per second. Tedious manual preparation of invoices, credit notes and payments can be performed at electronic speeds, and the accounting entries done simultaneously. Although preparatory work must still be performed, for example, when an order is received, all the operations which follow from that order – e.g. invoicing, accounting records, statements, etc. – can be carried out automatically.

1 *Computer hardware*

Whilst a detailed knowledge of computer hardware is not necessary, it is useful to be familiar with the names of the units and the parts they play. Figure 5.3 shows a typical commercial configuration, with alternative input and output devices.

The three essential elements in computerisation are **inputs, processing** and **outputs.** We must be able to put data into the computer, which will then process the data and put out the results so that they can be understood. These three elements are provided for in the following ways.

(a) *Input devices.* Some typical input devices are punched-card readers, paper-tape readers, key-edit devices and the console communicator, which is like an electronic typewriter. All these devices are relatively slow in the preparation and checking stage. At the time of input the card reader operates at about 160 000 characters per minute – much slower than the computer's million operations per second. The key-edit device is faster, since

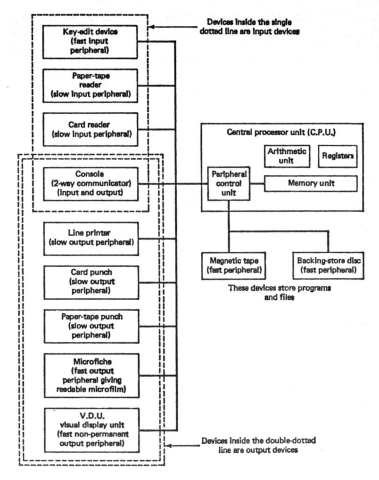

Figure 5.3 A commercial computer configuration

information is fed onto magnetic tape, rather than cards or paper tape. The term 'edit' refers to the ability of the device to detect when an operator miskeys and feeds an error into the system. When a collection of documents, such as purchases invoices, is to be put into the computer, the documents are 'batched up', coded with any necessary codes and passed to the punch or key operator. The resulting punched cards, paper tape or magnetic tape can then be used to pass data into the computer. This is called **data transfer.** The data can now be processed according to the programs already stored in the computer.

(b) *The central processor unit.* The CPU is the main section of

(1) Every transaction has an original document

(but now most of these documents will be produced by the computer automatically instead of manually)

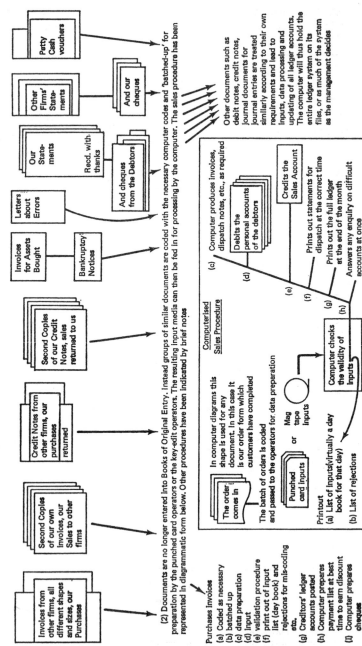

(2) Documents are no longer entered into Books of Original Entry. Instead groups of similar documents are coded with the necessary computer codes and 'batched-up' for preparation by the punched card operators or the key-edit operators. The resulting input media can then be fed in for processing by the computer. The sales procedure has been represented in diagrammatic form below. Other procedures have been indicated by brief notes

Other documents such as debit notes, credit notes, journal documents for journal entries are treated similarly according to their own requirements and lead to inputs, data processing and updating of all ledger accounts. The computer will thus hold the entire ledger system on its files, or as much of the system as the management decides

Computerised Sales Procedure

In computer diagrams this shape is used for any document. In this case it is our order form which customers have completed

The order comes in

The batch of orders is coded and passed to the operators for data preparation

Punched card inputs   or   Mag tape inputs

Computer checks the validity of inputs

Printout
(a) List of inputs(virtually a day book for that day)
(b) List of rejections

(c) Computer produces invoices, dispatch notes, etc., as required

(d) Debits the personal accounts of the debtors

(e) Credits the Sales Account

(f) Prints out statements for dispatch at the correct time

(g) Prints out the full ledger at the end of the month

(h) Answers any enquiry on difficult accounts at once

Purchases Invoices
(a) Coded as necessary
(b) batched up
(c) data preparation
(d) Input
(e) validation procedure
(f) print out of input list (day book) and rejections for mis-coding etc.
(g) Creditors' ledger accounts posted
(h) Computer prepares payment list at best time to earn discount
(i) Computer prepares cheques

Invoices from other firms, all different shapes and sizes, our Purchases

Second Copies of our own Invoices, our Sales to other firms

Credit Notes from other firms, our purchases returned

Second Copies of our Credit Notes, sales returned to us

Letters about Errors

Invoices for Assets Bought

Bankruptcy Notices

Our Statements   Recd. with thanks

And cheques from the Debtors

Other Firms' Statements   And our cheques

Petty Cash vouchers

Figure 5.4(a)

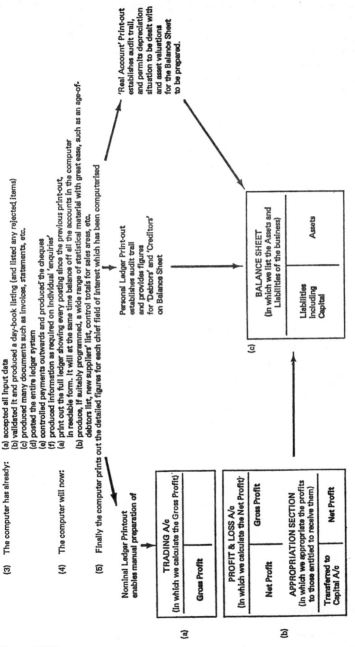

Figure 5.4(b)

(3) The computer has already:
(a) accepted all input data
(b) validated it and produced a day-book listing (and listed any rejected items)
(c) produced many documents such as invoices, statements, etc.
(d) posted the entire ledger system
(e) controlled payments outwards and produced the cheques
(f) produced information as required on individual 'enquiries'

(4) The computer will now:
(a) print out the full ledger showing every posting since the previous print-out, in readable form. It will at the same time balance off all the accounts in the computer
(b) produce, if suitably programmed, a wide range of statistical material with great ease, such as an age-of-debtors list, new suppliers' list, control totals for sales areas, etc.

(5) Finally the computer prints out the detailed figures for each chief field of interest which has been computerised

Nominal Ledger Printout enables manual preparation of

TRADING A/c
(In which we calculate the Gross Profit)

| Gross Profit | |

(a)

PROFIT & LOSS A/c
(In which we calculate the Net Profit)

| Net Profit | Gross Profit |

APPROPRIATION SECTION
(In which we appropriate the profits to those entitled to receive them)

| Transferred to Capital A/c | Net Profit |

(b)

Personal Ledger Print-out establishes audit trail and provides figures for 'Debtors' and 'Creditors' on Balance Sheet

'Real Account' Print-out establishes audit trail and permits depreciation situation to be dealt with and asset valuations for the Balance Sheet to be prepared.

BALANCE SHEET
(In which we list the Assets and Liabilities of the business)

| Liabilities Including Capital | Assets |

(c)

the computer and contained within it are the **memory unit,** the **peripheral control unit or units,** the **arithmetic unit** and the **registers.**

The memory unit of the CPU determines the power of the computer, since it is here that the actual processing of data according to programmed instructions takes place.

The arithmetic unit is located in the CPU, and here the calculations such as multiplication and division are performed. The answers, and partial answers, to the calculations are stored in the registers temporarily, from where they may be transferred to the memory unit for subsequent output to tape or disc storage.

Peripheral control units are designed to deal with all the ancillary equipment used for input and output of information. Outside components are known as peripherals. The word 'periphery' means 'outside boundary' and the peripherals may be regarded as surrounding the CPU. Note that in some instances the peripheral control units are themselves peripheral to the CPU.

(c) *Output devices.* The chief method of output in the final stage is the line printer. This prints out the result of the processed data. It is the computer's most convenient method of communication since it can be read by the human user. Speeds vary with the type of device but an output of 1 300 lines per minute, each line having a maximum of 132 characters, is representative. Other output devices such as punched cards or paper tape are less easily understood by the human user. As can be imagined, the production of output information is governed by the printer speed, which is low. To overcome this difficulty matter for printing is 'queued' on a fast medium, such as tape or disc, and then printed by a specialist program divorced from the original program. This is known as 'off-line' printing. Another method which avoids vast collections of paper computer print-out is the development of microfiche output, which can be produced direct from a magnetic tape file, so that no printing is required. The computer output consists of a succession of microfilm exposures photographed from a cathode ray tube. They can be read in a microfilm reader.

2   *How computers have changed book-keeping*

On pages 38–9 a chart shows how the double entry book-keeping system works. If we wish to see how computers have modified book-keeping it is useful to redraw this chart, in computerized form, and this is done in Figure 5.4 (see pages 80–1). The chart is largely self-explanatory.

It is not usual for computers to prepare final accounts, although they can be programmed to do so. The point here is that the cost of a program to make decisions at the final accounts level is greater than the cost of the work saved. Generally speaking the preparation of final accounts from the print-outs of the ledgers supplied by the computer is a straightforward task easily carried out manually. A study of the chart will reveal how the batched-up documents which would formerly have been entered in the day books are now recorded in the ledger accounts and on a printed list of inputs (the day book) electronically. The reader should now study the chart on pages 80–1.

5.6   Exercises set 5.1 – saving work on the Day Books

1. (a) What is meant by a 'simultaneous-entry' system? (b) How can this system by applied to a debtors' ledger?

2. Explain briefly what is meant by the following terms in the computer industry:

(a) Central processor unit
(b) Peripheral units
(c) Console
(d) Batching-up
(e) Off-line printing
(f) Program

3. What is meant in the computerization of accounts by:

(a) Input validation
(b) A day-book listing
(c) Mag tape input
(d) Visual display
(e) Arithmetic unit
(f) Disc storage

4. What is meant by the slip system of book-keeping? What sort of slips are available from banks to facilitate this type of book-keeping?

6
The Three-column Cash Book

6.1 Introduction

In Chapter 2 we learned how to keep the Ledger, with its collection of personal, nominal, and real accounts. As businesses grew bigger two problems presented themselves to the business-man. Firstly, the ledger grew thicker and thicker as more and more customers and creditors entered into business relationships with the firm. Secondly, some sub-division of the work became necessary as it is impossible for two clerks to work with only one book.

A natural subdivision of the work occurs if we remove from the ledger the two busiest accounts of all, the Cash Account and the Bank Account. These two accounts are extremely active accounts; hardly a day goes by without twenty or thirty items being paid or received by the normal small business, and large businesses may handle hundreds of items daily. It therefore seems sensible to move these two accounts from the ledger and put them them into a separate book in the special charge of one person, called the **Cashier.**

6.2 Cashiers, Bound Books, and Fidelity Bonds

Of all the valuable items in which a business deals, cash is the most easily misappropriated. Many small businessmen try to keep control of the cash themselves, or ask their wives to handle the cash side of the business. If this is not possible the cashier may be a trusted employee whose reliability is beyond doubt, and who will be paid a salary commensurate with the responsibilities of the post. Even then it is usual to take precautions against defalcations.

One such precaution is to have a bound book for a Cash Book. A loose-leaf book is most unsuitable, because it is possible to rewrite pages and insert them without the owner's knowledge.

Loose-leaf books are unsafe even for ordinary Ledger Accounts; for the Cash Book they are particularly unwise. If a cashier keeps the records in a bound book it makes it extremely difficult to rewrite a page.

A second precaution is to take out a Fidelity Bond on the cashier. This is an insurance policy to cover any defalcations up to a limit of, say £15 000.00, that may occur while keeping the Cash Book. A firm employing personnel as cashiers safeguards itself in this way. It is usual for the employee to be asked to agree to take out the policy, the premium for which is deducted from the employee's salary. Naturally a cashier is paid a salary commensurate with the responsibilities of the post, so that the premium deductions are hardly noticed as the new cashier is being paid on a higher scale than formerly. There is one important feature of these policies that students should known about: compensation is only paid to the employer when the employee has been convicted in the courts. The employer cannot say: 'You have been dishonest but I will forgive you this time, and collect my compensation from the insurance company.' It is against public policy, that is to say crime would only be encouraged, to allow the criminal to escape the rigour of the law at the expense of the insurance company.

6.3　Why have a Three-column Cash Book?

We shall understand this most easily if we consider a two-column Cash Book first. We have decided to remove the Cash Account and the Bank Account from the Ledger, and put them into a special bound book, called the Cash Book, kept by a responsible employee, the cashier. We are doing this firstly because they are very busy accounts, and the cashier can be fully employed entering up the cash and cheques; secondly because they are very vulnerable accounts and we want to protect them. We may even build our cashier a small separate office where the safe, the cash till, and the cash book can all be locked up securely.

What will be the point of having these two accounts on separate pages? The cashier will have to keep turning the pages from one account to the other, and if the book is a big one, with about 300 pages, will suffer considerable physical strain turning to the page required if we have the Cash Account at the beginning and the bank account half-way through.

The genius who decided to put the two accounts side by side has been lost in history, like the man who invented the wheel, but it was certainly a very happy idea. The Two-column Cash Book had been invented.

No doubt a few years went by before some other genius added a discount column to either side and changed the Two-column Cash Book into the Three-column Cash Book, but we shall see that this book is most appropriate to our needs.

Explanation of Figure 6.1

(a) The Three-column Cash Book is really two ledger accounts, the Cash Account and the Bank Account set out side by side. They are completely unconnected; each is a separate account with a debit side and a credit side.

(b) The Discount Column is not an account. The Discount Allowed Account and Discount Received Account are both in the ordinary Ledger – two Nominal Accounts. These columns are **Memorandum Columns** only; they help us remember how much discount has been allowed or received.

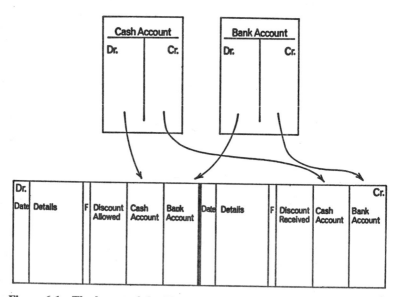

Figure 6.1   The layout of the Three-Column Cash Book

(c) In order to give plenty of room in the column for details a Three-column Cash Book is spread out across the whole double page of a book. It follows that when you first open a new Three-column Cash Book the first page you come to just inside the cover is only half a page; you have to ignore it and turn over to the first full width double page.

6.4 Original documents for the Three-column Cash Book

Just as purchases, sales, and returns all begin with the preparation of original documents so the entries made in the Cash Book start with an originating document.

These documents are the **Statement,** the **Cheque,** the **Receipt,** and the **Cheque Book Counterfoil.** Small items may be vouched for by a Petty Cash Voucher, but as these are usually dealt with in the Petty Cash Book a discussion of them is postponed until later.

The Statement
Figure 6.2 is a picture of a simple statement. It is a business document which is sent out at the end of the month to all the debtors of our firm, reminding them what they owe us for the purchases they have made during the past month. The phrase 'To account rendered' is used to save the trouble of listing the various invoices, debit notes, credit notes, and receipts which have been sent to them during the month.

```
                    STATEMENT
        In account with Tom Jones & Co. Ltd.,
                    20 Hill Road,
                        Newcastle.
   □                              □
      Messrs. Briggs & Bolton
         24 High Road,
            Newtown,
              Essex.
   □                    □
                                  July 31, 19. .

      To Account rendered              147.15

      Terms: 5 per cent Cash 30 days
```

Figure 6.2   A simple Statement

Computerized Statements
Many firms today are using computerized forms of book-keeping. There are many such systems. The statement shown in Figure 6.3 is printed by kind permission of British Olivetti Limited. You will notice that it does not just contain the words 'To account rendered' but instead contains details of all payments by the debtor and of goods sent to him and items returned by him. This is because under computerized book-keeping the statement is printed automatically from the entire data file for the month concerned. At electronic speeds it is no trouble for the computer

to give all the details. Most firms use some system of **cyclical billing** and print 4% of statements every day, to avoid a mad rush at the end of the month.

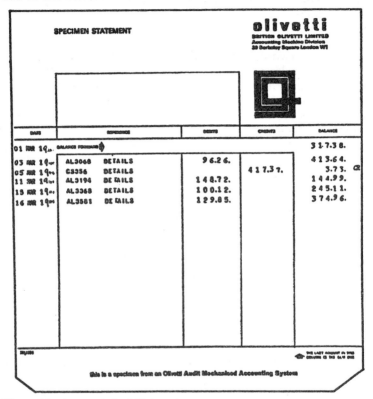

Figure 6.3   A computerized Statement

What happens to the Statements we send out?
The debtor who receives our statement first checks it against his book-keeping records. If it is correct he then uses it as a covering document for his cheque, which he draws up and sends with the covering statement to our accounts department. If he is entitled to deduct 5 per cent cash discount he will write on the statement 'Less 5 per cent Cash Discount', deduct it, and send us the cheque to cover the net amount.

Some computerized systems send out the statements in duplicate form, and label the copy **Remittance Advice Note.** This enables the customer to keep the statement, and use the remittance advice note to act as a covering document for the cheque.

What happens to the Statement we receive?
The same process as above, because we are now the debtor and it is up to us to pay our debt after deducting Cash Discount if we are entitled to do so.

Cheques
A cheque is an order to a banker to pay money to someone at once. Technically it may be written on any piece of paper or indeed on anything. One wag wrote a cheque out on his cricket bat. These days bankers prefer cheques to be of a certain size because they are dealt with by machines, so they issue books of cheques to their customers. Odd bits of paper do not fit the machines. This is also true of cricket bats.

The advantages of paying money by cheque

(a) It is just as easy to pay £1 000.00 as it is to pay £5.00. You do not need 200 pieces of paper as you do with £5.00 notes.
(b) A cheque can be safeguarded by crossing it so that even if it is stolen it is useless to the thief.
(c) The money never leaves the bank so it is perfectly safe.
(d) In some countries, for instance in the United Kingdom (by the Cheques Act of 1957), the cheque is a receipt. It is proof, once it has been cleared, that you did pay the money.

Explanation of the four cheques in Figure 6.4
(a) This is an open cheque; it can be cashed at the bank by anyone who presents it and says he is T. Jones. He will have to endorse it. This means he must sign his name on the back when he cashes the cheque. Although this is not much of a safeguard it does have a deterrent effect on thieves, because signing the name T. Jones on the cheque when you are not Mr Jones means you have committed the crime of forgery, which is more severely punished than mere theft. There is an even more unsafe cheque, called a 'Bearer' cheque, which is made out 'Pay Bearer'. This is very unsafe indeed and does not require endorsement, because the name of the Bearer is not important. Anyone who presents it is entitled to payment on it. Generally speaking it is safer to cross a cheque, and banks issue books of cheques that are already crossed for those who prefer to play safe.

(b) This is a general crossing – two lines with or without '& Co.'. It will not be cashed across the counter of the bank but must be cleared into a bank account. It is therefore much safer than (a), but it can be cleared by anyone so long as R. T. McGuiness (Camside) Ltd have endorsed it (written their name on the back).

(a)

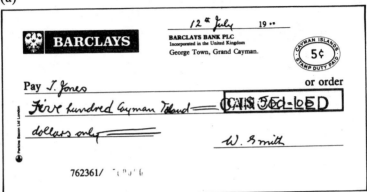

(b)

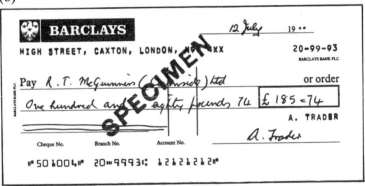

(c)

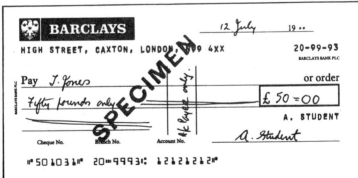

(d)

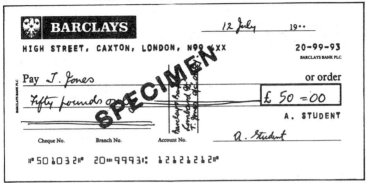

Figure 6.4 Safeguarding a cheque

Notice that it is possible to pay this cheque into *any* account. It does not have to go into the account of the person named on the cheque, McGuinness. This is possible because it is an Order Cheque. At the end of the line it says 'Pay R. T. McGuiness (Camside) Ltd .... or Order'. This means that if McGuiness Ltd endorse it 'Pay R. Brown' and sign their name, the bank concerned will obey the order and pay R. Brown not McGuiness Ltd.

The simpler rules about endorsement are as follows:

(i) No endorsement is necessary if the payee pays an order cheque into his own account.
(ii) If the payee orders the bank to pay someone else he must endorse the cheque. The new payee will also endorse it when he pays it into his account.

(c) Crossed A/c Payee. Another general crossing! The payer safeguards himself by suggesting that it should be paid only into the account of the payee. If the cheque is paid into any other account the bank is 'put upon inquiry' over the circumstances; that is, they will be liable to the payer if an unauthorized person should collect the money. The bank must inquire whether the payee has given authority for the cheque to be cleared through the account of the person who has paid it in.

(d) This is a special crossing, since the bank into which it is to be paid is clearly stated.

What happens to the cheques we receive?
Cheques that arrive from debtors are taken to the cashier who enters them on the debit side of the Bank Account. If a receipt is

required he/she writes a receipt, acknowledging that the debt has been settled by this payment, and returns it to the debtor. In the United Kingdom cheques marked 'Paid' are accepted as receipts under the Cheques Act 1957, but a debtor who wishes to do so may still demand a receipt. After entering the cheques in the Cash Book they are paid into the bank, the same day usually, and the bank collects payment from the debtors' banks through the clearing system. The entries are shown in Figure 6.5.

What happens to the cheques we make out to pay our creditors?
They are entered on the Cheque Book Counterfoil and are then posted off to the creditors so that they can collect payment. The Cheque Book Counterfoils are then used as the entry media for the Cash Book. The entries are made in the Bank Account on the credit side (see Figure 6.5).

What is a receipt?
A receipt is a business document which is given to a debtor when he pays a debt; as proof of payment. It should be made out at once on receiving the payment and be either given to, or sent through the post to the debtor.

As explained in the section on cheques, the law has been changed in the United Kingdom by the Cheques Act 1957 so that receipts are not really necessary now when payments are made by cheque.

6.5   Explanation of the Three-column Cash Book – including contra entries

Figure 6.6 shows a typical Three-Column Cash Book, with the Cash Account lying alongside the Bank Account.

Like any other real account the Cash Account and the Bank Account are debited with increases in value and credited with decreases in value. Looking more closely at the entries (see page 96) we notice the following points:

Debit side
January 1 – The opening balances are those that the Cash Account and Bank Account have received from the owner of the business. The folio number says J1 because this is coming from a Journal Entry, which is dealt with in Chapter 7.

January 2 – When goods are sold for cash, the amount of cash increases, so that the Cash Account is debited.

January 3 – H. Kemp has sent us a cheque, so that the bank

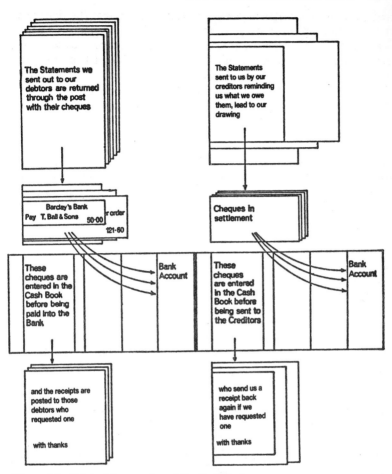

Figure 6.5 Original documents and the Cash Book

balance increases in size. The discount we allowed him for paying promptly is recorded in the Discount Allowed column.

January 4 – Robson has also sent us a cheque, which is debited in the Bank Account.

January 7 – More cash sales, as on January 2. The entries on January 11, 13, and 15 are similar to those already discussed except for the very important entry 'Cash', on January 15.

Contra entries in the Cash Book

In any account you can only have one-half of a double entry. An account cannot receive and give both at the same time; but in the Three-column Cash Book we have two accounts, the Cash

Account and the Bank Account. It is possible to have both a debit entry and a credit entry at the same time. The two halves of the double entry on January 15 both appear on opposite sides of the Three-column Cash Book, but not on opposite sides of the same account. The debit entry is in the Bank Account but the credit entry is in the Cash Account. Such entries are called Contra Entries, from the Latin prefix *contra* meaning 'opposite or against'. The folio column has a letter 'c' in it.

The kind of contra entry we have in this specimen Cash Book is one in which cash has been taken out of the Cash Account on the credit side (the Cash Account has given) and has been put into the Bank Account (the Bank Account has received). This paying of cash into the bank is a frequent occurrence; whenever we have excess cash we have to go to the bank and pay it in for safe-keeping.

It is possible to have a contra entry that is the exact reverse of this. If we buy a great many goods for cash the amount of cash in the till will decrease and we may need to draw more. This involves a credit entry for the Bank Account, which is *giving*, and a debit entry for the Cash Account, which is *receiving*.

Contra Entries are a very important part of the Three-column Cash Book; they can only occur because there are two accounts side by side, and it is quite untrue to say, as thoughtless students often do, that the Cash Book is the only account that can have a debit entry and a credit entry on it at the same time. *The Cash Book is not an account; it is two accounts, laid side by side for the greater convenience of the Cashier.*

Credit side

Whenever payment is made, either in cash or by cheque, the account concerned suffers a reduction in value.

January 2 – The Cash Account is credited with £5.00 which has been spent on postage stamps. Similar cash expenditure on wages takes place on January 7 and 15 respectively.

January 4 – R. Leverhulme, a creditor, is paid by cheque the sum of £129.20, in full settlement of a debt of £136.00. In other words he allows us discount, which is recorded in the Discount Received column. The same kind of entry occurs on January 5, 13, and 14.

January 12 – On this date the proprietor withdrew £112.50 from the bank for his own use. This is rather like wages; it is money for him to support his family during the coming week. As the proprietor of a business is not entitled to wages it is called **Drawings.** It implies that he has drawn out some of the capital invested in the business. Even this is not quite a fair picture, for what he has really drawn out is some of the profit he hopes that he has made during the period in which he has been operating. If the student likes to regard Drawings as 'Drawings in expectation of profits made', then he probably has the best picture of what Drawings really is.

January 14 – F. Fish is paid a small account, not by cheque but in cash. The Cash Account has to be credited with this decrease in value.

January 15 – Here we see the other half of the contra entry already described.

On the same date the two accounts are balanced off and the balances are brought down. In many businesses it would be necessary to do this daily and 'cash up' – check the cash in the till and see it agreed with the cash balances as shown on the books.

What is the best wording for the Details Column?

It is often a problem to a book-keeper to know what words to use in the Details Column. There is a very simple rule which solves the problem for him. Whenever a debit entry is made on an account we write **the name of the account where the other half of the double entry is to be found.** The only exception is where we write 'Opening Balance'. All other entries show the account where the other half of the double entry may be seen, and the folio column tells us on which page to find it in the ledger. This rule even applies for the Contra Entry, since the word 'Bank' tells us that the other half of the double entry is in the Bank Account and the folio number 'C' tells us it is 'contra' or 'opposite'.

Similarly, when a credit entry is made in an account we write **the name of the account where the double entry is to be found.** On January 2 it will be found in the Postage Account, etc.

What happens to the Discount Columns?

The Discount Columns are added up as shown in Figure 6.6. They are then posted into the Discount Allowed Account and Discount Received Account. The student must pay particular attention to the posting of these two accounts, which is dealt with in Section 6.7. The posting of these entries is the only difficult thing in the Cash Book, and a cause of very common errors in book-keeping. The folio numbers of these accounts are written just below the totals, as shown in Figure 6.6. Before considering these postings let us consider VAT and the Three-column Cash Book.

Date 19.. Jan.	Details	F	Discount Allowed	Cash £	Bank £
1	Opening Balances	J1		24.50	17 035.35
2	Cash Sales			242.25	
3	H. Kemp	L7	7.70		146.30
4	R. Robson	L3			11.63
7	Cash Sales	L11		834.40	
11	M. Starr	L7			17.10
13	North London Rail (Refund)	L14	0.90		10.65
15	M. Jordan	L29	11.33		215.35
15	Cash	L42			520.00
15	R. Peters	C	1.20		17.80
15	H. Kemp	L15			12.24
		L11	21.13	1 101.15	17 986.42
			L79		
Jan. 16	To Balances	c/d		63.95	17 518.89

Date 19.. Jan.	Details	F	Discount Received	Cash £	Bank £
2	Postage	L49	6.80	5.00	
4	R. Leverhulme	L27	1.44		129.20
5	R. Morgenthal	L28			27.35
7	Wages	L50		250.65	
12	Drawings	L38			112.50
13	L. Amaranth	L5	1.35		25.65
14	J. Jarvis	L12	1.47		27.95
14	P. Heron	L26	0.91		17.25
14	F. Fish	L23			
15	Bank	C		20.65	
15	Rates	L55		520.00	
15	Wages	L50		240.90	127.63
15	Balances	c/d		63.95	17 518.89
			11.97	1 101.15	17 986.42
			L80		

Figure 6.6 Specimen Three-column Cash Book

6.6   VAT and the Three-column Cash Book

In the United Kingdom there can be a problem in recording VAT where items are not entered in any day book, but are entered directly into the Three-column Cash Book. For example in Figure 6.6 the two items of Cash Sales on January 2 and January 7 must include some VAT and instead of being posted in full to Sales Account should be posted partly to Sales Account and partly to VAT Account. The difficulty is knowing how much VAT is included in the sales when we cash up the tills at the end of the day. There are actually nine different ways of doing the calculation, and traders must adopt one of the nine Special Retailer's Schemes, which are called A–J (there is no Scheme I). We can understand best if we consider first the question of VAT fractions.

It is obvious that some fraction of the Daily Takings is VAT. What the VAT fraction is depends upon the rate of VAT charged. Suppose this is 10 per cent. Then:

Selling Price without VAT	= 100%
Add VAT at 10%	= 10%
Total Takings	= 110%

We can see that the VAT fraction in the total takings is not (as we might suppose) $\frac{1}{10}$, it is $\frac{10}{110} = \frac{1}{11}$.

If VAT is charged at 15% we have:

Selling Price without VAT	= 100%
Add VAT at 15%	= 15%
Total takings	= 115%

VAT fraction = $\frac{15}{115} = \frac{3}{23}$

So VAT fractions are not at all easy to work out, and if takings are £834.40 the VAT element with a 10 per cent rate is $\frac{1}{11}$ of £834.40 = £75.85.

However, that was just a simple case. Many things are sold at zero rate VAT so the takings in any given day of £834.40 may contain some things on which VAT was not charged and other things on which VAT was charged. If we have a multi-rate system of VAT – some zero rated goods, some standard rated goods and some luxury goods at higher rate it all becomes very muddling indeed. Hence the nine different schemes.

It would be possible to work out the VAT element everyday and enter it in the Cash Book as follows:

July 19   Cash Sales (VAT £75.85)   £834.40

When we post this to the ledger accounts we would have to credit the £75.85 to VAT Account and only enter £834.40 − £75.85 = £758.55 in the Sales Account.

The more sensible thing is to do the calculation once a month only, according to your special scheme, and taking the total Cash Sales for the month. We can then get the VAT which has been posted to Sales Account out of the Sales Account very simply, by a Journal Entry. This is explained in Section 7.20.

As far as the Three-column Cash Book is concerned we have ignored VAT in this book (which is used all over the world in countries where VAT is not used). Please refer to Section 7.20 if you wish to see what is done to remove VAT from daily takings (cash sales).

6.7   Posting the Three-column Cash Book to the Ledger

When we removed the Cash Account and the Bank Account from the Ledger and put them into the Cash Book they did not cease to be accounts. We now have two accounts which are not in the Ledger. Only one-half of the double entries in these accounts has already been done. The other half is done when we post the Cash

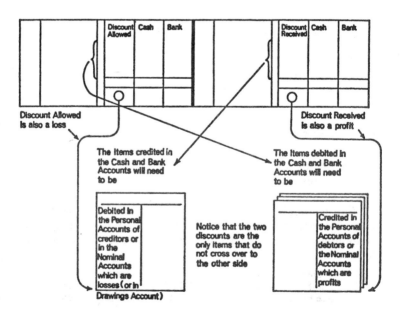

Figure 6.7   How to post the Three-column Cash Book

Book to the Ledger. Every item on the debit side of the Three-column Cash Book requires a credit entry on the credit side of some other account. Similarly every item on the credit side of the Cash Book requires a debit entry on the debit side of some other account. There is also a rather difficult little matter of the Discounts to deal with. These are the **only entries that do not change sides,** as shown in Figure 6.7.

The Ledger Accounts connected with the Three-column Cash Book shown in Figure 6.6 will therefore appear as in Figures 6.8 and 6.9. To save space only the first personal account on each side has been shown; the others will be exactly the same. Notice that it would be **absolutely wrong to post the contra entries,** both halves of the double entry being already done in the Cash Book.

		SALES ACCOUNT				L7
			19. .			£
			Jan. 2	Cash	CB1	242.25
			7	Cash	CB1	834.40

				H KEMP ACCOUNT				L11
19. .			£	19. .				£
Jan. 2	Balance	B/d	154.00	Jan. 3	Bank	CB1	146.30
12	Goods	SDB	12.24	3	Discount	CB1	7.70

(These are invented to make sense – a debtor must owe money before he pays it.) | 15 | Bank | | 12.24
(Notice that both the cheque and the discount are entered.)

All the other debtors' accounts will look the same as H. Kemp's Account.

		DISCOUNT ALLOWED ACCOUNT		L79
19. .		£		
Jan. 15	Sundry Discounts	21.13		

Notice that discount is the only entry that does not cross over to the credit side.

Figure 6.8   Ledger Accounts posted from the Cash Book: debit side

6.8   Why do the discount figures, when they are posted, not cross over to the other side?

Consider the double entry for the payment by H. Kemp on January 3. Remember every debit entry must be balanced up by a corresponding credit entry. In this case we have a double entry as follows:

Debit side	*Credit side*
£146.30 in the Bank Account	£146.30 in H. Kemp's Account
(see Figure 6.6)	£7.70 in H. Kemp's Account

Clearly this does not balance and we cannot count the £7.70 in the Discount column of the Cash Book because the Discount column is **not an account.**

If we do post this £7.70 into the Discount Allowed Account it must not go over to the credit side; to do so would unbalance the double entry even more.

The £7.70 must go on the debit side of the Discount Allowed Account, to record the loss and get the double entry correct.

The student should now develop a similar line of argument to explain why the Discount Received Account does not change over sides.

			POSTAGE ACCOUNT				L49
19. .			£				
Jan. 2	Cash	CB1	5.00				

			R. LEVERHULME ACCOUNT				L27
19. .			£	19. .			£
4	Bank	CB1	129.20	Jan. 1	Balance	SDB1	136.00
4	Discount	CB1	6.80				

All the other personal accounts of creditors will appear exactly like the one above.

			WAGES ACCOUNT			L50
19. .			£			
Jan. 7	Cash	CB1	250.65			
15	Cash	CB1	240.90			

			DRAWINGS ACCOUNT			L38
19. .			£			
Jan. 12	Bank	CB1	112.50			

			RATES ACCOUNT			L55
19. .			£			
Jan. 15	Cash	CB1	127.63			

	DISCOUNT RECEIVED ACCOUNT				L80
	19. .				£
	Jan. 15	Sundry Discounts	CB1	11.97	
	(Notice that this account is the only one that does not cross over to the debit side.)				

Fig. 6.9 Ledger Accounts posted from the Cash Book: credit side

6.9   Bank overdrafts

Sometimes the local bank manager will permit us to draw cheques to a greater value than the money that we have in the bank. Such **overdrafts** represent a loan to us of the outstanding balance. Of course, the bank will charge interest on the sum borrowed in this way, and if it exceeds a purely nominal amount the bank may even ask for **Collateral Security.** This is a security lying alongside the debt, which gives the bank a chance to recover its money should we not repay it when asked. Collateral Security is dealt with more fully in Chapter 7.

When a Bank Account is overdrawn in this way the account ceases to be an asset and becomes a liability. It cannot have a debit balance, like an asset account; the balance will be a credit balance.

In these circumstances our Three-column Cash Book has a debit balance on the Cash Account, but a credit balance on the Bank Account reading: Bank Overdraft. It is impossible to have a credit balance on the Cash Account, since, unlike a bank, you cannot get more out of a cash box than you put into it.

The student is now ready to try some entries in the Three-column Cash Book. The first four exercises in Set 6.1 merely ask you to record the entries in the Three-column Cash Book. The remainder ask you to post the Cash Book to the Ledger when you have finished making the entries, putting in the folio numbers as you do so.

6.10   Exercises set 6.1 – the Three-column Cash Book

1. Enter the following items in the Three-column Cash Book, and balance off the book on January 5:

19. .
Jan.   1 T. Brophy commences business with cash £5 000.00; he pays £4 750.00 into the Bank Account from the cash box (Contra Entry); he buys goods (purchases) for cheque £1 150.00.
2 He pays rent £225.00; pays legal costs £36.75, both by cheque.
3 He settles a debt of £125.00 due to H. Jones by cheque, deducting discount at 5%.
4 P. Brown pays Brophy a debt of £53.00 by cheque, less 5% discount.
5 Pays wages £57.50 in cash; draws £100.00 for personal use (Drawings) from the cash box.

2. Enter the following items in B. Jorgensen's Three-column Cash Book, and balance off at October 6:

19. .
Oct.   1 Balances in hand, cash £335.50 and bank £3 977.50.

Paid to R. Jones by cheque £1 062.50; discount £55.92.

2 Received from B. Morse cheque for £205.00. Allowed him discount £5.26.

Paid water rate £47.39; paid for repairs to office safe £38.65, paid office cleaner £38.50, all these payments made in cash.

3 Drew £100.00 from bank for office cash (Contra Entry).

Paid R. Tompkins cash £13.40; received discount £0.70.

4 Received from E. Lyne cash £79.75; gave him discount £4.20.

Paid to F. Acomb cheque £1 800.50, discount £46.16.

5 Received cheque from Docherty & Sons £105.00; they were allowed discount £5.53.

6 Paid cheque to F. Handsome £55.95.

Drew cheque for wages £180.50.

Drew cash for personal use £125.00 (Drawings).

3. Enter the following in T. Charles' Cash Book:

19. .

Feb.   1 T. Charles had a balance of cash in hand of £230.50 and a balance at the bank of £1 882.75.

Paid E. Cremer in cash £176.70, being allowed discount £9.30 by him.

2 Received from T. Horwell cheque for £260.50; gave him discount £13.71.

Paid for carriage on goods sold £7.75 in cash.

3 Drew from bank for office cash £125.00.

Received from J. Farmer cash £99.25; allowed him discount £2.54.

Paid by cheque £158.75 to Horton & Co., being allowed discount £8.36.

4 Bought goods at sale of bankrupt stock for cash £126.80 (Purchases).

Paid M. Jenner by cheque £199.50 being allowed discount £10.50.

5 Received from M. Waters cheque £75.00.

Balanced off the Cash Book and brought down the balances.

4. Enter the following in R. Jollyboy's Cash Book and balance off on May 5:

19. .

May   1 Balances: Cash Box £136.25; Bank £6 501.30; paid R. Brown (by cheque) £48.75; discount £1.25.

2 M. Slow paid by cheque £122.80; allowed him discount £6.46.

3 Paid postage in cash £6.30; rent £60.00 in cash; paid T. Brownjohn by cheque £210.50, receiving discount £11.08.

Drew cash from bank for office use £100.00.

4 R. Little sent us a cheque for £643.62 in full settlement of his account of £677.50.

Cash sales for week £2 625.50.

5 Bought machinery at auction for cash £475.50; paid wages in

cash £162.50; paid for stamps in cash £4.75. Banked £1 800.00 from tills.

5. L. Lewis's cash book is a Three-column Cash Book. Make the following entries in it for the first week of July:

19. .
July 1 Balances in hand: cash £288.45; bank £8 250.75.
   Bought goods for re-sale for cash £213.00.
2 Drew cash from bank for office use £200.00; R. Long paid cash £28.50, allowed him discount £1.50.
   Paid J. Roberson cheque £188.80.
3 Paid telephone account £36.25; sundry expenses £4.25; postage £13.20, all in cash.
4 Paid R. Matthias £190.00 by cheque; received discount £10.00.
   Received from T. Jonah cash, £17.75.
5 Paid salaries £82.50 in cash; paid sundry expenses £27.50 cash; paid for goods to be re-sold, by cheque £70.50; entered cash sales from till £1 195.85. Banked £1 000.00.
Balance off the Cash book and post it to the Ledger.

6. On May 1, 19. ., R. Jolson set up in business by putting £7 500.00 in his Bank Account. He then paid rent £500.00, by cheque, bought goods £112.50 by cheque and paid electricity connexion charges £45.50 by cheque. He also drew out £100.00 for the office cash. Enter these items and also the following in his Cash Book, and post them to the Ledger:

19. .
May 2 Cash sales £371.40; paid postage £3.20 cash; R. Brownjohn paid by cheque £38.00, gave him discount £2.00.
3 Paid for repairs to window £23.25 in cash; paid signwriter £14.35 in cash.
4 Johnson & Co. paid £103.35 by cheque; gave them disount £2.65.
5 R. Thomas sent a bill for £218.00; paid it by cheque; paid wages £75.75 in cash.

The following two questions, Numbers 7 and 8, require special care. They have bank overdrafts to begin with.

7. On May 1 R. Lunnis has the following balances in his Cash Book: cash £138.00, bank overdraft £877.25. Enter these balances and record the following in his Cash Book. Post to the Ledger.

19. .
May 1 R. Brown paid £637.80 by cheque; Lunnis allowed him discount of £33.57.
2 M. Jones sent a cheque for £562.80; no discount given as it was overdue.
   Sent P. Robinson a cheque for £213.75; discount received £11.25; paid wages £82.50 in cash; paid for repairs £8.25 in cash.
3 R. Thompson paid £160.00 in cash; cash sales £1 572.50.

5 Paid carriage on parcel £13.20 in cash; paid £1 500.00 into the bank from the cash box.

8. On May 1 John Brown had £137.50 in his cash box and was overdrawn at the bank by £1 353.25. Enter these opening balances in his Cash Book, enter the following items, balance off the Cash Book and post it to Ledger:

19. .
May   2 Paid for postage stamps £13.00 in cash; paid for repairs £7.35 in cash; paid to R. Jones a cheque for £137.75. Jones gave discount £7.25.

3 R. Wich paid in cash £25.00 to Brown; paid travelling expenses £11.75 in cash.

4 Cash sales £438.50; paid £250.00 out of the cash box into the bank.

5 Bought goods by cheque at an auction £465.00; paid rent for month £147.50 by cheque; paid wages £80.00 in cash.

6 R. Libbey paid by cheque £487.50 in full settlement of £500.00 which he owed us.

7 Rates paid by cheque £113.25; drew for personal use from cash box £75.00; Cash Sales £1 325. Banked £1 000.00.

6.11 A page to test you on the Three-column Cash Book

Cover the page with a sheet of paper, then read one question at a time.

Answers	Questions
—	1 Why do we take the Cash Account and the Bank Account out of the Ledger?
1 (a) Because they are busy accounts; (b) because they are vulnerable.	2 What do we call the theft of money by a trusted employee?
2 Embezzlement.	3 What is the missing money called?
3 A defalcation.	4 What insurance policies cover this risk?
4 Fidelity bonds	5 Why are there three columns on each side of the Three-column Cash Book?
5 (a) One for the Cash Account; (b) one for the Bank Account; (c) one for the Discount column.	6 Do the Discount columns form an account?
6 No. They are only memorandum columns.	7 What type of accounts are the Cash Account and Bank Account?
7 They are both real accounts.	8 What is the rule for these accounts?
8 (a) Debit increases in value; (b) credit decreases in value.	9 What is a contra entry in the Cash Book?
9 A contra entry is one where both the debit and credit entries appear on the page at once, one in the Cash Account and one in the Bank Account.	10 Can a contra entry like this appear anywhere else in the ledger?
10 No – because this is the only place where two accounts are written side by side.	11 How do we post the Cash Book to the Ledger?
11 (a) Everything on the debit side of the Cash Account and Bank Account is posted to the credit side of an account in the Ledger; (b) everything on the credit side of the Cash Account and Bank Account is posted over to the debit side of the Ledger.	12 Is there anything that does not change sides?
12 Yes. The totals of the Discount Allowed column and Discount Received column do not change sides.	

6.12   A page to test you on Statements and Receipts

Answers	Questions
—	1 What is a Statement?
1 A business document which is sent out at the end of the month to all our debtors.	2 What does it tell them?
2 How much they owe us altogether on the last day of the month.	3 What words are used on it?
3 'To A/c Rendered.'	4 What does the debtor do when the Statement arrives.
4 (a) He checks it; (b) he deducts Cash Discount if he is paying it promptly, and if the terms of sale allow it; (c) he pays it, usually by cheque returning the statement with the cheque.	5 How does a computerized statement differ from an ordinary statement written out by the ledger clerk at the end of the month?
5 The computerized statement is printed out from the computer's memory so that it is an exact copy of the Ledger Account and shows all the debits and credits on the Account, giving the final balance owing to the debtor.	6 What happens when the cheque and the statement are returned to the creditor?
6 (a) The cheque is entered in the Cash Book; (b) the statement is receipted, if a receipt is required, and posted back to the debtor.	7 Why may a receipt not be needed?
7 Because under the Cheques Act, 1957, a cheque itself is a receipt.	8 What is a receipt?
8 A legal proof of payment.	9 What form does it take?
9 A document on which is written 'received with thanks', followed by the amount, and the signature of the creditor.	

6.13 A page to test you on Discounts

Answers	Questions
—	1 What are the three kinds of Discount?
1 Cash Discount, Settlement Discount and Trade Discount.	2 What are Cash Discount and Settlement Discount.
2 Amounts deducted from a purchase or a statement paid promptly.	3 When should a debtor pay his debts?
3 When the period of credit expires, which is usually at the end of the month.	4 What do we call it if a debtor does not pay when he should?
4 A breach of 'Good Faith'.	5 What are the usual rates of discount?
5 2½% and 5%	6 Suppose you owe £50.00 and receive a statement that allows 5% discount. What do you do?
6 Write on the statement below the total figure = 50.00 Less 5% Discount = 2.50 Cheque enclosed £47.50 and send a cheque for £47.50.	7 What do 'Terms Cash Net' or 'Terms Strictly Net' mean?
7 They mean that no Cash Discount is allowed.	8 What is Trade Discount?
8 It is a reduction in the catalogue price of a branded good to enable the retailer to make a profit when he sells at this catalogue price.	9 What are the usual rates of Trade Discount?
9 10–45% are quite common.	10 When is the rate of Trade Discount small?
10 When the turnover is rapid, i.e. chocolates, cigarettes.	11 When is it large?
11 When the items are slow-moving, i.e. furniture.	12 Why is it large with these items?
12 To enable the retailer to cover the overhead expenses of a longer period.	13 Who writes the Trade Discount on the invoice?
13 The supplier before he sends it out.	14 Does cash discount go in the books?
14 Yes. It is entered in the Cash Book and posted to the Ledger.	15 Does Trade Discount go in the books?
15 It is entered in the Day Book but is *never* posted to the Ledger.	16 Is there a Trade Discount Account?
16 No. It never goes in the Ledger.	

7
The Journal Proper

7.1 Introduction

We have now dealt with most of the really common transactions in business: the purchases, sales and return of goods, and the payment and receipt of cash. We now turn to a consideration of some of the less common items which occur, not every day, but a few times a year only. These items are usually dealt with through the **Journal Proper,** a Day Book which has been in use since the Middle Ages.

The ruling of this Day Book is a traditional ruling which is illustrated in Figure 7.1.

19. . Date		Dr.	F	£ 20.55	£
	Account to be debited				
	Account to be Credited		F		20.55
	Being, etc.				

Figure 7.1   Paper for Journal Entries

There are about nine chief types of entry that are made through the Journal Proper, but as this is the *residual* Day Book, that is, the only Day Book left to accommodate all other items, the range of entries made through the Journal is very great indeed. The nine commonest items are

   (a) Opening entries.
   (b) Closing entries.
   (c) Purchase of assets.
   (d) Depreciation of assets.
   (e) Sale of worn-out or obsolete assets.
   (f) Bad debts entries.
   (g) Correction of errors.

(h) Dishonoured cheques.

(i) Bank loans, interest and charges.

Some other entries that would be passed through the Journal Proper are the issue of shares and debentures, goodwill valuations, dissolution of partnership entries, and some adjustments for Final Accounts.

7.2 Journal Proper paper

Explanation of Journal paper

(a) The paper for the Journal Proper is ruled as shown in Figure 7.1. There is a date column, a 'particulars' column where we can explain which accounts are to be debited and which are to be credited, a folio column and two cash columns. The first of these is the debit column and the second is the credit column.

(b) The date is put in once on each Journal Entry.

(c) The account that is to be debited is named at the beginning of the line; the letters 'Dr.' come at the end of the line, and the money value is inserted in the first column.

(d) On the next line we indent a little way, write the name of the account to be credited, and enter the money value in the second money column.

(e) Lastly we write a short **narration** – an explanation of the entry. A narration accompanies every Journal Entry because they are all so different from one another. Usually the narration begins with the word 'Being . . .' and explains exactly what has been done.

(f) Finally we post the Journal Entry to the Ledger, debiting the account that has to be debited and crediting the account that has to be credited. We put the folio numbers in and rule off across the wording column.

(g) Except for Opening Journal Entries, which are rather special, Journal Entries are *not* added up, though usually each page is totted up in the Journal just to see that the debits and credits do balance.

Notice therefore that the Journal Proper is a rather special book. It tells us what unusual entries are being made in the Ledger, and why. Often there will only be two accounts mentioned, one to be debited and the other to be credited, but often there will be three accounts affected and sometimes several. Whatever the number, the debits and the credits must be equal to give a proper double entry.

Figure 7.2 is a typical Journal Entry.

It so happens that this is the purchase of an asset, a motor vehicle. Motor Vehicles Account has received value, £3 500.50,

19. . Jan. 7	Motor Vehicles Account Dr. Rex Garages Ltd. Being a Morris Mini 3XYZ127 pur- chased on this date on credit	L7 L19	£ 3 500.50	£ 3 500.50

Figure 7.2   A typical Journal Entry

which is obviously the value of a motor car. Since we have not paid for the car the supplier Rex Garages Ltd has become a creditor, and must be credited with the amount due. The narration explains what has happened. We will now look at the nine common types of Journal Entry.

7.3   Journal Entries no. 1 – the Opening Journal Entry

When business first begins, the owner of the business puts some money into the firm. This is his capital and usually it is in the form of a current account balance in the bank.

Supposing Tom Brown sets up in business on July 1 with a capital of £50.00 in the cash box and £950.00 in the bank. The Cash and Bank Accounts will receive value and must be debited. The Capital Account must be credited since it is the capitalist (or owner of the capital) who has given value. The cash and bank moneys are assets of the business; things the business owns. The capital is a liability of the business, since the business owes it to the owner of the business. Many students think that capital is an asset, but it is *not*; it is a *liability* of the business.

Here is the opening Journal Entry for Tom Brown. Notice that as this is an Opening Journal Entry, and marks a special point in the existence of the business, we do add it up and put a clear currency sign. I have put the £ sign but readers in other countries will use their own signs of course.

The usual narration for an opening Journal Entry is the one shown here.

19. . July 1	Cash A/c Dr. Bank A/c Dr. Capital A/c Being assets and liabilities at this date	CB1 CB1 L1 £	£ 50.00 950.00 1 000.00	£ 1 000.00 1 000.00

Figure 7.3   A simple Opening Journal Entry

Once the opening Journal Entry has been made it must be posted to the Ledger, and where necessary the Cash Book to open up the ledger accounts and start the books of the business. A typical set of entries is shown in Figure 7.4(b) later.

We also may record an opening entry on the first day of every year if we wish, to bring the record of the owner's assets up to date. In the rather artificial world of a book-keeping textbook, where we are asking students to pretend that an exercise represents a real-life business, we may have to open up each exercise as if a new business was beginning. You will be expected to do this in Chapter 9, which is about book-keeping to the Trial Balance.

This kind of opening entry has rather more accounts to be opened because we usually assume that the business has been in existence for some time. The example given below, and illustrated in Figure 7.4, has nine accounts to be opened.

Example

John Brown is a master carpenter, and on January 1 his assets and liabilities are as follows: Cash £50.00; Bank balance £1 320.00; Tools and equipment £1 400.00; Premises £21 200.00; Debtors, A. Pearce £45.00; B. Lebon £27.55; he owes £36.50 to Wood Suppliers Ltd, and £11 000.00 to the Master Builders' Building Society. Do the opening Journal Entry.

Rough work: Make a list of all the assets and liabilities:

Assets		Liabilities	
Cash	50.00	Wood Suppliers Ltd.	36.50
Bank	1 320.00	Mortgage	11 000.00
Tools, etc.	1 400.00	Capital	?
Premises	21 200.00		
A. Pearce	45.00		
B. Lebon	27.55		

The assets and liabilities are the Dr. items and the Cr. items for the Journal Entry. They must be equal, but clearly they are not. This is because we have been left to work out the capital. The capital is practically always a liability; if you ever get a debit balance on capital account it is called a 'deficiency' and means that the trader concerned is insolvent, and will soon be out of business. In this case the capital works out at £13 006.05.

The Journal Entry and the resulting Cash Book and Ledger entries are shown in Figures 7.4(a) and (b).

In the exercises which follow, you are asked to draw up the opening Journal Entries and then to post them to the Cash Book and the Ledger. Remember that the accounts are the really important records, and in order to open the accounts in a formal way we need the opening Journal Entry.

7.4 Exercises set 7.1 – Opening Journal Entries

1. Tom Cortes starts up in business as a jobbing carpenter on January 1. He has £250.00 which he puts into a Bank Account, his kit of tools worth £425.00, and general equipment valued at £125.00. Work out the capital he has invested in his business; do the opening Journal Entry and post it to the Cash Book and the Ledger.

2. Elmer Ridge sets up in business on 1 May 19. . as a music dealer, with the following assets: Cash £500.00; Cash at bank £12 500.00; Stocks of instruments £2 400.00; Records £925.00; Musical manuscripts £325.00; Furniture and fittings £2 400.00. Work out the total capital he has invested in the business and do the opening Journal Entry. You need not post it to the Cash Book and the Ledger, but invent sensible folio numbers.

3. Arthur Bryants opens up in business as a Turf Accountant on 1 August 19. ., with the following assets and liabilities: Cash £2 000.00; Bank moneys £25 000.00; Furniture and fittings £1 400.00; Premises £27 000.00. He has two debtors. T. Train and B. Bridges, for £20.00 and £200.00 respectively, and he also owes M. Tanner £900.00 for equipment supplied. Calculate the total capital he has invested in the venture and do the opening Journal Entry. Invent sensible folio numbers.

4. M. Price is in business as a retail tobaconnist. On 1 January he has assets and liabilities as follows: Cash £250.00; Cash at bank £900.00; Stocks £3 800.00; Premises £17 000.00; Debtors, R. Hood £135.50 and L. John £73.00; Creditors, Universal Tobacco Co. Ltd. £1 470.50. Richmond Tobacco Co. Ltd. £900.00; Bank loan £750.00. Work out his total capital and do the opening Journal Entry. Post it to the Cash Book and the Ledger.

5. M. Longshore is in business as a fish merchant. On 1 April 19. . he has the following assets and liabilities: Herring Drifter £135 000.00; Nets £5 000.00; Premises £34 000.00; Refrigerators £21 500.00; Stores of spare

19. .				£	£ J1
Jan. 1	Cash A/c	Dr.	CB1	50.00	
	Bank A/c	Dr.	CB1	1 320.00	
	Tools and Equipment A/c	Dr.	L1	1 400.00	
	Premises A/c	Dr.	L2	21 200.00	
	A. Pearce A/c	Dr.	L3	45.00	
	B. Lebon A/c	Dr.	L4	27.55	
	Wood Suppliers Ltd.		L5		36.50
	Mortgage		L6		11 000.00
	Capital		L7		13 006.05
	Being assets and liabilities at this date		£	24 042.55	24 042.55

Figure 7.4(a) **A more difficult Opening Journal Entry**

THREE COLUMN CASH BOOK (DEBIT SIDE ONLY)

19. . Jan 1	Opening Balance	F J1	£	£ 50.00	£ 1 320.00

TOOLS AND EQUIPMENT A/C   L1

19. . Jan. 1	Opening Balance	£ 1 400.00	

PREMISES A/C   L2

19. . Jan. 1	Opening Balance	£ 21 200.00	

A. PEARCE A/C   L3

19. . Jan. 1	Opening Balance	£ 45.00	

B. LEBON A/C   L4

19. . Jan. 1	Opening Balance	£ 27.55	

WOOD SUPPLIERS LTD   L5

		19. . Jan. 1	Opening Balance	£ 36.00

MORTGAGE A/C   L6

		19. . Jan. 1	Opening Balance	£ 11 000.00

CAPITAL A/C   L7

		19. . Jan. 1	Opening Balance	£ 13 006.05

Figure 7.4(b) Opening the Cash Book and Ledger Accounts

parts for ship and machinery £4 200.00; Furniture and fittings £1 400.00; he has Cash £120.50; Bank moneys £66 442.50; and debtors as follows: L. Jones £25.00; Ice Packers Ltd. £2 430.50; and R. Billingsgate £420.60. He has creditors, M. Ramsey £1 240.00 and L. Liverpool £2 483.30. Work out the total capital invested; do the opening Journal Entry and invent sensible folio numbers, but you need not post the entries to the Cash Book and Ledger.

6. A. Jordan and C. French are in partnership equally as booksellers. They have the following assets and liabilities on 1 April: Cash £1 350.00; Cash at bank £21 500.00; Stock £23 500.00; Computer £2 150.00; Office equipment £1 400.00; Furniture and fittings £3 780.00; Premises £27 000.00; Investments £2 250.00; Creditors, £1 380.00 owing to R. Keen, and £1 900.00 owing to B. Bunyan; Debtors £2 025.00 owing by B. Trotman, and £3 300.00 owing by M. Wrenn. Work out the capital, do the opening Journal Entry, and post to the Cash Book and Ledger.

7.5   Journal Entries no. 2 – Closing Entries

Opening Entries are made when a business is started, and are repeated once a year on the first day of the year. Closing Entries are made at the end of a financial year, when the losses and profits of a business are set against one another, and the success or otherwise of the year's activities is determined. Closing Entries are dealt with in Chapter 17, page 230.

7.6   Journal Entries no. 3 – Purchases of Assets

When we purchase anything we receive an invoice from the seller. Invoices can be divided into three types:

(a) Invoices dealing with 'goods' for resale – these are entered in the Purchases Day Book.

(b) Invoices dealing with expense items, like stationery, advertising, materials, motor vehicle repairs, etc. These are entered in the Expenses Day Book (see Chapter 4, page 54).

(c) Invoices dealing with the purchase of assets. These are the subject of Journal Entries.

Example 1
On January 15 we bought from Typebetta Ltd:

1 new electronic computer value £2 600.00, on credit, ref. no. of machine 12708/5/CD.

The rules for purchasing an asset are:

(a) **Always debit the Asset Account.**

(b) **Always credit** (i) *the Cash Account* if you paid cash, (ii) *the Bank Account* if you paid by cheque, (iii) *the Creditor* if you bought on credit.

In our example we bought on credit. The Journal Entry therefore looks like this:

| 19. .
Jan. 15 | Office Machinery A/c   Dr.
        Typebetta Ltd. A/c
Being the purchase of electronic
  computer Ref. 12708/5/CD at this
  date | L27
L38 | £
2 600.00 | £ J5

2 600.00 |

Figure 7.5   The purchase of an asset

Notice that this Journal Entry has not been added up. Also notice that the recording of reference numbers is very desirable on all office equipment, which is easily stolen and finds a ready market. Typewriters, for instance, should always be recorded officially on the books, where the reference numbers are available for police purposes in the event of a burglary.

When posted to the Ledger Accounts these appear as follows:

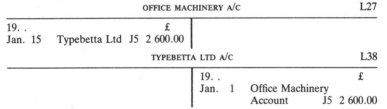

OFFICE MACHINERY A/C   L27

| 19. .
Jan. 15 Typebetta Ltd   J5   2 600.00 | |

TYPEBETTA LTD A/C   L38

| | 19. .   £
Jan.   1   Office Machinery
                     Account   J5   2 600.00 |

Figure 7.6   Ledger Accounts for the purchase of an asset

Example 2
On January 16 we attended a sale of bankrupt's effects and purchased the following, paying by cheque:

2 Filing Cabinets (ref. nos. 1786/5 and 1786/6), £60.00 the pair; 1 Motor Vehicle (XZ 1274), £677.50; goods for resale £227.50.

Clearly the Journal Entry here will involve a number of accounts. Some of the items purchased are assets and some are our normal goods for resale. As we have paid by cheque there is no creditor, but the credit entry will be in the Cash Book, a credit to Bank Account. The Journal Entry will now appear like this:

| 19. .
Jan. 16 | Office Equipment Account   Dr.
Motor Vehicle Account   Dr.
Purchases Account   Dr.
        Bank Account
Being assets and goods for resale
  purchased at bankrupt's sale. Fil-
  ing Cabinets Ref. Nos. 1786/5 and
  1786/6. Motor Vehicle XZ 1274. | L1
L2
L3
CB1 | £
60.00
677.50
227.50 | £ J1

965.00 |

Figure 7.7   Assets bought for cash

Some book-keepers consider there is no real need to journalize entries which are cash transactions since the Cash Book is the appropriate book of original entry. It is true that many firms 'cut corners' and leave out the occasional journal entry, but in doing so, useful details may be left out. For instance, in Figure 7.7 we have recorded the reference numbers of the filing cabinets; these may prove useful one day. In book-keeping you may cut as many corners as you like when you are really confident you know what you are doing, but when studying at an elementary level it is best to keep to the rules.

7.7   Exercises set 7.2 – Purchases of assets

1. On July 14 Thomas & Co. Ltd purchased a new typewriter for cash from Reditype Ltd for £375.00, paid in notes. Do the Journal Entry and post it to the Ledger. Serial no. 17065/2.

2. On October 15 Mears Ltd purchased a second-hand planing machine for £825.00 by cheque at an auction of property involved in a bankruptcy case. Do the Journal Entry and post it to the Ledger. Serial no. 2599/4a/65.

3. On November 11 your firm buys on credit a new piece of property (Land and Buildings Account) valued at £28 000.00 from the Loamshire Property Development Trust Ltd. Do the Journal Entry and post it to the Ledger. The property is situated at 23 High Street, Newtown.

4. On August 1 we purchased on credit a yacht for the use of our sports club members for £1 400.00 from Seaway Ltd. Do the Journal Entry and post it to the Ledger. You will have to decide on a suitable name for the Asset Account.

5. On August 1 K. Khamis sets up in business. Next day he purchases on credit the following from Business Supplies Ltd: 1 office desk £142.50; 2 filing cabinets at £99.00 each; 1 electronic typewriter, Serial no. 72/69310, £487.50; and a letter-folding machine £321.25.
   These items are to be kept on his books in two Asset Accounts only. Do the Journal Entry for the purchases, inventing sensible folio numbers. You need not post the entries to the Ledger.

6. Dry Gulch Rural District Council purchases equipment as follows: Irrigation pipe layer £5 000.00; Trench cutter £9 250.00; Water bulk transport truck £7 250.00; 2 electric pumps at £4 250.00 each. The Council's rule is that equipment whose initial cost is £5 000.00 or more will be recorded in a separate Asset Account of its own. Equipment costing less than this will be recorded in the General Equipment Account. The whole of these purchases were paid for by cheque on the day of delivery, August 11, when the Journal Entry was made. Make this Journal Entry, inventing sensible folio numbers.

7. John Lowson recently started in business with capital in the bank of

£50 000.00, bequeathed to him by a rich aunt. On February 1 he purchased the following, paying by cheque: Plant and machinery £11 000.00; Motor vehicle £2 250.00; Word processor £4 000.00; Furniture £1 400.00. Make the Journal Entry for these purchases, inventing sensible folio numbers.

7.8 Journal Entries no. 4 – depreciation of assets

A full account of the different methods of depreciation is dealt with in Chapter 14, but we will here take a preliminary look at depreciation.

What is depreciation?
Depreciation is a reduction in the book value of an asset due to fair wear and tear. For instance, a new motor-car bought this year may be worth £5 000.00. By next year it will be worth less than this, about £4 000.00, and in ten years' time it will be ready for the scrap heap. We cannot keep the motor-car on our books valued at £5 000.00 down the years. Every year we depreciate it by a fair amount. Just how much we deduct from its value depends on our estimate of its fall in value, but at best it can only be a guess. Here is such an account, showing the reduction for depreciation over the years:

MOTOR VEHICLE ACCOUNT   L25

19. .		£	19. .		£
Jan. 1	New Vehicle	5 000.00	Dec. 31	Depreciation	1 000.00
			31	Balance	4 000.00
		£5 000.00			£5 000.00
19. .		£	19. .		£
Jan. 1	Balance	4 000.00	Dec. 31	Depreciation	1 000.00
			31	Balance	3 000.00
		£4 000.00			£4 000.00
19. .		£	19. .		£
Jan. 1	Balance	3 000.00	Dec. 31	Depreciation	1 000.00
			31	Balance	2 000.00
		£3 000.00			£3 000.00
19. .		£	19. .		£
Jan. 1	Balance	2 000.00			

Figure 7.8 The depreciation of an asset over the years

Below is the type of Journal Entry which would authorize the reduction in value.

19. .
Dec. 31
	Depreciation Account Dr.
	    Motor Vehicles Account
	Being the writing off of fair wear and
	   tear at this date.
		L73
		L25
			£
			1 000.00
				£ J7
				
				1 000.00

Figure 7.9 A depreciation Journal Entry

The amount transferred to Depreciation Account would be written off the profits at the end of the year. The Depreciation Account is one of those Nominal Accounts where losses are collected together preparatory to being written off.

DEPRECIATION ACCOUNT   L73

19. . Dec.			£	19. . Dec.			£
	31	Motor Vehicles	J17	1 000.00	31	Transfer to Profit and Loss	J24	3 250.00
	31	Furniture and Fittings	J18	250.00			
	31	Plant and Machinery	J21	2 000.00			
				3 250.00				3 250.00

Figure 7.10 Collecting losses together before writing them off

7.9 Exercises set 7.3 – Depreciation of assets

1. Show the Journal Entry required when the Motor Vehicles Account is depreciated by £1 000.00. Show also the Ledger Accounts, assuming that the motor vehicle was new on January 1, cost £5 000.00, and today's date is December 31, the same year.

2. My furniture and fittings are valued at £4 400.00; of which £3 000.00 is furniture. Do the Journal Entry for depreciation at 20 per cent on furniture and 10 per cent on fittings. Post to the Ledger.

3. Plant and Machinery for Cross Ltd is valued at £19 000.00 at June 30. At December 31 they depreciate it by 10 per cent per annum. (Careful, it's only a half-year.) Show the Journal Entry and both Ledger Accounts.

4. Michael Saunders is a bookmaker, and his electronic computer was valued at £20 000.00 on January 1. On December 31 of that year he depreciates it by 10 per cent, and on December 31 of the next year he depreciates it by a further 10 per cent on the original valuation. Show the Computer Account on the three dates named, bringing down the balance at the end of each year.

5. A Farmer depreciates his equipment December each year as follows: Tractors 20 per cent; Ploughs, harrows, and other tools 10 per cent; Fencing and gates 25 per cent; Barns 10 per cent; Buildings 5 per cent. Show the Journal Entry for a year's depreciation on Tractors £7 500.00;

Ploughs, etc. £1 950.00; Fencing, etc. £2 500.00; Barns £14 000.00; Buildings £75 000.00. Do not do the Ledger postings.

More advanced questions on depreciation appear at the end of Chapter 14.

7.10 Journal Entries no. 5 – the sale of worn-out assets

When most fixed assets get old they lose their value, for two reasons:

(a) Repairs get more frequent, so that both the cost of the repairs, and the loss of production and convenience while the machine is idle, increase.
(b) The machine becomes obsolete, that is, newer ideas which are an improvement on the machine we are using make it uneconomical to continue with the old one.

When this happens we usually sell the old machine and buy an up-to-date model. Very often we get a 'trade-in' allowance for the old model from the supplier of the new one.

What this means in terms of book-keeping depends upon the value of the old asset on the books, and its value when we actually sell it. There are three possibilities:

(a) The book value may be exactly the same as the real value on the market.
(b) The book value may be excessive, the market value is less than the book value.
(c) The book value may be too small – the real value on the market is greater than we expected.

Let us consider these cases, but remember that all three can only result from our *guesses* about depreciation. If we guess accurately, situation (a) will face us; if we guess poorly, either situation (b) or (c) will apply.

Example 1 The sale of a worn-out asset at its book value.
We have on our books a machine value at £500.00. We sell it on May 31 for exactly £500.00 in cash. Clearly the asset will disappear from our books and be replaced by an exactly equal asset, cash.
The Journal Entry will be as follows:

19. .				£	£ J8
May 31	Cash Account Dr.	CB9		500.00	
	Machinery Account	L27			500.00
	Being sale of machine 7/71656/d at this date.				

Figure 7.11 Selling machinery at book value

When posted to the credit side of the Machinery Account this entry will remove the £500.00 machine from the books, replacing it with the cash debited to Cash Account.

Example 2   The sale of a worn-out asset for less than its book value

Imagine that we are disposing of the same machine but find we can only get £300.00 for it. This means we have guessed the depreciation wrongly over the years, which is hardly surprising. Remember that depreciation is, at best, an informed guess.

Clearly we shall only have £300.00 cash to replace £500.00 worth of machine, but we must write off the total book value of the machine. We cannot leave £200.00 of a non-existent machine on the books. Whatever we get for our worn-out machine the rule is:

Always credit the Asset Account with the book value of the old asset.

Always debit Cash Account with the cash received.

Debit the loss in Sale of Machinery Account, rather than in Depreciation Account since it is usual to show the item separately in the Profit and Loss Account at the end of the year.

19. . May 31	Cash Account Dr. Sale of Machinery Account Dr. Machinery Account Being sale of machine 7/71656/d at a loss on its book value.	CB9 L21 L17	£ 300.00 200.00	£ J9 500.00

Figure 7.12   **Selling machinery at less than its book value**

Example 3   The sale of a worn-out asset at more than its book value

The third possibility is that the asset realizes more than its book value. When this happens we have clearly been guessing too great a figure for depreciation. The machine has not depreciated as much as we expected. In real life scrap values vary so much with the world political situation that no one can be blamed for guessing inaccurately. A machine containing valuable metal may fetch a top price, or a rock-bottom price, according to what is happening in the economic world.

Imagine that the machine in Example 1 fetches £850.00 when sold for scrap. Clearly this time a new asset Cash, value £850.00, will replace the old asset, value £500.00. We cannot take more than £500.00 off the Machinery Account; to do so would be to remove part of some other machine's value as well. The rule is the same: deduct the book value of the old machine from the Machinery Account. The rest will have to be treated as a profit (credit item) on Sale of Machinery Account, rather than crediting Depreciation Account, since it should be shown separately on the Profit and Loss Account at the end of the year.

The Journal Entry will look like this:

19. .
May 31
	Cash Account Dr.
	    Machinery Account
	    Sale of Machinery Account
	Being sale of machine 7/71656/d at a
	figure in excess of its book value.
		CB9
		L17
		L21
			£
			850
				£ J1
				
				500.00
				350.00

Figure 7.13 **Selling a machine at more than its book value**

The student should now try the following exercises on the sale of worn-out assets. Note that it is necessary to use one's own common sense when deciding on the name of the accounts to be used when recording profits or losses on the sale of worn-out assets.

7.11 Exercises set 7.4 – The sale of worn-out assets

1. On May 20 we sell a typewriter valued on the books at £50.00 for exactly that sum in cash. Do the Journal Entry.

2. On May 21 we sell a machine valued on the books at £500.00 to R. Dealer, who will pay for it at the end of the month. Do the Journal Entry. Price to R. Dealer is £500.00.

3. On May 23 we sell a typewriter valued on the books at £20.00 for £12.50 to Anne Employee, who pays in cash. Do the Journal Entry.

4. On July 27 we sell a combine harvester valued on the books at £4 050.00 for £4 000.00 to A. Farmer. He pays later. Do the Journal Entry.

5. On August 31 L. Lebon purchases from us a tool shed, valued on our books at £40.00, for £60.00 cash. Do the Journal Entry.

6. On May 7, R. Cooper buys from us on credit a motor vehicle, valued at £1 250.00, for £1 450. Do the Journal Entry.

7. On December 12 we sell T. Thomas a pile-driver valued at £1 900.00, for cash £1 500.00, and 2 office machines valued at £500.00 each. Do the entry as it would appear in our Journal Proper. Post the entry to the Ledger.

7.12   Journal Entries no. 6 – simple bad debts

When a debtor owes us money and is unable to pay there is very little point in keeping the debt on our books as if we shall be paid very soon. We must either take steps to force the debtor to pay, or recognize the fact that we have lost our money.

If we decide to take legal action through the Courts to force payment of the debt, the result will eventually be a Receiving Order by the Court, which puts the debtor in the hands of the Official Receiver. This government official will then seize the debtor's assets and sell them to pay the debts. If the sale of the debtor's assets realizes sufficient to pay the debts the debtor will not be made a **bankrupt,** but usually the proceeds are insufficient and bankruptcy follows. The whole affair is conducted under carefully devised rules, the aim of which is to set the debtor free from the burden of debts so that he/she may start life anew, but with certain safeguards that will prevent the same muddle again.

A visit to the Bankruptcy Court in your own area is the best way of gaining experience of the law's attitude to the bankrupt. Overseas readers should check the law of their own countries on these matters.

Sometimes we do not bother to have a debtor bankrupted, either out of pity, or because it would be 'throwing good money after bad', or because adverse criticism in Court may affect our own goodwill with the public. In such cases we will merely write off the money owing as a **bad debt**.

Three possible situations arise:

(a) A debt that is wholly bad.
(b) A debt that is partially bad.
(c) A bad debt recovered, with interest.

Example 1   A debt that is wholly bad
On March 13 we hear that A. Debtor who owes £125.00 has died in tragic circumstances, leaving a widow and five children. We decide to write off the debt as a loss, to Bad Debts Account.

The Journal Entry and the accounts would appear as follows:

19. .				£	£ J1
Mar. 13	Bad Debts Account Dr.	L12	125.00	
	A. Debtor Account	L15		£125.00
	Being bad debt written off at this date – debtor killed in bank raid			

Figure 7.14   A debt that is wholly bad

A DEBTOR (before death)   L15

19. .			£		
Mar. 18	Balance	b/d	125.00		

A. DEBTOR (after writing off debt)   L15

19. .			£	19. .			£
Mar. 1	Balance	b/d	125.00	Mar. 13	Bad Debt	J1	125.00

BAD DEBTS ACCOUNT   L12

19. .			£		
Mar. 13	A. Debtor	J1	125.00		

Fig. 7.15 Clearing a debtor's account

Note that the debit item on the Debtor's Account – when it is cleared – is replaced by a debit item on a Loss Account, the Bad Debts Account.

Usually we also take the precaution of writing clearly in *red ink* across the Debtor's Account. This warns any member of staff who may receive inquiries about the debtor, or even requests for further supplies, that we no longer wish to deal with him.

Figure 7.16   A Warning Sign on a bad debtor's account

Example 2   A bed debt that is partially bad
Imagine the same debt as before, but this time A. Debtor has not died in tragic circumstances, he is simply a bad payer. We do not feel any sympathy at all for this type of debtor, and after doing our best to collect the money we take action through the Courts. The action eventually results in a Receiver taking over the debtor's assets. We are not being vindictive in taking this action; if a debtor cannot live by the normal standards of honourable business, then he has no right to be in business at all. For the good of the community we should take such action as will prevent him buying on credit in future. If he is not a rogue but just a fool, then for his own good we should put him out of business before he gets even deeper in debt.

The result of the Receiver's activities will be that such sums of money as can be collected by the sale of the debtor's effects are collected, and made available to the creditors. The amount available after paying the Receiver's expenses is shared among the creditors as a certain fraction in the £1. Suppose that the Receiver is able to pay 30 pence in the £1, or 30 cents in the Dollar. We have a debt of £125.00. We shall therefore receive

$$125 \times £0.30 = £37.50$$

the rest of the debt having to be written off as bad.

The Journal Entry will appear as follows:

19. .				£	£
July 15	Bank Account Dr.	CB7		37.50	
	Bad Debts Account Dr.	L12		87.50	
	A Debtor	L15			125.00
	Being the writing off of a bad debt on receiving cheque from the Receiver at £0.30 in the £1.00				

Figure 7.17   A debt that is partially bad

Note that the date is much later than the actual debt; legal process always take a considerable time. In this case we would certainly write 'Bad Debtor' clearly across the face of the account.

Example 3   A bad debt recovered

The Bankruptcy Laws set a man free from debt so that he can begin life again, but he may not enter business life again (except as an employee) without permission from the Court. It is an offence to obtain goods, etc., on credit while an undischarged bankrupt, and this is one reason why many bankrupts do their best to pay up their debts, with interest. Cases are recorded every month of people doing this many years after their bankruptcies, and thus re-establishing their good names.

Imagine that A. Debtor pays up his outstanding debt of £87.50, with interest at 10 per cent, which we will imagine adds a further £17.50 to the debt. One morning our postbag will include an unexpected £105.00. We shall, of course, be agreeably surprised by this, and the cheque will be banked in our Bank Account on the debit side. Which account shall we credit? We have already cleared the Debtor's Account and probably, if we have a loose-leaf system, the 'dead' page will have been removed after a while from the book.

The part which represents interest on the original debt is pure profit; it is a payment for the use of our capital in the months that have passed by, and it should be credited to Interest Received

Account. The other part, which represents the actual debt itself is best treated as a credit (profit) item in the Bad Debts Recovered Account; it will reduce this year's bad debts by £87.50 when transferred to Profit and Loss Account.

The Journal Entry and Ledger accounts will be as shown in Figures 7.18 and 7.19.

19. .
Oct. 31
	Bank Account Dr.
	  Interest Received Account
	  Bad Debts Recovered Account
	Being bad debt recovered with interest from A. Debtor at this date.
		CB19
		
		L77
		
		L12
			£
			105.00
				£
				
				17.50
				
				87.50

Figure 7.18 A bad debt recovered

	INTEREST RECEIVED ACCOUNT		L77
	19. . Oct. 31 By Bank	J1	£ 17.50

	BAD DEBTS RECOVERED ACCOUNT		L12
	19. . Oct. 31 By Bank	J1	£ 87.50

Figure 7.19 Two nominal accounts with profits on them

7.13 Exercises set 7.5 – Simple bad debts

1. On July 9 we hear that A. Debtor who owes us £15.60 has disappeared without trace. Do the Journal Entry to clear the debt.

2. On August 14 we hear that A. Borrower who owes us £250.00 has been killed in a railway disaster. As a gesture of goodwill to his bereaved relatives the debt is written off. Show the Journal Entry.

3. On July 19 a debtor, Anne Alien, who owes £500.00 informs us that in view of difficult economic circumstances the government of her country will only sanction the payment of half the money. It is decided to clear the whole debt in view of the political situation in the country concerned. Do the Journal Entry.

4. A debtor, B. Henriques, who owes us £1 200.00 is declared a bankrupt. He pays £0.05 in the £1.00, and the debt is written off. Do the Journal Entry, and post it to Henriques' Account, the Bank Account, and the Bad Debts Account.

5. On June 17 X sold goods on credit to Y valued at £2 000.00. In November he learned that Y had become bankrupt, and on November 30 he received a cheque for a final settlement of £0.70 in the £1.00. Show the Account of Y in X's Ledger and the Journal Entry for November 30.

6. R. Losalamos was written off as a debtor some time ago for £1 400.00. On July 12 he sends us a cheque for £1 475.00 in full settlement. Show the Journal Entry, the Bank Account, and any other accounts.

7. J. Houston was written off as a debtor some time ago for £1 500.00. On November 5 he sends us a cheque for £1 575.00 representing the complete payment of the debt and interest thereon for the intervening time. Do the Journal Entry.

8. F. Worth sends you a cheque for £365.75 which represents payment in full of a bad debt of £300.00, and interest on it for the outstanding period. Show the Journal Entry on May 8.

9. R. Galveston sends you a cheque for £500.00, and a supply of spare tyres valued at £400.00. This is in complete payment of a debt previously written off as bad. This debt was for £775.00, legal charges were £65.00 and £60.00 represents interest on the debt. Do the Journal Entry.

7.14 Journal Entries no. 7 – the correction of errors

Countless errors can occur in a set of books if they are kept by inefficient book-keepers, and it would be impossible to describe them all and show how they should be corrected. The great thing is to learn one's book-keeping as fully as possible, paying real attention to detail.

The basic rule is this: examine the error that has been made and do what you must to put it right. This will usually involve a double entry of some sort; very rarely do we get a matter that only requires a single-sided entry.

Here are some typical errors:

Example 1 Item debited to the wrong debtor
On January 14 it is discovered that Mr H. Smith has been debited with £75.00 which is actually owing from Mr H. B. Smith. Mr. H. Smith's Account and the Journal Entry to correct it are shown in Figure 7.20, while the corrected accounts are shown in Figure 7.21.

		H. SMITH ACCOUNT		L1
19. .			£	
Jan. 12	Sales	SDB1	75.00	

19. . Jan. 14	H. B. Smith Account Dr. H. Smith Account Being correction of error in posting	L2 L1	£ 75.00	£ 75.00

Figure 7.20   An incorrect account and the Journal Entry to correct it

H. SMITH ACCOUNT   L1

19. . Jan. 12	Sales	J1	£ 75.00	19. . Jan. 14	H. B. Smith	J1	£ 75.00

H. B. SMITH ACCOUNT   L2

19. . Jan. 14	H. Smith	J1	£ 75.00		

Figure 7.21   Correcting an error in posting to the Ledger

Example 2   Purchase of an asset entered in the Purchases Day Book

If an invoice for an asset is mistakenly entered in the Purchases Day Book with invoices for goods, the Asset Account will not be debited. Instead the Purchases Account will be debited and as this account is used for working out the profits or losses at the end of the year, this mistake will make our calculations wrong.

It is an error of principle to treat assets as if they were goods, and if such an error is made, a Journal Entry is required to correct it. Consider the following case:

T. Hansard, a bookseller, bought a delivery van for £4 000.00 on August 4. On August 31 it was noticed that the invoice had been treated not as the purchase of an asset but as an ordinary purchase in the Purchases Day Book.

It is clear here that the £4 000.00 will have been posted to the Purchases Account on the debit side, instead of being debited in the Motor Vehicles Account. To get the matter right we must debit the Motor Vehicles Account and credit the Purchases Account, so that the £4 000.00 is removed.

The Journal Entry will therefore be as shown in Figure 7.22.

19. . Aug. 31	Motor Vehicles Account Dr. Purchases Account Being an error of principle in which an asset was treated as goods.	L27 L32	£ 4 000.00	£ 4 000.00

Figure 7.22   Assets mistaken for goods

Example 3   A single-sided error
When adding up the Sales Day Book on July 31 an error of £100.00 was made in the addition, so that the total posted to the Sales Account was £100.00 more than it should have been. How is the error corrected on August 4?

In this case there is nothing wrong with the amounts posted to the debit side of the Ledger Accounts of the debtors. The only error is the £100.00 mistake on the Credit side of the Sales Account.

To put it right we simply debit the Sales Account with £100.00. This is a one-sided entry.

The Journal Entry will look like Figure 7.23.

19. . Aug. 4	Sales Account Dr. .... Being a single-sided entry required to correct an over-addition in the Sales Day Book.	L121	£ 100.00	£ —

Figure 7.23   An unusual entry

An alternative way of dealing with this is actually to cross out the Sales Account figure and rewrite it correctly, initialling the alteration.

If a **Suspense Account** had been open at the end of July this would change the treatment again, but this will be dealt with in the section on Suspense Accounts, Chapter 10, page 168.

7.15   Exercises set 7.6 – The correction of errors

1. Prepare Journal Entries for the following, showing the narrative used:

(a) The purchase of a typewriter, value £377.50, has been wrongly included in purchases.
(b) A credit note issued to R. Morgan for goods returned to the value of £300.00, less 25 per cent trade discount, has been posted to the account of R. Morton.

2. Show by means of Journal Entries how the following errors would be corrected in the books of C. Careless:

(a) Machinery valued at £2 500.00 purchased on credit from Excel Engineering Company had been debited to the Purchases Account.
(b) When paying J. Johnson, a creditor, Careless had deducted £25.00 discount. Johnson had disallowed this discount.
(c) Depreciation of £1 000.00 on motor vehicles had been credited to the Fixtures and fittings Account.

(RSA – Adapted)

3. A Sales Invoice made out to Alan Gee for goods supplied to him valued at £1 150.00 was posted by mistake to G. Allen's account in the Ledger. Correct this error on December 5.

(East Anglian Examination Board – Adapted)

4. Show by means of Journal Entries how the following errors would be corrected in the books of V. Slack:

(a) Depreciation of £500.00 on motor vehicles had been credited to the Machinery Account.
(b) When paying S. Jones, a creditor, Slack had deducted £37.50 as cash discount. Jones had disallowed this discount.
(c) Machinery valued at £5 000.00, purchased on credit from Steel Engineering Company, had been debited to the Purchases Account.
(d) A sale to Derby & Co. amounting to £1 377.50 had been entered in the Sales Day Book as £1 737.50 and this latter figure had been posted to the respective Ledger Accounts.

(RSA – Adapted)

5. Correct by means of Journal Entries the following mistakes in the books of E. Nartey, a retail draper:

(a) Sale of a suit on credit to M. Haji for £100.00 was wrongly entered in G. Haji's account.
(b) The total of the Purchases Day Book was wrongly brought forward as £5 250.00 instead of £5 520.00.
(c) An office typewriter costing £327.50 was wrongly entered in the Purchases Day Book instead of Typewriter Account.
(d) The total of the Discount Allowed Column, £135.75, was wrongly posted to the Credit side of Discount Allowed Account. (Be careful with this entry.)

6. Correct the following errors by Journal Entries:

(a) An allowance of £7.00 made to a debtor R. Cornish had been entered in the Sales Returns Book as £70.00 and posted to Cornish's Account at that figure.
(b) Stators (the stationary part of electric motors), purchased for electric motor assemblies, value £750.00, which should have been recorded in the Purchases Account, were incorrectly debited in the Stationery Account.
(c) Sales to P. Robson of £225.00 were posted in error to P. Robison's Account.
(d) The purchase of an oil-fired boiler for £5 000.00 had been entered in the Purchases Day Book instead of the Fixed Machinery Account.

7. Give Journal Entries to correct the following Items:

(a) A credit entry of £300.00 was made in the books of E. Kemp instead of E. Kempster.
(b) A lorry was recorded in the books of C. Phillips at £950.00. It was bought by Garage Ltd. at an agreed value of £750.00, but the

book-keeper did not remove the £200.00 extra from the Motor Lorry Account.

(c) Goods sold to L. Bates valued at £442.00 were entered in the Sales Day Book as £244.00 and posted at that figure to the accounts.

(RSA – Adapted)

8. Correct the following items by means of Journal Entries (a Suspense Account has *not* been opened up):

(a) The total of the Discount Received Column in the Cash Book was posted on May 31 to the wrong side of the Discount Account. The figure was £158.90.

(b) A final dividend of £180.00 from a bankrupt, R. J., was received from the Official Receiver and posted to the credit side of R. J.'s Account. R. J.'s Account had already been cleared to Bad Debts Account the previous December 31.

(c) The sale of an obsolete machine for £212.50 on credit to Sun Garage Ltd. was entered in the Sales Day Book in error and posted to the accounts. The machine had been sold at book value.

7.16   Journal Entries no. 8 – dishonoured cheques

When a cheque is received from a debtor there is no guarantee that he has funds in his account to cover the cheque. When we enter the cheque on the debit side of the Cash Book and post it to the credit side of his account there is always the possibility that we shall have to reverse the process later.

If a cheque is dishonoured in this way it is returned to us marked **Refer to Drawer.** Such a cheque should immediately be referred to the person who drew it.

It is an offence to pass a cheque in this way. Often the explanation will be acceptable to us; the drawer will phone his bank and arrange for the cheque to be honoured. We shall present it again and this time all will be well. If the explanation is unsatisfactory we shall refer the matter to the police. In the meantime we have to put through a Journal Entry which cancels the original entry for the cheque.

The rule for dishonoured cheques is:

Restore the debt to the debtor
Remove the bad cheque from the Cash Book (i.e. **Debit** the debtor, **Credit** the Bank Account)

Example 1
A. Brown sends us a cheque for £282.50 which is banked and credited to his account. Subsequently it is returned 'refer to drawer' and we find that A. Brown is temporarily in difficulties.

The Journal Entry will appear as shown in Figure 7.24.

19. .
July 12
	A. Brown Dr.
	    Bank Account
	Being a dishonoured Cheque – debt
	  restored to debtor
		L17
		CB9
			£
			282.50
				£
				
				282.50

Figure 7.24 Clearing a dishonoured cheque

A further complication arises where a debtor whose cheque subsequently 'bounces' has been given discount for prompt payment. Since he has not now paid promptly we must clearly restore the full debt, not just the amount of the cheque. The following example illustrates this point:

Example 2
On April 4 A. Morton pays a debt of £750.00 by sending a cheque for £735.00, the rest being discount. This cheque is returned 'refer to drawer' on April 6. Restore the debt to the debtor.
   The Journal Entry now becomes:

19. .
Apr. 6
	A. Morton Dr.
	    Bank Account
	    Discount Allowed Account
	Being debt restored in full to A.
	  Morton's Account on dishonour of
	  cheque.
		L173
		CB19
		L29
			£
			750.00
				£
				
				735.00
				15.00

Figure 7.25 A dishonoured cheque, where discount has been given

The discount debited in the Discount Allowed Account as a loss must be credited to remove the loss – we are not suffering this loss any more. Of course we may suffer a much bigger loss if Morton does not pay, but that remains to be seen in the future.

7.17 Exercises set 7.7 – Dishonoured Cheques

1. On May 19 a cheque for £262.50 received two days earlier from R. Thomas was returned marked 'refer to drawer'. Restore the debt to the debtor.

2. On July 11 two cheques are returned marked 'refer to drawer'. One was for £254.75 from L. Jones and the other £132.25 from T. Peterson. Do the Journal Entry restoring these debts to the Debtors' Accounts.

3. M. Lucas paid us £211.00 on May 5. On May 8 the cheque was returned marked 'refer to drawer'. Restore the debt to Lucas.

4. R. Jowett, who paid us £282.75 in full settlement of a debt of £297.50 on May 8, dishonours his cheque. It is returned 'refer to drawer', on May 11. Restore the debt to the debtor with a Journal Entry.

5. M. Cole's cheque for £1 822.50, which was in full settlement of a debt of £1 850.00 is returned dishonoured. Restore the debt to the debtor with a Journal Entry dated June 11.

6. T. Cruiser dishonours a cheque for £904.00 which was in full settlement of a debt of £920.00. Do a Journal Entry to restore the debt to his account.

7.18   Journal Entries no. 9 – bank loans, interest, and charges

Where a bank lends money other than by means of an overdraft an agreement will be drawn up and signed covering the terms of the loan. This agreement will usually specify the amount of the loan, the rate of interest payable, the period over which it is to be repaid, the amount of the monthly repayment, and the collateral security to be provided.

Once this agreement is signed the bank puts the amount of the loan into our ordinary Current Account, but also opens up a **Loan Account,** which records the amount loaned, and to which our monthly repayments will be credited. We shall do the same in our books, as shown by the following example:

Example 1
Briggs Bank Ltd. agree to lend us the sum of £5 000.00 against the security of a life assurance policy on the proprietor. The Loans Agreement is signed on April 1. Repayments are to be at the rate of £200.00 per month.

The Journal Entry will be as shown in Figure 7.26.

19. .			£	£
Apr. 1	Bank Account Dr.	CB1	5 000.00	
	Briggs Bank Loan Account	L29		5 000.00
	Being loan received on this date against life assurance policy			

Figure 7.26   Recording a loan

The Loan Account is credited with £5 000.00, but as the repayments are made, the sums credited in the Bank Account are debited to the Loan Account, as shown in Figure 7.28.

Bank interest payable
Interest charged by the bank is a loss to the person paying it, and a profit to the bank.

The periodic amounts of interest charged will be credited to the Loan Account, since the bank becomes a creditor for the amount of the interest, and will be debited to **Loan Interest Account** as one of the losses of the business. The Journal Entry for this will be as follows, taking £141.00 as the interest due:

19. . July 1	Loan Interest Account Dr. Loan Account, Briggs Bank Being interest due for quarter	L28 L27	£ 141.00	£ 141.00

Figure 7.27 Recording loan interest

The Loan Account now looks as shown in Figure 7.28, with the three monthly repayments of £200.00.

			LOAN ACCOUNT					L27
19. .			£	19. .				£
Apr. 30	Bank	CB7	200.00	Apr. 1	Bank	CB5	5 000.00	
May 31	Bank	CB9	200.00	1	Interest	CB13	141.00	
June 30	Bank	CB13	200.00					

Figure 7.28 Repaying a loan

Bank interest receivable
Bank interest is paid on loans, but it may also be received if we have a Deposit Account. There are two kinds of Bank Account used by traders: the Current Account and the Deposit Account.

Current Accounts do not earn interest, because the bank cannot rely upon the use of money in a Current Account. We make use of the bank's services, the cheque system and the credit transfer system, etc. and we must expect to pay for them. With a Current Account, therefore, it is usual for the bank to make bank charges. Sometimes, if a fairly substantial sum is left unused in the Current Account the Bank will not charge 'bank charges', but will carry out these services free in return for the use of the stable portion of our funds.

With Deposit Accounts the depositor agrees to give the bank seven days' notice before withdrawing the deposit. The bank is then able to use the funds we have deposited to lend to borrowers at a rate of interest which is usually 2–5% above bank base rate. The Bank, in return for this use of our money shares its earnings with us, by giving us some of the interest it is receiving from the borrower; usually 2 per cent less than the bank base rate. In this way we could receive **Bank Interest** – this time as a profit of our business.

Such interest is added by the bank to the Deposit Account. To record this profit in our books we need a Journal Entry that looks like Figure 7.29.

19. .
Oct. 1
	Bank Deposit Account Dr.
	        Interest Received Account
	Being interest from the bank at this
	   date.
		L45
		L47
			£
			37.50
				£
				
				37.50

Figure 7.29   Recording interest received

Bank charges

Like bank interest payable, bank charges are a loss to the business. If the bank charges us sums of money for using its services it will deduct these sums from our Bank Account. When we find that this has been done we have clearly to deduct the bank charges from our Cash Book, or we shall find that our Cash Book differs from the Bank Account. Strictly speaking a Journal Entry is not absolutely necessary for this, but if we do decide to journalize, the Journal Entry will appear as in Figure 7.30.

19. .
Aug. 4
	Bank Charges Account Dr.
	        Bank Account
	Being Bank Charges deducted at this
	   date.
		L17
		CB24
			£
			27.50
				£
				
				27.50

Figure 7.30   Journalizing bank charges

7.19   Exercises set 7.8 – Bank loans, interest, and charges

1. On May 14 the General Bank Ltd agreed to lend us £2 500.00 against the security of the deeds to our shop. Record this loan in a Journal Entry.

2. On December 31 R. Pace borrows £5 000.00 privately from A. Friend, giving his life assurance policy as collateral. Record this loan in R. Pace's books, through a Journal Entry. This £5 000.00 is banked.

3. Steady Bank Ltd lend Overdrawn Ltd £50 000.00 secured on the plant and machinery of the firm. Record the Journal Entry as it would appear in the books of Overdrawn Ltd on March 31.

4. On September 30 Steady Bank Ltd charge Overdrawn Ltd £3 000.00 interest on the loan described in Question 3. Record this interest charge in the Journal of Overdrawn Ltd.

5. On October 1 R. Smith is notified by his bank that interest on his gilt-edged securites has been received from the Bank of Australia and credited to his account. The payment is £150.00. Record this interest received in his Journal.

6. On December 31 T. Jones asks his bankers for a Bank Statement and finds that on December 15 they charged him Bank Charges of £13.75 Record this in his Journal and post to the Ledger and Cash Book.

7. On December 31 R. Moy is notified by his Building Society that business deposits in his Savings Account have earned interest of £138.25 for the half year. Do the Journal Entry for this profit and post to the Ledger. (Debit Building Society Savings Account.)

7.20   VAT in cash takings

In Section 6.6 reference was made to the problem of calculating VAT in cash takings. There are actually nine different schemes for calculating VAT on cash takings and unless the system is computerized so that the VAT element in the day's takings can be very easily calculated it is much easier to do the calculations once a month only.

What we have to do is deduct from the cash sales figures posted to the Sales Account every day when the daily takings is recorded, the element of VAT included. This requires a Journal Entry. The following example shows the entries required.

Example
A. Brown has takings in cash (cash sales) of £13 725.60 in the month of February. His VAT calculations under his special scheme show that £1 625.42 is VAT. Do the Journal Entry to remove the VAT element from the Sales Account.

Answer
Clearly the VAT has to be debited in Sales Account (to remove the VAT element from the sales) and credited in VAT Account (because the £1 625.42 is Output Tax charged to customers, and must be paid to the VAT authorities in due course). The Journal Entry and ledger postings are therefore as shown in Figure 7.31 below.

19. .					J17
Feb. 28	Sales A/c	Dr.	L12	1 625.42	
	VAT A/c		L93		1 625.42
	Being VAT element in cash sales removed from total sales figure.				

SALES ACCOUNT

19. .			£	19. .		£
Feb. 28 VAT A/c	J17	1 625.42		Feb. 28 Total sales (both cash and credit) say		29 205.00

VAT ACCOUNT   L15

				19. .		£
				Feb. 28 Balance (say)		3 125.00
				28 Sales A/c	J17	1 625.42

7.31   Removing VAT from a 'cash sales' figure

7.21   Exercises set 7.9 – Exercises on VAT in cash takings

1. M. Sharpe has cash takings in the month of March 19. . which (including VAT) total £24 715. At the end of the month his scheme calculations reveal that £3 217.20 of this is VAT. Do the Journal Entry to remove this from the Sales Account.

2. R. Seager has cash takings in the month of January 19. . (including VAT) of £37 259.94. His scheme calculation reveals that £5 105.25 of this is VAT. Do the journal entry to remove this VAT from Sales Account to VAT Account.

3. At the end of April 19. ., R. Longstaff's VAT Account has the following entries on it. Input tax £275.85 Output tax on credit sales £3 824.50. His Sales Account includes cash sales of £14 256.50 which has an element of VAT in it totalling £1 762.50. Show (a) the Journal Entry for removing this VAT from the Sales Account and (b) the VAT Account at the end of April 19. ., balanced off to show the balance payable to Customs and Excise.

8
The Columnar Petty Cash Book – Imprest System

8.1 Introduction

There are many items of quite small importance in business which nevertheless must be accurately recorded, especially if a code of honesty is to be established in the business. For instance, postage stamps must be accurately recorded or they may be used by staff for their own purposes. Telephone calls are very cheap but if staff use the telephone for private calls they will increase the bills payable by the business. All such items are called **Petty Cash** items.

The word 'petty' comes from the French word 'petit' meaning small, and the Petty Cash Book is a book where small items are recorded by the 'Petty Cashier'. We have already seen that the cashier is an important and trusted servant, paid a salary commensurate with his/her responsibilities. The petty cashier is usually a young and inexperienced person, whose honesty has not been entirely proved yet, although we have every reason to believe him/her trustworthy. Many cashiers begin life as petty cashiers, and this is one of the useful functions of the petty cash system; it develops inexperienced staff and makes them responsible. It has certain safeguards built into it, one of which gives the system its name – the **Imprest System.**

8.2 The Imprest System

An imprest is a certain sum of money which has been set aside for a particular purpose. It is an advance of cash, with an implied promise that there is more to come later whenever it is needed, and when the present imprest has been accounted for by the petty cashier. The main cashier starts the petty cashier off with a sum deemed to be sufficient for the office's needs for a limited time, say one week. Since postage is the commonest use for this system, the postal clerk is often the petty cashier. Given an imprest of £50 he/she will buy the stamps, pay for fares, cleaning materials, etc., and will also pay out petty cash to anyone who needs it. The office boy may need petty cash for bus fares, or money to buy odd items required in a hurry, like string, cellulose tape or similar office sundries.

When the petty cashier begins to run short of money, the postal clerk completes the Petty Cash Book in the way shown on page 142, and goes with it, and the Petty Cash Box, to the cashier. The cashier then checks the books, agrees that the record has been properly kept, counts what is left in the till, and **restores the imprest.** This means he gives the petty cashier the amount of money spent, **so that he/she finishes up with the original imprest again, ready to start the next week.**

This is the really important point about the Imprest System; the petty cashier is not given a further sum of £50.00 because with what is left over the total would be more than the agreed imprest. The petty cashier is simply given enough money to bring the total to £50.00 again, thus **restoring the imprest position.**

Advantages of the Imprest System

(a) It saves the main cashier, being endlessly bothered for trifling sums of money, and enables him/her to get on with other work.

(b) It trains young and inexperienced staff and develops their sense of responsibility.

(c) The sum of money chosen for the imprest is not large enough to present much of a temptation either to the petty cashier or to the other employees. This does not mean that care should not be taken with petty cash. In most cities the majority of crimes connected with offices involves thefts of petty cash, usually at lunch-time. The petty cashier should always lock the till before leaving the desk, and should lock it away in a safe as well before going to lunch.

(d) Even if it is stolen the loss does not represent a serious one to the firm.

(e) There is a very great saving **in the posting of expenses to the Nominal Accounts, because of the analysis system.** This is dealt with on page 143.

(f) At any time the till can quickly be checked, for the cash left + the value of the **payment vouchers** = the original imprest.

8.3   Original documents – the Petty Cash Voucher

Every transaction in business starts off with its original document and in the case of petty cash items the document concerned is the

White — **Customer's copy**
Buff — **Store copy**

**Customer's
receipt for
cash purchase**

(U.K.) V.A.T. Registration No. 232 5555 75
(R.I.) V.A.T. Registration No. 8/K/56287

Ref. No. 728149

Store address stamp

F. W. WOOLWORTH P.L.C.

19-24 Sidney Street
Cambridge OB2 3HI

Sales receipt   Date 14 July 19..

Qty.	Item Group like rated items together	Unit S.P.	V.A.T. %	Incl. V.A.T. £	p
6	100 Watt light bulbs	75p		4	50
1	Candle Lamp	7·95		7	95
1	13 Amp plug	1·15		1	15

| Received
with thanks | R.T. | | | | Total | £ 13 | 60 |

Complete this section only if requested by customer	Totals excl. V.A.T. £ p	V.A.T. %	Amount of V.A.T. £ p	Totals incl. V.A.T. £ p
		Zero		
Totals				

Customer's name   G. M. Whitehead

Address   2174 Camside

                              Cambridge

S.75 (V.A.T.) – 11/80

Figure 8.1 An external Petty Cash Voucher

Petty Cash Voucher. 'To vouch' is to certify the honesty of something, and the Petty Cash Voucher certifies the honesty of the petty cash disbursement made. Petty Cash Vouchers may be receipts obtained from someone outside the business or may be an internal voucher. The former are preferable since they give less opportunity for dishonesty to the employee. Even then one cannot always be certain. If the office boy is sent to buy a ball of string he/she is expected to produce a bill for it. Any shop-keeper will provide one on request when a purchase is made. In this way a check can be kept of the money actually spent, but fraudulent conspiracies are not uncommon, as any newspaper will show. Every week one reads in the police reports about such minor cases. A van driver who has been told to buy petrol and to ask for a receipt when he buys it, may give the garage employee a fat tip and ask him for a receipt showing a quantity greater than that really issued and paid for. When he shows the false receipt and is reimbursed from the petty cash, the driver is cheating his employer. This sort of practice can easily be detected if regular checks are made of the mileage per gallon. The low-mileage-per-gallon vehicle which is as new as other vehicles but unaccountably uses more petrol may have a dishonest driver.

Petty Cash Vouchers may be very small – bus tickets are an example. Such tickets may be stuck in books, or on larger sheets of paper, but they are proof of money spent and are therefore valid as vouchers. Where it is impossible to produce a voucher from

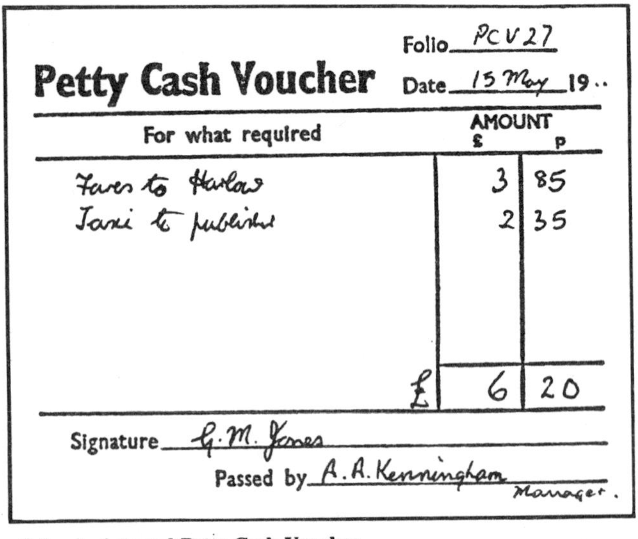

Petty Cash Voucher

Folio PCV 27

Date 15 May 19..

For what required	AMOUNT £	p
Fares to Harlow	3	85
Taxi to publisher	2	35
£	6	20

Signature G. M. Jones

Passed by A. A. Kenningham Manager.

Figure 8.2 An internal Petty Cash Voucher

outside the business – for instance when letters are posted – it is usual to provide an internal voucher, signed by the manager or some person in authority, to vouch for the expense.

These vouchers are numbered, and the numbers are recorded in the PCV column in the Petty Cash Book. They are then filed away in numerical order, so that if required the auditors may inspect them.

8.4 The Columnar Petty Cash Book (see pages 142–3)

For the reader's convenience the explanation of the layout of the Petty Cash Book has been given facing the illustration on page 142. Read this section now.

The student should now try several petty cash exercises. It is possible to buy petty cash paper from a stationer, but as in examinations one usually has to rule up paper for Petty Cash exercises, it is better to rule up a few sheets, even though this is rather laborious. Another way is to rule up one sheet and photocopy it if you have access to a photocopying machine.

(*Section 8.5 continues on page 145.*)

Dr. £	Date	Details	PCV	Total £	Postage £	Fares £	Cleaning £	Sundry Expenses £	Stationery £	Folio	Ledger A/cs £ (Cr.)
50.00	19.. Mar. 25	Imprest	CB9								
	25	Stamps	1	7.50	7.50						
	26	Postage	2	3.25	3.25						
	26	Cleaning	3	2.25			2.25				
	27	Sundries	4	1.60				1.60			
	27	Fares	5	7.25		7.25					
17.50	28	Telephone Calls	L3								
	28	R. Jones	7	6.70						L19	6.70
	29	Cleaning	8	3.25			3.25				
	29	Sundries	9	2.00				2.00			
	29	Travelling	10	8.25		8.25					
	30	Envelopes	11	2.25					2.25		
	30	Office Equipment	12	8.25						L15	8.25
	30	Sundries	13	0.75				0.75			
	31	Totals	—	53.30	10.75	15.50	5.50	4.35	2.25		14.95
	31	Balance	c/d	14.20	L5	L11	L27	L36	L49		
£67.50			£	67.50							
14.20	Apr. 1	Balance	b/d								
35.80	1	Restored Imprest	CB11								

Figure 8.3   The Petty Cash Book

Notes:

(a) Notice that the centre of the book is misplaced to the left, so that the debit side has only a cash column. This is done to save paper, which would otherwise be wasted, since the receipt of cash is quite a rare item. The petty cashier usually receives cash only from the cashier when he collects the imprest at the beginning of the week. About the only other cash he receives is when staff pay for private telephone calls, as may be seen in Figure 8.3 on March 28.

(b) Since there is no 'Details' column on the left-hand side, the petty cashier writes all the details on the right-hand side, being careful to leave the credit side of the book blank on lines where a debit entry is written in the 'Details' column.

(c) These credit entries are not only entered in the Total column but are analysed into columns farther over; this enables us to collect the total expenses, under the various headings, into one sub-total. This is one of the great advantages of the columnar Petty Cash Book; it saves a great deal of posting. Instead of posting each item of expenditure to the various accounts we need only post the totals once a week.

(d) As the expenses are paid they are entered into the total and the analysis columns. There is one special column at the end, the Ledger Account column. Notice that it has a folio column next to it. This Ledger Account column is used to collect any items for Personal or Real Accounts. The expenses (losses) will be going into Nominal Accounts and can be collected from the subtotal columns. While it is sensible to post all the postage to the Postage Account it would not be sensible to post Mr Jones's £6.70 with Office Equipment £8.25. These are posted to their own accounts and the folio number is put in the folio column.

(e) At the end of the week the book is totalled, then cross-totalled to double check the entries; the balance of cash in hand is calculated and carried down to the credit side. Clearly this balance must agree with the cash in hand, and before going to the cashier, the petty cashier will obviously check that the book agrees with the Cash Box. He will also post the subtotals to the debit side of the Loss Accounts concerned, and post the items in the Ledger Accounts column to the debit side of the respective Ledger Accounts. If there should be any debit items in the debit column (like the telephone calls in this example) the petty cashier will post these sums to the credit side of the appropriate account. In this case the Telephone Account is, of course, a Loss Account, but the amount paid by the members of staff for private calls will reduce the total loss to be charged against the profits at the end of the financial year.

This posting is really fairly complex, but Figure 8.4 explains it.

(f) When the cashier has checked the book he restores the imprest, by giving the petty cashier the amount needed to restore the cash box to the full amount of the imprest. This is debited by the petty cashier in the Petty Cash Book; the other half of the double entry is credited in the cashier's main Cash Book as he pays out the money.

(g) Notice carefully all the positions of the folio numbers, especially the Cash Book folios, the folio numbers at the bottom of the columns, the folio numbers in the Ledger Account folio column, and the folio number in the Petty Cash Voucher column against the telephone entry.

Now return to Section 8.4.

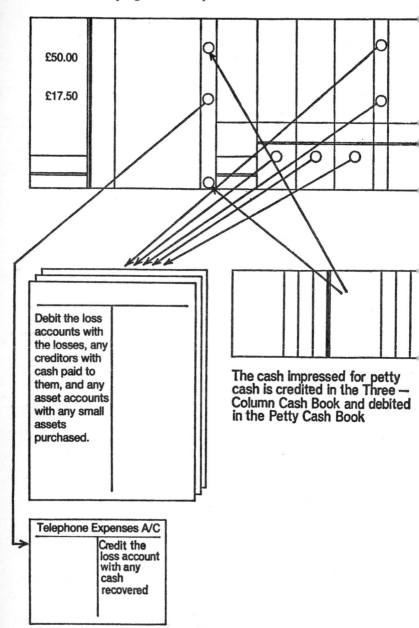

£50.00

£17.50

Debit the loss accounts with the losses, any creditors with cash paid to them, and any asset accounts with any small assets purchased.

The cash impressed for petty cash is credited in the Three — Column Cash Book and debited in the Petty Cash Book

Telephone Expenses A/C

Credit the loss account with any cash recovered

Figure 8.4   Posting the Petty Cash Book

8.5   A page to test you on the Petty Cash Book

Cover the page with a sheet of paper, then read one question at a time.

Answers	*Questions*
—	1 What does 'petty' mean?
1 Small or unimportant.	2 What system is used for Petty Cash?
2 The Imprest System.	3 What is an imprest?
3 A sum of money set aside for a particular purpose.	4 What are the advantages of the Imprest System?
4 (a) It saves bothering the main cashier; (b) little risk, and little temptation; (c) trains young staff; (d) saves time on posting to the Ledger because of the analysis columns (e) is easily checked.	5 Where is the 'middle' of a page in a Petty Cash Book?
5 Set towards the left-hand side of the page.	6 Why is this done?
6 Because the petty cashier doesn't often receive money.	7 When does he receive money?
7 (a) When he draws the imprest from the cashier; (b) when members of staff pay for telephone calls, etc.	8 Why does the credit side need more room than in an ordinary Cash Book?
8 Because there are extra analysis columns.	9 What is the point of these analysis columns?
9 To collect together similar minor expenses and to make it possible to post the total each week in only one posting per column.	10 Why is the end column different?
10 Because where postings are to either Personal or Real Accounts they must be kept separate. Only expenses for the Nominal Accounts can be added together.	11 How do you finish off a Petty Cash Book?
11 (a) Add the columns, then add across to check the work; (b) find the balance, check that the till is right, balance the books and bring down the balance; (c) ask the cashier to restore the Imprest.	12 What is the document for which the Petty Cash Book is the book of original entry?
12 The Petty Cash Voucher.	13 Where should a Petty Cash Voucher come from ideally?
13 From outside the business.	14 As we post the Petty Cash Book what must we write on it?
14 The folio numbers of the Ledger pages.	—

8.6   Exercises Set 8.1 The Petty Cash Book

1. Rule up a Petty Cash Book for five columns: Sundry Expenses, Fares, Stationery, Postage and Ledger Accounts. Enter the following items:

19. .
Jan.   1 Drew imprest £100.00 from the chief cashier; paid for office teas
          £1.75 postage stamps £6.75, fares £2.75.
       2 Paid for envelopes £11.40; paid P. Jones £13.65.
       3 Paid fares £1.60; paid cleaning materials £3.15.
       4 Paid stationery £6.65; paid P. Brown £5.80.
       5 Paid for cleaning materials £6.25; paid fares £2.65.
       6 Paid for ball of string £0.70.
       7 Paid for sundry items for office use £4.30.

Balance off the Petty Cash Book and restore the imprest.

2. Enter the following items in a Petty Cash Book which is kept on the Imprest System. At the end, balance off the book and restore the original imprest. Use analysis columns for Fares, Postage, Sundry Expenses, Stationery, and Ledger Accounts, and invent appropriate folio numbers and Petty Cash Voucher numbers.

19. .
Oct.   1 Drew Imprest from cashier £50.00.
       2 Paid fares £2.65; bought postage stamps £1.90.
       3 Paid for office teas £2.25; paid for stationery £3.30; paid for ball
          of string £0.75; collected for private telephone calls £17.27.
       4 Paid fares £5.75; paid for gum for office £1.15.
       5 Postage stamps £1.40; paid General Insurance Co. Ltd £4.25;
          paid J. Thomas £5.40.
       6 Paid fares £1.65; paid cleaner £1.25; paid dustman £0.50.

3. Tom Brown runs his office petty cash on the Imprest System. He has five columns: Postage, Travelling Expenses, Cleaning, Sundry Expenses, and a column for Ledger Accounts. Enter the following items, balancing the book at the end of the week, and restoring the imprest:

19. .
Mar. 25 Drew Petty Cash Imprest £100.00; bought stamps £5.50.
      26 Paid postage £1.80; paid cleaner's wages £7.50.
      27 Paid for string £0.75; fares £7.25; postage £1.75.
      28 Paid sum of £8.75 to R. Jones. Collected for private telephone
          calls £8.22.
      29 Paid for cleaning materials £2.25; sundry expenses £1.25;
          postage £7.25.
      30 Paid £6.25 to L. Robbins; bought scales for office use (Furniture
          and Fittings Account) £6.90; paid travelling expenses £3.15.

Note: The scales are clearly the purchase of an asset and should be the subject of a Journal Entry. This does not affect the Petty Cash Book which will still credit the sum paid and record the analysis in the Ledger Accounts column.

4. Enter the following in a Petty Cash Book with six columns, for Postage, Fares, Office Sundries, Cleaning, Repairs, and Ledger Accounts. Invent appropriate folio numbers and Petty Cash Voucher numbers.

19. .
Oct. 15 Drew petty cash Imprest £100.00; paid postage £7.50.
   16 Paid fares £2.40; bought ball of string £0.75; paid window-cleaner £4.25 and a creditor, T. Brown, £8.25.
   17 Paid postage £7.75; bought envelopes £12.50; bought cleaning materials £3.25.
   18 Paid R. Johnson £8.75; member of staff paid £2.25 for private telephone call; paid fares £1.65.
   19 Paid fares £13.75; paid cleaner's wages £7.75; paid for repairs to window catch £4.25; paid M. Smith £5.75; paid postage £2.50.

Balance the book and restore the imprest.

5. Make out the Petty Cash Book for a firm which gives its petty cashier an imprest of £75.00 and requires her to analyse expenses under the headings: Postage, Travelling Expenses, Sundry Expenses, Wages, Repairs and Ledger Accounts.

19. .
Jan. 1 Received imprest from cashier £75.00; paid for postage stamps £12.50.
   2 Repairs to lock, after burglary, £12.25; paid dustman £0.50; paid for postage £1.25; R. Morgan called in and paid Petty Cashier £8.75.
   3 Paid sundry expenses £3.10; cleaner's wages £12.50.
   4 Paid postage on parcel £1.80; travelling expenses £1.25.
   5 Sundry expenses paid £2.75; stamps £7.25.
   6 Postage £7.15; paid M. Clark £18.25.

Balance off the book and restore the imprest, inventing appropriate folio numbers and Petty Cash Voucher numbers.

6.
(a) J. Peach keeps his Petty Cash Book on the Imprest System. What does this mean?

(b) What are the advantages of the Imprest System?
(c) Peach's book has the following matters recorded in the first week of the year. Draw up the book, balance it off, and restore the imprest, inventing suitable folio numbers and Petty Cash Voucher numbers. Use columns for Postage, Fares, Sundry Expenses, and Ledger Accounts.

19. .
Jan. 1 Drew imprest of £50.00 from cashier; paid postage £8.25.
   2 Paid fares £2.25; postage £1.15; collected private telephone call money from staff £7.10.
   3 Paid for paper and string £1.10; paid L. French £13.80.

4 R. Peters paid J. Peach £8.25 which was put into the Petty Cash till; paid postage £7.25.

5 Paid fares £0.75; taxi for visitor £2.25.

7. A Petty Cash Book is kept on the Imprest System, the amount of the imprest being £100.00. It has five analysis columns: Postage and Stationery, Travelling Expenses, Carriage, Office Expenses and Ledger Accounts. Give the ruling for the book and enter the following transactions:

19. .

Jan.   4 Petty Cash in hand £7.50; received cash to make up the Imprest; bought stamps £10.00.

7 Paid railway fares £1.25; bus fares £0.65; paid T. Jones £5.65.

8 Paid carriage on small parcels £2.10; paid railway fares £4.60; bought envelopes £4.45.

10 Paid for repairs to typewriters £13.75; paid A. Supplier's account for December £11.05.

11 Paid office tea lady £7.50. Sold old typewriter to member of staff £10.00, its book value.

Balance the Petty Cash Book as on January 11 and bring down the balance.

(RSA – Adapted)

8. On June 30 the debit (or receipts) side of a trader's Petty Cash Book showed a total of £100.00 this being the amount of the fixed imprest; on the same date the Total Payments column showed a total of £85.85, and the analysis columns showed individual totals as follows: Carriage Inwards £20.80; General Expenses £10.75; Postage £10.50; Stationery £0.75; Travelling Expenses £25.65, and Ledger Accounts £17.40. There was only one item in the Ledger Accounts column, and it was written up in the Particulars column as follows: 'A/c Clerys Ltd for air-freight charges to Dublin'.

Answer the following questions:

(a) On June 30 how much would the petty cashier collect from the principal cashier in order to restore his balance in hand to the imprest figure?

(b) Which Ledger Accounts would be debited, and with what amounts, in order to complete the double entry:

(c) Which Ledger Account would have its page number written in the Ledger folio column against the item of £17.40.

(RSA – Adapted)

9
Book-keeping to the Trial Balance

9.1 Introduction

Advertisements will often be seen in the press offering employment to persons who can keep books to the Trial Balance level.
This is the first stage of book-keeping work, and the student who
approaches this chapter with a good sense of achievement on the
work of earlier chapters is about to make a breakthrough to the
point where he can call himself a 'Book-keeper to the Trial
Balance'. Such a student should not feel too disappointed if his
Trial Balances do not come out first time. It is a lucky book-keeper
who does not make some slip in his month's work, and it takes a
good level of experience to get even a textbook exercise right first
time. The important thing is to persevere; by the time you have
done six or seven of these major exercises you will begin to know
what you are doing.

9.2 What is involved in book-keeping to the Trial Balance?

Trial Balances in small offices are usually done once a month, on
the last day of the month. They cannot be done more frequently
because the work involved is too great, nor should they be done
less frequently. The purpose of the Trial Balance is to discover any
mistake; if there is one, it may be a long task finding it, even if
there is only one month's work to look through. To delay making a
Trial Balance for five or six months would mean Herculean labour
if a mistake were discovered.

During one month we have been recording a wide range of
transactions:

(a) Opening the books, with an Opening Journal Entry, unless of
    course they were already open from last month, in which case
    we start with last month's balances already on the books.
(b) Recording a great many Purchases, Sales, Purchases Returns,

and Sales Returns in the Day Books, and posting them to the Ledger.
(c)   Recording in the Cash Book cash received and paid, and posting it to the Ledger Accounts.
(d)   Recording Petty Cash received and paid, and posting it to the Ledger Accounts.
(e)   Recording several less common items like the Purchase of Assets and the Correction of Errors in the Journal Proper and posting them to the Ledger.

The final result of all these activities is a set of Ledger Accounts which have been entered accurately on the double entry method, so that every debit entry has a corresponding credit entry. If everything has been done correctly, a list of the debit balances will exactly equal a list of the credit balances. This is what a Trial Balance is: *a list of all the debit balances and of all the credit balances, each totalled to see whether the two totals agree.* If they do agree we may conclude that our book-keeping has been correct. (In fact this may not be true because there are five classes of error which do not show up on the Trial Balance. These will be discussed in Chapter 10 page 166).

9.3   Tidying up the Ledger Accounts and extracting a Trial Balance

A Trial Balance is a list of the balances on the accounts. As we draw up the Trial Balance we usually 'tidy up' the accounts. This means balancing them off and bringing down the balances but there is no point in doing this if it looks exactly the same afterwards as before.

Example 1
Consider this account:

			R. JONES		L27
19. .				£	
Jan.	14	Goods	SDB1	2 137.50	

Figure 9.1   A 'tidy' Personal Account

This account is as clear as it can possibly be. R. Jones is a debtor for £2 137.50, and even if we balance it off and bring down the balance the account will be no clearer than it is already. This is shown opposite:

							L27
			R. JONES				

				£	19. .				£
19. .									
Jan.	14	Goods	SDB1	2 137.50	Jan.	31	Balance	c/d	2 137.50
				£2 137.50					£2 137.50
19. .				£					
Feb.	1	Balance	b/d	2 137.50					

Figure 9.2   No tidier than Figure 9.1

As there is no point in balancing off in this way, we simply take the balance as shown in Figure 9.1, direct to the Trial Balance like this:

<u>M. BROWN AND T. JOHNSON</u>

<u>TRIAL BALANCE</u>

<u>as at January 31st, 19. .</u>

	Dr.	Cr.
R. Jones	2 137.50	

Figure 9.3   Starting a Trial Balance

Notice the following points:

(a) The firm's name is written at the top.
(b) The heading 'Trial Balance' always has a date on it – in this case 'as at January 31' – because a Trial Balance is only the same for one moment of time. As soon as February 1 comes a new set of transactions will alter the balances we have listed. For instance, Jones may pay his debt and his account will then be cleared. An account that is clear need not be brought into the Trial Balance at all.
(c) The debit balance is put in the debit column; a credit balance is put in the credit column.

Example 2
Now consider the following account:

			M. LICHMAN			L33

19. .				£	
Jan.	15	Goods	SDB1	181.25	
	17	Goods	SDB1	247.50	
	27	Goods	SDB1	802.50	
	27	Carriage	SDB1	26.25	

Figure 9.4   An account with entries on one side only

There is no real point in balancing off this account either. All we want to know on any account is: how big is the balance, and is it a debit or a credit balance? In this case it is clearly a debit balance and all we do is add it up and pencil in the total using small figures. This account adds up to £1 257.50.

M. Lichman's balance is now ready to be taken to the Trial Balance as shown in Figure 9.5.

M. LICHMAN						L33
19. .				£		
Jan.	15	Goods	SDB1	181.25		
	17	Goods	SDB1	247.50		
	27	Goods	SDB1	802.50		
	27	Carriage	SDB1	26.25		
				1 257.50	← Pencil figures – the Balance owing – to be taken into the Trial Balance.	

Figure 9.5   Totalling in pencil for Trial Balance purposes

Example 3
The last of our three examples of Personal Accounts shows an account that does need 'tidying up'. We cannot see clearly what the balance is at present.

J. OUTRED									L52
19. .				£	19. .				£
Jan.	4	Cash	CB7	625.00	Jan.	1	Balance	b/d	637.50
	4	Discount	CB7	12.50		12	Purchases	PDB5	702.25
	14	Returns	PRB4	27.50		18	Purchases	PDB7	681.25
						18	Carriage	EDB17	27.50
						27	Purchases	PDB15	926.25
						27	Insurance	EDB25	23.75

Figure 9.6   A busy account that needs balancing off

If we balance this account off and bring down the balance we shall find the figure we need for the Trial Balance, and at the same time clarify the account. Imagine that the phone rings. J. Outred is

J. OUTRED									L52
19. .				£	19. .				£
Jan.	4	Cash	CB7	625.00	Jan.	1	Balance	b/d	637.50
	4	Discount	CB7	12.50		12	Purchases	PDB5	702.25
	14	Returns	PRB4	27.50		18	Purchases	PDB7	681.25
	31	Balance	c/d	2 333.50		18	Carriage	EDB17	27.50
						27	Purchases	PDB15	926.25
						27	Insurance	EDB25	23.75
				£2 998.50					£2 998.50
					Feb.	1,	Balance	b/d	2 333.50

Figure 9.7   Clarifying an account
Note: EDB stands for Expenses Day Book

on the other end, inquiring if we can oblige him by settling our account by tomorrow. Before he agrees the manager will probably ask the ledger clerk to tell him what the balance is on the Ledger Account. At the moment the picture is confused. The ledger clerk will need a pencil and paper to sort it out. Imagine what a muddle it would be if it had not been tidied up for five or six months. If the account is tidied up at the end of each month it will be easy to see the present state of affairs.

It is now quite clear that the balance on this account is £2 333.50 and that this is a credit balance. Our Trial Balance now looks like this:

M. BROWN AND T. JOHNSON

TRIAL BALANCE

as at January 31, 19. .

	Dr.	Cr.
R. Jones	2 137.50	
M. Lichman	1 257.50	
J. Outred		2 333.50

Figure 9.8   Building up a Trial Balance

D. GOOCH AND SON

TRIAL BALANCE

as at December 31, 19. .

	Dr.	Cr.
Cash	350.00	
Bank	10 426.25	
Motor Vehicles	11 925.00	
Plant and Machinery	8 926.75	
Land and Buildings	20 179.75	
Debtors and Creditors	8 095.25	12 045.00
Sales Returns and Purchases Returns	727.00	1 000.00
Purchases and Sales	22 977.50	63 850.00
Carriage In	417.50	
Wages	6 407.00	
Salaries	3 078.00	
Opening Stock	5 926.00	
Rent and Rates	779.00	
Light and Heat	1 078.75	
Sundry Expenses	346.25	
Loan from Bank		20 000.00
Postage	330.00	
Discount Allowed and Received	298.00	432.50
Investments	22 677.00	
Capital		27 617.50
	£124 945.00	£124 945.00

Figure 9.9   A Trial Balance

If we continue to go through the accounts, tidying them up if necessary, we shall eventually produce a complete Trial Balance, like the one shown on page 153.

When the Trial Balance agrees in this way we say that – *prima facie* (at a first look) – the book-keeping has been well done. However, it is still possible that hidden errors could be present (see page 166).

9.4 How to keep a sole trader's books for one month and check for accuracy

Before a book-keeper can call himself a 'book-keeper to the Trial Balance' he must be able to keep the books of a small business for one month, and then prove by means of a Trial Balance that he has done the work accurately. The procedure is as follows:

(a) Do the Opening Journal Entry, and post it to the Ledger and the Cash Book. This will open up the Cash Book with a cash and bank balance on these two accounts, and open up the Ledger with any other assets or liabilities, including the proprietor's Capital Account.

(b) Now begin the month's transactions. This means that the documents for any sales or returns are made out and sent off, the duplicates being recorded in the Sales Day Book and Sales Returns Book. Any purchases invoices or purchases returns credit notes are recorded in the Purchases Day Book and Purchases Returns Book and all these four books are posted to the Ledger. Any of the rarer items that require Journal entries are journalized, and then posted to the Ledger. All cash and cheques received are debited in the Cash Book, and all cash and cheques paid are credited in the Cash Book. The Cash Book is then posted to the Ledger. Lastly, if a Petty Cash Book is kept the petty cash payments and receipts are recorded and posted to the Ledger.

This sounds rather involved but the student should console him/herself with the thought that once he/she masters the procedure he/she will really understand the mystery of book-keeping, and the many advantages of the double entry system. Whatever the problems, they will already have been dealt with in the earlier chapters.

(c) At the end of the month the totals of the Day Books must be posted to the respective accounts – the Purchases Account, the Sales Account, the Purchases Returns Account, and the Sales Returns Account. This is a vital process that many students forget. The final thing on these books is the posting of the totals to the Ledger Accounts. It is this that **completes the double entry** for the hundreds of invoices and credit notes recorded.

(d) Lastly draw up the Trial Balance. After heading the paper properly and putting the date, the Ledger Accounts must be inspected, tidied up if necessary, and the balances brought into the debit and credit columns. Do *not* forget the balances on the Cash Account (including the Petty Cash) and the Bank Account. These are the only two accounts that are not in the Ledger and are often forgotten. Do not forget the Discount Allowed and Discount Received columns of the Cash Book, which have to be posted to the Discount Accounts. Remember they do not change sides.

Do not forget that every account that has a balance on it must appear on the Trial Balance. If an account is clear there is no need to bring it into the Trial Balance, since there is no debit or credit balance to record.

9.5 What to do if a Trial Balance does not agree

If a Trial Balance does not agree there is a systematic procedure for discovering the error. Some of the steps in this procedure are rather complex and the reader will not yet fully understand them; they are discussed in detail later. The stages of the work in tracing errors are as follows:

(a) Add up the Debit and Credit columns again. It is easy to make a slip in addition, and a recheck is advisable.

(b) If the Trial Balance still does not agree take the total of one side from the other and find the difference. Imagine it is £137.80. Someone in the office may now have a bright idea like, '£137.80 – that's what we paid for the second-hand duplicator we bought at the auction'. This kind of happy thought may save hours of work. When we check the item we find that it has been left off the Office Machinery Account.

(c) If no one has a happy thought like that, the next thing is to halve the difference and look for something on the wrong side of the Trial Balance. Half of £137.80 is £68.90. If a figure of £68.90 appears on the Trial Balance check to see if it is on the proper side. £68.90 for example, put on the debit side when it should be on the credit side will make the debit side £68.90 too large and the credit side £68.90 too small – making a difference of £137.80.

(d) If we can't correct the Trial Balance this way then our problem is more serious, but before we go on to other possibilities let us notice two more simple things. Firstly, if an error is 1, or 10, or 100, or 1 000, or 0.10, or 0.01 it is probably due to a slip in addition. Somewhere we may have made a mistake in arithmetic that has put a balance out. For mistakes of this type a systematic check-up on all additions and subtractions is desirable.

Secondly, if an error divides by 9 it may be due to the transposition of figures. For instance, if a book-keeper writes 72 instead of 27 the error will be 45, which divides by 9. If an error divides by 9, then this is a possible cause of the trouble. Some people are very prone to make this kind of error because they are 'crossed laterals' – people whose dominant eye is not the same as their dominant hand. They may be right-handed and left-eyed, or left-handed and right-eyed. If you find that one book-keeper repeatedly makes this kind of mistake warn him to be especially careful about it.

(e) The next step is to check the extractions from the accounts into the Trial Balance. It is easy to make a slip here, and a quick 'calling over' of the Ledger Accounts to see if they have been extracted correctly will discover the error.

(f) If this has been done properly and the Trial Balance still does not agree, then we may be able to isolate certain sections of the work and prove that they are right by taking out **Control Accounts.** This is an important process which requires a whole chapter to itself, and the student is advised to disregard it for the present. It is dealt with in Chapter 30 page 436.

(g) We must now check the entire month's activities, going over every single item and checking that a perfect double entry has been made in every case. This means checking all the additions, carrying forward, etc. It is a great labour, but to find the mistake it may be necessary.

(h) Finally, if we cannot find our mistake, we can open a Suspense Account. This means we take a new page in the Ledger and open up an account with the difference on the books. In the case we imagined earlier we would put £137.80 on the Suspense Account on the side where it was needed to make the books balance. The books will now agree, for the debits balance the credits; but, of course, sooner or later the mistakes are going to be discovered. The Suspense Account is a last resort solution to the problem.

The student should now work through the following specimen exercise (see page 158).

These ledger accounts to the specimen exercise have been printed here to enable the reader to see pages 158 and 159 without turning a page

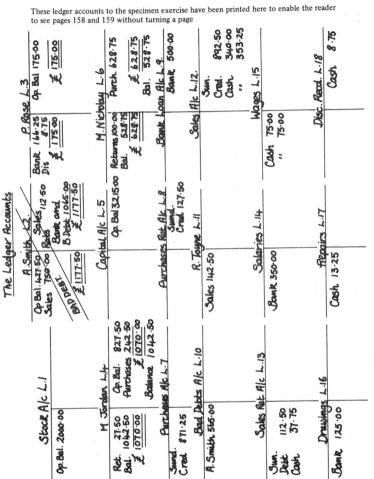

Figure 9.10(e) The Ledger Accounts

9.6   A Specimen exercise to the Trial Balance

Robert Morgan started business with these assets and liabilities on July 1:

Cash in hand £140.00, Cash at Bank £1 650.00, Stock £2 000.00, Debtor: A. Smith £427.50, Creditors: P. Rose £175.00, M. Jordan £827.50.

Open the accounts by means of an Opening Journal Entry, posted to the Ledger and the Cash Book. Then enter the following transactions in the appropriate Book of Original Entry, post them to the Ledger, and extract a Trial Balance to prove the accuracy of your work.

19. .
July 1 Sold goods for cash £340.00.
      3 Received a loan from the bank £500.00.
      4 Sold goods on credit to A. Smith for £1 000.00 less 25%
         Trade Discount.
      5 Paid salaries by cheque £350.00.
     10 A. Smith returns goods, catalogue price £150.00.
     11 Paid wages in cash £75.00.
     13 Settled P. Rose's account in full, by cheque £166.25.
     15 Purchased goods on credit from M. Jordan £242.50.
     18 Cash Sales £353.25.
     20 Banked £500.00 from cash box.
     21 Drew from bank for private use £125.00.
     22 Refunded cash to a customer for goods returned £37.75.
     23 Sold goods on credit to R. Toyne £142.50.
     24 Purchased goods on credit from M. Nickolay £628.75.
     25 Paid for minor repairs £13.25 cash.
     26 Returned goods to M. Nickolay £100.00.
     27 A. Smith is in difficulties; agreed to accept £500.00 cheque
         in full settlement – rest treated as a bad debt.
     28 Paid wages in cash £75.00.
     31 Received a credit note from M. Jordan (allowance)
         £27.50.

The solution is shown on the next few pages. After careful study the student should try *several* exercises from Set 9.1.

Notes on specimen exercises opposite:
First we must do the Opening Journal Entry, and post it to the Ledger and the Cash Book. We are then ready to begin the July transactions.

If you treat each line as a separate problem and ask yourself in which book of original entry you should enter the transaction, and then think carefully how to post the transaction to the Ledger, you should have little difficulty in doing this type of exercise. In an office the same problems arise; the book-keeper decides what to do and then makes the necessary entries. Here are a few hints:

19. .
July 1 This is Cash Sales; debit the Cash Book.
       3 We have to do a Journal Entry for a Bank Loan.
       4 Sold goods on credit is a Sales Day Book item.
       5 Credit the Cash Book for salaries paid.
      10 Goods returned go in the Sales Returns Book (beware – Trade Discount).
      11 Cash Book – credit side of Cash Account – money is going out.
      13 Credit the Cash Book – Bank Account – cheque is going out. There is also discount to be recorded.
      15 Purchases on credit go in the Purchases Day Book.
      18 Cash Book – debit side of Cash Account.
      20 This is a Contra Entry – Cash Book, both sides.
      21 Drawings – credit Cash Book – Bank Account.
      22 Sales Returns, but cash not credit; money going out of Cash Book. Credit side of Cash Account.
      23 Sales Day Book item.
      24 Purchases Day Book item.
      25 Credit Cash Book – Cash Account.
      26 Purchases Return Book item.
      27 Journal entry – Bad Debt.
      28 Cash Book item – Cash Account.
      31 Purchases Returns Book item.

The actual entries are shown in Figure 9.10(a)–(f). After studying these entries carefully you should attempt the exercises in Set 9.1. (*Note: 9.10(e) is on page 157.*)

19..	Particulars	F.	£	£	£	19..	Particulars	F.	£	£	£
July 1	Opening Balances	J1		140.00	1 650.00	July 5	Salaries	L14			350.00
1	Cash Sales	L12		340.00		11	Wages	L15	8.75	75.00	
3	Bank Loan Account	J1			500.00	13	P. Rose	L3			166.25
18	Cash Sales	L12		353.25		20	Bank	C		500.00	
20	Cash	C			500.00	21	Drawings	L16		37.75	
27	A. Smith	J1			500.00	22	Cash Sales Returns	L13		13.25	
						25	Repairs	L17		75.00	
						28	Wages	L15		75.00	125.00
						31	Balances	c/d		132.25	2 508.75
		£	—	833.25	3 150.00			£	8.75	833.25	3 150.00
				132.25	2 508.75						
Aug. 1	To Balances	b/d		132.25	2 508.75			L18			

Figure 9.10(b)   The Three Column Cash Book

19. .					J1
July 1	Cash Account	Dr.	CB1	140.00	
	Bank Account	Dr.	CB1	1 650.00	
	Stock Account	Dr.	L1	2 000.00	
	A. Smith Account	Dr.	L2	427.50	
	P. Rose Account		L3		175.00
	M. Jordan Account		L4		827.50
	Capital Account		L5		3 215.00
	Being assets and liabilities at this date		£	4 217.50	4 217.50

Figure 9.10(a) **A merchant's books to the Trial Balance – opening the books at the start of the month**

19. .					
July 3	Bank Account	Dr.	CB1	500.00	
	Bank Loan Account		L9		500.00
	Being loan granted by bank at this date				
27	Bank Account	Dr.	CB1	500.00	
	Bad Debts Account	Dr.	L10	565.00	
	A. Smith		L2		1 065.00
	Being Bad Debt written off				

Figure 9.10(c) **Other entries in the Journal**

SALES DAY BOOK

19. .				£
July 4	<u>A. Smith</u>			
	Goods		1 000.00	
	Less 25% Trade Discount		250.00	
	<u>R. Toyne</u>	L2		750.00
23	Goods	L11		142.50
		£		892.50
				L12

SALES RETURNS BOOK

19. .				£
July	<u>A. Smith</u>			
	Returns		150.00	
	Less 25% Trade Discount		37.50	
		L2		112.50
		£		112.50
				L13

PURCHASES DAY BOOK

19. .					£
July 15	M. Jordan				
	Goods	L4			242.50
24	M. Nicholay				
	Goods	L5			628.75
				£	871.25
					L7

PURCHASES RETURNS BOOK

19. .					£
July 26	M. Nicholay				
	Goods	L6			100.00
31	M. Jordan				
	Allowance	L4			27.50
				£	127.50
					L8

Figure 9.10(d)   The four day books

ROBERT MORGAN

TRIAL BALANCE AS AT JULY 31, 19. .

	Dr.	Cr.
Cash	132.25	
Bank	2 508.75	
Stock	2 000.00	
M. Jordan		1 042.50
Capital		3 215.00
M. Nicholay		528.75
Purchases	871.25	
Purchases Returns		127.50
Bank Loan		500.00
Bad Debts	565.00	
R. Toyne	142.50	
Sales		1 585.75
Sales Returns	150.25	
Salaries	350.00	
Wages	150.00	
Drawings	125.00	
Repairs	13.25	
Discount Received		8.75
	£7 008.25	7 008.25

Figure 9.10(f)   The Trial Balance

9.7 Exercises set 9.1 – book-keeping to the Trial Balance

1. Peter Newman had the following balances on his books on 1 October: Cash in hand £330.00; Cash in bank £4 000.00; Premises £34 000.00; Debtors: A. New £2 000.00; B. Castle £450.00; Stock £3 000.00; Creditors: J. Horne £4 250.00; J. Harper £900.00. Make the opening Journal Entry and post it to the Ledger and to the Cash Book.

The following transactions then took place:

19. .
Oct. 1 Cash sales £450.00.
    3 Paid office expenses in cash £25.00.
    5 Purchased furniture for office use by cheque £900.00.
    8 Paid wages in cash £97.50.
  10 Sold goods to B. Castle on credit, £200.00.
  12 A. New settled his account by cheque, less 2½% cash discount.
  14 Received a loan from the bank, £1 250.00 secured on a Life Assurance Policy. (Interest on this loan will not be paid until December.)
  16 Paid J. Horne on account £2 500.00 by cheque.
  19 Sent B. Castle a credit note for goods returned £40.00.
  21 Bought goods on credit from J. Harper £200.00.
  24 Paid rates by cheque £123.75.
  26 Withdrew from bank for private use £100.00.
  28 Cash sales £600.00.
  29 Brought goods on credit from J. Horne £427.75.
  30 Paid office-cleaning expenses £31.25 in cash.
  31 Paid into bank from office cash £500.00; paid salaries by cheque £620.00.

Enter them in the appropriate books of Original Entry, post to the Ledger, and extract a Trial Balance.

2. Alan Dawlish has the following balance on his books on June 1: Cash in hand £250.00; Cash at bank £1 900.00; Premises £25 000.00; Furniture and fittings £3 000.00; Debtors: R. Sind £500.00, P. Quilter £750.00; Stock £2 500.00; Creditors: A. Jolson £350.00, L. Toft £900.00. Show the opening Journal Entry and post to the Ledger.

These are his transactions for the month of June. Enter them in the appropriate subsidiary books, post to the Ledger, and extract a Trial Balance.

19. .
June 1 Cash sales £202.50.
    4 Purchased machinery by cheque £900.00.
    5 Paid wages in cash £98.75.
    9 Paid office expenses by cash £36.75.
  10 R. Sind settled his account by cheque less 2½% cash discount.
  13 Sold goods to P. Quilter £750.00 on credit.
  14 Sent a credit note for goods returned by P. Quilter £200.00.
  16 Received a loan from the bank £2 500.00.

19 Paid A. Jolson cheque in full settlement less 5% cash discount.

22 Withdrew from bank for private use £150.00.

24 Bought goods on credit from L. Toft £327.50.

27 Paid rates by cheque £120.00.

28 Brought goods on credit from L. Toft £350.00.

29 Cash sales £653.25.

30 Paid into bank from cash box £500.00; paid salaries by cheque £300.00.

3. Derek Webster was in business as a retail furniture dealer and his financial position on July 1 was as follows: Cash in hand £280.50; Cash at bank £5 182.50; Stock £6 920.00; Furniture and fittings £1 350.50, Debtors: A. Evans £135.95, B. Turner £190.75; Creditors: A. Presley £1 450.85. Make the opening Journal Entry, and post it to the Ledger and Cash Book.

His transactions for the month of July were as follows:

19. .

July 1 Sold goods on credit to A. Evans £800.00 less 25% trade discount.

2 Received from B. Turner a cheque for £185.00 in full settlement.

4 Paid rent by cheque £150.00.

5 Bought on credit from Redditype Ltd. typewriter for office use £375.00.

6 Paid cash for stationery £70.00.

7 Paid postage in cash £15.00.

8 Drew cash for personal use from bank £150.00.

9 Sent A. Presley cheque for £1 400.00 in full settlement.

12 Bought goods at auction for cheque £150.00. A. Evans returned goods, catalogue price £200.00 (not up to specification).

19 Cash sales £500.00 of which £375.00 was banked.

20 Paid cash for stationery £15.50.

23 Sold to A. Jorgensen goods on credit £200.00.

25 A. Jorgensen sent cheque on account £100.00.

26 Paid wages in cash £75.00.

28 A. Jorgensen's cheque returned dishonoured.

31 Cash returned to a customer £20.60 for goods returned.

Record the transactions, post to the Ledger, and extract a Trial Balance.

4. R. Palmer is a young man who enters the building trade with a capital of £17 500.00, which he puts in the bank on January 1, 19. .. The same day he purchases for £400.00 on credit furniture and fittings from Shopfitters Ltd and for £1 900.00 tools and equipment from Builders' Materials Ltd. Here are his first month's transactions. Enter them in the appropriate books of original entry, post to the Ledger, and take out a Trial Balance.

19. .

Jan. 1 Drew £125.00 for cash from bank; bought typewriter £200.00 by cheque; Lea Builders Supply sent goods £1 200.00 on credit.

2 Received from R. Brown £250.00 in cash – deposit on house; paid rent £75.00 in cash.

3 Sold goods to R. Ellis £121.25 on credit; paid Shopfitters Ltd the amount owed, less 2½% discount by cheque.

14 Bought goods, £125.00 on credit, from Builders' Materials Ltd; paid wages £137.50 cash; bought stationery for cash £8.25.

15 Sold goods to R. Ellis £72.50 on credit; cash sales £401.50.

18 Paid rent £75.00.

19 Lea Builders Supply Ltd sent goods, value £400.00, on credit.

20 R. Ellis returned goods valued at £15.50 (wrong colour).

21 Paid Builders' Materials Ltd the amount owed on January 1, less 5% cash discount by cheque.

28 Paid wages £137.50 cash; paid rent £75.00 cash; personal drawings £200.00 by cheque.

31 Received cash from R. Brown £500.00 further payment on house being erected.

5. On June 1 the following balances were extracted from George Dickens's books: Machinery £10 000.00; Stock £3 750.00; Cash in hand £500.00; Sundry Debtors: M. Mysore £410.00; S. Hyderabad £330.00, Bank overdraft £200.00; Sundry Creditors: R. Robot £300.00; S. Electra £1 100.00.

Make the opening Journal Entry, enter the transactions, post to the Ledger, and extract a Trial Balance.

19. .
June 1 Paid wages in cash £125.00.

2 Cash sales £600.00 of which £500.00 was banked.

3 M. Mysore pays his account by cheque less 5% cash discount.

4 Sold goods on credit to S. Hyderabad £750.00.

10 Purchased goods on credit from S. Electra £500.00.

12 Cash purchases £125.00.

13 Bought office equipment on credit from Comfichairs Ltd, £2 750.00.

14 Sold machinery for £2 500.00 (its proper value on the books). The buyer paid by cheque.

15 Cash sales £425.00.

18 Paid wages in cash £120.00.

19 Refunded cash to a customer £52.50 for goods returned.

20 Paid rent by cheque £177.50.

22 Paid for repairs to premises £175.00 by cheque.

23 S. Hyderabad returns goods valued at £188.75 (poor quality).

24 Paid carriage charges £25.00 in cash.

25 S. Hyderabad settles the account owing at June 1 with 5% discount deducted, by cheque.

29 Paid S. Electra a cheque on account £800.00.

30 Paid salaries by cheque £200.00; banked £400.00 from cash box. Dickens paid Robot's account in full with a cheque for £292.50.

10
Limitations of the Trial Balance: Suspense Accounts and the correction of errors

10.1 Introduction

We have already seen that the chief use of the Trial Balance is to check the accuracy of the book-keeping. The agreement of the debit and credit totals is reasonably good evidence that the book-keepers have done their work well, but it is not conclusive.

Sometimes we are unable to find the cause of a disagreement between the sides, and are reduced to inventing a Suspense Account which will hold the balance until the true reason for the difference is discovered. Indeed, some firms make it a matter of policy not to look for the mistakes on their books, since this is time-consuming and expensive. Such firms simply open a Suspense Account at once, and allow the problems to solve themselves in the course of time. Sooner or later someone will complain that his account has been underpaid, for instance.

10.2 Errors that the Trial Balance does not disclose

Earlier (Section 9.3) we said that if a Trial Balance balances it is some indication that the book-keepers have done their work well. *Prima facie* (at a first glance) the books are correct, but we may later find that even so there is an error in the books, because there are some types of errors which are not revealed by a Trial Balance.

There are five classes of error which the Trial Balance does not disclose. They are:

(a) Original Errors.
(b) Errors of Omission.
(c) Errors of Commission.
(d) Errors of Principle.
(e) Compensating Errors.

(a) *Original Errors*

These are errors in the original entries – errors made in copying from the documents from which all book-keeping entries are made. If we take an invoice for £2 500.00 and enter it as £2 550.00 in the Purchases Day Book, posting it correctly to the creditor's account, and posting the total correctly to the Purchases Account, our Trial Balance will come out correctly, and the mistake will not be discovered. Our books are *prima facie* (at a first look) correct – but in fact there is an error on them.

(b) *Errors of Omission*

If something is omitted completely from the books it will appear on neither the debit nor credit side of the Trial Balance. A book-keeper was once given thirty invoices to enter in the Purchases Day Book. As he dropped the heavy Day Book on to his desk, the top invoice blew away unnoticed down the back of a filing cabinet. The Trial Balance was correct at the end of the month, and the staff congratulated one another on an excellent month's work, until the irate creditor wrote in demanding payment.

One way to avoid such errors today is to use an adding-listing machine to add up the total of the invoices received every day. This 'list' and the invoices can be clipped together and when the Day Book has been entered, the day's entries can be checked with the 'list'.

As explained in Section 5.2, some firms do not bother to keep a Purchases Day Book at all, but use the file of invoices as a Day Book. This saves work, but gives a less permanent and reliable record. In such cases the adding-listing machine 'list' gives the total figure for the day to be entered in the Purchases Account. Instead of a monthly total to be debited in the Purchases Account, we have a daily total. Some of our gain in not having to keep a Purchases Day Book is lost on more frequent entries into the Purchases Account.

(c) *Errors of Commission*

These are errors in the actual performance of an operation like posting. The word 'commission' here means 'doing'. If we do something wrongly – for instance enter a debt in the wrong debtor's account – the Trial Balance will balance but there will be a hidden error in the books. If J. Smith is debited instead of T. Smith the Trial Balance will not be affected, but J. Smith will resent receiving a statement at the end of the month, while T. Smith will be delighted not to receive one.

168   *Book-keeping Made Simple*

(b) *Errors of Principle*

An error of principle is an error which offends against the basic ideas of book-keeping. One of these basic ideas (dealt with fully in Chapter 20, page 261) is the distinction between capital and revenue expenditure. This has already been referred to briefly in the section on the correction of errors in Chapter 7.

If we buy goods for resale the invoice is recorded in the Purchases Day Book. If we buy assets, the invoice is recorded in the Journal Proper as the purchase of assets. To record the purchase of assets as the purchase of goods for resale offends against the basic principles of book-keeping.

Such an error would not show up in the Trial Balance. Our debit in the Purchases Account would enable the Trial Balance to balance, even though it should really be a debit in the Asset Account.

(e) *Compensating Errors*

These are errors which make up for one another. They usually arise from two pieces of bad arithmetic. Imagine that in adding up the Purchases Day Book we make a slip, and the total is £10.00 out. Clearly this should show in the Trial Balance, but if it is compensated for by another £10.00 error in the addition of the Sales Day Book the debit and credit sides will appear to balance, although each has a £10.00 error.

Routine checking of additions with an electronic calculator will prevent this kind of error from slipping through.

10.3   Suspense Accounts and the correction of errors

If a Trial Balance has been put right by the invention of a Suspense Account, this account will only stay on the books as long as is necessary. As soon as the mistake is discovered the Suspense Account can be cleared off.

Consider the following examples:

Example 1

A Trial Balance will not agree; the debit side is £202.50 greater than the credit side. A Suspense Account is therefore opened. Here it is:

SUSPENSE ACCOUNT		L171
	19. .	£
	Aug. 31 Difference on books	202.50

Figure 10.1   A simple Suspense Account

Notice that the £202.50 has been put on the credit side so that both sides agree; the debit side is no longer £202.50 greater than the credit side.

Subsequently it was discovered that the mistake was due to the duplication of an invoice to R. Jones. R. Jones's premises had caught fire and our invoice for £202.50 had been burnt. Jones had asked for a duplicate invoice, which, before dispatch, had been debited in Jones's Account. It had not been passed through the Day Book, otherwise it would have been credited in the Sales Account too, and would have been an Error of Commission, one not discovered by the Trial Balance.

The real error in the Trial Balance therefore was that the debit side was £202.50 too much. We could remove this error by crediting R. Jones with £202.50. This would now leave the credit side £202.50 too much because of the balance in the Suspense Account. If we debit the Suspense Account as we credit Jones, we should put the books right.

This obviously requires a Journal Entry like the one below, posted into the two accounts. The books would then be correct.

19. . Sept. 9	Suspense Account Dr. R. Jones Being correction of error due to double posting of an invoice	L171 L39	£ 202.50	£ J1 202.50

				R. JONES ACCOUNT			L39
19. . Aug. 4 17	Sales Sales	SDB1 SDB	£ 202.50 202.50	19. . Sept. 3 3 7	Cash Discount Suspense Account	CB1 CB J1	£ 195.00 7.50 202.50

SUSPENSE ACCOUNT   L171

19. . Sept. 9	R. Jones	J1	£ 202.50	19. . Aug. 31	Difference on books		£ 202.50

Figure 10.2   Writing off the Suspense Account

Example 2

A Trial Balance will not agree; the debit side is £153.25 less than the credit side. A Suspense Account for this amount is accordingly opened.

SUSPENSE ACCOUNT   L161

19. . Aug. 31	Difference on books	£ 153.25	

Figure 10.3   Another Suspense Account

Afterwards the following mistakes are discovered:

(a) A sum of cash received from a debtor was debited correctly in the Cash Book, but credited twice to the debtor's account. The amount was £61.25 from R. Jordan.

(b) Instead of the Discount Account being debited with £558.75 discount allowed, and credited with £671.75 discount received, these items had been crossed over. The £671.25 had been debited and the £558.75 had been credited.

(c) Purchases Returns of £317.00 to a creditor J. Miles had not been posted at all to his account, but the credit note had been properly entered in the Purchases Returns Book.

It is clear that the Suspense Account balance is not caused by a single error, but by a series of errors. Each of these errors now has to be put right and this involves careful, logical thought. Taking the errors in turn, we find:

(a) The debtor's account will look like this:

				R. JORDAN				L12
19. .				£	19. .			£
July	15	Sales	SDB5	61.25	Aug. 14	Cash	CB12	61.25
					14	Cash	CB12	61.25

Figure 10.4   A Debtor's Account which has been posted twice

The book-keeper who made the second entry was not thinking what he was doing, and it is obvious that this entry will give trouble later on. To put it right we shall need to debit R. Jordan, and credit the Suspense Account.

(b) The Discount Account mistake is a more difficult one. This firm puts both Discount Allowed and Discount Received in the one Discount Account, but the mistake has resulted in a debit balance of £112.50 instead of a credit balance of £112.50.

To correct this error we have to change the present debit balance of £112.50 into a credit balance of £112.50, which means we must credit the account with £225.00. This means debiting the Suspense Account with £225.00. Figure 10.5 opposite shows the error that has been made in the Discount Account, and Figure 10.6 shows the Journal Entry required to correct the error.

DISCOUNT ACCOUNT   L94

19. .		£	19. .		£
Aug. 31	Discount Received	671.25	Aug. 31	Discount Allowed	558.75
			31	Balance c/d	112.50
		£671.25			£671.25
Sept. 1	Balance b/d	112.50			

(*a*) The Account as it looks at present.

DISCOUNT ACCOUNT   L94

19. .		£	19. .		£
Aug. 31	Discount Allowed	558.75	Aug. 31	Discount Received	671.25
31	Balance c/d	112.50			
		£671.25			£671.25
			Sept. 1	Balance b/d	112.50

(*b*) The Account as it should be.

Figure 10.5   Mistakes on the Discount Account

(c) The third error is straightforward enough. J. Miles, the creditor to whom we have returned goods worth £317.00, should have been debited with £317.00. If we debit his account, the Suspense Account will have to be credited. The Journal Entries for these corrections are like this:

19. .				£	£ J1
Sept. 4	R. Jordan	Dr.	L12	61.25	
	Suspense Account		L161		61.25
	Being correction of posting error				
11	Suspense Account	Dr.	L161	225.00	
	Discount Account		L94		225.00
	Being correction of mis-posting				
13	J. Miles	Dr.	L48	317.00	
	Suspense Account		L161		317.00
	Being correction of mis-posting				

Figure 10.6   Journal entries to clear the Suspense Account

Figure 10.7 on page 172 shows the postings from the Journal which correct all the errors and clear the Suspense Account.

R. JORDAN   L12

19. .				£	19. .				£
July	15	Sales	SDB5	61.25	Aug.	14	Cash	CB12	61.25
Sept.	4	Suspense				14	Cash	CB12	61.25
		Account	J1	61.25					
				£122.50					£122.50

DISCOUNT ACCOUNT   L94

19. .			£	19. .				£
Aug.	31	Discount Received	671.25	Aug.	31	Discount Allowed		558.75
					31	Balance	c/d	112.50
			£671.25					£671.25
			£	Sept.	11	Suspense		£
Sept.	1	Balance	b/d 112.50			Account	J1	225.00

J. MILES   L48

19. .				£	19. .			£
Sept.	13	Suspense			Aug.	14	Purchases (say)	580.00
		Account	J1	317.00				

SUSPENSE ACCOUNT   L161

19. .				£	19. .				£
Aug.	31	Difference on books		153.25	Sept.	4	R. Jordan	J1	61.25
Sept.	11	Discount				13	J. Miles	J1	317.00
		Account	J1	225.00					
				£378.25					£378.25

Figure 10.7 Clearing the Suspense Account

10.4 A page to test you on the Trial Balance

Answers	Questions
—	1 What is a Trial Balance?
1 It is a list of all the accounts that have balances on them.	2 When is it taken out?
2 At least once a month.	3 What do we take it out for?
3 To discover whether the book-keeping has been carefully done.	4 What will happen if we have done our book-keeping properly?
4 The Trial Balance will balance – that is the debit balances will exactly equal the credit balances.	5 Is the agreement of the Trial Balance conclusive evidence that the books are correct?
5 No – only *prima facie* evidence.	6 Why is it not quite conclusive?
6 Because five types of errors do not show up on the Trial Balance.	7 What are these five types of errors?
7 (a) Original Errors; (b) Errors of Omission; (c) Errors of Commission; (d) Errors of Principle; (e) Compensating Errors.	8 Explain each of these in turn.
8 Original Errors are errors in the original documents to be recorded; Errors of Omission occur when we leave something out altogether; Errors of Commission are errors where we make a slip in doing the work, i.e. enter an item for D. Brown in G. Brown's books; Errors of Principle are errors where we do not understand our basic principles of book-keeping, i.e. Purchase of Assets treated as Purchases of Goods. Compensating Errors are Errors that compensate for one another, i.e. a £10 adding up mistake on each side.	9 What do you do if a Trial Balance does not agree?
9 (a) Add it up again in case we've made a slip; (b) see if anyone remembers an amount for the difference, say £240.00; (c) if this doesn't help, divide by 2 and see if £120.00 is on the wrong side; (d) if this doesn't help, check the extractions to the Trial Balance from the Ledger; (e) if this doesn't help, take out Control Accounts on the Sales and Purchases Ledgers; (f) if this doesn't help, check everything; (g) If we still haven't found the mistake, open up a Suspense Account.	10 Go over this again until you are perfectly sure of it all.

10.5 Exercises set 10.1 – Trial Balances and Suspense Accounts

1. What is a Trial Balance? What steps would you take if a Trial Balance failed to agree? Describe these steps in the order in which you would take them.

2. 'An agreed Trial Balance is only proof of arithmetical accuracy. It does not mean that the book-keeping is correct.' Do you agree or disagree with these statements?

3. Certain types of book-keeping error do not affect the agreement of the Trial Balance. One such error is called an 'Error of Principle'. What is an 'Error of Principle', and why does it not affect the Trial Balance?

4. Explain 'Error of Omission' and 'Error of Commission'. In what way are these errors similar?

5. What are: (a) an 'Error in the Original Entry' and (b) a 'Compensating Error'? What is their significance with regard to a Trial Balance that agrees?

6. On March 31 A. Lauderdale's Trial Balance failed to agree and he opened a Suspense Account for £500 on the credit side. The error subsequently proved to be a miscasting in the Bank Account which caused his favourable Bank Balance of £3 283.00 to be carried down as £3 783.00. Show (a) the Journal Entry correcting this error on April 6, and (b) the Suspense Account after the Journal Entry had been posted.

7. On August 31 R. Meson's Trial Balance failed to agree, the debit side being £138.00 greater than the credit side. He opened a Suspense Account. The errors proved to be as follows:

(a) A debtor R. Lang had paid his account, £107.50, in full but this had not been credited to his account.

(b) The total of discount received for one week, £30.50, had not been posted to the appropriate account. Show (i) the Journal entries to correct these errors, and (ii) the Suspense Account after the corrections had been completed.

8. During the half year ending June 30 a book-keeper of the Y-Z Company made the following errors (the rest of his work was accurate):

(a) Goods valued at £50.00 sold to E. Bates were debited to E. Bateson.

(b) Expenditure of £4.25 for stationery was charged to the nominal account as £42.50.

(c) The Purchases Book was undercast by £100.00.

(d) An item of £46.35 discount allowed was not posted to the Discount Allowed account.

    (i) Considering each error separately, state which column – debit or credit – of the Trial Balance, dated June 30, would be the greater and by how much.

    (ii) What entry would you make in a Suspense Account prior to the correction of the above errors?

(RSA – Adapted)

9. A book-keeper finds his Trial Balance to be £96.75 in excess on the Debit Side. A Suspense Account is opened to get the Trial Balance right, but later is cleared by the following discoveries:

(a) A balance due to R. Haggerty had been omitted from the Trial Balance although Haggerty's account was correct at £57.75.
(b) A motor lorry purchased for £825.00 cash was entered correctly in the Cash Book but posted to the Motor Lorry Account as £852.00.
(c) Bank interest received of £12.00 had been entered in the Cash Book but not posted to the Nominal Account.

Make the Journal Entries and show the Suspense Account as it will finally appear. (Be careful with Journal Entry (a).)

10. A book-keeper failed to balance his Trial Balance on August 31 19. ., the debits exceeding the credits by £235.50. This amount was entered in a Suspense Account. Later these errors were discovered:

(a) The Sales Day Book had been undercast by £50.00.
(b) £50.75 received from A. Debtor whose debt was already written off as bad had been debited correctly in the Cash Book but credited both to the Debtor and to the Bad Debts Recovered Account.
(c) A credit balance on Rent Received Account of £302.25 had been entered in the Trial Balance as £320.25.
(d) A cash payment of £254.25 made by B. Debtor had been entered properly in the Cash Book but had not been posted to the Debtor's Account.

Make the Journal Entries and show the Suspense Account as it would finally appear.

11. On April 30 R. Jones extracted a Trial Balance from his Ledgers. The Trial Balance did not agree and a Suspense Account was opened for the difference. The Suspense Account was debited with £368.70. A further check revealed the following errors:

(a) The Discount Account had been debited with £780.00 with discounts received and credited £901.50 with discounts allowed.
(b) A cheque was paid to R. Lee in payment of his account of £1 000, less 5 per cent cash discount. This was correctly entered in the Cash Book. No entry for the discount had been made in Lee's account.
(c) A cheque for £122.90 paid for heating had been correctly entered in the Cash Book, but had been debited to the Heating Account as £212.90.
(d) A credit note for £83.00 received from F. Brown had been correctly entered in the appropriate subsidiary book, but had been posted to Brown's Account as £8.30.
(e) A sale of goods, value £91.00 to J. Place had been correctly entered in the Sales Book but had not been posted to Place's account.

Show by means of Journal entries how the above errors would be corrected and show the Suspense Account as it should appear after the correction of errors.

11
Bank Reconciliation Statements

11.1 Introduction – the meaning of reconciliation

If two friends quarrel, or fail to agree about some matter the disagreement may temporarily end the friendship between them. When they become friends again we say they have been reconciled with one another. Reconciliation is therefore the resuming of friendly relations as a result, very often, of reasonable explanations. In business we often have sets of figures which are apparently in disagreement with one another, but reasonable explanations for the difference will reconcile the two sets of figures and show that, in fact, **both are right.**

The two figures for 'bank' moneys
In business we keep our Bank Account in the Cash Book, as part of the Three-column Cash Book. It is made up every day, and we enter in the account all cheques received, and take from the account all cheques paid. We shall also have several contra entries every month, recording cash takings paid in or cash drawn out when required for office use. We therefore have in our Cash Book a bank balance (as per the Cash Book).

The bank are also keeping a record of our Bank Account, and they too enter into our account every day what is paid in and what is drawn out. At the end of any day they will gladly tell us our bank balance (as per the bank).

11.2 Why do the Cash Book figure and the bank's figure disagree?

There are three reasons why these figures are rarely the same:

(a) One party may lack knowledge of the actions performed by the other.
(b) There is always an unavoidable delay between one party doing something and the other party knowing about it.
(c) Errors often occur.

Before looking at a Bank Reconciliation Statement it is helpful to revise our knowledge of how money is paid into and removed from accounts. The chief methods are:

(a) *Cheques paid in.* These are cheques received from our debtors, which are paid in on a paying-in slip, and are credited in our account at the bank (of course they are debited in our Cash Book).

(b) *Cheques drawn out.* These are our cheques, which we have written to our creditors and they have paid them into their accounts. They will be cleared through the clearing mechanism of the banking system, and will be debited in our account at the bank to reduce our balance – we have paid the money away.

(c) *Standing orders.* A standing order is used where we have to pay a sum of money regularly – for example a mortgage payment of £160.00 a month. We give the bank a standing order to pay this money on the same date every month and they will tell the computer to debit our account and credit the Building Society or other mortgagor. This prevents us from forgetting to make the payment. It is also used for paying hire purchase debts or any debt which is *the same amount every month, or year* (if it is an annual payment). For example many people give an annual payment to a charity such as Dr Barnardo's Homes.

(d) *Direct debits.* A direct debit is a way of arranging payments, in which the creditor is allowed to ask the bank for money from the debtor's account instead of the usual method of where the debtor writes a cheque ordering the bank to pay the money. The reason this was introduced some years ago was that where the amount varies each year (as it does, for example, with rates paid to the local council) the standing order method is not much use, as the debtor does not know how much to pay. It is the creditor (the local authority for example) who knows how much to ask for. There have to be certain safeguards on these arrangements and the debtor has to sign a **Direct debit mandate** giving the creditor the power to ask for the money.

(e) *Bank giro credit (sometimes called Credit Transfer).* A bank giro credit is a transfer into an account made by the debtor to the creditor's account. This service was given its name a few years ago, when National Girobank was presenting the other banks with competition. The inference is that the money is going round within the banking system like a giroscope – a rather meaningless idea. What a bank giro payment does is transfer money to the credit of an account, so credit transfer is the better name. It is used chiefly to pay wages, but also to pay such things as dividends or interest payments to shareholders and debenture holders of companies. It is also used by customers of mail order houses and managers of branches of multiple shops and chain stores to pay funds over the counter of banks for credit transfer to the head office account.

The last three of these methods of payment will be carried out through the banking system and the ordinary customer will not necessarily remember them, or be aware of them, until a bank statement is received from the bank.

The idea of a Bank Reconciliation Statement is to discover the various things the bank has done which the cashier was not aware of, put right anything that is wrong, and draw up a logical explanation of the remaining differences, which are not wrong, but are delayed from being right by the time lag.

Consider the following information from A. Dealer's Cash Book and Bank Statement:

CASH BOOK (BANK COLUMN ONLY)

Dr.						Cr.
19. .			£	19. .		£
Feb. 1	Balance		1 125.00	Feb. 2	Green	238.00
10	Ambrose		253.75	14	Howard	142.50
17	Bloggs		313.10	19	Ives	183.50
28	Crayford		367.50			

A rough calculation shows that the balance on this Cash Book is £1 495.35 – a debit balance.

BANK STATEMENT
A. Dealer in account with Barclay's Bank Limited

Date	Details	Dr.	Cr.	Balance
19. .				
Feb. 1	Balance Forward			1 125.00
2	Green	238.00		887.00
4	Direct debit (UDC)	185.00		702.00
12	Ambrose		253.75	955.75
16	Howard	142.50		813.25
16	Charges	26.25		787.00
17	Bloggs		313.10	1 100.10
28	Bank of England (bonds)		62.90	1 163.00
28	Anglia Building Society (s/o)	140.00		1 023.00

A careful look at these two accounts will show:

(a) The balances do not agree. £1 495.35 according to the Cash Book, £1 023.00 according to the Bank Statement.

(b) Both accounts did agree on February 1, so the problem is quite recent. Sometimes we may find a time lag lasting months, usually because someone has failed to bank a cheque.

(c) Ives's cheque sent to him on February 19 has not yet been paid in by Ives. He may be a sole trader who only bothers to go to the bank once a week or so. On the other hand, it may have blown down the back of the radiator when someone opened the window. This is one example of a time lag.

(d) Crayford's cheque received by February 28, that is today, has been paid in by Dealer but is not recorded on the statement. This is another kind of time lag; the bank will probably credit it tomorrow to the account.

(e) On February 4 the bank statement shows that the Urban District Council (UDC) put through a direct debit asking the Bank to deduct £185.00 from Dealer's account. This would obviously be for rates. Dealer is not aware that this has been done on February 4 until the statement arrives.

(f) The bank has charged Dealer £26.25 Bank Charges. Dealer did not know about this deduction from his funds, but now he does know he should clearly put it right by deducting it from his Bank Account.

(g) The bank has received some interest from the Bank of England for Dealer. Dealer has not been told about this increase in his funds but now that he knows he will obviously enter it into his Cash Book. This is an example of a bank giro credit transfer, in this case for interest on a gilt-edged security (Government loan stock).

(h) On February 28 the bank has paid a standing order to the Anglia Building society for A. Dealer's mortgage payment. Although A. Dealer will be expecting this payment he would not enter it in his Cash Book until the Bank Statement confirms that it has actually been paid.

(e), (f), (g) and (h) are examples of a lack of knowledge existing between Dealer and his bankers. Dealer did not know that the bank had taken away or received on his behalf, these moneys.

11.3 How to draw up a Bank Reconciliation Statement

In examinations we are sometimes asked to reconcile the two balances using all the items that are outstanding, but in business the following is the programme:

(a) Compare the two accounts and note all the items of disagreement, as we have done in (a)–(h) in the last section.
(b) Adjust all items that can be put right in the Cash Book – items which are only wrong because of our lack of knowledge of what the bankers have done.
(c) Reconcile the rest in a reasonable statement, starting with one balance and finishing with the other.

If we cannot reconcile them there must be some mistake, either on our part or on the bank's part. Carefully scrutinize every figure. (The author once went heavily 'in the red' because his bankers paid the mortgage twice every month for six months. A bad figure on the Standing Order for payment was being read by one Clerk as 'Pay on the 1st' and by another clerk as 'Pay on the 7th'.)

Our calculations now look like this:

REVISED CASH BOOK (BANK COLUMNS ONLY)

Dr. 19. .				£	Cr. 19. .				£
Feb.	1	Balance		1 125.00	Feb.	2	Green		238.00
	10	Ambrose		253.75		14	Howard		142.50
	17	Bloggs		313.10		19	Ives		183.50
	28	Crayford		367.50		28	Rates (UDC)		185.00
	28	Interest Received		62.90		28	Bank charges		26.25
						28	Anglia B/S		140.00
						28	Balance		1 207.00
				£2 122.25					£2 122.25

19. . Mar.	1	Balance	£ 1 207.00	

BANK RECONCILIATION STATEMENT
(as at February 28)

	£
Balance as per Cash Book	1 207.00
Add back the cheque not yet presented	183.50
(because the bank has not yet been asked for the money)	
	1 390.50
Deduct the Crayford cheque not yet cleared	367.50
(because the bank are not yet crediting us with the money)	
Balance as per Bank Statement	£1 023.00

Clearly we have been able to explain the disagreement successfully. Bank Reconciliation Statements are typed out neatly and filed away for inspection when required.

Note also that we could just as easily have shown the working the other way round. We could have started with the 'Balance as per Bank Statement' and worked towards the Cash Book figure.

BANK RECONCILIATION STATEMENT
(as at February 28)

	£
Balance as per Bank Statement	1 023.00
Add the Crayford cheque not yet cleared	
(because the Cash Book already knows about this cheque and has already debited it)	367.50
	1 390.50
Deduct the cheque paid to Ives (because the Cash Book already knows about this and has deducted it from the Bank Account)	183.50
Balance as per Cash Book	£1 207.00

11.4 Exercises set 11.1 – Bank Reconciliation Statements

1. On June 30 W. Evans's Cash Book shows a bank balance of £2 020.90, but at the same date the monthly statement from his bank showed a balance of £2 103.20.

The difference between the two balances was found to be due to the following

(a) On June 10 a charge of £12.00 for foreign exchange commission had been made by the bank. Evans had not entered this in his Cash Book.
(b) An annual subscription of £15.00 had been paid by a banker's Standing Order on June 25.
(c) Cheques for £129.00 and £185.95 issued by Evans had not been presented for payment.
(d) A cheque for £205.65 from A. Jones paid into the bank on June 15 had been returned marked 'No Account'. No entry of this dishonour had been made in the Cash Book.

You are asked to open Evans's Bank Account in his Cash Book with the opening balance given above, £2 020.90; to enter such items as have been omitted; to find the new balance that results, and to draw up a Bank Reconciliation Statement to reconcile this new balance with the balance given on the Bank Statement.

(RSA – Adapted)

2. The following shows the entries in T. Fitt's Cash Book in March:

19. .		£	19. .			£
Mar. 1	Balance at bank brought forward	575.00	Mar. 5	Drawings – self	100.00	
			15	Noah	400.00	
16	Brown	125.00		Oliver	125.00	
25	Abel	925.00	29	Rigg	475.00	
31	Warner	1 430.00		Lee	75.00	
			31	Balance at bank carried forward	1 880.00	

Early in April he received this statement from his bank:

T. FITT: IN ACCOUNT WITH THE LOANSHIRE BANK LIMITED

Date	Particulars	Debit	Credit	Balance
Mar. 1	Balance Forward			575.00
5	Self – T. Fitt	100.00		475.00
17	Sundries		125.00	600.00
18	Oliver	125.00		
18	Noah	400.00		75.00
26	Sundries		925.00	1 000.00
28	Cheque returned unpaid	125.00		875.00
31	Charges (export services)	20.00		855.00
31	Lee	75.00		780.00

(a) Draw up a Cash Book, starting with the present balance of £1 880.00 and correct such differences as are caused by a lack of knowledge of the bank's activities. Then reconcile the revised cash balance with the balance at the bank in a Bank Reconciliation Statement.
(b) Whose cheque was returned unpaid?

3. On December 31 the Woodlands Girls' School Fund Cash Book showed a balance at the bank of £235.60, whereas the Bank Statement showed a balance of £162.55. On checking these against one another it was found that Mrs Austerberry, the Treasurer, had entered a cheque for £200.60 in the Cash Book as £200.65. This cheque was paid out to 'War on Want'. Two cheques paid into the school fund had not yet been credited by the bank. These were from A. Governor, £27.50, and from A. Parent, £35.00. The bank had charged £10.60 for arranging foreign exchange for a school visit, and this had not been entered in the Cash Book. Get the Cash Book right first and then do the Bank Reconciliation Statement.

4. On July 31 R. Heron's Cash Book shows a balance at the bank of £1 315.95. On asking the bank for a statement he finds it shows that he has £1 645.55. On checking he sees the following differences: he has forgotten to write £22.50 off his Cash Book for a standing order, and the bank have also charged him £13.80 charges. Two cheques sent to R. Blood £137.55, and B. Thunder £228.35, have not yet been presented by them.

You are asked (a) to put the Cash Book right where it is wrong; (b) to make out a Bank Reconciliation Statement for the remaining items.

5. On August 31 J. Trueman asks his bank for a statement. It shows a balance of cash at the bank £814.75, whereas according to his Cash Book he has exactly £1 000.00 at the bank. He finds that a cheque for £749.75 which he sent on August 30 to P. Brown has not yet been presented by Brown, and also that two cheques paid into the bank for £800.00 and £135.00 have not yet been credited by the bank. These cheques were from J. Jones and R. Elvidge. Reconcile the two balances.

6. On March 31, J. Cooper's Cash Book showed a balance of £2 250.00 and his Statement of Account from the bank showed a balance in his favour of £4 000.00. On comparing the statement with his Cash Book he found that the following entries in the Cash Book had not yet been entered on the statement:

Cheques paid in on March 31, £800.00
Cheques drawn up to March 31, £1 750.00

and the following entries on the statement had not yet been entered in his Cash Book:

Direct debit for rates for Council £100.00
Credit transfer to the bank by a debtor £900.00

You are asked (a) to draw up a new Cash Book balance bearing in mind such of the above figures as are relevant; (b) to reconcile this new Cash Book balance with the bank balance shown above.

(RSA – Adapted)

7. The following are copies of the Bank Column of R. Miller's Cash Book and of his Bank Statement as rendered by the bank. You are asked to bring the Cash Book up to date and reconcile the remaining items, in a well-presented Bank Reconciliation Statement.

CASH BOOK (BANK COLUMN ONLY)

Dr. 19. .		£	Cr. 19. .			£
June 20	Balance	992.00	June 21	A		32.80
25	C	142.30	23	B		86.60
30	E	73.00	29	D		147.70
			30	Balance	c/d	940.20
		£1 207.30				1 207.30
July 1	Balance b/d	940.20				

R. Miller in account with Royal Bank Ltd

19. .	Details	Dr.	Cr.	Balance
June 20	Balance			992.00
23	Cheque	32.80		959.20
25	Sundries		142.30	1 101.50
29	Cheque	147.70		953.80
30	Direct debit (UDC)	23.25		930.55
30	Credit transfer		87.75	1 018.30

8. F. Graham's Cash Book showed a balance of £2 700.90 cash at bank on December 31. On that date his bank pass book showed a balance of £2 629.80 cash at bank. The difference arose as follows:

Cheques drawn by F. Graham for £143.85 in favour of Smith and £360.80 in favour of Williams had not been presented by them for payment and £498.55 received on December 31 was not shown in the pass book until January 2. The bank charged £77.20 for a foreign exchange transaction which has not yet been entered in the Cash Book.

You are required to prepare a Reconciliation Statement in correct form.

9. On August 31 R. Herd's Cash Book shows a balance at the bank of £1 343.50. The Bank Statement on the same date shows £1 730.70. On carefully checking the two statements he finds:

(a) Two cheques sent to B. Disraeli and K. Gladstone during the month, for £360.60 and £155.50 have not yet been presented by them.
(b) The takings paid in on August 31 have not yet been entered. These were £93.00.
(c) Bank Charges of £14.90 have been deducted by the bank without notice, and also a direct debit for £21.00 subscription to Herd's professional body. This had been forgotten in the Cash Book.

Reconcile the two balances.

10. On January 1, R. Jones has a balance at the bank, according to his Cash Book, of £1 500.75. He asks his bank for a statement and is told that he has a balance of £2 394.20. He is also able to discover that the bank charged him £20.60 Bank Charges, and had collected from the Treasury interest on his War Loan amounting to £800.00. A cheque for £114.05 sent by Jones to a supplier, Best Biscuits Ltd, on December 31 had not yet been presented by them. You are asked: (a) to correct the Cash Book; (b) to reconcile the amended Cash Book with the Bank Statement.

11. R. Barnaby's Cash Book for July was as follows: 6 14

19. .				19. .			
July	1	Balance	2 628.75	July	2	Cromer & Co.	127.25
	4	Cash Sales	250.00		10	Folkstone Ltd	238.85
	7	Jones & Co.	1 833.75		22	Drawings	125.00
	24	Cash Sales	300.75		27	Lee & Co.	242.80
	31	B. Smith	213.25		29	Zenith Ltd	148.25
					29	Charges	12.50

His bank statement showed:

19. .				19. .			
July	17	Folkstone	238.85	July	1	Balance	3 002.50
	18	Cromer & Co.	127.25		4	Sundries	250.00
	19	Hugh & Co.	272.25			Sundries	1 833.75
	22	Drawings	125.00		24	Sundries	300.75
	22	Toffer	101.50			Credit transfer	
	29	Charges	12.50			(Peters)	202.25

You are asked to correct the Cash Book for items which are the result of Barnaby's not knowing what the bank had done, and then to do a Bank Reconciliation Statement for the remaining items.

12. From the following prepare a Bank Reconciliation Statement as at June 30, after first bringing the Cash Book up to date if this is required:

J. JONES & CO.

CASH BOOK ON JUNE 30, 19. .

19. .				19. .			
June	4	Bank Loan	2 500.00	June	1	Balance	1 135.50
	11	R. Gee	16.00		8	T. Smith	203.00
	30	L. Mitre	20.00		15	R. Port	24.80
					29	B. Lemon	310.50

BANK STATEMENT AS AT JUNE 30, 19. .

Date		Particulars	Debit	Credit	Balance
June	1			(Red)Dr.	1 135.50
	4	Loan		2 500.00	1 364.50
	8	Sundries	203.00		1 161.50
	11	Sundries		16.00	1 177.50
	16	Bank of S. Australia Div.		62.00	1 239.50
	29	Sundries	310.50		929.00
	30	Charges	12.50		916.50

12
Analytical or
Columnar Day Books

12.1 Introduction

Where a firm has departments, or lines of goods which are
distinctive from other lines, the proprietor may prefer to calculate
the profits on each department separately. This is to prevent good
work in one department hiding bad work in another. One
department may be well run by an efficient departmental manager
who is careful to keep costs as low as possible and to buy astutely
when prices are right. Another department may be run very badly,
its buying policy weak, with articles of poor value for the price,
and its sales only maintained because of the low profit margin
added. Such a department may actually be running at a loss, yet
because of the good work done in other departments the weakness
is hidden. The business as a whole is making reasonable profits.

Such weak points in a firm can be discovered if Departmental
Accounts are kept. This will be discussed more fully in Chapter 26,
page 367, the section on Departmental Accounts. Before we can
prepare such accounts we must provide the figures, and this means
analysis of the Purchases, Sales, and Returns made by the
departments. We can then discover what each department has
bought and sold.

12.2 Columnar sales and purchases rulings

A simple Day Book is written on two column Journal Paper, or if
VAT is used, a third column is added. One column is used only for
collecting together the items that occur on one invoice, or for
deducting Trade Discount. A second column is used for VAT and
the right-hand column is the important one that is used to post the
original entry into the Ledger Accounts.

With an analytical or columnar Day Book, extra columns are
added to analyse the amounts relating to separate departments. In

the specimen paper shown here we have allowed only five analysis columns, but in business as many as thirty-eight columns can be provided. Naturally this makes a very large book indeed, and if the Day Book is typewritten a very long carriage on the typewriter is desirable. Alternatively, the analysis can be computerized, codes being used to capture the data for each department and a print-out of the analysis being made available when required.

Figure 12.1 shows an analysis book for a garage. Sales are analysed under five headings, and the columns can be totalled to produce the departmental figures required. The ordinary Day Book work is unchanged. We still record the invoice details in the details column and add them up into the next column. Then if VAT applies we add on the VAT and carry the total into the Total column. Note that VAT is not allowed to be reclaimed from motor vehicles. The total of the Sales column is posted to Sales A/c, VAT is credited to VAT A/c and the debtors are debited with the invoice values. The extra columns simply help us, as they did in the Petty Cash Book, to collect into subtotals information we require about each department of the firm.

At the end of the page the totals of the columns are carried forward to the next page, but before we do this it is usual to *cross-tot*. This gives us a useful check on the arithmetical work performed.

When columnar Sales and Purchases Books become very cumbersome, for example where every product is to be analysed off, separate books can be used for each department; so can separate Sales Accounts instead of the Departmental Sales Account shown in Figure 12.2.

Page
Centre   SALES ACCOUNT (CREDIT SIDE ONLY)

Date	Petrol and Oil	New Vehicles	Repairs	Accessories	Spare Parts	F	L162 Total
19 July 31	£ 8 932.50	£ 28 390.00	£ 4 937.50	£ 1 628.00	£ 7 367.50	SDB 41	£ 51 255.50

Figure 12.2   A Columnar Departmental Sales Account

12.3   Posting the Totals of an Analysis Book

As the month goes by we post the various invoices to the debtors' accounts, but when we come to the end of the month the sales total for the month is posted to a special type of Sales Account, a Departmental Sales Account. Figure 12.2 is an example, but the figures are not those shown in Figure 12.1 since clearly July 2 is not the last day of the month.

Date	Details	Petrol and Oil	New Vehicles	Repairs	Access-sories	Parts	F	Details	Sales	VAT	Total
19 July 1	Moore & King 5 gallons petrol 4 pints oil De-mister	29.70 3.56			6.52		L27	29.70 3.56 6.52	39.78	3.98	43.76
1	Lewis & Co. Mercedes-Benz		12 256.00				L25		12 256.00	–	12 256.00
2	Colt & Lewis 5 000-mile service Plugs, etc. Spot Lamp			37.50	49.50	6.54	L13	37.50 6.54 49.50	93.54	9.35	102.89
		33.26	12 256.00	37.50	56.02	6.54	c/f		12 389.32	13.33	12 402.65
									L71	L72	

Figure 12.1 A Columnar Sales Day Book

Purchases Day Books and Returns Books can be ruled in similar styles to provide departmental figures for Purchases, Purchases Returns, and Sales Returns.

12.4 Computerized analysis of retail trade

In the earlier sections of this chapter we have been referring to sales and purchases records where an invoice is available. In many cases invoices are not made out at all, for example in retail trade. When we go to the supermarket and buy our weekly supplies of groceries etc., we pay at the check-out and receive a **till receipt**. This receipt records not only the price of the item but a code which identifies the nature of the item sold, for example groceries, butcher's meat, greengroceries, etc. The computer detects this coding and captures the data in the appropriate register to record the sale. A daily print-out of the sales in each department can thus be made.

Note that with retail trade VAT has to be calculated by one of the 'Special Schemes for Retailers', and the computer's VAT program will be geared to the necessary scheme and will extract the output tax automatically.

Even the smallest computerized systems have these facilities, usually for up to twenty departments, and the necessary p.o.s. (point of sale) programs can not only detect the sales of each department, but can also detect the item of stock sold for stock-taking purposes if required – though this requires the keying-in of a more complicated code.

DEPARTMENT	SUN	MON	TUE	WED	THU	FRI	SAT	TOTALS
GROCERY	–	85.65	105.29	89.72	136.25	278.60	295.85	991.36
BUTCHERY	–	46.55	73.25	69.70	85.65	136.54	172.91	584.60
GREEN GROCERY	–	56.80	76.80	34.25	95.60	121.50	185.64	570.59
WINES & SPIRITS	216.25	31.80	34.80	75.20	64.30	155.20	180.44	757.99
TOTALS	216.25	220.80	290.14	268.87	381.80	691.84	834.84	2904.54

Figure 12.3 Computerized sales analysis on a daily basis (courtesy of Micro-Simplex Ltd)

12.5 Exercises set 12.1 – analysis Day Books

1. Give the ruling of a Sales Book suitable for a business divided into three departments and insert three specimen entries, supplying your own dates, names, etc. VAT is at 10%.

2. Give the ruling of a Purchases book for a businesswoman who buys silk, cotton, and woollen goods, so that she may ascertain her total monthly purchases of each class of goods, as well as the gross total. Make three specimen entries. VAT is at 10%.

3. Rock N. Roll is a retailer selling music centres, records and musical instruments, and keeps a separate Purchases Account for each department. You are asked to prepare a suitable Purchases Day Book in columnar form and enter in it the following purchases. VAT is at 10%.

19. .

Mar. 1 Bought from Adam & Co. 6 Violins at £50.00 each less $33\frac{1}{3}$% Trade discount.

     12 Bought from Nippon Ltd 12 music centres at £277.50 less 25% Trade discount.

     18 Bought from Caleb & Co. 3 'Cellos at £200.00 each.

     21 Bought from Abel Swinger three Saxophones at £445.00 each, less 25% Trade discount.

     29 Bought from Western Records Ltd 300 records at £3.50 each, less 30% Trade discount.

Rule off the Day Book at the end of the month and insert the totals.

(RSA – Adapted)

4. B. Whittington is in business as a wholesale florist. He deals in four main classes of goods: seeds, bulbs, cut flowers, and pot plants. Record the following invoices in a suitable Sales Day Book – analysed for these four departments. VAT is added to all orders at 10%

19. .

Oct. 3 R. Mulligan purchases goods as follows:

200 packets assorted flower seeds	=£ 23.75
200 packets assorted vegetable seeds	=£ 18.75
5 sacks bulk Daffodils	=£ 61.25

    10 M. Bews purchases goods as follows:

6 boxes cut Chrysanthemums	=£ 47.50
12 boxes cut Roses	=£ 72.50
200 packets Iris bulbs (packets of 12)	=£ 52.00

    17 R. Peachey purchases goods as follows:

40 boxes cut Scabious	=£182.50
2000 packets flower seeds	=£237.50
2000 packets vegetable seeds	=£187.50

    27 M. Lupin purchases goods as follows:

6 boxes cut Chrysanthemums	=£ 47.50
100 pot plants (various)	=£ 80.00
200 packets flower seeds	=£ 23.75

5. Floris Brandt runs a business which has four departments: stationery, confectionery, chemists' sundries, and toys. He keeps a Purchases Day Book on the columnar basis which analyses the purchases under these four headings. Enter the following invoices on special paper ruled up for the purpose and total the book at the end of the month: VAT is added at 10% to all invoices received.

19. .
Aug. 4 R. Rector sold Brandt goods as follows:

500 packets envelopes at 25 pence each	=£125.00
200 writing pads at 30 pence each	=£ 60.00
30 dolls at £2.25 each	=£ 67.50
20 'Mini Model' cars at £1.30 each	=£ 26.00

  12 B. Vicar sold Brandt goods as follows:

6 jars liquorice drops at £4.75 jar	=£ 28.50
10 jars fruit drops at £5.50 jar	=£ 55.00
40 packets Snacktime chocolates at £1.79	=£ 71.60
200 aspirin tubes at 35 pence each	=£ 70.00

  18 A. Priest sold to Brandt goods as follows:

200 boxes cough tablets at £1.15 per box	=£230.00
100 infants' dummies at £0.30 each	=£ 30.00

  29 G. Monk sold to Brandt as follows:

100 bars chocolate at 43 pence each	=£ 43.00
100 bars chocolate at 48 pence each	=£ 48.00
200 memo pads at 25 pence each	=£ 50.00

Insert appropriate folio numbers in suitable places.

13
The Bank Cash Book

13.1 Introduction

As a firm grows larger the problems of controlling the firm grow too, especially that of finding enough good workers. This does not mean that reliable workers are not available, or that workers are more dishonest than they used to be. It means that the number of posts available to workers has increased and they are able to pick and choose their firms, and demand higher wages as a result. If we can devise schemes which permit us to use less skilled or less reliable labour we can keep the wage bill down.

The Bank Cash Book is such a device. It gives efficient control of the cash, enabling Head Office to see what is happening in all branches at the shortest possible notice, and to descend suddenly upon branches where they suspect inefficiency or even crime.

13.2 The Principle of the Bank Cash Book

The basic idea of the Bank Cash Book, which replaces the Three-column Cash Book, is that the cashier does not disburse cash at all, and if he receives any he pays it into the bank as if it was a cheque. Any cash that has to be paid out will be dealt with through the Petty Cash Book, on the Imprest System.

If this is how we intend to deal with the cash, then the cash column in the Three-column Cash Book will not be required at all, and may be used for another purpose which will be illustrated shortly.

The cashier is now receiving money, probably from daily takings in the tills, and possibly from debtors, but that money will be banked each night in full, probably in the night safe of the local bank. Head Office usually has an arrangement with the bank that if the daily takings are not banked in the night safe, Head Office will be informed at once. This enables Head Office to send someone down to see the branch manager immediately.

Head Office will also watch the amounts of the daily takings. If a particular day's takings seem lower than usual, or if takings generally are declining, Head Office will investigate. There may be a thousand and one reasons: the manager is stealing the money; the assistants are not ringing up the tills for the right amounts; the manager is bad-tempered, and is alienating customers; the shop is facing cut-price competition from other shopkeepers. This is the way to control a business – to investigate immediately all unusual matters, from every possible point of view.

13.3   Layout of the Bank Cash Book

The difference between this book and the Three-column Cash Book is that cash will not be handled at all, except as daily takings to be paid into the bank. This means that the cash column is not needed and may be used instead as a details column for bank payments, the total paid into the bank being the only figure to appear in the bank column. This is a great advantage since it enables us to compare the bank figures very easily with the Bank Statement sent to us by the bank. The Bank Statement usually has the amount paid in, both cheques and cash, lumped together in one figure as Sundries. It is a great help to have this one figure, lumped together, also in our Cash Book.

The lines ruled across the details column are for the addition of the day's total for the bank. Usually the last item on the debit side will be the daily cash takings as the tills are cashed up at the end of the day and paid into the bank.

In all other respects the Bank Cash Book is exactly like the Three-column Cash Book.

13.4   The Cash Book as a Book of Original Entry

In discussing the books of Original Entry we have not yet considered the position of the Cash Book. It is unusual in that it is both a book of Original Entry, and a part of the Ledger.

It is a book of Original Entry because documents – cheques and receipts – are entered directly into it. The Cash Book therefore constitutes the prime entry for cheques and receipts. There is no real need to Journalize cash, since the Cash Book is itself the Day Book. For very formal matters, like the purchase of valuable assets for cash, a Journal Entry would probably be done in order to record the serial number, if any, of the asset purchased.

The entries in the Petty Cash Book are similarly original entries, and yet form part of the Ledger itself. The Petty Cash Book is an

Date	Details	Folio	Discount Allowed	Details	Bank	Date	Details	Folio	Discount Received	Details	Bank
19 Jan.			£	£	£	19 July			£	£	£
1	Balance	b/d			1 893.25	3	Marshal & Co.	L62	7.22	137.25	137.25
1	D. Williams	L79	3.32	36.75		4	M. Fox	L33		23.10	
1	Grout & Co.	L26		63.00		4	T. Green	L37		36.75	
1	Cash Sales	L34		226.60	326.35	4	M. Larkin	L42	33.59	638.25	
2	R Jones	L45	7.46	141.75		4	Petty Cash	PCB 5		20.90	719.00
2	P. Masters	L49		21.25		4	Balance	c/d			3 133.20
2	Cash Sales	L34		328.75	491.75						
4	J. Cornwell	L27	47.24	897.50							
4	D. Davis	L29		73.75							
4	R. Morgan	L38		63.25							
4	Cash Sales	L34		243.60	1 278.10						
		£	58.02	£	3 989.45				40.81		3 989.45
			L81						L82		
5	Balance	b/d			3 133.20						

Figure 13.1   The Bank Cash Book

extension of the Cash Account, to cover small cash receipts and disbursements.

13.5   Exercises set. 13.1 – the Bank Cash Book

1. Write up a trader's Bank Cash Book from the following information:

19. .

May 1 Balance as per Cash Book £3638.25; total paid in £488.24, consisting of £238.24 from M. Jones in full settlement of his debt of £250.78, and £250.00 cash sales; cheques drawn: R. Fowler £83.75, M. Lewis £66.25.

2 Total paid in £638.25, all cash sales; cheque drawn: Urban Council £126.25, Petty Cash £75.00.

3 Total paid in £636.60; consisting of cheques from M. Cantor, £39.00, in full settlement of his debt of £40.00; and R. Lessor, £225.00. The rest was cash takings; cheques drawn: T. Clive £23.75; R. Loosely £38.10.

Balance off the book and bring down the balance. Insert appropriate folio numbers in suitable places.

2. Write up a trader's Bank Cash Book from the following:

19. .

July 1 Balance as per Cash Book £3 458.75; total paid in £423.10, consisting of cheques from R. Roper, £28.75, P. Lucas, £34.35, and cash sales £360.00; cheques drawn: A. Landlord £202.50.

2 Cheques drawn: J. Morgan £263.75 in full settlement of a debt of £277.63.

3 Total paid in £881.25, consisting of a cheque for £76.25 from R. Lauder and the rest cash sales; cheques drawn: Petty Cash £43.75.

4 Total paid in £378.25, of which there were cheques from T. Sampson £21.75 and D. Lyler £56.50; the rest was cash sales; cheques drawn: M. Gyler £322.50 in full settlement of her account of £339.47.

3. Write up a trader's Bank Cash Book from the following information:

(a) his balance at the bank at the close of business on May 27, according to his Cash Book, was £4 362.65.

(b) the counterfoils of his Paying-in Book give these details:

19. .

May 28 Total paid in £1 016.50, consisting of cash from sales £226.50, a cheque from B. Bath for £302.50, and a cheque from L. Poole for £487.50; Poole's cheque was accepted in full settlement of £500.00 owed by him.

30 Total paid in £220.75, consisting entirely of cash from sales.

31 Total paid in £403.00 consisting of cash from sales £195.00 and a

cheque from H. Winton for £208.00. This was accepted in full settelement of his debt of £218.95.

(c) The counterfoils of his cheque book show:

19. .
May 28 J. Battle and Co. Ltd   £1 493.25
     30 W. Thorley and Co.   £975.00
     31 Petty Cash   £131.50
        Self   £250.00
        Elton's Garage   £88.25

The cheque to Thorley and Co. was accepted in full settlement of £1 000.00 owing to them. The cheque to Elton's Garage was for petrol, oil, and maintenance of the delivery van for the previous month, and no previous record of this transaction had gone through the books. (The implication of this statement is that Elton's Garage are not creditors with an outstanding balance, and the payment should be treated as Motor Vehicle Expenses. When posted from the Cash Book this amount would be debited in Motor Vehicle Expenses A/c and not in an account for the garage.)

The details columns of the Cash Book should indicate clearly which Ledger Account is to be debited or credited in respect of each entry. Rule off and balance the Cash Book as at the close of business onMay 31.

(RSA – Adapted)

4. The Cash Book of Thomas, a wholesaler, shows a balance at the bank of £4 382.75 on January 1. He pays all receipts into the bank and pays all payments by cheque except for Petty Cash items. Enter the following items in correct date order and balance off the account. Invent suitable folio numbers for each item.

Receipts in Receipts Book

			£		£
Jan.	1 Nigel and Co.	Cheque	887.72	Discount	46.69
	5 Ravel and Co.	Cheque	428.00	Discount	22.53
	8 Purcell and Co.	Cheque	386.25	Discount	20.33
	11 Mozart Ltd	Cheque	728.25	Discount	38.33

Cash Sales from Till
Jan. 2 £673.00
     6 £637.50
     8 £694.00
   10 £392.50

Cheques drawn

		£		£
Jan.	1 Haji and Co.	213.75	Discount	11.25
	2 Nartey and Co.	153.25		
	3 M. Thompson	39.25	Discount	2.07
	5 R. Fidler	98.65		
	6 L. Shane	82.25		
	8 R. Mackay	63.75		
	10 S. Lucas	568.75	Discount	29.93
	11 R. Theron	73.00		

14
More about depreciation

14.1 A 'true and fair view' of the assets

Depreciation is the reduction in value of an asset as a result of fair wear and tear. As an asset loses value we reduce the book valuation of it in line with our estimate of the loss. In Chapter 7 we saw how to do this by means of a simple Journal Entry. We now need to learn a little more about depreciation, a fairly complex subject, where book-keeping merges into accountancy.

The accounting principle which motivates accountants to try different methods of depreciation, is that we are seeking in our accounting to achieve a 'true and fair view' of the position of the business. As far as Limited Companies are concerned in Great Britain, this is positively required by law. The Companies' Act 1985 requires all businesses to keep accounts in such a way as to give a 'true and fair view' of the Company's affairs. This 'true and fair view' requires two things:

(a) The assets must be valued on the books at a fair value so far as we can estimate it.
(b) If a loss has been suffered it must be charged against the profits – to do otherwise would overstate the profitability of the business.

Applying these two rules to the problem of depreciation, we see that if an asset wears out the loss suffered as a result of wear and tear must be written off the profits. At the same time the asset will be reduced in value to show only its present value now that it has been partly worn out.

There are about eight different methods of calculating depreciation, but for *Book-keeping Made Simple* we will discuss the three commonest methods. These are:

(a) The straight line or equal instalment method.

(b) The diminishing balance method (sometimes called the double-declining method).

(c) The revaluation method.

Before considering each of these methods in turn there is one further part of the Companies Act 1985 which is important. This section requires that in order to help shareholders and investors judge the value of a company's assets the assets must appear in such a way as to show them at cost, less depreciation to date. For a typical company we might therefore have a display like the one shown below:

Fixed assets	At cost	Less depreciation to date	Net Value
	£	£	£
Machinery	27 000	13 500	13 500
Furniture, etc.	18 000	16 000	2 000
Motor vehicles	23 000	2 300	20 700
	68 000	31 800	36 200

We can see from these figures that the machinery is about half worn out, the furniture is practically valueless – it must be very old – but the motor vehicles appear to be almost new.

Although this rule only (strictly speaking) applies to companies, accountants do tend to copy a good idea into other areas of their work, and the same sort of display might be used for sole traders, partnerships, etc. The procedure for obtaining the figures needed is explained in the sections which follow.

14.2 The equal instalment or straight line method

When we buy an asset the value of the asset is its cost price. When it comes to the end of its useful life it will usually have some remaining value, which is called its **residual value**, or the term **scrap value** is often used. It will also have an **estimated working life**. For example machinery usually lasts about ten years (newer versions of the same machine will have come onto the market by that time). Motor cars usually last about five years. Ships last about fifteen years and computers about six years.

For the equal-instalment method the accountant first calculates the amount of the annual charge for depreciation necessary to reduce the asset to its scrap value, or residual value, over the lifetime of the asset. To do this we use the following formula:

$$Annual\ charge = \frac{Cost\ price\ less\ scrap\ value}{Estimated\ lifetime\ in\ years}$$

Example

A motor vehicle is purchased for £3 750 on January 1. It is estimated that it will need replacing in four years and will then fetch £1 250 on trade-in. Using the formula, we have:

$$Annual\ charge = \frac{£3\ 750 - £1\ 250}{} $$
$$= \frac{£2\ 500}{4}$$
$$= \underline{\underline{£625.00}}$$

The asset will be depreciated by four equal instalments of £625.00 and will then be reduced on the books to a value of £1 250.00. Using the traditional method, where the depreciation is

MOTOR VEHICLE ACCOUNT							L11
Year 1			£	Year 1			£
Jan. 1	Rex Garages	J1	3 750.00	Dec. 31	Depreciation L17		625.00
				31	Balance	c/d	3 125.00
			£3 750.00				£3 750.00
Year 2			£	Year 2			£
Jan. 1	Balance	b/d	3 125.00	Dec. 31	Depreciation L17		625.00
				31	Balance	c/d	2 500.00
			£3 125.00				£3 125.00
Year 3			£	Year 3			£
Jan. 1	Balance	b/d	2 500.00	Dec. 31	Depreciation L17		625.00
				31	Balance	c/d	1 875.00
			£2 500.00				£2 500.00
Year 4			£	Year 4			£
Jan. 1	Balance	b/d	1 875.00	Dec. 31	Depreciation L17		625.00
				31	Balance	c/d	1 250.00
			£1 875.00				£1 875.00
Year 5			£				
Jan. 1	Balance	b/d	1 250.00				

Depreciation Account					L17
Year 1		£	Year 1		£
Dec. 31	Motor Vehicles	625.00	Dec. 31	Profit & Loss A/cL95	625.00

Figure 14.1 Depreciation by the 'straight-line' method

actually deducted from the asset account, the Motor Vehicle Account will be as shown in Figure 14.1, over the five year period. Only the first year entry is shown in the Depreciation Account. It would be the same each year, the depreciation for this (and any other assets) being written off the Profit and Loss Account.

Leaving assets on the books at cost price

As explained earlier, the better method of recording depreciation today is to use the method called for in the Companies Act 1985. This requires us to leave the asset on the books unchanged (at cost price) instead of reducing the value each year as shown in Figure 14.1. Instead we credit the depreciation, not in the Asset Account, but in a separate Provision for Depreciation Account, which collects the depreciation over the years, leaving the asset on the books in the Asset Account at cost price. The two accounts would look like this at the end of the third year, using the example illustrated previously in Figure 14.1. The four years depreciation are shown in Figure 14.2.

	MOTOR VEHICLES ACCOUNT			L11
19. . Jan. 1	Rex Garages	J1	£ 3 750.00	

	PROVISION FOR DEPRECIATION ON MOTOR VEHICLES ACCOUNT	L12
	19. . (Year 1) Dec. 31	£ 625.00
	19. . (Year 2) Dec. 31	625.00
	19. . (Year 3) Dec. 31	625.00
	19. . (Year 4) Dec. 31	625.00

Figure 14.2 Leaving the asset on the books at cost price

The value of the asset at any given time is therefore the book-value (i.e. cost price), less the accumulated depreciation to date. At the end of Year 3 in this case it would be:

	£
Cost price	3 750.00
Less depreciation	1 875.00
Present value of asset	£1 875.00

which is the same as the balance on the Asset Account shown in Figure 14.1 at the end of the third year.

Advantages and disadvantages of the straight line method

Advantages

(a) It is straightforward and easily understood.
(b) It writes the asset down over a definite period to a predicted minimum value below which the business would not normally keep the asset.

Disadvantages

(a) Whenever new assets are bought or old assets are sold the depreciation for the asset must be recalculated.
(b) There is an increasing charge to the Profit and Loss Account over the years, because the repairs on an old machine increase. As the depreciation charge is steady the total cost – depreciation plus repairs – must increase over the years. This offends against another book-keeping principle, that we should try to even out the burden to Profit and Loss Account over the years from the use of the same asset.
(c) There is no provision made for replacing the asset when it is worn out. This is discussed later in the chapter.

14.3   The diminishing balance method

Under this method the asset is depreciated by a fixed percentage every year on the diminishing balance of the account. There is a formula for calculating the desirable percentage but it is too advanced for this book. In fact is usually comes out to about twice the percentage one would expect. For example, an asset is expected to last eight years (so one would think we should write off 12½ per cent per annum) the formula would give an answer of about 25 per cent. For this reason it is sometimes called the **double-declining method**.

Once again, the traditional method was to debit Depreciation Account and credit the Asset Account as shown in the Journal entry Figure 7.9 (see page 118). This would give us an asset account like the one shown in the example below

Example

A firm's depreciation policy for motor vehicles requires the book-keeper to write 25 per cent off the diminishing balance of the asset every year. Show the Depreciation Account for a motor vehicle valued at £3 750.00 bought on January 1, 19. ., for the first four years. By the traditional method the Motor Vehicles Account will appear as shown in Figure 14.3 below, while by the more modern method the Motor Vehicles Account and the Provision for Depreciation on Motor Vehicles Account will be as shown in Figure 14.4

				£						£
		MOTOR VEHICLES ACCOUNT								L11
Year 1				£	Year 1					£
Jan. 1	Rex Garages	J1	3 750.00		Dec. 31	Depreciation	L17			937.50
					31	Balance	c/d			2 812.50
			£3 750.00							£3 750.00
Year 2				£	Year 2					£
Jan. 1	Balance	b/d	2 812.50		Dec. 31	Depreciation	L17			703.12
					31	Balance	c/d			2 109.38
			£2 812.50							£2 812.50
Year 3				£	Year 3					£
Jan. 1	Balance	b/d	2 109.38		Dec. 31	Depreciation	L17			527.34
					31	Balance	c/d			1 582.04
			£2 109.38							£2 109.38
Year 4				£	Year 4					£
Jan. 1	Balance	b/d	1 582.04		Dec. 31	Depreciation	L17			395.51
					31	Balance	c/d			1 186.53
			£1 582.04							£1 582.04
Year 5				£						
Jan. 1	To Balance	b/d	1 186.34							

Figure 14.3   Depreciation by the Diminishing Balance Method

Advantages and disadvantages of the diminishing balance method

Advantages
(a) It is straightforward and recalculations are not required when new assets are purchased or old assets sold.
(b) The charge against the profits for the use of the asset is more even over the years, since the diminishing charge for depreciation offsets the increasing charge for repairs. Notice how the charges fall year by year in Figure 14.4.

Disadvantages
(a) The asset is never completely written off.
(b) Where a very short life is normal for an asset the percentage method is unsatisfactory, since the percentage required to

MOTOR VEHICLES ACCOUNT				L11
19. .			£	
Jan. 1	Rex Garages	J1	3 750.00	

PROVISION FOR DEPRECIATION ON MOTOR VEHICLES ACCOUNT			L12
	19. .	(Year 1)	£
	Dec. 31	Depreciation L17	937.50
	19. .	(Year 2)	
	Dec. 31	Depreciation L17	703.12
	19. .	(Year 3)	
	Dec. 31	Depreciation L17	527.34
	19. .	(Year 4)	
	Dec. 31	Depreciation L17	395.51

DEPRECIATION ACCOUNT (SIMILAR EACH YEAR)				L17
19. .		£	19. .	£
Dec. 31	Motor Vehicles	937.50	Dec. 31 Profit and Loss L95 4 235.50	
	(other items would also be			
	be depreciated —			
	say)	3 298.00		
		£4 235.50		4 235.50

Figure 14.4   Using a Provision for Depreciation Account and the Diminishing Balance Method

write the asset off is very high. For instance, to write off £500.00 completely over three years requires a 90 per cent depreciation rate, i.e. £450.00 the first year, £45.00 the second year, and £4.50 the next year. This charge is so uneven as to be unsatisfactory.

(c)   Again there is no provision for replacing the asset at the end of its useful life.

14.4   The revaluation method

With some businesses it is quite impossible to treat depreciation by the normal method. For instance, a farmer can hardly say with certainty 'This old cow has declined by 20 per cent this year'. She may have had two fine calves this year. Where a firm has many loose tools, for instance shovels, spades, hoes, and rakes for a landscape gardening firm, it is often difficult to depreciate these items.

The sensible method in these cases is the revaluation method.

This may result in a loss, a depreciation charge, or a profit – an appreciation in value caused by a rise in the asset's value. The valuation should always be carried out by an appropriately qualified person, a valuation is only acceptable (for example to the Inalnd Revenue Department) if made by a person who is professionally qualified in the area concerned – for example landed estate valuation, jewellery valuation, engineering valuation, etc etc.

Example

Farmer Giles's herd was valued at £63 625.00 on January 1 by the local valuer called in for the purpose. On December 31 the same valuer estimated the herd to be worth £60 325.00 show the depreciation entry and the Herd Account.

Clearly the herd is worth less on December 31 than at the start of the year. To adjust the asset account to its correct value we must reduce it by £3 300. The Journal and Ledger entries are shown in Figure 14.5.

19. . Dec. 31	Depreciation Account Dr. Herd Account Being decrease in value of herd dur- ing year	L7 L5	£ 3 300.00	£ 3 300.00

HERD ACCOUNT   L5

19. . Jan. 1 To Balance	£ b/d 63 625.00	19. . Dec. 31 By Depreciation L17 By Balance c/d	£ 3 300.00 60 325.00
	£63 625.00		£63 625.00
19. . Jan. 1 To Balance	£ b/d 60 325.00		

Figure 14.5 Depreciation by revaluation

Some accountants claim that this sort of entry does not give a fair picture, since it appears that we have tried to depreciate animals. They argue that a better way is to write off the whole of the herd as at 1 January and take on the new valuation at 31 December. Whichever way is adapted the result is the same, we end up with the Herd Account at the new valuation of £60 325.00.

Of course the valuer could have valued the herd at a greater value than at the start of the year; indeed normally this would be what a farmer hoped for. In that case there would not be any depreciation, instead we should have an appreciation of Herd Account, and this would be taken to Profit and Loss Account as a profit for the year.

14.5   Providing for the replacement of an asset

Unfortunately depreciation in the way we have described does nothing at all to provide cash to replace an asset when it finally becomes obsolete or worn out. Depreciation reduces the profit available for the use of the proprietor, but it leaves this undistributed wealth in the business. Since uncommitted wealth has a way of getting used up in the ordinary conduct of the business, it is unwise to leave this wealth lying about. Sooner or later someone will put it to use in an 'extravagant' way. To purchase extra equipment, replace existing assets, or pay higher wages out of money that should be accumulating for the purchase of new machinery in the future, is an extravagance the business cannot afford.

Prudent managers therefore take a second step in depreciation policy. Not only do they write depreciation off the profits in the Profit and Loss Account and thus reduce the value of the asset as already shown – **they also invest an equal amount of money in securities outside the business**. When the day comes to replace the asset the investments can be sold to provide the purchase price of the new equipment. This prevents the wealth accumulating inside the firm where anyone who notices it can find a use for it. The Journal Entry for this type of investment might read:

19. . Dec. 31	Plant and Machinery Replacement Investment Account Dr. Bank Account Being cash invested at this date	L85 CB27	£ 625.00	£ J21 625.00

Figure 14.6   **Investing to Provide for the Renewal of Machinery**

The asset, cash at bank, has been reduced and the portion given up has been replaced by a further asset, investments, which will not be touched until the order for new machinery is placed. A further point is that these investments will earn profits which can be reinvested to enlarge the portfolio of investments available for sale by the proprietors when required. This type of fund is called a **Sinking Fund**.

14.6 Leases – a special case of the straight-line method

When we purchase the lease of a property, we purchase the right to live in that property for a given number of years, after which time it is returnable to the landlord. The commonest period for a long-term lease is ninety-nine years, but some leases are now being given for 999 years. Short leases are very common too.

If we purchase a lease for £25 000 which has twenty years to run, we should write off one-twentieth of its value every year, that is £1 250.00 each year. This is called **amortizing the lease**, that is, writing off the dead part of the life of the lease. *This is treated here as a special case of the straight-line method of depreciation, but more advanced treatments are possible.*

Two other points worth mentioning on leases are dilapidations and lease replacement sinking funds.

Dilapidations
When a property is returned to the landlord he is entitled to demand that it be in as good as condition as when he leased it to us. For this reason leaseholders often put away certain sums each year to provide for any dilapidations that may need to be put right when the property is returned.

Lease replacement sinking funds
When we surrender our lease we shall have to find alternative property, or pay a lump sum to renew the lease if the landlord is prepared to renew it. To provide for this, sums of money are invested each year to provide the necessary cash when it is required. The method is the same as the one described in the previous section.

14.7 Exercises set 14.1 – Depreciation

1. On January 1 a firm bought a machine for £9 000.00. Its probable working life was estimated at ten years and its probable scrap value at the end of that time at £1 000.00. It was decided to write off depreciation by the fixed instalment method. Show the Machinery Account for the first two years.

(RSA – Adapted)

2. On January 1 M. Rook bought a machine for £10 000. Its probably working life was estimated at 8 years and its probably scrap value at the end of that time at £800. It was decided to write off depreciation by the fixed instalment method. This will not be deducted from Machinery Account but will be collected over the years in a Provision for Depreciation on Machinery Account. Show:

(a) The Journal entry for Year 1.
(b) The Machinery Account and the Provision Account for the first two years.
(c) The value of the Machinery on the books at the end of Year 2.

3. L. Jericho has a machine on his books which he purchased on July 1, 19. . for £15 000. He depreciates it at a rate of 10 per cent *per annum* on December 31 of every year. In 19. . this is based on cost price, but in subsequent years it is based on the value at the start of the year (i.e. he uses the diminishing balance method). Show the Machinery Account for Years 1, 2, and 3, bringing down the balance each year. (*Be careful in Year 1 – it is only half a year's depreciation*.)

4. R. Babylon has a machine on his books which he purchased on July 1, 19. . for £12 000. He depreciates it at a rate of 20 per cent *per annum* on December 31 of every year. In 19. . this is based on cost price, but in subsequent years it is based on the value at the start of the year (i.e. he uses the diminishing balance method). This is the only machine Babylon owns.

(a) Show the Machinery Account on July 1 19. .
(b) Babylon does not allow depreciation to be deducted direct from the Machinery Account; it is collected together over the years in a provision for Depreciation Account. Show this account for the first three years.
(c) Show the value of the machine on Babylon's books on 1 January Year 4.

5. A and B who set up in partnership as builders on January 1 19. ., had a motor van the value of which was £1 600.00. On the same day the firm bought (for cash) a further motor van for £2 800.00 and a car for £5 000.00.

It is decided to write off depreciation at 25 per cent per annum on the reducing balance system. This depreciation will actually be deducted on the Motor Vehicles Account, and will be calculated correct to the nearest £1.

On December 31, two years later, the car was sold for £2 000.00 cash.

You are asked to prepare the Motor Vehicles Account as it would appear in the partnership books for each financial year ended 31 December Year 1 and Year 2, showing the amount written off as depreciation each year, and the adjustment for the sale of the car. Show the Journal entry for this sale, and your calculations.

6. R. Long who set up in business as a fashion designer on January 1 19. ., purchased on that day for cash a motor van the value of which was £3 600.00. Later she purchased a larger vehicle for deliveries. This was purchased on October 1 the same year, for £5 700.00, cash.

She decided to write off depreciation at 20 per cent per annum on the reducing balance system, to be collected together year by year in a provision for Depreciation Account. On December 31, Year 2 the van was sold for £2 000.00 (cheque).

You are asked to prepare the Motor Vehicles Account and the

provision for depreciation on Vehicles Account as they would appear in her books for the financial years ended 31 December Year 1 and Year 2, showing the amount written off as depreciation each year, and the calculations and entries for the disposal of the van.

7. A Farmer has a herd valued at £78 750.00 on March 31, 19. . One year later, when he has the herd revalued, it is only valued at £66 375.00. Show the Journal entry for the depreciation, and the 'Herd Account' for the year, balanced off and brought down.

8. Gardening Ltd use great quantities of small tools whose working life is fairly short. All purchases of such tools are entered in the Loose Tools Account, but the stock of loose tools, is valued on December 31 of each year. On January 1, 19. ., they were valued at £2 075. New tools to the value of £1 135 were added in the year, on June 30. On December 31 the stock of loose tools to be carried forward to the next year was valued at £2 200. Show the Journal entry for depreciation and the Loose Tools Account for the year.

15
The Wages Book and wages systems

15.1 Introduction

Wage payment has become more and more involved in recent years as most countries introduce some elements of welfare, paid for by deductions from the pay packet. Liability to pay Income Tax has also increased as world wage levels have risen and the activities of governments in providing public education and other facilities have grown. Some sort of 'Pay As You Earn' system of taxation is necessary for lower income earners, who cannot be expected to save up a year's tax and pay it in one lump sum. An employer must keep a clear record of the wage earned, the deductions for welfare payments (called in the United Kingdom the 'National Insurance Scheme'), the PAYE tax deductions, and other deductions of a voluntary nature. In many firms these include charitable contributions or contributions for sports club facilities. Britian's PAYE scheme is shortly to be improved by a 'Tax Credit' system, and also includes an element of statutory sick pay (SSP).

15.2 Wages calculations

Wages are calculated in various ways. Those paid on a weekly or monthly basis start with the basic wage, from which various deductions have to be made. Where wages are paid hourly the number of hours must be worked out from some sort of timing mechanism and the number of hours is then multiplied by the hourly rate of pay; often overtime rates are based on 'time and a quarter', or 'time and a half', or even 'double time'. Thus an employee paid £3 per hour and time and a half for overtime over 40 hours might work 47 hours in the week. The calculation is:

40 hours + 7 hours overtime = 40 + $10\frac{1}{2}$ hours = $50\frac{1}{2}$ hours.
$50\frac{1}{2} \times £3 = £151\frac{1}{2} = \underline{\underline{£151.50}}$

Another element in pay is *Statutory Sick Pay*, an amount of sick pay paid by employers for short periods of sickness. This may be reclaimed by the employer from official sources. It usually appears on the wages slip as 'Other Pay' or 'SSP' (statutory sick pay).

A further element of pay, under discussion at present, is the *tax credit system*. This is a system which will enable those employees entitled to social security benefits of one sort or another – say, Family Income Supplement for large families – to be paid direct into the wage packet by the employer, who would then claim it back from tax moneys collected from other employees.

The deductions made from wages may be as follows:

(a) *Superannuation*. Where an employee has to pay a contribution towards a pension fund this is usually deducted first. This is because the tax system in the United Kingdom disregards superannuation pay and only taxes the pay received after superannuation has been deducted.

(b) *Tax Payable under the PAYE (Pay As You Earn) Scheme*. This is calculated by reference to Tax Tables supplied by the Inland Revenue Department. They are referred to later.

(c) *National Insurance Contributions (NIC)*. These are contributions to the National Insurance Scheme for sickness benefit, unemployment benefit, state pensions, etc. They are referred to later.

(d) *Voluntary Contributions*. These are contributions to charities, trade unions, etc., which the employer agrees to deduct at source to assist the charities and trade unions concerned. They may also deduct SAYE (Save As You Earn) contributions for employees who wish to save in Government Savings Schemes.

The result is that an employee's gross wage is reduced by a number of compulsory deductions (pension contributions, income tax and national insurance contributions) and then by a further series of voluntary deductions (trade union contributions, charitable contributions and savings). The balance left is called, the net pay, which actually goes into the pay packet or is transferred into the employee's bank account. Sometimes, where a change in family circumstances produces a tax refund, the refund will be added to the net pay to recognize the new arrangements.

Some simple wages calculations are given in Exercises set 15.1. Try these now.

15.3 Exercises set 15.1 – simple wages calculations

1. M. Lucas is paid a basic weekly wage of £140 for a 35 hour week. Any overtime is paid at time and a quarter. During the week ended November 22 he worked a total of 43 hours.
Deductions were as follows:

Company pension scheme: 8% of Gross Wage
National Insurance 9% of gross wage
Income Tax £27.50.
Voluntary deductions: Charity £0.50, Trade Union £1.

You are required to:

(a) Find the gross pay for the week ending 22 November
(b) Calculate the amount of each deduction and hence find the take-home pay for the week.

2. R. Smith is paid a basic weekly wage of £100 for a 40 hour week. Any overtime is paid at time and a half. During the week ended August 30 he worked a total of 52 hours. He was also paid a productivity bonus of £30. Deductions were as follows:

Company Pension Scheme: 6% of gross wage
National Insurance 9% of gross wage
Income Tax – a *refund* of £28.00
Voluntary deductions: Trade Union £1., Save as You Earn £3.

You are required to:

(a) Find the gross pay for the week ending August 30.
(b) Calculate the amount of each deduction and hence find the take-home pay for the week.

3. Rita Ford is paid a basic monthly salary of £420. In January she also earned an overtime payment of £12.50.
Deductions were as follows:

Company pension scheme 5% of gross salary
National Insurance 9% of gross salary
Income Tax £81.75
Voluntary deductions: Save as You Earn £10, Charity £1.

You are required to:

(a) Find the gross pay for the month.
(b) Calculate the amount of each deduction and hence find the amount transferred by bank giro to the credit of her bank account on pay day.

4. Michael Smith is paid a basic monthly salary of £300 and also earns commission of £40 per £1 000 sales. In March his sales totalled £12 500. Deductions were as follows:

Company pension scheme 6% of gross salary
National Insurance 9% of gross salary
Income Tax £84.50
Voluntary deductions: union £1.50; savings £25; charity £2.

You are required to:

(a) Find the gross salary for the month of March.
(b) Calculate the amount of the deductions and hence find the take home pay for the month.

15.4 The traditional Wages Book

A traditional Wages Book is illustrated in Figure 15.1 and explained in the notes facing it. A careful study of the columns will show the student how the final sums due to the employee have been calculated, and what other payments must be made to outside bodies like the Inland Revenue and charitable organizations.

15.5 Exercises set 15.2 – simple Wages Books

Rule up a wages book similar to the one in Figure 15.1, and make entries for the following firms. Wages details for employees are shown for Week 1 of the financial year. (*Note:* In Week 1 of the financial year 'Gross Pay for tax purposes' and 'Gross Pay to date for tax purposes' are the same.) Bring out the totals payable for wages, tax, etc.

1. T. Roberts and Co. Employee details are as follows:

Name	Basic pay £	Other pay £	Superannuation £	Tax-free pay £	Tax due £
A.B.	85.50	3.20	4.40	13.65	21.00
C.D.	102.60	15.40	5.90	34.25	23.10
E.F.	73.50	8.50	4.10	25.60	15.60
G.H.	64.70	4.20	3.40	17.50	14.40

	National Insurance £	Trade union £	Charity £	SAYE £	Employer's National Insurance £
A.B.	6.53	0.50	0.15	5.00	11.54
C.D.	8.69	0.50	—	—	15.36
E.F.	6.03	0.50	0.15	5.00	10.15
G.H.	5.07	0.50	0.10	—	8.96

2. M. Davies and Co. Employee details are as follows:

Name	Basic pay £	Other pay £	Superannuation £	Tax-free pay £	Tax due £
R.S.	96.50	4.60	6.07	8.25	25.80
T.U.	74.50	5.40	4.79	14.80	18.00
V.W.	126.20	32.80	9.36	32.70	34.80
Y.Z.	132.50	46.50	10.74	17.30	45.00

	National Insurance £	Trade union £	Charity £	SAYE £	Employer's National Insurance £
R.S.	7.36	0.65	0.25	—	13.01
T.U.	5.82	0.65	—	5.00	10.29
V.W.	11.60	0.65	—	5.00	20.50
Y.Z.	13.04	0.65	0.15	15.00	23.05

No.	Name of employee	Earnings week 5 May 4-10					Tax details to date							Deductions						Net pay	Refunds, etc.	Amounts payable	Employer's National Insurance
		Basic pay	Overtime	Other	Gross pay	Super-annuation	Gross pay for tax purposes	Gross to date for tax purposes	Tax-free pay	Taxable pay to date	Tax due to date	Tax paid	Refunds (if any)	Tax	National Insurance	T.U.	Charity	SAVE	Total deducts				
		(i)	(ii)	(iii)	(iv)	(v)	(vi)	(vii)	(viii)	(ix)	(x)	(xi)	(xii)	(xiii)	(xiv)	(xv)	(xvi)	(xvii)	(xviii)	(xix)	(xx)	(xxi)	(xxii)
1	A. Smith	56.00	–	5.00	61.00	3.05	57.95	275.70	82.75	192.95	57.60	46.80	–	10.80	4.49	0.41	0.03	–	15.73	42.22		42.22	7.94
2	B. Taylor	65.25	3.25		68.50	3.42	65.08	318.50	110.50	208.00	62.40	49.60	–	12.80	5.04	0.41	0.02	–	18.27	46.81		46.81	8.91
3	C. Baker	72.40	–	17.50	89.90	4.50	85.40	426.30	261.00	175.30	52.50	43.20	–	9.30	6.62	0.41	0.01	5.00	21.34	64.06		64.06	11.70
4	D. Porter	48.20	–	22.30	70.50	3.52	66.98	328.20	123.00	205.20	61.50	63.50	2.00	–	5.19	0.41	0.02	3.00	8.62	58.36	2.00	60.36	9.17
		241.85	3.25	44.80	289.90	14.49								32.90	21.34	1.64	0.08	8.00	63.96	211.45	2.00	213.45	37.72

Figures for management to use in controlling costs and fixing selling prices →

Due to Inland Revenue (less refund of £2.00)

Due to trade union

Due to charity

Due to National Savings Office

Due to employees in wage packets or to bank accounts

Due to Inland Revenue

Figure 15.1   A simple Wages Book

Notes

(i) The first section shows earnings of various sorts, totalled to give the gross pay.

(ii) From this gross pay superannuation is deducted to give the gross pay for tax purposes. The employee will draw this amount, less the deductions.

(iii) Working out the tax deductions can be a little difficult. The stages are:

(a) What did the employee earn this week, after superannuation? (column VI)
(b) What is the gross pay to date after superannuation? (column VII)
(c) How much of this is tax free? We have to look at Tax Table A from the tax office to find this out. (column VIII)
(d) That gives us the total taxable pay to date (column VII minus column VIII). (see column IX)
(e) What is the tax on this amount? We need to look at Tax Table B to find this out. (column X)
(f) We look at the employee's record last week. How much tax has been paid so far this year? Clearly Smith has to pay some more this week, and so must Taylor and Baker, but Porter has paid too much and is entitled to a refund.

(iv) Finally the tax, national insurance and other deductions are totalled to give column XVIII, from which the net pay (column XIX) can be calculated. Porter, who is entitled to a refund, has this added to the net pay, to give the amount payable. (column XXI).

(v) The employer's national insurance contribution, which is payable for each employee employed, is now entered in column XXII.

(vi) The cashier now goes to the bank to draw the payroll money and makes up the wage packets. Alternatively, those who have agreed to be paid by credit transfer have the money transferred into their bank accounts.

(vii) Once a month the employer will pay the Inland Revenue, the trade union, etc., the sums due.

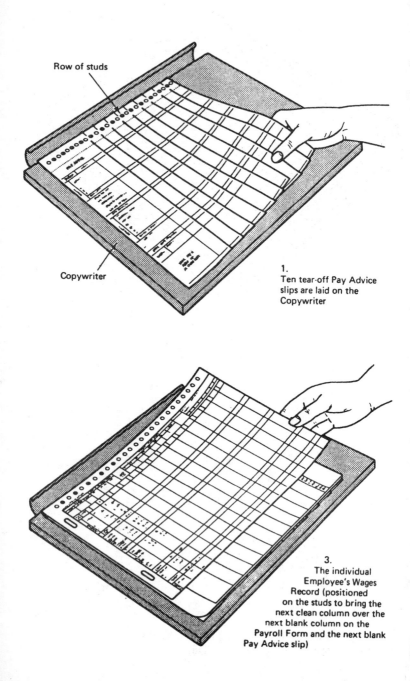

Row of studs

Copywriter

1.
Ten tear-off Pay Advice slips are laid on the Copywriter

3.
The individual Employee's Wages Record (positioned on the studs to bring the next clean column over the next blank column on the Payroll Form and the next blank Pay Advice slip)

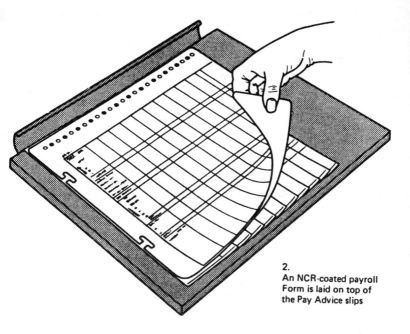

2.
An NCR-coated payroll
Form is laid on top of
the Pay Advice slips

4.
The torn-off Pay Advice slips
folded once to go into the
pay packets. If paid in cash
the money is inserted in the
same envelope

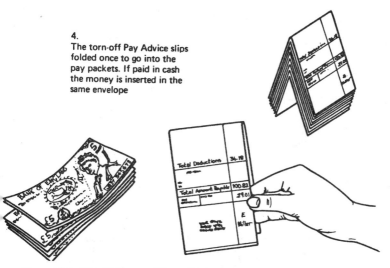

Figure 15.2 The Kalamazoo Wages System
(Reproduced by courtesy of Kalamazoo Ltd)

15.6   The Kalamazoo Wages System

Some three million people in the United Kingdom alone are paid their wages weekly or monthly using the Kalamazoo Wages System. This system is an example of **simultaneous records**, a system which avoids copying errors by preparing several sets of records simultaneously using 'no carbon required' paper. A few words of explanation are helpful. To keep proper records of wages three things are required:

(a) A **pay advice note** which shows the employee exactly how the pay has been calculated. This is used to make up the wage packet, and enables the employee to check the pay on receipt. Sometimes the packet has small holes in it so that coins can be counted, and the notes can be checked, before opening the packet.

(b) A **payroll** which lists all payments made for the week or month, and which is the firm's record retained in a special loose-leaf binder.

(c) An individual **employee's record card**, which lists all the employee's pay for the year. In any query about pay we can produce this record to discuss it with the employee. We do not want to produce the payroll, for this would enable the employee to see what other staff earn.

In the Kalamazoo system a flat board, called a **copy-writer** is used as a backing sheet as shown in Figure 15.2. It has a row of studs at the top over which the various documents can be placed. First comes a set of ten wages advice notes. On top of this is placed the NCR coated payroll form. Then the individual's record card is placed over the top of the payroll form. The week's pay is then entered on the record card. Naturally the entry is copied on to the payroll form and the advice note because of the 'no carbon required' paper. When the entry is complete the wages clerk takes the next employee's record card, and positions it over the next clean column on the payroll – a few studs up from the previous entry. The perforations in the forms can be seen in Figure 15.2 and in Figure 15.3. Figure 15.2 shows how the system works. The final result is a full set of records (a), (b) and (c) as explained above. A pay advice note is shown in detail in Figure 15.3.

Notes to Figure 15.3:

   (i)   The week or month number is shown and the date it commences.
   (ii)   There are six lines for types of earning, such as basic wage, overtime, commission, etc. One of these lines is for statutory sick pay. The total of these gives the gross pay.
   (iii) Superannuation is then deducted, because it is not taxable.

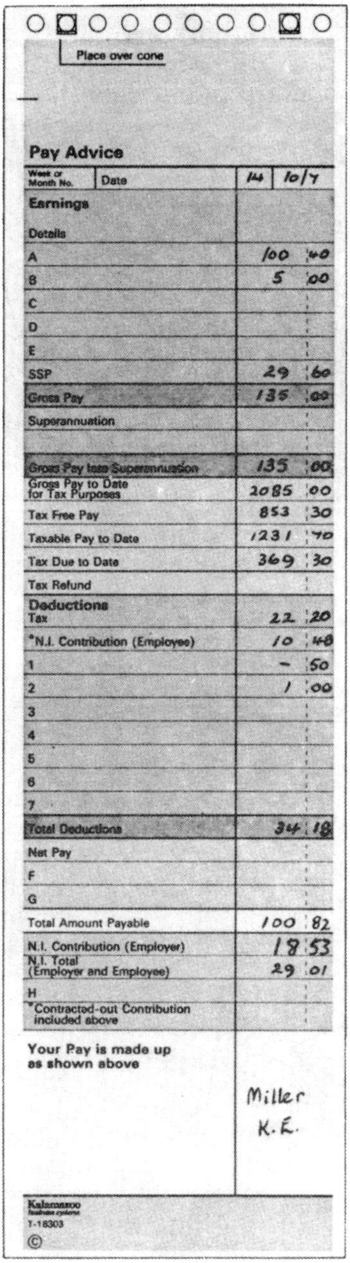

Pay Advice			
Week or Month No.	Date	14	10/7
Earnings			
Details			
A		100	40
B		5	00
C			
D			
E			
SSP		29	60
Gross Pay		135	00
Superannuation			
Gross Pay less Superannuation		135	00
Gross Pay to Date for Tax Purposes		2085	00
Tax Free Pay		853	30
Taxable Pay to Date		1231	70
Tax Due to Date		369	30
Tax Refund			
Deductions Tax		22	20
*N.I. Contribution (Employee)		10	48
1		–	50
2		1	00
3			
4			
5			
6			
7			
Total Deductions		34	18
Net Pay			
F			
G			
Total Amount Payable		100	82
N.I. Contribution (Employer)		18	53
N.I. Total (Employer and Employee)		29	01
H			
*Contracted-out Contribution included above			

Your Pay is made up
as shown above

Miller
K. E.

Kalamazoo
business systems
1-18303
©

Figure 15.3 A Kalamazoo pay advice slip

(iv) The gross pay for tax purposes is then used to find the tax payable – using the Tax Tables provided by the Inland Revenue.

(v) The deductions are then listed, which gives the net pay.

(vi) There are then two lines for any additions to net pay – such as refunds of tax overpaid or expenses incurred. This gives the total amount payable.

(vii) The employer also needs to know what the total cost was for National Insurance – in this case the employer had to pay £18.53, making £29.01 in all.

15.7 Exercises set 15.3 – the Kalamazoo Wages System

(*Note:* To complete a full set of Kalamazoo wages records it is essential to have the correct stationery and invent imaginary names, code numbers, etc. School and colleges wishing to purchase such stationery should approach the Education Department of Kalamazoo Ltd, Mill Lane, Northfield, Birmingham, B31 2RW. For the purpose of the exercises below it is suggested that pay advice notes similar to Figure 15.3 should be ruled up.)

Complete wages advice notes for the four employees shown below whose pay details are as follows:

	1 A.B.	2 C.D.	3 E.F.	4 G.H.
Week	1	7	9	16
Date	12.4.19. .	24.5.19. .	7.6.19. .	26.7.19. .
Earnings A	66.50	122.50	79.80	84.60
Earnings B	4.55	3.80	17.24	16.60
Gross pay	?	?	?	?
Superannuation	3.55	6.32	4.85	5.06
Gross pay for tax purposes	?	?	?	?
Gross pay to date for tax purposes	?	836.50	902.60	1582.50
	(*Note:* It is week 1)			
Free pay	26.15	189.70	297.90	553.60
Taxable pay to date	?	?	?	?
Tax due to date	12.30	193.80	181.20	308.40
Tax paid up to last week	—	202.90	166.70	291.20
Tax	?	?	?	?
		(*careful*)		
NI contribution	5.23	9.30	7.14	7.21
Charity	0.25	0.15	0.15	0.20
Total deductions	?	?	?	?
Net pay	?	?	?	?
Refunds (if any)	?	?	?	?
Total amount payable	?	?	?	?
NI contribution (employer)	9.25	16.44	12.63	13.17
NI Total	?	?	?	?

15.8 Wages and the Bank Giro credit system

More and more people today receive nothing in their wages envelopes but an advice note similar to that described in the last section. The money is simply credited to their Bank Accounts and no actual cash is handled. This is the Bank Giro Credit system and it is stongly recommended as the best way to pay wages.

The basic idea is this: the pay roll is done in the usual way, but instead of going to the bank to draw the pay roll in cash and notes, from which the wage packets may be prepared, the cashier takes to the bank a list of the employees' names. Against each name is the sum due to that employee, which the bank will now transfer to the employee's account. The cashier gives the bank an authorization to debit the firm's account with the total pay roll. The firm has thus paid the wages in a very safe and economical way. No security guards are needed; no tedious counting of notes or handling of coins. For the employee, there is no queuing up to collect his pay packet, and no chance of spending it before he gets home.

16
Book-keeping to 'Final Accounts' – part one: the Trial Balance

16.1 Introduction – what are Final Accounts?

In a free enterprise society businessmen go into business with the idea of making profits, which are the reward of enterprise. But whatever the society, people are likely to be best served in the long run if the utmost economic gain can be achieved at the smallest economic cost.

Final Accounts enable us to check on the conduct of our enterprise, and to discover whether it is being run efficiently. A great variety of statistical control figures can be deduced from the Final Accounts, which enable us to check on our business. Is the manager embezzling the money? Are the staff stealing the stock? Is Mrs Jones, the buyer, an old fuddy-duddy? Does Brown, the office manager, collect too many pretty young typists? Does the dog-lover in the Pet's Corner hold a bigger stock of expensive dog-collars than the public will ever buy? These are the sort of questions you should be able to answer from studying a set of final accounts. If you are able to answer them correctly someone should give you a bonus for promoting the efficiency of the business.

To begin with we will learn the simplest type of Final Accounts: a Trading Account followed by a Profit and Loss Account. The starting-point for these two accounts is the Trial Balance. We prepare from the Trial Balance a Trading Account and a Profit and Loss Account, and by the time we have finished, we have a very much smaller Trial Balance which we then rearrange into a Balance Sheet.

16.2 A closer look at the Trial Balance

A real understanding of Final Accounts must be based first of all on a real understanding of the Trial Balance. Before we try to draw up Trading and Profit and Loss Accounts we must be quite

(*continues on page 222*)

R. JONES
TRIAL BALANCE
as at December 31, 19. .

Ledger Accounts	Notes	£ Dr.	£ Cr.	Notes
Premises Account	Asset	22 450.00		
Capital Account			30 500.00	Liability
Debtors:				
R. Johnson Account	Asset	4 000.00		
M. Thompson Account	Asset	3 530.00		
Creditors:				
R. Lupin Account			600.00	Liability
M. Chuzzlewit Account			1 800.00	Liability
Plant and Machinery Account	Asset	10 250.00		
Office Furniture Account	Asset	8 000.00		
Cash Account	Asset	1 500.00		
Bank Account	Asset	4 000.00		
Bad Debts Account	Loss	500.00		
Carriage in Account	Loss	600.00		
Commission Paid Account	Loss	2 320.00		
Discount Allowed Account	Loss	500.00		
Discount Received Account			300.00	Profit
Rent and Rates Account	Loss	1 000.00		
Carriage Out Account	Loss	300.00		
Salaries Account	Loss	11 800.00		
Warehouse Wages Account	Loss	2 600.00		
Rent Received Account			450.00	Profit
Stock at January 1, 19. .	Trading A/c Item	10 500.00		
Purchases Account	Trading A/c Item	26 000.00		
Sales Account			87 500.00	Trading A/c Item
Purchases Returns Account			450.00	Trading A/c Item
Sales Returns Account	Trading A/c Item	2 250.00		
Drawings Special Item		9 500.00		
		£121 600.00	121 600.00	

In abbreviated form these notes can be condensed into the following groups:

TRIAL BALANCE		Dr.	Cr.
	(a)	Assets	Liabilities
	(b)	Losses	Profits
	(c)	3 Trading Items	2 Trading Items
	(d)	Drawings	

sure we can always draw up a Trial Balance from any given set of figures.

Consider the Trial Balance on page 221, which has had notes added on each line:

The student here has the key to a real understanding of the Trial Balance. The following points are important:

(a)   *Assets and liabilities*. If an account is an Asset Account it must have a debit balance and come in the debit column. The moment it ceases to have a debit balance it crosses over the columns and becomes a liability. The best example of this is the Bank Account. The moment it ceases to be an asset, because we draw a cheque that is greater than the money on deposit, the account becomes a bank overdraft and becomes a liability. As fast as the bank computer prints its warning sign about the overdraft, the Bank Account crosses from the debit column to the credit column of the Trial Balance.

In the same way capital is nearly always a liability, but when the proprietor loses all his capital, and develops a **deficit on Capital Account**, the Capital Account ceases to have a credit balance. It crosses over from the credit side to the debit side, becoming an asset of the business – but a rather unsatisfactory one. The next thing that usually happens is that the proprietor goes out of business, or is bankrupted and forced out of business.

(b)   *Losses and profits*. These are the items which will be taken into account in the Final Accounts when we try to work out the profitability or otherwise of the business. Some of them will go into the Trading Account with the Trading Account items shown in part (c) but most of them will be dealt with in the Profit and Loss Account. (It is a pity we call it the 'Profit and Loss Account'; 'Loss and Profit' Account would be so much more sensible. The losses are the debits and the profits are the credits.) When asked to arrange a list of balances into a Trial Balance, the student can be sure that any losses will be debit balances and any profits will be credit balances.

(c)   *Trading Account Items*. A full explanation will be given of these items in the next chapter. For the present the student should learn by heart the layout of these accounts in the Trial Balance, which is shown below:

TRADING ACCOUNT ITEMS IN THE TRIAL BALANCE

Dr.	Cr.
Stock at beginning of year	—
Purchases	Sales
Sales Returns	Purchases Returns

(d)   *Drawings*. This is a rather special item. It actually represents some of the future profits drawn out. As profits are added to the capital, which is always a credit item, drawings will clearly be a debit item. A full discussion of what is implied by drawings is given later in 'Drawings and Interest on Drawings'.

16.3   Causes of confusion in the Trial Balance

There are one or two confusing items in a Trial Balance. A word of warning will save you hours of looking for mistakes.

(a)   *Returns In and Returns Out*. One of these is a debit balance and one is a credit balance.

Returns In is the return of something we have sold, which the purchaser is dissatisfied with. It is therefore a sale returned, and is a debit balance, as shown in the Trial Balance above and in note (c) above.

Returns Out is the return of something we do not want that we have purchased previously. It is therefore a purchase returned and is a credit balance as shown in the Trial Balance and note (c).

(b)   *Carriage In and Carriage Out*. If Returns In and Returns Out are on opposite sides of the Trial Balance it seems as if Carriage In and Carriage Out ought to be on opposite sides too. This is very deceptive, but in fact both are *losses* and must therefore be debit balances. Carriage In and Carriage Out have to be kept separate because one is dealt with in the Trading Account and one in the Profit and Loss Account. Carriage In is explained on page 234, Carriage Out on page 244. Remember then, Carriage In and Carriage Out are both debit balances.

(c)   *Provisions for bad debts and provisions for depreciation*. These are dealt with in due course, but for the present it is important to realize that they are not losses. They do not come into the debit column. In fact they are sums of profit tucked away in anticipation of bad debts and wear and tear on assets. They really belong to the owner of the business since they are some of his profits earned in years gone by. They must be put in the credit column, and a full discussion of them follows in the chapter on Adjustments (page 296 and page 307).

Now consider the following example:

Example
Prepare a Trial Balance from the following balances which were extracted from the books of R. Gosling on May 31, 19. .:

	£
Trade Expenses	2 602.50
Sales	24 000.00
Purchases	5 300.00
Cash in Hand	303.25
Freehold Property	34 000.00
Sundry Debtors	4 002.50
Stock in Trade at start	6 903.75
Sundry Creditors	2 504.75
Bank Overdraft	1 504.25
Plant and Machinery	10 000.00
Returns Inward	501.50
Discount Received	504.50
Capital	27 100.00
Rent and Rates	3 100.00
Office Expenses	3 900.00
Loan from A. Friend	15 000.00

A quick check through will enable us to write the following notes by each item, and prepare the Trial Balance.

TRIAL BALANCE
as at May 31 19. .

Name of Account	Note	£ Dr.	£ Cr.
Trade Expenses	Loss	2 602.50	
Sales	Trading Account item		24 000.00
Purchases	Trading Account item	5 300.00	
Cash in Hand	Asset	303.25	
Freehold Property	Asset	34 000.00	
Sundry Debtors	Asset	4 002.50	
Stock in Trade at start	Trading Account item	6 903.75	
Sundry Creditors	Liability		2 504.75
Bank Overdraft	Liability		1 504.25
Plant and Machinery	Asset	10 000.00	
Returns Inwards (Sales Returns)	Trading Account item	501.50	
Discount Received	Profit		504.50
Capital	Liability		27 100.00
Rent and Rates	Loss	3 100.00	
Offices Expenses	Loss	3 900.00	
Loan from A. Friend	Liability		15 000.00
		£70 613.50	70 613.50

You should now prepare several Trial Balances from the information given in the exercises that follow, so that you develop facility at placing these balances properly in the Dr. or Cr. columns.

16.4 Exercises set 16.1 – The Trial Balance

1. Prepare a Trial Balance from the following details taken from R. George's Ledger on December 31.

	£
Sundry Debtors	33 750.00
Sundry Creditors	2 500.00
Premises	120 000.00
Furniture and Fittings	30 000.00
Rates	4 500.00
Cash in Hand	750.00
Cash at Bank	13 000.00
Capital	135 500.00
Drawings	13 750.00
Purchases	130 000.00
Sales	287 500.00
Returns Inwards	10 500.00
Returns Outwards	17 125.00
Factory Wages	34 250.00
Carriage Inwards	1 250.00
Carriage Outwards	500.00
Salaries	27 500.00
Rent received	5 750.00
Stock, January 1	26 000.00
Insurance	2 125.00
Bad Debts	500.00

2. The following is the list of a trader's accounts at March 31. Take out the Trial Balance.

Bad Debts Account £700.00
Carriage Inwards £635.00
Discount Received £925.00
Lighting and Heating Account
£1 400.00
Factory Wages £24 625.00
Office Salaries £23 045.00
Rent Account £6 500.00
Sales Account £132 955.00
Drawings £13 830.00
Debtors: A. Jones £3 100.00, B. Brown
£550.00
Creditors: C. Richards £6 250.00
Postage Account £1 080.00

Bank Account £4 595.00
Discount Allowed £680.00
General Expenses Account £2 980.00
Machinery £27 500.00
Motor Vehicles Account £14 000.00
Purchases Account £46 080.00
Returns Outwards £2 180.00
M. Tyler's Capital Account £47 360.00
Stock at April 1 last £18 370.00

(RSA – Adapted)

3. The following is the list of Peter Hyde's accounts at March 31. Prepare the Trial Balance.

Stock at April 1 last £75 000.00
Sales Account £425 000.00
Carriage Inwards £500.00
Rents and Rates £1 875.00
Postage Account £425.00
Printing and Stationery £1 400.00
Bank Interest Paid £450.00
Creditor: C. Bryant £3 800.00
Cash in Hand £550.00
Machinery and Plant £85 000.00
Carriage Out £250.00
Drawings £8 800.00

Purchases Account £185 000.00
Factory Wages Account £37 500.00
Repairs £11 250.00
Insurance £3 750.00
Travelling Expenses £4 750.00
Discount Received £1 250.00
Debtors: R. Cross £5 800.00
B. Thomas £2 750.00
Bank Overdraft £4 800.00
Buildings £170 000.00
Capital £165 700.00
Advertising £5 500.00

4. The following is a list of a trader's accounts at March 31. Take out a Trial Balance.

Bad Debts £480.00
Bank Account £8 113.00
Discounts Received £1 754.50
Travelling Expenses £953.00
Machinery £53 000.00
Motor Vehicles £12 500.00
Purchases £87 752.50
Returns Outward £2 302.50
M. Jones's Capital £92 720.00
Stock at April 1 last £19 810.00
Creditor: A. Richards £2 502.50

Light and heating £2 272.50
Repairs to plant £5 260.00
General Expenses £2 951.00
Redecorations £2 802.50
Factory Wages £31 252.50
Salaries £12 002.50
Rents Account £9 500.00
Sales Account £165 020.00
Drawings £9 700.00
Debtors: R. Thomas £3 750.00
B. Brown £1 500.00
Postage Account £700.00

5. From the following prepare B. Perkins's Trial Balance, as at December 31:

	£
Capital	426 000.00
Rates and Insurance	5 400.50
Light and Heat	3 684.00
Purchases	941 915.50
General Factory Expenses	27 500.00
Sales	1 697 500.00
Stock at beginning of year	148 500.00
Postage	3 525.80
Office Expenses	4 025.20
Bank Loan	83 000.00
Returns In	25 000.00
Returns Out	20 000.00
Cash in Hand	2 775.50
Machinery	396 000.00
Office Salaries	74 949.00

Warehouse Wages	106 850.00
Discount Received	7 850.00
Creditors	93 000.00
Debtors	171 000.00
Carriage In	6 224.50
Bad Debts	4 250.00
Commission Received	2 250.00
Motor Vehicles	22 500.00
Furniture	65 000.00
Premises	230 000.00
Goodwill (asset)	24 000.00
Cash at Bank	26 500.00
Investment in Harrow Ltd	40 000.00

6. In a Trial Balance you are asked to prepare, the following items appear. Copy out and complete:

Name of Account	*Does it go in the Dr. or Cr. Column?*	*Why?*
1 Motor Vehicles		
2 Creditor A. Jones		
3 Capital		
4 Light and Heat Account		
5 Rent Received Account		
6 Drawings		

7. A. Jaffa extracts the following balances from his Ledger on December 31. Present them in the form of a Trial Balance.

	£
Cash in Hand	125
Cash at Bank	3 125
Sales	36 325
Purchases	11 750
Motor Vehicles	6 250
Rent and Rates	625
Light and Heat	300
Carriage In	250
Carriage Out	175
Opening Stock at January 1	9 125
Commission Received	675
Capital	40 000
Drawings	4 250
Returns Outwards	800
Returns Inwards	825
Warehouse Wages	7 600
Office Salaries	4 900
Debtors	11 825
Creditors	2 825
Furniture and Fittings	4 000

Land and Buildings	23 000
Loan from Bank	
(borrowed on December 30)	7 500

(East Anglian Examination Board – Adapted)

8. M. Lucas extracts the following balances from his Ledger on December 31. Present them in the form of a Trial Balance.

	£
Capital at July 1	90 000
Rent and Rates	1 750
Purchases	77 500
Audit Fee	650
Sales	127 500
Stock at July 1	25 000
Telephone	500
Bank Overdraft	2 750
Returns Inward	1 250
Returns Outward	2 500
Cash in Hand	850
Machinery	25 000
Salaries	16 250
Factory Wages	19 500
Discount Received	1 250
Creditors	7 750
Debtors	13 500
Carriage Outwards	500
Bad Debts	750
Commission Received	250
Furniture	8 000
Premises	37 000
Goodwill	4 000

9. The following Trial Balance has been prepared from R. Joiner's books by an inefficient book-keeper. You are asked to rewrite it correctly.

TRIAL BALANCE
as at 28 February, 19. .

	Dr. £	Cr. £
Capital at start		33 000
Premises	27 000	
Drawings		4 750
Plant and Machinery	14 850	
Stock at March 1		4 500
Office Furniture, March 1	3 500	
Insurance	425	
Office Salaries		9 950
Commission Received		800
Bank Loan	5 000	

Cash at Bank	3 250	
Bad Debt	325	
Discount Allowed		450
Debtors and Creditors	3 100	2 900
Returns Inwards		400
Returns Outwards	200	
Purchases and Sales	28 500	61 250
Rent Paid	2 150	
	£88 300	£118 000

10. The following Trial Balance of a sole trader is incorrect, although it adds up to the same total on both sides.

TRIAL BALANCE
as at June 30, 19. .

	Dr. £	Cr. £
Capital at July 1	44 752.50	
Drawings		5 252.50
Stock at July 1	18 675.00	
Purchases	117 001.25	
Sales		197 126.25
Wages and Salaries	31 025.00	
Bank Overdraft	4 875.00	
Equipment	18 000.00	
Carriage Outwards		1 152.50
Returns Inwards	525.00	
Provision for Bad Debts	1 752.50	
Returns Outwards		1 450.00
Discount Allowed	1 428.75	
Discount Received		1 578.75
Rent, Rates, and Insurance	5 575.00	
Motor Vehicles	7 375.00	
Cash in Hand	550.00	
Sundry Creditors	24 626.25	
Sundry Debtors		69 601.25
	£276 161.25	£276 161.25

Draw up a corrected Trial Balance.

17
Book-keeping to 'Final Accounts' – part two: the Trading Account

17.1 The profit on a simple transaction

Imagine a simple transaction. I buy a bar of chocolate for £0.20 and sell it for £0.25. Clearly the profit on trading is £0.05, for profit is the difference between the cost price and selling price.

The very simple Trading Account recording this set of transactions would read as follows:

TRADING ACCOUNT
for year ending December 31, 19. .

	£		£
Purchases	0.20	Sales	0.25
Gross Profit	0.05		
	£0.25		£0.25

Note these points

(a) Every Trading Account must bear at the top the phrase '*for .... ending .... 19. .*' In this case it was a year ending on December 31.

(b) The profit at the end of a Trading Account is called the **Gross Profit** which means 'Fat Profit' or 'Overall Profit'. The reason will be made clear later.

(c) The Gross Profit is the difference between the selling price and the cost of the sales.

17.2 Final Accounts and Closing Journal Entries

In Chapter 6 (on Journal Entries), the only common type of Journal Entry that was not discussed was a Closing Journal Entry. These are used to close off the Nominal Accounts and to transfer their balances to the Trading Account or the Profit and Loss Account.

Consider the Sales Account in the Trial Balance of Section 16.2 page 221. It has a credit balance of £87 500.00. When we transfer this to the Trading Account in order to work out the Gross Profit, we close off the Sales Account.

Here it is before and after closure.

SALES ACCOUNT   L49

		£
	Jan., Feb., Mar., etc., for 12 months totalling	87 500.00

Figure 17.1   A Sales Account before closure

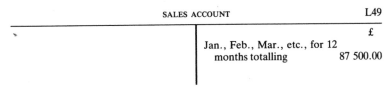

| 19. . Dec. 31 | Sales Account   Dr. Trading Account Being transfer of Sales figure to Trading Account to determine gross profit | L49 L186 | £ 87 500.00 | £ J1 87 500.00 |

Figure 17.2   A closing Journal Entry

SALES ACCOUNT   L49

19. . Dec. 31	Trading Account	£ 87 500.00	19. . Jan., Feb., Mar., etc., for 12 months totalling	£ 87 500.00
		£87 500.00		£87 500.00

Figure 17.3   The Sales Account closed off for the year

The result of this Closing Entry is that the Sales Account no longer has a balance on it, it is clear, and therefore vanishes from the Trial Balance. Its place has been taken by the entry in the Trading Account which now reads:

TRADING ACCOUNT   L186
for year ended December 31, 19. .

		£
	Sales	87 500.00

Figure 17.4   Starting the Trading Account

In every transfer into the Trading Account we shall be doing the same sort of Closing Entry, clearing off completely the balances on the Nominal Accounts we close, and transferring their balances to the Trading Account.

17.3   The true sales figure

We now have an entry for sales in our Trading Account which reads £87 500.00. But is this the true sales figure for our business? Did we really sell £87 500.00 worth of goods? If we are going to find the Gross Profit we must know the correct purchase price and the correct selling price. This figure of £87 500.00 is not the correct sales figure because there were some Sales Returns. Looking back to the Trial Balance again, page 221 we find that the Sales Returns Account has a balance of £2 250.00. It looks like this:

	SALES RETURNS ACCOUNT		L65
	£		
Jan., Feb., Mar., etc., coming to a total of	2 250.00		

Figure 17.5   **The Sales Returns Account before closure**

Clearly this should be closed off and the entry transferred to the Trading Account. Sticking to the rules of strict double entry we must this time debit the Trading Account and credit the Sales Returns Account. This will clear the Sales Returns Account and leave the Trading Account looking like this:

	TRADING ACCOUNT		L186
	for year ending December 31, 19. .		
	£		£
Sales Returns	2 250.00	Sales	87 500.00

Figure 17.6   **Sales on the Trading Account (by strict Double Entry)**

In fact this is very awkward, for it leaves us not knowing quite what the sales figure really was: we have to do some mental arithmetic to find out. For the sake of greater clarity, and 'good style', we adopt a little trick. Instead of debiting the Trading Account with the £2 250.00 returns we *deduct* these returns from the credit side. Since deducting them from the credit side is exactly the same as adding them to the debit side, we still keep a good double entry. We have, in order to get a really clear picture of the sales for the year, abandoned strict double entry. All students should appreciate that **clear presentation is the vital thing in Final Accounts. We must be able to see the important figure instantly.**

Our Trading Account now looks like this:

<table>
<thead>
<tr><th>TRADING ACCOUNT
for year ending December 31, 19. .</th><th>L186</th></tr>
</thead>
<tbody>
<tr><td></td><td>£</td></tr>
<tr><td>Sales</td><td>87 500.00</td></tr>
<tr><td>*Less* Returns</td><td>2 250.00</td></tr>
<tr><td>Net Turnover</td><td>85 250.00</td></tr>
</tbody>
</table>

Figure 17.7   Trading Account showing the true Sales Figure

The turnover of a business

In the Trading Account of Figure 17.7 we have now brought out one of the vital figures of business. Whenever a business is bought or sold one of the important things to be taken into account in determining the price is the turnover figure, or **net turnover**. The word 'net' means 'clean', and implies that the returns have been deducted from the sales figure to give a clear figure of actual turnover.

Why is turnover so important? Naturally it reflects the 'busy-ness' of the business. If a business is prosperous, the public are buying and the proprietor will make good profits. If a business has only a small turnover it offers poor prospects to the purchaser, so that he will not pay a high price for it. Some businessmen specialize in curing the ills of bad businesses; they take over a firm cheaply because it has a poor turnover, improve it and restore it to good heart. They then sell it at a profit. It now offers a new owner a good prospect of profitability.

The reason we adopt the good style shown in Figure 17.7 is because it brings out clearly the net turnover figure.

17.4   The true purchases figure

Having found the true sales figure we now have to discover what these sales cost us, because the Gross Profit is the difference between the sales figure and the **cost of the sales**. To find the cost of the sales is much more difficult than finding the true sales figure, because some of the things that we sold were purchased last year, and the purchases figure on the Purchases Account does not include them. They are to be found on the Stock Account. We must build up our idea on the **Cost of sales** figure in stages.

17.5   Finding the cost of the sales

Stage 1 of finding the cost of sales – finding the net purchases figure
This is the same as the calculation of the true sales figure. Referring back to the Trial Balance on page 221 we find that the

Purchases Account and the Purchases Returns Account are as follows:

PURCHASES ACCOUNT		L101
	£	
Total balances for year	26 000.00	

PURCHASES RETURNS ACCOUNT		L102
		£
	Total balances for year	450.00

Figure 17.8   Purchases Account and Purchases Returns Account before closure

Closing these off in the same way as before, and adopting the good style used to produce the sales figure, we now have a Trading Account that reads:

TRADING ACCOUNT					L186
for year ending December 31, 19. .					
	£				£
Purchases	26 000.00		Sales		87 500.00
Less Returns	450.00		*Less* Returns		2 250.00
Net Purchases		25 550.00	Net Turnover		85 250.00

Figure 17.9   Stage 1 – finding the net purchases figure

Stage 2 of finding the cost of sales – carriage in and other increases in the purchase price

We must now deal with the difficulty referred to in 17.4 above. Is the figure shown in Figure 17.9 the true purchases figure? In fact it is not, because the goods that we purchased probably cost us more than this. In the Trial Balance we find that Carriage In was £600.00 for the year. Carriage In is the carriage paid on goods coming into the business, which have been purchased at an **ex works** price. If we pay £500 for goods ex works, and pay £25 delivery charges, the true purchase price is £525. Everyone who buys a car finds to his disgust that a charge for delivery is added to the price quoted by the dealer. The true purchase price of the car is the list price plus the delivery charge.

Carriage In is not the only charge that may be added, another very common one is Customs Duty on imported goods. These again represent an increase in the purchase price, and should really be added to the purchases figure.

If we now transfer the Carriage In to the Trading Account by a Closing Journal Entry we have:

TRADING ACCOUNT   L186
for year ending December 31, 19. .

	£			£
Purchases	26 000.00		Sales	87 500.00
Carriage In	600.00		*Less* Returns	2 250.00
	26 600.00		Net Turnover	85 250.00
Less Returns	450.00			
Net Purchases		26 150.00		

Figure 17.10   **Stage 2 – taking Carriage In into account**

Note: The best place to add the Carriage In is as shown in the illustration. It is added in business life *before* we even think of returns.

Stage 3 of finding the cost of sales – stock at beginning of year

We now have a figure of £26 150.00 for the net purchases figure. Is this the cost price of the goods we sold? Unfortunately not, because if we are running our business sensibly we shall sell off goods that are already in stock at the beginning of the year before we sell off the purchases we are buying in January, February, etc. Most businesses operate a first-in, first-out system of dealing with stock, to clear goods before they depreciate. Stage 3 of finding the cost of sales figure involves transferring the Opening Stock at January 1, valued on the Trading Account at £10 500.00, to the Trading Account. This is why the figures for Purchases in Figures 17.9 and 17.10 were indented a little, to have a clear line for the addition of this stock and the net purchase figure. We have now:

TRADING ACCOUNT   L186
for year ending December 31, 19. .

	£	£		£
Opening Stock		10 500.00	Sales	87 500.00
Purchases	26 000.00		*Less* Returns	2 250.00
Carriage In	600.00			
			Net Turnover	85 250.00
	26 600.00			
Less Returns	450.00			
Net Purchases		26 150.00		
Total Stock Available		36 650.00		

Figure 17.11   **Stage 3 – taking account of 'stock at start'**

Note: The phrase 'total stock available' accurately describes the sum of £36 650.00 since this is the stock we had at the beginning of the year, plus the stock purchased (and not returned) during the year. It is therefore the stock that has been available during the present year.

Stage 4 of finding the cost of sales – closing stock
We now come to one of the vital things in Final Accounts, the adjustment needed for closing stock. Stock valuation is a subject of sufficient importance to merit a chapter by itself, and is dealt with in Chapter 21, page 271. All we need say here is that stock still in hand at the close of the financial year, must be counted, valued, and totalled up. This gives us the valuation of stock in hand that has not been sold.

Having found the stock figure, which must be given to us in any exercise we do on the Trading Account, but which in real life must be found by actually taking stock, we need to bring this figure into the Trading Account. Here again good style is important. First let us look at the Stock Account as it is at present. We see that it is actually clear.

		STOCK ACCOUNT					L37
19. . Jan. 1	Balance	b/d	£ 10 500.00	19. . Dec. 31	Transfer to Trading Account		£ 10 500.00

Figure 17.12 The Stock Account with 'opening stock' closed off to Trading Account

Taking the new figure for closing stock as £7 800 we must now record this stock figure on the Stock Account because it is one of the assets of the business. This requires a Journal Entry debiting the Stock Account with the stock value £7 800.00. Here is this Journal Entry:

19. . Dec. 31	Stock Account Dr. Trading Account Being stock at close of year re- corded in books at this date	L37 L186	£ 7 800.00	£ 7 800.00

Figure 17.13   Journalizing Closing Stock

and the Stock Account now reads as follows:

		STOCK ACCOUNT				L37
19. . Jan. 1	Balance	£ 10 500.00	19. . Dec. 31	Transfer to Trading Account		£ 10 500.00
19. . Jan. 1	New valuation	£ 7 800.00				

Figure 17.14   Re-opening Stock Account with the closing stock figure

When we do the other half of the double entry we should, according to strict double entry, credit the Trading Account with the closing stock. This will unfortunately spoil the clarity of the figures we are trying to produce. What we want to bring out clearly is the cost of the stock sold. If we deduct the closing stock from the total stock available we shall produce the cost of the stock sold, for what is not left in stock must have been sold. As the stock and the purchases are at cost price we shall have the sales at cost price, i.e. the cost of stock sold. Our Trading Account how looks like this:

TRADING ACCOUNT   L186
for year ending December 31, 19. .

	£	£		£
Opening Stock		10 500.00	By Sales	87 500.00
Purchases	26 000.00		*Less* Returns	2 250.00
Carriage In	600.00			
			Net Turnover	85 250.00
	26 600.00			
Less Returns	450.00			
Net Purchases		26 150.00		
Total Stock Available		36 650.00		
Less Closing Stock		7 800.00		
Cost of Stock Sold		28 850.00		

Figure 17.15   Bringing out the cost of the stock sold

Stage 5 of finding the cost of sales – factory or warehouse expenses

The last stage in finding the Gross Profit is to enter in the Trading Account any items of expenses which are better dealt with there than in the Profit and Loss Account. This is one of those grey areas, neither black nor white, where people often argue about whether expenses should go in the Trading Account at all, and if so, which.

Probably the best guide is that the Profit and Loss Account should be kept for the selling and administrative expenses. Any expense which is concerned with the production or warehousing of the goods should be dealt with at this stage in the Trading Account. Later we shall learn how to keep a Manufacturing Account, but at present the best policy is to put such items in the Trading Account.

The only expense of this type in our Trial Balance is the Warehouse Wages Account, £2 600.00

When we close the Warehouse Wages Account and transfer the wages to the Trading Account we finish up with the following Trading Account which shows us the Gross Profit on trading clearly and easily. The cost of sales, deducted from the net turnover gives us the Gross Profit.

TRADING ACCOUNT   L186
for year ending December 31, 19. .

	£	£		£
Opening Stock		10 500.00	Sales	87 500.00
Purchases	26 000.00		*Less* Returns	2 250.00
Carriage In	600.00			
			Net Turnover	85 250.00
	26 600.00			
Less Returns	450.00			
Net Purchases		26 150.00		
Total Stock Available		36 650.00		
Less Closing Stock		7 800.00		
Cost of Stock Sold		28 850.00		
Warehouse Wages		2 600.00		
Cost of Sales		31 450.00		
Gross Profit (transferred to Profit and Loss Account)		53 800.00		
		£85 250.00		£85 250.00

Figure 17.16   A Trading Account in good style

The Profit and Loss Account is now open and looks as follows:

PROFIT AND LOSS ACCOUNT   L187
for year ending December 31, 19. .

	£
Gross Profit (transferred from Trading Account)	53 800.00

Figure 17.17   Starting the Profit and Loss Account with the gross profit

17.6   Some definintions connected with the Trading Account

The following definitions are worth learning:

Gross Profit – is the difference between the net sales of the business, and the cost of these sales.

Cost of stock sold – is the cost of the stock we had at first, plus the cost of the net purchases, minus the cost of the unsold portion of the stock.

Cost of sales – is the cost of the stock sold, plus the expenses of handling that stock.

The turnover of a business – is the net sales, that is the sales less sales returns.

The student should now practise preparing Trading Accounts in good style, to bring out the net turnover and the cost of sales.

17.7 Exercises set 17.1 – Trading Accounts

1. From the following particulars prepare the Trading Account of J. Weaver for the year ended December 31 19. .:
   Sales £135 282.50; Purchases £76 378.75; Sales Returns £782.50; Purchases Returns £878.75; Stock January 1 £8 827.50; Stock December 31 £9 272.00.

2. From the following particulars prepare the Trading Account of C. Cooper for the year ended December 31, 19. .
   Stock January 1 £6 398.25; Purchases £236 632.00; Purchases Returns £3 432.00; Sales £376 316.25 Sales Returns £6 316.25; Stock December 31 £13 677.50; Factory Wages £13 732.50.

3. Prepare the Trading Account of A. S. Brewis for the year ended December 31 19. .:
   Stock January 1 £2 628.25 Cash Purchases £18 627.50; Credit Purchases £36 282.00; Carriage In £1 378.25; Returns Outwards £2 132.50; Cash Sales £28 252.50 Credit Sales £48 362.50; Returns Inwards £362.50; Stock December 31 £3 378.75.

4. Prepare a Trading Account for the year ended December 31, 19. . for J. Lyons from the following information:
   Opening Stock £8 532.50; Purchases £28 632.50; Carriage In £632.50; Customs Duty on Imported Purchases £2 932.50; Purchases Returns £1 381.25; Closing Stock £7 046.00; Wages of warehouse workers £7 397.50; Warehouse expenses £4 132.25 Sales £61 326.50; Sales Returns £1 027.50.

5. At December 31, 19. ., the Trial Balance of E. Randall contained the following items:

	£
Stock at January 1, 19. .	13 925.00
Purchases	34 540.00
Sales	58 210.00
Returns Outwards	975.00
Returns Inwards	1 310
Warehouse Wages	3 500
Wages Owing	100.00
Import Charges	630.00

Randall's Stock at December 31, 19. ., was valued at £12 200.00. Prepare the Trading Account for the year ending December 31, 19. .
                                                        (RSA – Adapted)

6. The following figures relating to a dressmaking business were extracted from the Trial Balance taken out on March 31, 19. . From them select those items you consider should be used in the Trading Account of the business and prepare this account for the quarter ended on that date.

	£
Sales for the quarter	40 000.00
Purchases of cloth, etc.	12 770.00
Purchases of sewing machines	1 900.00
Carriage on goods sold	235.00
Returns to and allowances from suppliers	270.00

Purchases of cardboard boxes, wrapping paper, etc.	150.00
Office heating and lighting	515.00
Heating and lighting of workrooms	1 060.00
Office salaries and expenses	4 360.00
Workroom Wages	8 250.00

Advertising	100.00
Rent and rates (three-quarters workroom, one-quarter office)	2 400.00
Electric power for machines	750.00
Carriage on purchases	160.00
Discounts allowed	180.00

Discounts received	250.00
Stocks of cloth, etc.:	
January 1, 19. .	3 000.00
March 31, 19. .	3 830.00

(*RSA – Adapted*)

7.
(a) From the following information prepare the Trading Account of W. Wigg for the year ending June 30, 19. .:

	£
Stock at start	12 000.00
Purchases	76 025.00
Sales	104 300.00
Stock at close	19 200.00

Returns Outwards	925.00
Returns Inwards	4 300.00
Manufacturing Wages	14 480.00
Carriage Inwards	2 620.00

(b) If the Stock at June 30, 19. ., had been valued at £15 000.00 what would the gross profit have been?

(*RSA – Adapted*)

8. Give the effect of *each* of the following errors on the *Gross Profit* of a business, stating exactly by how much the Gross Profit will be increased or decreased. If you think there would be no change write 'None'.

(a) The sales Returns Book was over-added by £100.
(b) The entries in respect of an invoice for goods bought totalling £300 were omitted from the books.
(c) Carriage on sales had been entered in the Ledger Account as £605 instead of £560.
(d) The closing stock was under-valued by £3 245.
(e) Carriage on purchases had been entered in the Ledger Account as £945 instead of £495.
(f) An amount of £400 in respect of goods returned to a supplier was entered in the Sales Book instead of the Purchases Returns Book.

(RSA – Adapted)

18

Book-keeping to 'Final Accounts' – part three: the Profit and Loss Account

18.1 A revised Trial Balance

Consider what has happened to the Trial Balance drawn up in section 16.2, page 221.

Because of the transfer of items to the Trading Account, a number of the balances shown on that Trial Balance have been cleared off completely, and, as a result, have disappeared from the Trial Balance. In addition, one of the accounts shown on that Trial Balance has changed from one figure to another, and has also changed its character. This is the Stock Account, which formerly was a Nominal Account with a balance of £10 500.00. It was a Nominal Account because the £10 500.00 was there 'in name only', in fact this stock had been sold and replaced by other stock purchased in the year. At first we transferred this £10 500.00 to the Trading Account, leaving the Stock Account clear for a short while, but then we reopened it with the closing stock. This closing stock is not a nominal figure, it is real. (Anyone who likes to check it can count the stock and value it.) It is therefore an asset, but, of course, tomorrow we begin a new year and we shall start selling our stock, so that the real figure today of £7 800 will soon become a nominal figure again. To be really clear about this is a vital part of understanding the stock. Our figure of £7 800.00 is an asset for today, but it will soon become a Nominal Account again, when dealings in stock change the real stock figure from £7 800.00 to some other figure.

If we now look at the revised Trial Balance, after doing the Trading Account, we find that it now appears as in Figure 18.1.

Note: The Trading Account items, and the losses that are best dealt with in the Trading Account have disappeared from the Trial Balance, and have been replaced by the Gross Profit, which starts off the Profit and Loss Account.

R. JONES
TRIAL BALANCE
as at December 31, 19. .

Ledger Account	Notes	£ Dr.	£ Cr.	Notes
Premises Account	Asset	22 450.00		
Capital Account			30 500.00	Liability
Debtors:				
R. Johnson Account	Asset	4 000.00		
M. Thompson Account	Asset	3 530.00		
Creditors:				
R. Lupin Account			600.00	Liability
M. Chuzzlewit Account			1 800.00	Liability
Plant and Machinery Account	Asset	10 250.00		
Office Furniture Account	Asset	8 000.00		
Cash Account	Asset	1 500.00		
Bank Account	Asset	4 000.00		
Stock Account	Asset	7 800.00		
Bad Debts Account	Loss	500.00		
Commission Paid Account	Loss	2 320.00		
Discount Allowed Account	Loss	500.00		
Discount Received Account			300.00	Profit
Rent and Rates Account	Loss	1 000.00		
Carriage Out Account	Loss	300.00		
Salaries Account	Loss	11 800.00		
Rent Received Account			450.00	Profit
Drawings Account	Special Item	9 500.00		
Gross Profit (on Profit and Loss Account)			53 800.00	Profit
		£87 450.00	£87 450.00	

Figure 18.1   A revised Trial Balance after taking out a Trading Account

18.2   Finding the Net Profit – Stage I – transferring the losses

On the Trial Balance above we still have a number of Nominal Accounts, which are either losses or profits. The Loss Accounts are all debit balances. When we clear these accounts off we credit them, to clear the balances from the accounts, and hence from the Trial Balance, and debit the loss in the Profit and Loss Account.

A typical entry would be:

19. .				£	£
Dec. 31	Profit and Loss Account Dr.		L187	500.00	
	Bad Debts Account		L44		500.00
	Being Bad Debts transferred to Profit and Loss Account				

Figure 18.2   Transferring a loss to the Profit and Loss Account

The Bad Debts Account now looks like this:

BAD DEBTS ACCOUNT   L44

19. .		£	19. .		£
July 4	R. Smith	300.00	Dec. 31	Transfer to Profit and	
Oct. 17	M. Pierce	200.00		Loss Account	500.00
		£500.00			£500.00

Figure 18.3   A Loss Account closed

After similar entries in the Journal to close off the other Loss Accounts we have a Profit and Loss Account like this:

PROFIT AND LOSS ACCOUNT
(for year ending December 31, 19. .)

	£		£
Bad Debts	500.00	Gross Profit (transferred	
Commission Paid	2 320.00	from Trading Account)	53 800.00
Discount Allowed	500.00		
Rent and Rates	1 000.00		
Carriage Out	300.00		
Salaries	11 800.00		

Figure 18.4   Losses transferred to the Profit and Loss Account
Note: Carriage out – like most selling expenses – appears in the Profit and Loss Account.

18.3   Finding the Net Profit – Stage II – transferring the profits

It is now the turn of the profits to be transferred into the Profit and Loss Account. At present these nominal Accounts which are profits have credit balances. To clear them and transfer the profits to the Profit and Loss Account we must debit the Nominal Account and credit the Profit and Loss Account. A typical Journal Entry would be:

19. .				£	£
Dec. 31	Discount Received Account Dr.		L154	300.00	
	Profit and Loss Account		L187		300.00
	Being discount received in year transferred to Profit and Loss Account				

Figure 18.5   Transferring a Profit to the Profit and Loss Account

and the Discount Received Account would then be clear as in Figure 18.6.

	DISCOUNT RECEIVED ACCOUNT			L154
19. .		£	19. .	£
Dec. 31 Profit and Loss			Jan., Feb., etc., Sundry Discount	
Account		300.00	totalling	300.00
		£300.00		£300.00

Figure 18.6 A Profit Account closed off

After all the profits have been transferred in this way, the final Profit and Loss Account would be as Figure 18.7

	PROFIT AND LOSS ACCOUNT		L187
	for year ending December 31, 19. .		
	£		£
Bad Debts	500.00	Gross profit (transferred	
Commission Paid	2 320.00	from Trading Account)	53 800.00
Discount Allowed	500.00	Discount Received	300.00
Rent and Rates	1 000.00	Rent Received	450.00
Carriage Out	300.00		
Salaries	11 800.00	Total Profits	54 550.00
Total Expenses	16 420.00		
Net Profit (transferred to			
Capital Account)	38 130.00		
	£54 550.00		£54 550.00

Figure 18.7 A Profit and Loss Account in good style

18.4 Closing the Profit and Loss Account and the Drawings Account

When we have determined the Net Profit of the business the profit belongs to the proprietor, and he may appropriate it for his private use. Since the average small trader has no private means other than the capital invested in his business, he will probably have been drawing sums of money for private purposes during the year. These sums are really drawings in expectation of profits made, and he has therefore already appropriated a good deal of the profit for his private use.

The Net Profit is transferred to the owner's Capital Account as shown in Figure 18.8.

CAPITAL ACCOUNT				L11
	19. .			£
	Jan. 1	Opening		
		Balance		30 500.00
	Dec. 31	Profit and		
		Loss Account		38 130.00

Figure 18.8   The Net Profit transferred to the proprietor's Capital Account

We now want to close the Drawings Account, by transferring the total to the proprietor's Capital Account. The Journal Entry is as follows:

19. .				£	£
Dec. 31	Capital Account Dr.	L11	9 500.00	
	Drawings Account	L69		9 500.00
	Being Drawings for year transferred			

Figure 18.9   Closing the Drawings Account

The Drawings Account is now closed, (see Figure 18.10) and consequently no longer appears on the Trial Balance.

DRAWINGS ACCOUNT							L69
19. .				£	19. .		£
Mar. 31	Bank	CB1	2 000.00		Dec. 31	Transfer to	
June 30	Bank	CB7	2 000.00			Capital	
Sept. 30	Bank	CB12	2 500.00			Account L11	9 500.00
Dec. 31	Bank	CB15	3 000.00				
			£9 500.00				£9 500.00

Figure 18.10   The Drawings Account closed

The Capital Account can now be ruled off and brought down ready for the new financial year, as shown in Figure 18.11.

CAPITAL ACCOUNT						L11
19. .		£	19. .		£	
De. 31	Drawings	9 500.00	Jan. 1	Opening Balance	30 500.00	
31	Balance	59 130.00	Dec. 31	Profit and Loss		
				Account	38 130.00	
		£68 630.00			£68 630.00	
			19. .		£	
			Jan. 1	Balance	59 130.00	

Figure 18.11   The Final Entries in the Capital Account

Our double entry book-keeping has now been brought to a successful conclusion and all that is needed is to marshal the assets in a clear and well-presented Balance Sheet.

18.5 A Trading and Profit and Loss Account

Because a Trading Account is always followed immediately by a Profit and Loss Account some accountants run them in together and use a joint title, calling it a Trading and Profit and Loss Account. This makes absolutely no difference to the working out of these accounts the two parts simply run on from one to the other, as in Figure 18.12.

TRADING AND PROFIT AND LOSS ACCOUNT   L186
(for year ending December 31, 19. .)

	£	£		£
Opening Stock		10 500.00	Sales	87 500.00
Purchases	26 000.00		*Less* Returns	2 250.00
Carriage in	600.00			
			Net Turnover	85 250.00
	26 600.00			
Less Returns	450.00			
Net Purchases		26 150.00		
Total Stock Available		36 650.00		
Less Closing Stock		7 800.00		
Cost of Stock Sold		28 850.00		
To Warehouse Wages		2 600.00		
Cost of Sales		31 450.00		
Gross Profit transferred		53 800.00		
		£85 250.00		£85 250.00
Bad Debts		500.00	Gross Profit (transferred	
Commission Paid		2 320.00	from Trading Account)	53 800.00
Discount Allowed		500.00	Discount Received	300.00
Rent and Rates		1 000.00	Rent Received	450.00
Carriage Out		300.00		
Salaries		11 800.00	Total Profits	54 550.00
Total Expenses		16 420.00		
Net Profit (transferred to				
Capital Account)		38 130.00		
		£54 550.00		£54 550.00

Figure 18.12   A Trading and Profit and Loss Account

You should now prepare a few Profit and Loss Accounts in the exercises which follow. The last exercise, number 6 is of a joint Trading and Profit and Loss Account as in Figure 18.12.

18.6 Exercises set 18.1 – Profit and Loss Accounts

1. From the following figures prepare T. Stebbing's Profit and Loss Account for the half year ended June 30, 19. .:

	£
Gross Profit	26 382.50
Discount Allowed	121.25
Discount Received	682.75
Bad Debts	226.35
Rent and Rates	932.50
Light and Heat	426.25
Packing and Delivery Expenses	1 478.00
Commission Received	532.50
Salaries	11 875.00

2. From the following particulars prepare M. Fletcher's Profit and Loss Account for the year ended December 31, 19. .:

	£
Gross Profit from Trading	36 232.50
Selling Expenses	6 227.50
Salaries	11 826.25
Discount Allowed	1 263.25
Discount Received	1 432.00
Rent, Rates, and Insurance	4 132.50

3. R. Dwyer's Trial Balance contains the following items other than assets and liabilities. From them prepare his Profit and Loss Account for year ending December 31, 19. .:

	£
Gross Trading Profit	56 300.00
Salaries	17 252.50
Selling Expenses	2 132.50
Package Materials	7 127.75
Rent, etc.	9 232.50
Discount Received	239.25
Discount Allowed	717.50

Salaries of £322.50 are due to a member of staff who is absent and these are to be included in the Profit and Loss Account.

4. From the following particulars prepare the Trading Account and then the Profit and Loss Account of R. Mildred, for the year ending June 30, 19. .:

	£
Stock at start, July 1, 19. .	8 802.75
Discount allowed	387.50
Insurance Premiums	220.75
Salaries	22 132.50
Purchases	42 752.50
Returns Outwards	360.70
Printing and Stationery	429.40
Rent and Rates	2 211.25
Sales	122 583.00
Returns Inwards	1 384.25
General Expenses	14 625.75
Telephone Account	927.50
Stock, June 30, 19. .	7 928.25
Discount Received	410.25
Interest paid on loans	452.75
Light and Heat	323.25
Motor Vehicle Expenses	2 850.75

5. From the following list of balances you are required to prepare the Trading and Profit and Loss Accounts for the year ending March 31, 19. ., of Robert Dingley, a wholesale merchant:

	£
Returns Outwards	900.00
Carriage Outwards	1 050.50
Sales	239 756.25
Wages and Salaries	38 980.00
(Half to Trading Account; half to Profit and Loss Account)	
Returns Inwards	1 756.25
Commission Paid	9 085.80
Commission Received	1 285.00
Carriage Inwards	1 560.00
Motor Van Expenses	3 811.00
Stock, April 1, 19. .	27 530.00
Purchases	120 260.00
Bank Interest and Charges	575.00
Rent, Rates, and Insurance	5 720.50
General Expenses	19 252.50
Bad Debts	1 050.00
Discount Allowed	650.45
Discount Received	400.75

In preparing your account you should note the following:

(a) Stock on March 31, 19. ., was valued at £23 940.00
(b) *No* Trial Balance or Balance Sheet is required

(RSA – Adapted)

6. From the following prepare R. Mowler's Trading and Profit and Loss Account for the quarter ended September 30, 19. ., using such of the figures as you think should be used:

	£
Capital	356 000.00
Rent and Rates	5 250.00
Purchases	232 500.00
Audit Fee	3 750.00
Sales	367 500.00
Stock at July 1, 19. .	45 000.00
Telephone	1 500.00
Bank Overdraft	8 250.00
Returns Inwards	3 750.00
Returns Outwards	7 500.00
Cash in Hand	1 750.00
Machinery	75 000.00
Salaries	28 750.00
Factory Wages	28 500.00
Discount Received	3 750.00
Creditors	23 250.00
Debtors	40 500.00
Carriage Outwards	1 500.00
Bad Debts	2 250.00
Commission Received	750.00
Furniture, July 1, 19. .	24 000.00
Premises, July 1, 19. .	225 000.00
Goodwill (this is an asset)	48 000.00

Stock at September 30, 19. ., was valued at £38 750.00.

19
Book-keeping to 'Final Accounts' – part four: the Balance Sheet

19.1 The residue of the Trial Balance

The Trial Balance originally given in Section 16.2 page 221, and revised in Section 18.1 page 243 has now been reduced still more. By closing off further accounts and transferring them to the Profit and Loss Account we have caused all the accounts with debit balances, which were losses, to disappear from the Trial Balance, and all the accounts with credit balances, which were profits, to do likewise.

We have also closed off the Drawings Account into the Capital

		R. JONES			
		TRIAL BALANCE			
		as at December 31, 19. .			
Ledger Accounts	Notes	Dr. £		Cr. £	Notes
Premises Account	Asset	22 450.00			
Capital Account				59 130.00	Liability
Debtors:					
R. Johnson Account	Asset	4 000.00			
M. Thompson Account	Asset	3 530.00			
Creditors:					
R. Lupin Account				600.00	Liability
M. Chuzzlewit Account				1 800.00	Liability
Plant and Machinery Account	Asset	10 250.00			
Office Furniture Account	Asset	8 000.00			
Cash Account	Asset	1 500.00			
Bank Account	Asset	4 000.00			
Stock Account	Asset	7 800.00			
		£	61 530.00	61 530.00	

Figure 19.1 The residue of the Trial Balance

Account. The Capital Account, a liability of the business, has therefore changed from its original balance of £30 500.00 to a new balance of £59 130.00 since we now owe the proprietor not only what he put into the business but also the profit resulting from the year's activities, which has been added to Capital Account.

As a result of these activities the Trial Balance now contains only the residual items which will continue into the next year's business – the assets and liabilities of the firm which will go on being used, or honoured, over the course of the next year. The problem now is to present these in such a way as to show 'a true and fair view' of the business to anyone interested in it. This means to *the owner*, the *prospective buyer*, should the owner be thinking of selling, or anyone else interested, like the Tax Authorities. Our Trial Balance now looks as in Figure 19.1.

19.2   History makes a mess of things – the Balance Sheet reversed

In Section 1.7 page 5, it was pointed out that by a strange quirk of history it has become usual to write the Balance Sheet the wrong way round in Great Britain and countries associated with her. The historical circumstances are worth noting.

Simon Stevin of Bruges invented the Balance Sheet in the sixteenth century. He called it a 'Statement of Affairs' of the business, a phrase which we still use today in connexion with Single Entry, dealt with in Chapter 25, page 352. Unfortunately, in taking the totals of the Assets and Liabilities out of the books he crossed them over and wrote them down with the assets on the right-hand side and the liabilities on the left. We don't quite know why he did this, probably he was thinking of it as if he were posting the Cash Book. It was quite wrong, but as the Balance Sheet is only a sheet of paper, not part of the real books, it doesn't make any difference, except that it is misleading to the student.

What made matters worse was that the British Parliament, not knowing its book-keeping, passed an Act which made this type of Balance Sheet the law of Great Britain. The Company Act of 1856 included, in Table B, a set of model articles which referred to a Balance Sheet which 'shall be presented to the members at the Annual General Meeting in the form annexed to this table, or as near thereto as the circumstances permit' (Article 72, 1856 Act). The Balance Sheet given was in Simon Stevin's form, with the assets on the right-hand side, and the liabilities on the left-hand side.

A British Act of Parliament, even when it makes absolute rubbish, is so revered a document that we all obey it. Other nations, which have less respect for formal nonsense, produce their Balance Sheets in the sensible form; as the accounts appear in the Trial Balance; with the assets on the left-hand side and the liabilities on the right-hand side. Fortunately British policies do change in time, and harmonization with the EEC countries may yet produce a British Balance Sheet in correct style.

Remember, then that although it makes no difference at all it is customary in Great Britain and associated countries to put the Balance Sheet with sides reversed: assets on the right, liabilities on the left.

19.3 The Order of Permanence and the Order of Liquidity

In Chapter 1 the student prepared a number of Balance Sheets with the assets and liabilities arranged in the Order of Liquidity, that is to say with the most liquid assets first. An alternative order is the Order of Permanence, with the least liquid assets first. In order to make these two orders clear, the Balance Sheet of R. Jones drawn up from the residue of the Trial Balance in Figure 19.1 is presented twice. Note that the changes in the Capital Account have been brought into the Balance Sheet. This is a useful and popular idea, showing the owner exactly how his new capital figure was derived.

R. JONES
BALANCE SHEET
as at December 31, 19. .
Order of liquidity

	£		£
CURRENT LIABILITIES		CURRENT ASSETS	
Sundry Creditors	2 400.00	Cash in Hand	1 500.00
		Cash at Bank	4 000.00
		Sundry Debtors	7 530.00
LONG-TERM LIABILITIES	0.00	Stock	7 800.00
			20 830.00
CAPITAL	£	FIXED ASSETS	£
At Start	30 500.00	Office Furniture	8 000.00
Add		Plant and	
Profits 38 130.00		Machinery	10 250.00
Less		Premises	22 450.00
Drawings 9 500.00			40 700.00
	28 630.00		
	59 130.00		
	£61 530.00		£61 530.00

Figure 19.2   A Balance Sheet in the order of liquidity

R. JONES
BALANCE SHEET
as at December 31, 19. .
Order of permanence

CAPITAL		£	FIXED ASSETS		£
At Start		30 500.00	Premises		22 450.00
Add	£		Plant and		
Profits	38 130.00		Machinery		10 250.00
Less			Office Furniture		8 000.00
Drawings	9 500.00				
		28 630.00			40 700.00
		59 130.00			
			CURRENT ASSETS		£
			Stock	7 800.00	
LONG-TERM LIABILITIES		0.00	Sundry Debtors	7 530.00	
			Cash at Bank	4 000.00	
			Cash in Hand	1 500.00	
CURRENT LIABILITIES					
Sundry Creditors		2 400.00			20 830.00
		£61 530.00			£61 530.00

Figure 19.3   A Balance Sheet in the order of permanence

The really important thing to achieve with a Balance Sheet is that the assets are well displayed whichever order you choose. The two methods, the Order of Liquidity and the Order of Permanence, are simply the reverse order of one another. The student should think seriously about where to place each asset and each liability. It is clear that cash is the most liquid asset we have, for the word 'liquid' means 'in cash form'. Cash at bank is the second most liquid asset – we can easily obtain the cash if we want it by drawing it out. Which is more liquid, stock or debtors? This is debatable. Debtors have a contractual obligation to pay you. Has anyone a duty to buy your stock? Since the answer is 'No', we usually consider Debtors as more liquid than Stock. Similarly the fixed assets are more, or less, easily convertible into cash, and become more fixed and permanent as we move through the list shown.

19.4   For which type of business is each method suitable?

Banks have always used the Order of Liquidity, because liquidity is very important to a bank. It is a basic idea of banking that depositors shall be able to obtain their money whenever they ask for it. A bank is therefore at pains to maintain its assets in a sufficiently liquid form to meet every requirement of depositors.

Limited companies other than banks usually marshal their assets and liabilities in the Order of Permanence. They are less free to choose now than formerly, as the Companies Act 1985 lays down a choice of formats. The strength of a company is often reflected in the material wealth of assets it controls. One can never be sure though, and a large proportion of fixed assets may leave the firm short of working capital, or liquid capital. These matters are discussed later in Chapter 29 page 425, on Interpretation of Balance Sheets.

Sole traders and partnerships may be presented in either form; both are equally correct.

19.5 Book-keeping to Final Accounts

The student should now prepare a large number of exercises to the Final Accounts level. There are still many things to learn about Final Accounts, but we must first consolidate our present knowledge. Every time you begin to prepare a set of Final Accounts from a Trial Balance you should be prepared to do it first in rough. You should then make a really neat set of Final Accounts, perfect in layout and style, from the rough copy. The student who acquires real facility at these exercises will be able to do the rough work, and get the Balance Sheet to balance, in about twenty minutes. A really neat fair copy then takes about ten minutes to write out. Headings and sub-totals can be made to look attractive with suitable underlining in red (a ball-point pen is best). *Note*: In the exercises from this point on, unless pence actually occur in an exercise, the pence columns .00 will be omitted.

19.6 Exercises set 19.1 – simple Final Accounts

1. Here is the Trial Balance of A. Tacitus's books. From it prepare his Trading Account, Profit and Loss Account, and Balance Sheet.

TRIAL BALANCE
as at March 31, 19. .

	Dr. £	Cr. £
Stock at Start	27 800	
Debtors and Creditors	29 770	16 860
Freehold Land and Buildings	48 780	
Carriage In	1 990	
Purchases and Sales	83 610	141 970
Bad Debts	1 500	
Motor Vehicle Expenses	2 650	
Office Repairs Account	1 650	
Returns – In and Out	2 750	2 330
Fixtures and Fittings	7 500	

Motor Vans	8 000	
Office Expenses	3 750	
Capital at April 1 last year		63 650
Bank Loan		10 190
Drawings	13 750	
Salaries and Commission Received	18 250	24 580
Depreciation	1 100	
Carriage Out	1 400	
Cash in Hand	750	
Cash at Bank	4 580	
£	259 580	259 580

Closing Stock on March 31, 19. .: £22 500

2. Here is the Trial Balance of N. Carter's books on December 31, 19. ..
You are asked to prepare the Trading Account, Profit and Loss Account,
and a Balance Sheet at this date for the year that has just passed.

	Dr. £	Cr. £
Debtors and Creditors	22 501	12 103
Plant and Machinery	46 500	
Purchases and Sales	42 502	145 000
Capital at January 1, 19. .		111 500
Premises and Mortgage Outstanding	55 000	38 500
Cash in Hand	2 502	
Cash at Bank	37 500	
Discount Allowed and Received	1 252	2 002
Bad Debts	1 700	
Motor Vehicles	10 000	
Commission Paid	6 500	
Insurance Premiums	550	
Office Furniture	2 500	
Stock on January 1, 19. .	22 500	
Rent and Rates	4 500	
Drawings	12 500	
Returns – In and Out	750	2 302
Office Salaries	12 150	
Wages (to go in Trading Account)	27 500	
Light and Heat	2 500	
£	311 407	311 407

Stock at the end of December: £18 950

3. Here is the Trial Balance of P. Holden at March 31, 19. .. You are to
prepare his Trading Account and Profit and Loss Account for the year
ending March 31, 19. ., and his Balance Sheet at that date.

	Dr.	Cr.
	£	£
Office Salaries	13 176.25	
Discount Allowed and Received	1 178.75	2 476.25
Rent	2 052.50	
Capital		56 625.00
Debtors and Creditors	3 927.50	9 003.75
Cash	2 428.25	
Plant and Machinery	23 175.00	
Stock at April 1 previous year	8 500.00	
Carriage Inwards	376.75	
Carriage Outwards	650.00	
Purchases and Sales	19 675.00	59 001.25
Premises	35 425.00	
Cash at Bank	5 428.75	
Drawings	11 575.00	
Returns – In and Out	1 551.25	2 013.75
	£ 129 120.00	129 120.00

Stock on March 31, 19. ., was valued at £8 877.50

4. Mr R. Teasdale is in business as a master tailor. On December 31, 19. ., he takes out his Trial Balance as shown below. Prepare his Trading Account, Profit and Loss Account, and Balance Sheet.

	Dr.	Cr.
	£	£
Stock at January 1st, 19. .	6 750.00	
Purchases and Sales	42 500.00	92 500.00
Returns – In and Out	1 177.50	1 202.50
Carriage In	412.50	
Carriage Out	1 200.00	
Factory Wages	16 252.50	
Factory Light and Heat	1 600.00	
Premises	40 000.00	
Plant and Machinery	14 800.00	
Motor Vehicles	9 000.00	
Debtors and Creditors	4 003.75	11 502.50
Office Expenses	10 808.75	
Office Salaries	11 000.00	
Commission Paid	1 000.00	
Bad Debts Recovered		125.00
Cash	100.00	
Capital		68 425.00
Drawings	9 000.00	
Cash at Bank	4 150.00	
	£ 173 755.00	173 755.00

Closing stock was valued at £9 500.00.

5. Here is T. Lauder's Trial Balance as at December 31, 19. .. You are asked to prepare his Trading Account, Profit and Loss Account, and Balance Sheet as at that date.

	Dr.	Cr.
	£	£
Capital		55 500.00
Cash	220.00	
Cash at Bank	16 250.00	
Stock at January 1, 19. .	22 500.00	
Sales Returns and Sales	5 002.50	217 502.50
Purchases and Purchases Returns	87 501.25	598.75
Debtors and Creditors	19 950.00	4 000.00
Discount Allowed and Received	2 502.50	4 500.00
Factory Wages	16 002.50	
Carriage Inwards	600.00	
Power and Heat for Office	10 376.25	
Rent and Rates	7 503.75	
Motor Vehicle Expenses	2 502.50	
Salaries	7 140.00	
Drawings	20 000.00	
Office Expenses	4 000.00	
Freehold Premises	37 500.00	
Motor Vehicles	10 000.00	
Fixtures and Fittings	13 000.00	
Depreciation	1 753.75	
Interest and Commission Received		2 203.75
	£ 284 305.00	284 305.00

The stock at the end of the year was valued at £16 500.

6. Mr Pinch's Trial Balance is as follows on December 31, 19. .. Prepare his Trading Account, Profit and Loss Account, and Balance Sheet in good style.

	Dr.	Cr.
	£	£
Opening Stock	9 752.50	
Capital		35 882.50
Carriage on Sales	1 427.50	
Sundry Expenses	1 500.00	
Purchases and Sales	85 001.25	190 002.50
Returns – In and Out	2 427.50	1 176.25
Salaries	23 502.50	
Cash	128.75	
Land and Buildings	42 670.00	
Plant and Machinery	15 000.00	

Office Furniture	9 250.00	
Commission paid to Travellers	3 802.50	
Cash at Bank	14 375.00	
Rent and Rates	2 202.50	
Factory Wages	19 250.00	
Drawings	10 500.00	
Discount Allowed and Received	130.00	925.00
Debtors and Creditors	4 500.00	18 383.75
Light and Heat	950.00	
£	246 370.00	246 370.00

Stock at the end of the year: £15 000

7. Prepare a Trading Account, Profit and Loss Account, and Balance Sheet from the Trial Balance below as at December 31, 19. .

	Dr.	Cr.
	£	£
Capital		180 000
Travellers' Salaries and Commissions	19 740	
Drawings	14 000	
Office Furniture	7 000	
Purchases and Purchases Returns	104 420	8 480
Sales and Sales Returns	3 640	299 680
Cash in Hand	420	
Cash at Bank	28 800	
Stock at January 1, 19. .	22 920	
Salaries	12 560	
Sundry Debtors and Creditors	73 940	33 960
Discount Received		360
Factory Wages	77 120	
Freehold Factory, January 1, 19. .	50 000	
Rent and Rates	13 880	
Carriage In	4 620	
Carriage Out	6 480	
Factory Expenses	14 480	
Factory Fuel	15 900	
Plant and Machinery	48 000	
Office Expenses	4 560	
£	522 480	522 480

Closing stock was valued at £28 580.

8. Here is T. Lowe's Trial Balance as at December 31, 19. .. You are asked to prepare his Trading Account, Profit and Loss Account, and Balance Sheet as at that date.

	Dr.	Cr.
	£	£
Sales Returns and Sales	3 782.50	173 402.50
Capital		64 800.00
Cash	11 272.50	
Purchases and Purchases Returns	76 703.75	631.25
Cash at Bank	16 050.00	
Stock at January 1, 19. .	21 280.00	
Warehouse Wages	11 700.00	
Debtors and Creditors	31 502.50	52 502.50
Discount Allowed and Received	3 653.75	1 141.25
Carriage Inwards	577.50	
Power, Light, and Heat for machines	11 500.00	
Rent and Rates	6 250.00	
Motor Vehicle Expenses	2 607.50	
Salaries	23 650.00	
Drawings	10 500.00	
Office Expenses	3 150.00	
Freehold Premises	36 500.00	
Motor Vehicles	11 500.00	
Fixtures and Fittings	8 800.00	
Depreciation	2 000.00	
Interest Received		502.50
	£ 292 980.00	292 980.00

The stock at the end of the year was valued at £20 000.00.

20
Capital and revenue expenditure and receipts

20.1 Introduction

Whenever we spend money we exchange it for some useful good or service, but the benefit received from the expenditure varies in duration. If we buy a filing cabinet it may last thirty years, and still give quite satisfactory service at the end. If we buy a stamp and stick it on a letter it will last a much shorter time.

The difference between these two types of expenditure is the difference between capital expenditure and revenue expenditure. It is of fundamental importance in understanding Final Accounts, because it is the key that decides whether to write off the expenditure as a loss or to carry it forward to next year as an asset.

20.2 Capital and revenue expenditure defined

Capital expenditure. This is expenditure on fixed assets which last a long time and permanently increase the profit-making capacity of the business.

Revenue expenditure. This is expenditure on items which are useful to the business, but are used up in less than one year, and therefore only temporarily increase the profit-making capacity of the business. Such expenses include goods for resale.

The chief difference between the two types is the length of time the expenditure is of benefit to the business and since we have to draw a line somewhere the sensible line to draw is at one year. If a good, or a service, lasts *less than one year it is revenue expenditure*. If it lasts *longer than one year it is capital expenditure*.

Examples of capital and revenue expenditure

Capital expenditure	*Revenue Expenditure*
Purchase of factory	Wages of factory workers
Purchase of machines	Oil to lubricate machines

Purchase of electric motors	Power to drive the motors
Purchase of new vehicles	500-mile service at garage
Purchase of loose tools	Screws to be used in repair jobs
New set of garage doors	Repairs to padlock on door

Example of a Doubtful Case

Brewer redecorates his premises at a cost of £2 500.00. He calculates this will last for five years. Is it capital or revenue expenditure? It is a little difficult to say. We will discuss the answer to this question later in the chapter (page 263).

20.3   Capital and revenue receipts

When the business receives money it is again of two sorts. It may be a capital receipt, a contribution by the proprietor, either to start the business off or to increase the funds available to it. It might be a mortgage or a loan which brings money into the business of a capital nature, but in this case it is not the owner of the business but some other investor who is supplying the capital.

Alternatively the receipt may be a revenue receipt, one which is truly a profit of the business. It may be rent received, or commission received, or it may be cash for sales of goods made that day, or at some previous time. In each case the receipt should be taken to the Revenue Account, for it is a revenue receipt. What, then, is the Revenue Account?

20.4   The Revenue Account

The name Revenue Account is a general term in book-keeping for the accounts where the profit or loss of the business is determined. Revenue expenses are losses of the business and must therefore go to the debit side of the Revenue Account; revenue receipts are profits of the business and must therefore be taken to the credit side of the Revenue Account.

In fact, the name Revenue Account is only used today for professional firms: doctors, dentists, lawyers, and accountants are some of the commonest. Such firms cannot really talk about profits and losses. It would be comical and unprofessional to say, 'We made £67.50 out of Mrs Jones's liver this morning.' Such professional firms talk about 'fees' and 'expenses' instead of profits and losses.

The complete list of Revenue Accounts looks like this:

Names given to the Revenue Account
(a) Revenue Account – for professional firms.
(b) Trading Account and Profit and Loss Account – for merchants.
(c) Manufacturing, Trading, and Profit and Loss Accounts – for manufacturing firms.
(d) Income and Expenditure Accounts – for clubs and non-profit-making societies.

Each of these types of firm is dealt with in the course of this book and in each case the distinction between capital and revenue expenditure is important.

20.5 Importance of distinguishing between the two types of expenditure and receipt

In most countries today an annual check-up on the business is required by law, to discover how profitable it has been. This is necessary because every government is an interested party in the business, wanting to collect tax revenues from the proprietor. In order to ensure that the owner arrives at a fair and accurate profit figure the accountant is required by law to abide by certain rules and regulations in preparing the Final Accounts figure.

At the root of these rules lie the distinctions between capital and revenue receipts and expenditure. If a receipt is a revenue receipt it must have added to the profitability of the firm and should therefore be included in the calculation of profits. If it is left out, then the profit will be understated and the Income Tax Authorities will be cheated of the government's lawful share.

If an item of expenditure is a revenue expense the benefit derived from it was used up completely during the year, and clearly should be counted as a deduction from the profits. If an item of expenditure is a capital expense, its benefit lasts more than a year, perhaps for ever (like buying the freehold of a piece of land), and clearly it should not be counted as a loss to the business.

To define exactly the nature of a revenue expense leads to many difficulties. Entertaining a business friend may justifiably be regarded as an expense of the business. But if you agree to entertain him in return for him inviting you back later you are clearly both evading the law in order to dodge taxation.

This is a rather extreme example, but doubtful cases arise all the time. We have already referred to one such case on page 262: Brewer redecorates his premises at a cost of £2 500.00 and estimates that this will last five years. Is this capital expenditure or revenue expenditure? The crucial point here is: does this expenditure increase the value of Brewer's assets? To the extent that it does it is capital expenditure. If it merely maintains the premises so that they retain their present value it is revenue expenditure – which seems likely to be the case here.

Since it lasts longer than a year, this revenue expenditure has to be treated as an adjustment. Adjustments are dealt with fully in Chapter 22, page 283.

20.6   The rules with capital and revenue items

To deal properly with capital and revenue items a businessman must abide by the following rules:

Rule 1. **Let every Revenue Account for the year in question carry every penny of loss that the business has suffered, and every penny of gain that the business has achieved; no more and no less**.

It follows from this rule that if we have not paid some item which we should have paid – like rent or wages or salaries – we should still count in the expense as if it had been paid, otherwise we shall overstate our profits. Conversely, if some payment is due to us, like commission that we should have received, we must still count this in as profit, and must *adjust* the commission received to take account of this receipt that has accrued. Chapter 22 is about adjustments and explains fully how to make allowances for all accrued payments due.

If follows equally clearly from Rule 1 that if we have made some payment in advance for next year, it would be unfair to include that payment in this year's losses. We must adjust the loss to account for the overpayment, since this year cannot fairly be expected to carry next year's losses. Conversely, any profits received now which properly belong to next year must be disregarded. In Club Accounts there are always some members who pay their subscriptions in advance. If a member pays next year's subscription in December we must hold this 'profit' of the club over until next year; it cannot be counted in this year's receipts. Chapter 22 deals fully with Payments in Advance.

Rule 2. **Every Balance Sheet must carry the assets at their fair value at the date shown on the Balance Sheet, while the liabilities must also be stated at their correct figure.**

If an asset has worn out a little since last year we must depreciate it to its proper value, writing the loss off the profits as depreciation. An interesting case is the asset **debtors**. It is well known that some debtors do not pay, either because fate is unkind to them or because they are rogues. We must provide for possible

Bad Debts even though we do not know they have actually occurred, and deduct this provision from the debtors' figure to show the debtors at their true value. All these matters are dealt with in Chapter 22.

20.7 The capitalization of revenue expenditure

There is one particular type of expenditure that is of great interest because it involves an obvious revenue expense that has to be treated as a capital expense. Consider these two examples:

Example 1
A machine, purchased on credit from Thompson Tools Co. for £5 000.00 is erected by our own fitters while the factory is closed on a public holiday. The cost of this in wages is £1 150.00

Clearly wages is a revenue expense, but in this case the wages have been added to the value of the machine. The value of the machine as we purchased it is £5 000.00. The value of the machine installed in its place is £6 150.00 for it cost us £5 000.00 and £1 150.00 to install.

Let us say at present the Wages Account looks like Figure 20.1.

			WAGES ACCOUNT	L162
19. .	Sundry payments	£ 56 252.00		

Figure 20.1 Wages – a revenue expense

Included in the figure of £56 252 is £1 150 which has been paid to the workers but which is not really a revenue expense. It has to be removed from the Wages Account and capitalized. A simple Journal Entry will record the purchase of the asset and capitalize the revenue expense. Here it is:

19. . July 12	Machinery Account Dr. Thompson Tools Co. Wages Account Being purchase of Machine No. LZ. 123 and erection at this date	L2 L71 L162	£ 6 150.00	£ 5 000.00 1 150.00

Figure 20.2 Capitalization of a revenue expense – Wages

The Wages Account will now appear as shown below. Notice particularly that the amount to be written off the profits at the end of the year for the Revenue Expense, Wages, has been reduced by £1 150. This £1 150 has not been lost – it is still in the business, embodied in the asset, machinery.

			WAGES ACCOUNT				L162
19. .		£	19. .				£
	Sundry payments	56 252.00	July 12	Machinery	J1		1 150.00

Figure 20.3 Wages Account adjusted to the true 'loss' figure

Example 2
Jones is a builder, but weather is poor and his men are unable to proceed with his present building jobs. He decides to alter his own premises, enlarging the shop front, redesigning display counters, and altering storage facilities, shelving, etc. This involves the following expenses: (a) materials £1 400 (b) labour £1 600 – but it increases the value of the building by £5 000. Capitalize the revenue expenses.

This is an exercise in double entry:

(a) The asset, premises, has increased in value by £5 000.
(b) Materials (Purchases Account) has lost £1 400; the Wages Account has £1 600 on it that should not be there, and Jones has made a £2 000 profit on the men's work. This will be treated as a capital profit and be credited in the Capital Account.

We would do the following Journal Entry:

				£	£
19. .					
Nov. 27	Premises Account	Dr.	L12	5 000.00	
	Purchases Account		L27		1 400.00
	Wages Account		L33		1 600.00
	Capital Account		L187		2 000.00
	Being the capitalization of revenue expenses on improving the property				

Figure 20.4 Improving the assets of a business by revenue expenditure

20.8 Revenue expenses that show up as reduced stock

There is one type of business loss that never appears directly in either the Trading or Profit and Loss Accounts. That is the type of loss which has the effect of reducing the stock. Consider these cases:

(a) A customer in a china shop breaks a plate accidentally. She offers to pay, but the owner refuses to allow her to do so as it was a pure accident. The broken plate is put in the dustbin. Such a loss would not appear in the Profit and Loss Account because it already appears in the Trading Account. When we count the stock, the plate will not be there. We will therefore take account of it and to write it off the Profit and Loss account would be to take account of it twice.

(b) A greengrocer has some tomatoes go bad over the week-end. There is no need to take account of this loss, as it will be taken into account when we value the stock.

(c) A furniture dealer has to reduce the price of a piano because of a bad mark sustained in moving it. This loss will be taken into account when the piano is valued as part of the stock.

20.9 Exercise set 20.1 – capital and revenue expenditure

1. The following items appear in R. Smith's books for this year:
    Telephone expenses £120: Salaries for office workers £41 250; New weighing machines for shop £270.50; New counters £160; Wages of men fitting the counters £120.
(a) Would you call each of these a capital or a revenue expense? (b) Say where you would expect to find each of them when the Final Accounts of the year and the Final Balance Sheet have been completed.

2. The Newtown Zoological Company Ltd has the following expenses during the current year. Copy them out and put a tick in the appropriate column:

Expenses	£	Revenue Item	Capital Item	Trading Account	Profit and Loss Account	Balance Sheet
(a) Purchased gorilla	25 000					
(b) Paid keepers' wages	54 750					
(c) Hire of loudspeaker equipment	150					
(d) Built monkey house	14 000					
(e) Repairs to aquarium air pumps	25					

3. On December 31 you begin work on your Final Accounts. The owner of your business, Mr Watchit, points out to you that crockery valued at £165 was destroyed last year after an accident in the shop, but you have made no note of this loss in the Profit and Loss Account. Explain to him why none is necessary.

4. A.B. Ltd purchased a machine ex works for £11 750. They paid carriage of £425 and wages to their own fitters for erecting the machine on a Sunday, £375. Show the capitalization of these revenue expenses and the purchase of the new machine, by doing a Journal Entry and posting it to the Ledger. The machine is on credit from Wormco Engineering Ltd.

5. M. Stove's expenses in the first month of business include the following: (1) Purchase of motor van £4 500. (2) Postage and stationery £220. (3) Purchase of typewriter £440 (4) Purchase of goods for resale £1 950 (5) Repairs to garage lock £7.25 (6) Teas for staff £2.55.

Say which you think are capital expenses and which are revenue expenses, and make a list of those he would still have on his books in twelve months time.

6. Rapidfloors Ltd, a firm of linoleum manufacturers, have the following expenses on their books. Copy out this list and tick in the appropriate column.

			Type of Expense		Position in Final Accounts		
						Profit	
			Revenue	Capital	Trading	and Loss	Balance
Expenses		£	Item	Item	Account	Account	Sheet
(a)	Painting machine	41 000					
(b)	Paper and string	135					
(c)	Building new canteen	75 000					
(d)	Wages of workers building canteen	18 750					
(e)	Wages to workers making lino	60 000					
(f)	Pitch (raw material) purchased	7 250					

7. Your employer suggests to you that as fruit and vegetables to a total value of £750 have been wasted during the year because they became over-ripe and unfit for sale, you should debit these losses in the Profit and Loss Account. Would you accept the suggestion or not? Justify your answer.

8. Funfair Ltd employ maintenance staff who, in busy times, act as attendants in the fun fair, and in less busy times do repair work – repainting side shows, installing new items, etc. On analysing their working time at the end of the season the following was discovered:

(a) Wages earned while acting as attendants £29 000.
(b) Wages earned while repairing existing parts of the fair during slack times £11 000.
(c) Wages earned while erecting a new sideshow – the water chute £9 000.

Do you consider these to be capital or revenue expenses? Explain where they would appear in the Final Accounts.

9.
(a) In keeping the books of a business, why is it important to distinguish between capital expenditure and revenue expenditure?
(b) In connexion with the business of a restaurant proprietor, state whether you consider the following to be capital expenditure or revenue expenditure, giving your reasons:
  (i)   Purchase of a new electric cooker.
  (ii) Charge for hire of a refrigerator.
  (iii) Cost of structural alterations to the dining-room to increase seating capacity.
  (iv) Cost of repainting the kitchen and the outside of the premises.
                                                                    (*RSA – Stage I*)

10.
(a) What are the meanings of the two terms capital expenditure and revenue expenditure?
(b) Name *two* types of capital expenditure and *two* types of revenue expenditure.
(c) A. Smartfoot has his premises redecorated externally at a cost of £1 000. He estimates that this will only be necessary once every four years. Discuss whether this is capital or revenue expenditure.
                                          (*East Anglian Examination Board – Adapted*)

11. A stray dog chases a cat into your employer's china shop, smashing a quantity of cut-glass ware. Some time later, when the Trading Account for the period has been prepared, your employer complains that the figure for the net profit must be incorrect as he remembers the considerable damage which took place but no entry appears in the Final Accounts in respect of it. What explanation would you give him?
                                                                    (*RSA – Adapted*)

12.
(a) R. S. deals in typewriters and accessories. State whether the following items of expenditure are capital or revenue expenditure.

  (i)   Purchase of two typewriters as stock-in-trade and two for office use.
  (ii) Purchase of office adding-listing machine.
  (iii) Fire insurance premiums on warehouse.

(b) A firm's Profit and Loss Account included an item of £2 500 for repairs and alterations to premises. If it is decided to capitalize one-half of this expenditure, what would be the effect on the Balance Sheet of the firm?

13. W. Tanner Ltd owned freehold business premises of which the book value on January 1, 19. ., was £50 000. During that year the company engaged Builders Limited to repair, paint, decorate, and build extensions to these premises. The invoice from Builders Limited, dated November 30, 19. ., showed repairs £1 400, painting and decorating £1 750 and cost of building extensions £7 500. (This invoice was paid on December 7 by cheque.) The company also purchased adjoining premises during the year for the sum of £20 000 which was paid by cheque on December 16, 19. ..

Make the entries in the company's Ledger to record the above transactions.

(University of London – Adapted)

14.

(a) Give *three* examples of Capital Expenditure that might be undertaken by a garage proprietor, and *three* examples of Revenue Expenditure that might be undertaken by a cafe owner.

(b) Smartfront Ltd spend £3 000 improving and redecorating their shop premises. It is estimated that the improvements, which are of a permanent nature, represent two-thirds of the total cost. The redecorations are estimated to last five years and four-fifths of the amount spent on them is to be kept in a Decorations in Suspense Account. The balance is to be written off to Depreciation Account. At present the £3 000 spent is to be found as follows: £1 500 in the Wages Account, having been paid to the firm's workers, and £1 500 in Purchases Account, having been spent on building materials.

You are asked to show the Journal Entry or Entries recording these matters.

(East Anglian Examination Board – Adapted)

21
The valuation of stock

21.1 Introduction – the importance of correct stock valuation

In Chapter 17 the position of stock was discussed as part of the Trading Account. The valuation of closing stock is very important, since it affects the Gross Profit figure. If we overvalue closing stock we will overstate our profits, and if we undervalue closing stock we will understate our profits. Moreover, since closing stock appears on the Balance Sheet, an incorrect stock figure means an incorrect Balance Sheet. Since businesses are bought and sold on the basis of a Balance Sheet, the deliberate misrepresentation of a stock figure is fradulent. Many purchasers of businesses insist upon an independent valuation of the stock by a disinterested third party.

Accurate stock valuation is therefore essential for the production of an honest Trading Account and an honest Balance Sheet. On what basis should stock be valued?

21.2 The basis of stock valuation

The basis for valuation of stock is laid down in SSAP 9 (Statements of Standard Accounting Practice No. 9) laid down in 1973 by the Accounting Standards Committee. It says 'Stocks and work-in-progress normally need to be stated at cost, or, if lower, at net realizable value.'

Let us examine this proposal. To value stock at cost price, that is, what it cost us when we bought it, seems a fair enough idea. To value it above this figure, for example at selling price would not be very wise, because it would mean we were taking a profit on it while it was still in our hands. Before we sell it the price may fall again, and our so-called profit would have disappeared. Prudent businessmen never take a profit until they have actually realized it. If current stocks rise in value on the market, ignore the price change until you actually sell and realize the profit.

Now consider what happens if the value of our stock falls. The traditional caution of businessmen has always led them to accept a loss when it was reasonably certain to occur, but never to anticipate a profit. If the value of stock falls below cost price, either because it is damaged or has deteriorated in some way, or because the bottom has fallen out of world prices, we should value the stock at its net realizable value. The term 'net' implies, 'after deducting any costs of disposal (transport and commission payable, perhaps).

21.3 Stock records

In many situations it is desirable to keep 'running balance' records of stock so that stock arrivals can be recorded at once and added to the running balance, while stock requisitions from the various departments can be recorded and deducted as the stock is issued. Stock cards, bin cards and similar stationery are designed and printed to meet the storekeeper's requirements. A suitable ruling is shown in Figure 21.1 Study this card carefully.

bin card

Part Name Television Control Knobs	Maximum Stock	15 000
Location Bin 27	Re-order Period	2 weeks
Code RTX/510/1	Minimum Stock	2 000
Unit of Issue 1 000	Re-order Level	3 000
Supplier Works Dept. (Batch Production)	Re-order Quantity	10 000

Received			Issued			Balance
Date	Order no.	Qty	Date	Requisition no.	Qty	Qty
1 Jan 19. .						4 000
			4 Jan	1246	1 000	3 000
			9 Jan	1315	1 000	2 000
13 Jan 19. .	159	10 000				12 000
			21 Jan	1426	3 000	9 000
			28 Jan	1495	3 000	6 000

Figure 21.1   A bin card for small components.

Notes:
   (i) The various details at the top of the card help control stock levels.
   (ii) It would be usual to 'bag up' the re-order level stock of 3 000. A storekeeper forced to break open this re-order level stock would have to make out an immediate order for a further 10 000 (the re-order quantity).

21.4 Stock-taking at the end of the financial year

The process of valuing stock can be an arduous one, for it involves the physical checking of the stock, pricing it at cost price or net realizable value, multiplying the price by the number of units in stock, and adding the totals.

To reduce the work as much as possible it is usual to hold a stock-taking sale. This has a dual purpose. First it reduces the physical number of items to be counted, and second, it gives the proprietor an opportunity to appraise the stock. An astute owner will notice many significant things about stocks at sale-time. Certain lines will be found to have sold badly – the shop is cluttered up with huge supplies of slow-moving items. This may be due to the personal foibles of the buyer concerned. One may be 'terribly interested' in Polynesia and have the art department littered with Easter Island statuettes that do not command a ready sale. Another may be an old 'fuddy duddy', buying lines that were popular thirty years ago. Some lines may be traditional ones that the shop has always sold, but times have changed. The elimination of these slow-moving lines, clearing the shelves for newer, more popular, items will improve the profitability of the business.

One effect of stock-taking sales is that they reduce the expected rate of Gross Profit. A slow-moving line may be cut to clear it from stock. It will still probably make a profit, but a much lower profit than was originally hoped. We shall see when we come to consider Gross and Net Profit Percentages that this causes a fall in the Gross Profit Percentage. We may have to remove that 'fuddy duddy' buyer to stop the same thing happening next year – we have to make sure that this particular buyer doesn't buy any more. This may seem harsh, but if our competitors force us out of business other employees will suffer too.

21.5 A stock valuation question

Consider the following case:
  A firm's stock records show –

19..		Quantity	Cost Price
January 1	Stock	2500	7.50
January 1–31	Purchases	3000	8.25
February 1–28	Purchases	3000	8.50
March 1–31	Purchases	1000	7.25
January 1–31	Sales	4000	12.50
February 1–28	Sales	3500	12.75
March 1–31	Sales	1500	11.25
March 31	Stock	?	value?

The firm's policy is to sell all stock in strict rotation, first in, first out. All the stock is in good condition except 100 units which are discoloured and agreed to be worth only £5 per unit.

You are to discover:

(a) The value to be placed on closing stock.
(b) The Gross Profit for the 3-month period.

Calculations
We shall need to calculate all the figures for the Trading Account, but first deal with section (a):

Calculation of value of closing stock:

$$
\begin{array}{rl}
\text{Units at Start} & = 2500 \\
\text{Purchased} & = 7000 \\
\hline
\text{Total Available} & = 9500 \\
\textit{Less Sales} & \ 9000 \\
\hline
\therefore\ \text{Closing Stock} & = \ \ 500 \text{ units} \\
\hline
\end{array}
$$

These must have been part of the most recent batch bought, which cost £7.25 each. As 100 units are in poor condition with a net realizable value of only £5 per unit we must value the stock as follows:

$$
\begin{array}{lr}
& \text{£} \\
400 \text{ units @ £7.25} = & 2900 \\
100 \text{ units @ £5} \ \ = & 500 \\
\hline
& \text{£3400} \\
\hline
\end{array}
$$

For the gross profit calculation we need these other calculations:

Opening
Stock $= 2500 \times £7.50 = £18\ 750$
Purchases $= (3000 \times £8.25) + (3000 \times £8.50) + (1000 \times £7.25)$
           $= £24\ 750 + £25\ 500 + £7\ 250$
           $= £57\ 500$

Sales $= (4000 \times £12.50) + (3500 \times £12.75) + (1500 \times £11.25)$
           $= £50\ 000 + £44\ 625 + £16\ 875$
           $= £111\ 500$

We are now able to proceed with section (b).

TRADING ACCOUNT
for quarter ending March 31, 19. .

	£		£
Opening Stock	18 750	Sales	111 500
Purchases	57 500		
Total Stock Available	76 250		
Less Closing Stock	3 400		
Cost of Sales	72 850		
Gross Profit	38 650		
	£111 500		£111 500

The gross profit is therefore found to be £38 650.

The student might usefully amuse himself/herself with following through exactly what happens when stock is overvalued, or understated. Using the above Trading Account as an example, if the Closing Stock is overvalued – say at £4 000 – this will reduce the cost of sales and increase the Gross Profit:

Hence *overvalued stock = overstated profits*

Undervalued stock has the reverse effect.

Hence *undervalued stock = undervalued profits*

Carrying the idea a step further, what will happen next year?

In the next year, this year's closing stock becomes next year's opening stock. Therefore overstated profits this year will be followed by understated profits next year.

In tabulated form we have:

Error	Effect on this year	Effect on next year
Overstated Stock	Overstated Profits	Understated Profits
Understated Stock	Understated Profits	Overstated Profits

We shall see later that this is an important explanation of statistical differences between the years. (See Chapter 29, page 409, on Interpretation of Final Accounts.)

21.6 Delays in stock-taking

It is often difficult to take stock on exactly the right day of the year. It may be too big a job for one evening and we may not wish to shut the store for a whole day. To overcome this difficulty we can take stock at any time we like that is conveniently near the last day of the financial year, and then adjust the stock figure for any incoming or outgoing stock in the interval between stock-taking and the end of the year. Consider the following case:

Example
A firm decides to do its stock-taking on December 27, which is a public holiday. It finds its stock on that date is £39 130. In the four remaining days of the year the following transactions take place:

Goods purchases and entered into stock	= £4 175
Credit sales at selling prices	= £2 780
Cash sales at selling prices	= £1 670
Returns from a customer taken back into stock	= £60
(These returns valued at selling price.)	

The firm adds 33⅓ per cent to its cost prices to obtain its selling prices.

Calculations:
There are a number of points to discuss here, but we will deal with each as we come to it.

		£
(a) Stock on December 27 =		39 130
(b) Stock purchases	=	4 175
		£ 43 305

(As this stock is at cost price it is clearly correct to add it on to the stock at December 27, since it will be in stock on December 31.)
(c) Cash Sales and Credit Sales. Here we have a problem. These sales are clearly part of the December 27 stock which has been disposed of and will not be in stock on December 31. We must therefore deduct them – but at cost price.

Note: Students who are not very good at commercial arithmetic may not appreciate that 33⅓ per cent added on to cost price is the same as 25 per cent deducted from Selling Price. Here is the explanation:

$$\text{Cost Price} + \text{Profit} = \text{Selling Price}$$
$$\therefore \quad 100\% + 33\tfrac{1}{3}\% = 133\tfrac{1}{3}\%$$

If we want to remove 33⅓ per cent from 133⅓ per cent it is not one-third but one-quarter of it. There are 4 × 33⅓ per cent in 133⅓ per cent.

The full rule is:

$$\tfrac{1}{2} \text{ on to cost price} = \tfrac{1}{3} \text{ off selling price}$$
$$\tfrac{1}{3} \text{ on to cost price} = \tfrac{1}{4} \text{ off selling price}$$
$$\tfrac{1}{4} \text{ on to cost price} = \tfrac{1}{5} \text{ off selling price}$$
$$\tfrac{1}{5} \text{ on to cost price} = \tfrac{1}{6} \text{ off selling price}$$

For percentages that do not easily change to this type of proper fraction (like 40 per cent) we find the cost price by this formula:

$$CP = \frac{SP}{140} \times 100$$

i.e. the CP is $\frac{100}{140}$ths of the SP

Returning to our example;

Cash Sales + Credit Sales × $\tfrac{3}{4}$

$$= \frac{£2\ 780 + £1\ 670}{4} \times 3 = \frac{4\ 450}{4} \times 3 = \frac{13\ 350}{4} = \underline{\underline{£3\ 337.50}}$$

Deducting these sales at cost price we have

	£
	43 305.
	− 3 337.50
	= 39 967.50

(d) Returns have to be added back at *cost price*

$$= £60 \times \frac{3}{4} \qquad\qquad = \quad 45.00$$

Value to be placed on closing stock = $\underline{\underline{£40\ 012.50}}$

21.7 Burglaries, floods and fires

Occasionally situations arise where we have to take stock because of some unusual event, such as a burglary, a flood or a fire. We are usually covered by insurance against such events and it is necessary to make a claim. To start with we need to discover how much stock has been lost. The method used is the usual stock-taking procedure, to discover what stock is left because it was not stolen or not destroyed in the flood or fire. The stock-taking is usually done by a professional valuer. Our records will show what stock we had at the start of the period, and how much stock we had purchased since. They will also show our sales in the period before the event – but we shall need to bring this down to cost price – since these sales will be at selling price. We can now calculate the stock stolen (or destroyed) as follows:

Opening Stock + Purchases = Total Stock available in the period before the event.

Total Stock available − Sales (at cost price) = Balance of Stock that should be in hand.

Balance of Stock − Actual Stock as counted = Stock lost.

An example will illustrate the problem.

Example
A. Trader suffers a burglary in March 19. . in which a large part of his stock of electronic equipment is stolen. His shop window is also smashed. His records show a stock of £23 800 (at cost) in hand at the start of the year and purchases of £83 420 at cost during the period before the burglary. His sales during the period January −March were £112 200. He always adds 50% to cost price to fix his selling prices. Stock-taking shows that the goods left behind by the burglars are worth £18 500 at cost. The window repairs cost £85.00 and the valuer charges £120. What will be the amount of his claim?

The calculation is as follows:

	£
Opening Stock at cost price	23 800
Purchases during the period (at cost)	83 420
	107 220

Less sales at cost price

$$= \frac{£112.200}{3} \times 2 \quad (\tfrac{1}{2} \text{ on cost price} = \tfrac{1}{3} \text{ off selling price})$$

$= £37\ 400 \times 2$	=	74 800
Stock that should have been still available		32 420
Less Stock in hand (as valued)	=	18 500
Stock lost by burglary		13 920
Add: Repairs to window		85
Valuer's charges		120
Amount to be claimed	£	14 125

21.8   Exercises set 21.1 − stock valuation

1.
(a) Rule up a bin card similar to the one shown in Figure 21.1 and record on it the following orders and requisitions for brass change-over

valves. The location is Bin 42; the code no. is V 25; the unit of issue is 'units'; the supplier is Brassware Components Ltd; the maximum stock is 60 valves the re-order period is 4 weeks, the minimum stock 20 valves, the re-order level 25 valves and the re-order quantity 40 valves.

1 Jan. 19. .	Opening Balance	35 valves
13 Jan. 19. .	Requisition No. 2484	16 valves
25 Jan. 19. .	Order No. 1686	40 valves
27 Jan. 19. .	Requisition No. 2499	20 valves
29 Jan. 19. .	Requisition No. 2342	22 valves
30 Jan. 19. .	Order No. 1792	40 valves

(b) What is the stock value at 31 January if the valves cost £8.95 each?

2. Rule up a Bin Card similar to the one shown in Figure 21.1 and record on it the following orders and requisitions for drop-leaf hinges.

1 October 19. .	Opening balance	200
3 October 19. .	Requisition No. 2784	100
11 October 19. .	Order No. 39	1 500
12 October 19. .	Requisition No. 2798	100
19 October 19. .	Requisition No. 2896	300

Other details are: Location Bin 124; Code H27; Unit of issue 100; Supplier: Brassware Products Ltd.; maximum stock 2000; re-order period 4 weeks, minimum stock 200; re-order level 300; re-order quantity 1500.

3. John Dillon, a merchant in malting barley, prepares his Trading Account for the year ended December 31, 19. . On that date his stock consists of 200 tonnes bought at varying prices: 20 tonnes at £97 a tonne, 80 tonnes at £100 a tonne, and 100 tonnes at £98.75 a tonne. 5 tonnes of his stock, originally costing £100 per tonne had overheated and will be sold for cattle feed at £60 per tonne.

Draw up a statement showing how Dillon should value, for his Trading Account, his unsold stock of barley on December 31, 19. .

(RSA—Adapted)

4. The following information is available from Jones & Co.'s stock records:

19. .		Quantity	Price (£)
January 1	Stock	3000	3.75
January 1–31	Purchases	4000	3.85
February 1–28	Purchases	4000	3.95
January 1–31	Sales	4500	5.50
February 1–28	Sales	3500	5.75
February 28	Stock	?	

(a) State the usual basis of stock valuation at the end of any trading period.
(b) Work out the quantity and value of the stock on February 28, 19. . given that stock is used in strict rotation and 100 units were shopsoiled and valued as only likely to fetch £3 each.

5.
(a) On what basis is stock valued at the end of the financial year?
(b) Hans Memling had on January 1, 19. ., a stock of 3000 pairs of shoes valued at cost price £12 each. During January he sold 1800 pairs and bought 2500 pairs at £14 each. In February he bought a further 2500 at £15 and sold 3000 pairs. At the end of February he still has 100 pairs of the January 1 stock unsold. These are in an unfashionable colour and he decides to dispose of them for £10 per pair. The shoes bought in February have not yet been offered to his customers. Calculate the value of his stock on February 28, 19. .

(East Anglian Examination Board – Adapted)

6. A trader, dealing in a single standard article, follows strictly the rule of selling his goods in the order in which he has bought them. On January 1, 19. ., his stock was 1000 articles, which had cost him £3.75 each. His subsequent purchases were January 30, 2000 articles at £4.15 each; February 27, 2000 articles at £4.25 each; March 16, 2000 articles at £4.50 each. His sales were: January, 2400 articles at £6.25 each; February, 2000 articles at £6.45 each; March, 1800 articles at £6.60 each. Damaged articles are valued at half their cost price. On March 31 he had 80 damaged articles, 20 purchased in January and 60 in February.

Show the trader's Trading Account for the quarter ended March 31, 19. .

(RSA – Adapted)

7. A trader had in stock on 1 March 10 000 articles at £1.75 each. During March he purchased a further 14 000 costing £1.90 each, but was given an allowance of £0.50 on 1000 of these because they arrived in a damaged condition. His sales during the month, made in strict rotation, were 15 000 undamaged articles at £2.75 each and 680 of the damaged articles at £2.25 each. He now feels that the remaining damaged articles will only fetch £1.25 each, and values his stock accordingly.

Show the Trading Account of the trader for the month of March. (Goods are sold in strict rotation – first in, first out.)

(RSA – Adapted)

8. The following information was extracted from the records of a firm which only sells one product.

19. .		Quantity	Price (£)
January 1	Stock	2000 articles	3.75 each
January 1–31	Purchases	3000 articles	4.40 each
February 1 to March 31	Purchases	1000 articles	4.75 each
January 1–31	Sales	4000 articles	6.25 each
February 1 to March 31	Sales	1500 articles	6.50 each
March 31	Stock	? articles	? each

(a) Calculate the closing stock value assuming that 72 of the articles in stock had a net realizable value of only £1.50 due to weather damage.
(b) Show the firm's Trading Account for the above three months. (Articles were sold in the same order as that in which they were purchased.)

(RSA – Adapted)

9. From the following figures you are required to prepare an estimate of J. Wilson's stock at cost price on June 30, 19. .:

	£
Stock (January 1, 19. .) at cost	13 000
Purchases from January 1 to June 30, 19. .	77 000
Returns Outwards	1 750
Sales	99 253
Returns Inwards	1 400
Goods given away for advertising purposes at cost	500

J. Wilson adds 40 per cent to his cost prices to obtain selling prices.

(*RSA – Adapted*)

10. A firm sells its goods for cash and on credit; it adds 33⅓ per cent to its purchase prices to obtain the selling prices.

The stock of the concern, at cost, on December 27, 19. ., amounted to £26 600. In the remaining three working days of the financial year the following transactions took place:

	£
Purchases at cost	2 120.00
Credit sales at selling prices	620.00
Cash sales at selling prices	1 600.00

Goods previously sold to a customer for £60 were returned by him, undamaged, and taken back into stock.

Prepare a statement showing the value of the firm's stock at December 31, 19. .

11.
(a) It is sometimes said that stock should be valued at 'cost or net realizable value, whichever is the lower'. What is meant by this?
(b) B. & M. Sellers are retailers whose financial year closed on Thursday March 31, 19. .. It was found convenient to take stock on the following Saturday afternoon when the business was closed. From the following information calculate the value of the stock at the close of business on March 31, 19.:

	£
Stock at cost on Saturday, April 2, 19. .	14 310
Cost of goods delivered by suppliers on April 1 and 2 and taken into stock	2 130
Sales on April 1	725
Sales on April 2	1 100
Credit to customers (at sale price) for goods returned on April 1	200

Note: The Business earns 20 per cent Gross Profit on *selling price*.

12. A trader began stock-taking for the year ended March 31, 19. ., on that date. He did not complete the stock-taking until the close of business on April 4, 19. ., when he ascertained the value of stock at cost price as £19 480.

The following information is available for the period April 1 to 4, 19. .:

	£
Purchases included in stock figure	1 520
Sales of goods not included in stock figure	2 300

Goods invoiced to a customer on March 31, 19. ., at £400 but held in the warehouse pending instructions as to delivery, were included at cost price in the stock figure. Percentage of Gross Profit *on sales* is 25%.

Draw up a statement to show the correct value of stock at cost price on March 31, 19. .

(London University O-level – Adapted)

13. From the following figures you are required to prepare an estimate of a trader's loss due to a burglary on April 15 19. .

	£	
Stock at January 1, 19. . (at cost)	20 000	
Purchases from January 1 to 15 April 19. .	165 000	
Sales from January 1 to 15 April 19. .	210 000	
Goods given away for advertising purposes	1 500	(at cost price)
Stock valued at cost after burglary	3 550	

The trader adds 33⅓ per cent to his cost prices to ascertain his selling prices.

14. On May 4, 19. ., a fire occurred on the premises of a trader and part of the stock-in-trade was destroyed. From the following information estimate the value at cost price of the stock destroyed:

	£
Stock at cost price on April 1, 19. .	23 350
Purchases April 1 to May 4, 19. .	29 210
Sales April 1 to May 4, 19. .	56 721
Value at cost price of stock salvaged	7 130

Percentage of Gross Profit on cost is 50%

(University of London O-level – Adapted)

22
Adjustments in Final Accounts

22.1 Introduction – why are adjustments necessary?

The aim of a good book-keeper is to provide a 'true and fair view' of the profitability and present state of the business. The Revenue Accounts display profitability, the Balance Sheet displays the present state. If there is any item which is incorrectly stated in either the Revenue Accounts or the Balance Sheet, then these records will not give 'a true and fair view' of the business.

The purpose of adjustments is to clear up all such outstanding details and bring the books into perfect order.

The main adjustments necessary are:

1 Payments in advance by the firm.
2 Payments in advance to the firm.
3 Accrued expenses owed by the firm.
4 Accrued receipts due to the firm.
5 Bad debts.
6 Provision for bad debts.
7 Provision for discounts.
8 Depreciation of assets.
9 Depreciation of goodwill.

Before beginning a detailed discussion of these the student is advised to commit to memory this vital phrase:

The purpose of adjustments is to produce a perfectly accurate set of Final Accounts for the period under review, and a perfectly honest Balance Sheet as at the present date.

22.2 Payments in advance by the firm

Certain expenses are nearly always paid in advance. The best example is insurance since the insurance cover only begins on payment of the premium and then runs for a given period, usually one year. Rent is often payable in advance, so are rates.

If we use insurance as an example, consider the following Insurance Account which we propose to close off into the Profit and Loss Account.

INSURANCE ACCOUNT			L61
19. .		£	
Jan. 1	Balance	300	
June 30	Fire Insurance	90	
Sept. 30	Motor Vehicles	512	

Figure 22.1   Expenses, some of which are in advance

How much of these insurance expenses apply to the present year, assuming that they are all annual premiums? Clearly all the £300 on January 1, 19. ., has been used up by December 31, 19. ., and may fairly be treated as a loss. The Fire Insurance premium of £90 on June 30, 19. ., has been half consumed; the insurance company has still to cover us for a further six months. £45 of this £90 has to be treated as an expense of the year, the other £45 is an asset at present – it will become an expense of next year.

The £512 paid for Motor Vehicle Insurance on September 30 has only been one-quarter used up by December 31, 19. .. £384 of this is an asset; the insurance company owes us cover for this amount. The other £128 is a loss for the present year.

Our adjustment now reads as follows: instead of £902 being transferred to the Profit and Loss Account as a loss, only £300 + £45 + £128 = £473 should be transferred, leaving £429 still on the Insurance Account as an asset of the business.

The Journal Entry for this will be:

19. .				£	£
Dec. 31	Profit and Loss Account Dr.	L66		473	
	Insurance Account	L61			473
	Being Insurance Premiums for year transferred				

Figure 22.2   Transferring the adjusted amounts

and the Insurance Account now looks like this:

INSURANCE ACCOUNT   L61

19. .			£	19. .			£
Jan.	1	Balance	300	Dec. 31	Profit and Loss		
June	10	Fire Insurance	90		Account	473	
Sept.	30	Motor Vehicles	512	31	Balance c/d	429	
			£902			£902	
19. .			£				
Jan.	1	Balance b/d	429				

Figure 22.3 A Nominal Account that has become a temporary asset account

Notice that the Nominal Account, which has carried our losses on insurance for the year, is at present carrying a balance that is in effect an asset. It must appear on the assets side of the Balance Sheet, since the insurance company are virtually debtors for this amount of cover.

(*Note*: Some theoreticians argue that a Nominal Account cannot have a real balance, and say the correct thing to do is to transfer this balance to a Suspense Account for Balance Sheet purposes. This is a highly academic rule 'more honoured in the breach than in the observance'.)

The Balance Sheet will now have this balance on the assets side, under Current Assets. The best place is to put it as the most liquid item, since it is so liquid *you have already spent it*.

BALANCE SHEET
as at December 31, 19. .

FIXED ASSETS	
CURRENT ASSETS	
Stock	
Debtors	
Cash	
Insurance in Advance	429

Figure 22.4 The most liquid asset

In examination work, where a student is working from a Trial Balance without the actual accounts, it is usual to show the adjustment on the Trading Account or Profit and Loss Account itself, by indenting the main figure. The Profit and Loss Account in this case would look as follows:

PROFIT AND LOSS ACCOUNT
as at December 31, 19. .   L161

	£	£
Insurance	902	
Less Amount Paid in Advance	429	
		473

Figure 22.5 The best way to show adjustments for examination purposes

The payment in advance must still be shown on the Balance Sheet as in Figure 22.4

22.3 Payments in advance to the firm

If payments in advance by the firm should not be counted as losses of the present year, but regarded as assets carried over to the next year for use in the coming months, it seems only logical that payments in advance to the firm for services not yet rendered should not be treated as profits, but carried forward to the next year as liabilities.

Taking the example of insurance used in Section 22.2 on page 284, from the insurance company's point of view the position will be the reverse of payments in advance by the firm. They have received premiums, of perhaps £5 000 000. Of this figure, let us imagine that £1 250 000 represents premiums received in advance. Clearly only £3 750 000 should be transferred to the Revenue Account, the rest remaining on the books as a liability to the policy-holders. It will become a profit in the course of the coming year. Such an account might look like this after closure:

PREMIUMS RECEIVED ACCOUNT   L195

19. .		£	19. .			£
Dec. 31	Revenue Account	3 750 000			Sundry Premiums	5 000 000
31	Balance c/d	1 250 000				
		£5 000 000				£5 000 000
			19. .			£
			Jan. 1	Balance b/d		1 250 000

Figure 22.6 A Nominal Account that has temporarily become a liability

When the credit balance is taken into the Balance Sheet it will look like this:

BALANCE SHEET
for year ending December 31, 19. .

CURRENT LIABILITIES	£	
Premiums in Advance	1 250 000	

Figure 22.7   A very current liability

22.4   Exercises set 22.1 – payments in advance

1. Lomax's Rent Account shows payments made to his landlord on January 3, March 31, June 26, September 25, and December 20, 19. ., of £500 each time. The rent is £500 per quarter. Show the Rent Account for the year, including the transfer to Profit and Loss Account on December 31, 19. .

2. Phillipson's Insurance Account shows annual insurance payments as follows: Fire Policy on January 1, £136; Motor Vehicles on March 31, £620; Life Assurance on June 30, £180. Show the Insurance Account for the year, including the tranfer to Profit and Loss Account on December 31, 19. ..

3. The Snooker Enthusiasts' Club had a credit balance on its Subscriptions Account of £1 125, which represented subscriptions in advance, on January 1, 19. .. During the year subscriptions of £31 125 were received, but £1 425 of this was in advance for the next year. Show the Subscriptions Account, including the amount transferred to the club's Income and Expenditure Account (this is the same as the Profit and Loss Account, and is explained later, on page 342).

4. Robson & Co. receive commissions on the sales executed for Yamachita & Co.: 2½ per cent commission on cost price on accepting the authority to sell, and 2½ per cent on selling price when the sale is made. If they are unable to sell, the commission on cost price is returnable. They therefore do not count such commission as profit until they have made the sale.

On January 1, 19. ., there was £1 630 of such commission outstanding as profit earned, but subject to the 'returnable' clause. During the year other commission came to £28 930 and on December 31st there was £2 628 outstanding again.

Draw up the Commission Received Account and thus show how much was transferred as profit to the Profit and Loss Account.

22.5   Accrued expenses owed by the firm

Sometimes we are not in advance with our payments but in arrears. Rent may be accrued due, or commission to travellers may be accrued due.

The word 'accrued' simply means 'collected' or 'built up' over the weeks. Any accruals must sooner or later be paid and settled. One particularly common example is wages that are due. We will use the Wages Account as an example.

Wages are usually paid weekly or fortnightly, and rarely will the last day of the financial year fall on a pay day. Suppose we pay wages on Fridays and the last Friday in the year is December 27. Workers who work on the 28th, 29th, 30th, or 31st will not be paid for these four days until Friday, January 3. We must therefore adjust for these four days, otherwise this year will only be covering 361 days and next year will have 369 days.

To make this adjustment clear, consider the Wages Account as it is at present, as in Figure 22.8.

		WAGES ACCOUNT		L75
19. .			£	
Dec. 27	52 weekly payments coming to a total of		86 084	

Figure 22.8   Wages account before adjustment

The £86 084 is the amount paid out by the cashier in wages over the 52 weeks of the year. It would not be on the account in one piece as shown here, but there would be fifty-two entries, one for each week in the year. Is this figure the correct figure to show in the Trading Account for wages for the year? Clearly it is not, because there are still four days of the year to adjust. Suppose the wages due are £1 138 for these four days? Then the total figure to be transferred to the Trading Account is £86 084 + £1 138 = £87 222. The Journal Entry will read:

19. .				£	£
Dec. 31	Trading Account Dr.	L95	87 222	
	Wages Account	L75		87 222
	Being wages for year transferred			

Figure 22.9   Closing the Wages Account

and the wages account will now have a credit balance. Like all

WAGES ACCOUNT   L75

19. .		£	19. .		£
Dec. 27	52 weekly payments totalling	86 084	Dec. 31	Trading Account	87 222
Dec. 31	Balance c/d	1 138			
		£87 222			£87 222
			19. .		£
			Jan. 1	Balance b/d	1 138

Figure 22.10 **The wages due shown as an outstanding balance**

credit balances this is a liability and will appear on the Balance Sheet as shown below:

BALANCE SHEET
as at December 31, 19. .

CURRENT LIABILITIES	£
Wages Due	1 138

Figure 22.11 **An accrued expense appearing on the Balance Sheet**

As with all adjustments we have achieved a dual aim. The charge against the profits for wages has been adjusted to the exact figure for 365 days, while the liability due to the workers for their efforts in the last four days of the year appears on the Balance Sheet as a current liability.

What effect does this credit balance have next year? On January 3, 19. ., we shall pay a full week's wages, say £2 500. These wages will be recorded in the Cash Book and posted over to the debit side of the Wages Account. The credit balance of £1 138 will automatically reduce the amount of £2 500 to a figure of £1 362 which will be the charge for wages for the three days of the new year. If you feel that these figures have been badly chosen, since on the four days of the old year less wages are paid than in the three days of the new year, you should remember that those four days include Saturday and Sunday – two non-working days in most countries. The Wages Account now looks as follows:

WAGES ACCOUNT   L75

19. .			£	19. .			£
Jan. 3	Cash	CB7	2 500	Jan. 1	Balance	b/d	1 138

Figure 22.12 **The first week's wages in the New Year**

22.6   Accrued Receipts due to the firm

Expenses may have accrued that we owe to other firms, but clearly the reverse can also be true. Receipts that the firm should have received for goods or services supplied this year may still be outstanding at the end of the year. It would be unfair in principle to let next year receive the benefit of this year's work. We should include these profits, even if they have not actually arrived, as if they had done so. This means we must adjust our Revenue Accounts. Rent received is a good example of this type of adjustment. Many firms sub-let spare rooms in their buildings to smaller businesses and thus earn valuable rent. If such a sub-tenant is in arrears with his rent, and we feel quite sure he will pay, this rent should be included. What is needed in the Profit and Loss Account is a full year's rent from the sub-tenant, even if he has not paid in full.

Example
P. Brown sub-let a room to Homeless at a rent of £325 per quarter, payable in arrears: Homeless paid rent on March 27, June 29, and September 30, but had not paid his next quarter due December 31. Show the Rent Received Account for the year, after transferring the year's rent to the Profit and Loss Account. Homeless is deemed to be reliable.

Clearly the profit for the year on this tenancy is £1 300 and this figure should be carried to the Profit and Loss Account. The Rent Received Account will therefore look as follows:

| | RENT RECEIVED ACCOUNT | | | | L74 |

19. .		£	19. .			£
Dec. 31	Profit and Loss Account	1 300	Mar. 27	Cash	CB7	325
			June 29	Cash	CB17	325
			Sept. 30	Cash	CB27	325
			Dec. 31	Balance	c/d	325
		£1 300				£1 300
Jan. 1	Balance b/d	325				

Figure 22.13   A profit that has accrued as an asset

This balance will appear as a current asset on the Balance Sheet.

22.7   Exercises set 22.2 – Accrued expenses and accrued receipts

1. P. Carter, a retailer, sub-lets the flat over his shop at an annual rent of £1 784 payable quarterly in arrear. During the year the tenant paid rent due from him on March 23, June 25, and September 30, but at December

31 had not paid the quarter's rent due. Show the Rent Account in P. Carter's Ledger, after the preparation of his Profit and Loss Account for the year.

(RSA – Adapted)

2. From the following information prepare the Electricity Account in the Ledger of L. Welsh, a manufacturer:

	£
Amount due at January 1, 19. .	321.75
Payments during the year	
January 15	321.75
April 20	271.25
July 17	211.75
October 15	237.50

The bill for electricity supplied during the three months ended December 31 was £413.50 and was not paid until January 19, 19. . Two-thirds of the net cost is to be charged to the Manufacturing Account and one-third to Profit and Loss Account. Balance the account on December 31st, 19. .

(RSA – Adapted)

3. At January 1, 19. ., T. Tennant owed a quarter's rent, £260 in respect of business premises that he occupied.

During the next twelve months he paid £260 by cheque on each of the following dates: January 4, March 26, June 25, and December 27.

(a) Prepare Tennant's Rent payable Account as it would appear after his Profit and Loss Account for the year ending December 31, 19. ., had been drawn up.
(b) What entry relating to rent should appear in his Balance Sheet dated December 31, 19. .?

(RSA – Adapted)

4. H. & C. Ltd erect lifts and repair them. Their Repairs Revenue Account has a debit balance of £3 640 at January 1, 19. ., for repairs effected the previous year and not yet paid for. During the year £49 393 was paid by customers for repairs work, and at December 31 it was calculated that £5 104 was outstanding for repairs already executed. Show the Repairs Revenue Account for the year, after transferring the correct profit to the Trading Account.

Show also the entry in the Balance Sheet as at December 31 for the Repairs Account.

22.8 Exercises set 22.3 – Final Accounts exercises with payments in advance and accrued expenses

1. On January 1, 19. ., the Rates Account of C. Cooper showed a prepayment of £1 000. During the year ending December 31, 19. ., he paid £2 260 for rates and £10 610 in respect of salaries. At the end of the year Cooper calculated that a further £140 was owing for salaries and that the rates were then prepaid to the extent of £925.

(a) Show the Salaries and Rates Accounts after the preparation of the annual Profit and Loss Account.
(b) What difference would there have been in Cooper's profits if the amounts in advance or accrued at the *end* of the year had not been allowed for?

(RSA – Adapted)

2. C. Cone began business on April 1, 19. ., and ended his first financial period on December 31, 19. . . Rent, due at £350 per quarter on June 30, September 30, and December 31, was paid on the due dates except that the rent due on December 31, was not paid until January 3, 19. .. Rates paid were £318 for the half-year ended September 30, 19. . (paid April 1, 19. .) and £342 for the half-year to the following March 31, 19. . (paid October 1, 19. .).

Prepare the Rent and Rates Account as it would appear in C. Cone's books for the period of nine months ended December 31, 19. ., and balance it, showing the amount chargeable to the Profit and Loss Account for the period.

(RSA – Adapted)

3. A firm has in its Ledger a combined Rent and Rates Account, which on 1 July, 19. ., read:

RENT AND RATES

19. .		£	19. .		£
July 1	Balance b/d being rates prepaid to September 30	182.00	July 1	Balance b/d being rent due June 24	500.00

The transactions affecting this account, which took place during the following financial year ending June 30th, were:

(a) Rent due on June 24, 19. ., £500 was paid by cheque on July 4.
(b) Rent due on September 29, 19. . £500 was paid by cheque on the due date.
(c) Rates for the half-year October 1, 19. ., to March 31, 19. ., £384, were paid by cheque on October 31.
(d) Rent due on December 25, 19. ., £500 was paid by cheque on December 22, 19. ..
(e) Rent due on March 25, 19. ., £500 was paid by cheque on April 5, 19. ..
(f) Rates for the half-year April 1, 19. ., to September 30, 19. ., £384, were paid on May 1, 19. ..
(g) On June 18, 19. ., the usual reminder that a quarter's rent £500 was due and payable on June 24 was received from the landlord. This payment had not been made when the financial year ended on June 30.

You are required to copy the heading and opening balances in the firm's Rent and Rates Account, as given above, to complete the account for the financial year ended June 30, 19. ., and to rule it off and balance it at the close of business on that date, after doing the Final Accounts entries.

4. Here is the Trial Balance of Gerard Eliasson on December 31, 19. ..
You are asked to prepare his Trading Account and Profit and Loss
Account for the year, and his Balance Sheet as at this date, bearing in
mind the adjustments given below the Trial Balance.

TRIAL BALANCE
as at December 31, 19. .

	Dr. £	Cr. £
Cash in Hand	137.50	
Cash at Bank	12 325.00	
Purchases and Sales	41 241.25	98 062.50
Returns – In and Out	562.50	241.25
Stock at January 1, 19. .	8 900.00	
Wages	12 250.00	
Salaries	22 900.00	
Light and Heat	2 100.00	
Commission Received		13 251.25
Rent Received		1 650.00
Telephone Expenses	1 602.50	
Insurance	1 250.00	
Motor Vehicles	6 250.00	
Land and Buildings	40 000.00	
Plant and Machinery	17 000.00	
Loan from Southern Bank		15 000.00
Interest Paid	751.25	
Capital		50 695.00
Motor Expenses	1 630.00	
Drawings	10 000.00	
	£178 900.00	178 900.00

Notes
(a) At December 31, 19. ., stock was valued at £10 250
(b) Insurance has been paid in advance for 19. . £250
(c) Interest is due on the loan from the bank £156
     Wages are to be charged to Trading Account.

5. Prepare a Trading Account, Profit and Loss Account, and Balance
Sheet from B. Murray's Trial Balance as at March 31, 19. ..

	Dr. £	Cr. £
Capital (B. Murray)		49 330.00
Cash	125.00	
Bank	15 375.00	
Premises	40 000.00	
Motor Vehicles	4 250.00	

	Dr.	Cr.
Plant and Machinery	16 350.00	
Factory Wages	14 332.50	
Office Salaries	23 676.25	
Factory Light and Heat	2 622.50	
Office Light and Heat	492.50	
Commission Received		12 970.00
Loan from R. Cambridge		12 000.00
Office Expenses	2 136.25	
Stationery	820.00	
Discount Allowed and Received	135.00	183.75
Purchases and Sales	56 230.00	121 477.50
Sales Returns and Purchases Returns	620.00	730.00
Drawings (B. Murray)	13 000.00	
Stock at April 1, 19. .	6 600.00	
Debtors and Creditors	10 682.50	11 398.75
Carriage In	500.00	
Carriage Out	142.50	
	£208 090.00	208 090.00

Stock at the end of the year was valued at £11 500. £217.50 is owing for factory wages and is to be included in the above accounts. Commission amounting to £130 has not yet been received, but is to be included as part of the year's profits.

6. Mrs Brown runs a small clothing factory and on December 31, 19. ., takes out the following Trial Balance. From it prepare her Trading Account, Profit and Loss Account, and Balance Sheet. There are some adjustments given below:

	Dr. £	Cr. £
Stock at January 1, 19. .	9 000.00	
Purchases and Sales	111 500.00	193 625.00
Returns – In and Out	625.00	6 500.00
Carriage In	502.50	
Carriage Out	1 327.50	
Factory Wages	16 002.50	
Factory Light and Heat	2 003.25	
Land and Buildings	37 500.00	
Plant and Machinery	32 500.00	
Motor Vehicles	9 000.00	
Debtors and Creditors	12 001.25	9 002.50
Office Expenses	1 150.50	
Office Salaries	21 852.50	
Commission Paid	2 000.00	
Commission Received		12 952.50

Cash	4 250.00	
Capital		60 885.00
Motor Vehicle Expenses	3 250.00	
Drawings	18 500.00	
	£282 965.00	282 965.00

Closing stock was valued at £21 350.
Wages due amounted to £500.
An amount is owing for office expenses £150.
A sum is due to Mrs Brown for commission amounting to £132.50.

7. Prepare a Trial Balance from the following balances extracted from the books of R. Lasham on March 31, 19. ., and then produce a Trading Account, a Profit and Loss Account, and a Balance Sheet:

	£
Discount Allowed	1 105
Discount Received	2 233
Returns Inward	278
Returns Outward	450
Purchases	23 500
Sales	56 000
Bank Overdraft	1 627
Creditors	3 700
Debtors	8 727
Cash in Hand	450
Rent and Rates	2 404
Premises (Freehold)	42 500
Stock at April 1, 19. .	4 750
Machinery	15 000
Carriage Charges on Sales	2 346
Capital Account	44 250
Office Salaries	16 315
Travellers' Salaries	12 500
Drawings Account	12 200
Commission Received	15 815
Mortgage	18 000

You should also take into account the following adjustments:

(a) Rent and rates due £96.
(b) Office Salaries due £85.
(c) Travellers' salaries paid in advance £250.
(d) Commission received in advance £75.
(e) The stock on hand at March 31 amounted to £6 325.

22.9   Bad debts

One of the important figures on a Balance Sheet is the **Sundry Debtors** figure. This shows how much our debtors owe us, and naturally appears on the assets side of the Balance Sheet. At the end of the financial year, before the debtors figure is brought into the Balance Sheet, all debts should be scrutinized to see whether they are in fact good debts. If we leave a bad debtor on our books, and pretend that the debt is good, we are breaking both our rules. Rule 1 says that we must admit and write off every loss that has been suffered in the year. Rule 2 says we must have an honest Balance Sheet. Neither rule will be observed if we allow a bad debt to persist into the new year.

Any debt revealed in our scrutiny as being bad, should be written off to the Bad Debts Account as already described in Chapter 7 (page 122). This will leave us with a true valuation of the debtors on our Balance Sheet, and the Bad Debts Account will be written off the profits, so that the full loss for the year has been accepted.

22.10   Provision for bad debts

We may have achieved a true debtors figure, but is it also a 'fair' view? Even the best debtor can become a bad debtor if fate knocks unkindly on his door. Someone will die, or be maimed for life, or become seriously ill, and his affairs will deteriorate over the next few months. Every business suffers a percentage of bad debts, and the average businessman knows roughly what percentage of bad debts is normal for his type of business.

If we intend to be perfectly accurate in our figure for the debtors, we should adjust for this expected percentage of bad debts. This is one of the finer points of book-keeping and the student should follow this example with care.

Example
R. Brown's debtors total £4 260 and it is usual in his trade for 5 per cent of debts to prove to be bad. Brown decides to provide this amount out of his profits for the year.

Method
5 per cent of £4 260 = £213
Brown must write off £213 from his profits as shown in Figure 22.14

PROFIT AND LOSS ACCOUNT   L198

19. .	£	19. .	£
Provision for Bad Debts	213	Gross Profit	22 194

Figure 22.14 Providing for bad debts that have not yet occurred

This means he must debit the Profit and Loss Account. But which account must be credited? Will Jones die, or Smith, or Bryant? Will Higgins get ill, or will it be Morris? Clearly Brown cannot tell, and yet he has to credit some account. The solution to the problem is to credit a Nominal Account, the Provision for Bad Debts Account. This account is best regarded as a liability to the proprietor. It is his profits that have been taken and tucked away in this Provision Account where he cannot spend them. When bad debts occur in the first few months of the year, the profits set aside from last year will offset the loss suffered, so that the new year is not suffering last year's bad debts.

The really ingenious part of this arrangement is the way it is dealt with on the Balance Sheet. We have charged the £213 to the Profit and Loss Account so that the current year has suffered the loss. We have this credit balance on the Provision for Bad Debts Account. As it is a credit balance we should expect it to appear on the liabilities side of the Balance Sheet, thus:

BALANCE SHEET
as at December 31, 19. .

	£	CURRENT ASSETS	£
Provision for Bad Debts	213	Debtors	4 260

Figure 22.15 Provision for bad debts is a liability

In fact it is much better style to take it over to the assets side as a deduction from the asset, debtors. When we do this we make it perfectly clear to anyone reading the Balance Sheet that although the debtors' balances actually total £4 260 we only expect to collect £4 047. This gives a 'true and fair view' of the asset, debtors.

BALANCE SHEET
as at December 31, 19. .

	CURRENT ASSETS	£	£
	Debtors	4 260	
	Less Provision	213	
			4 047

Figure 22.16 The best way to display the debtors

22.11   What happens to the provision for bad debts in the next year?

Consider the present provision as shown in the last section. It has a credit balance. It represents a liability to the proprietor for profits

PROVISION FOR BAD DEBTS		L199
	19. .	£
	Jan. 1 Balance	213

Figure 22.17   The provision for Bad Debts Account

earned, but retained in the business in case bad debts occur.

Next year we shall suffer some bad debts, and at the end of the year the provision we shall need will certainly not be £213. It would be a very rare chance that our debtors figure for one year should be exactly the same as the debtors figure twelve months later. As the provision is tied to the debtors figure it must vary from year to year.

Method 1
The simplest way to deal with this problem is to **write the bad debts off the Provision Account and not off the Profit and Loss Account**, on December 31 next. We can then make a new charge to profits for the new provision. There are three possibilities, one of which is highly improbable.

(a) The bad debts could be less than the provision at present of £213.
(b) The bad debts could be exactly £213.
(c) The bad debts could be more than the present provision.

Example (a)
The next year R. Brown suffers bad debts of £132 and on December 31 his debtors balances are £5 800.

If we write the bad debts off against the provision and not against the Profit and Loss Account we will debit them in the Provision Account as we close off the Bad Debts Account. This figure of £132 deducted from £213 leaves a balance of £81 still in the Provision Account.

This year we need 5 per cent of £5 800 which is £290. As we already have £81 in the provision for Bad Debts Account we only need to take £209 from the profits in the Profit and Loss Account. When this sum is debited to Profit and Loss Account and credited to Provision Account we have an account which balances off with exactly the right provision, as in Figure 22.18.

PROVISION FOR BAD DEBTS ACCOUNT   L199

19. .			£	19. .			£
Dec. 31	Bad debts		132	Jan. 1	Balance	b/d	213
31	Balance	c/d	290	Dec. 31	Profit and Loss Account		209
			£422				£422
				19. .			£
				Jan. 1	Balance	b/d	290

Figure 22.18 The old provision changed to the new figure (case (a))

Example (b)
Too unlikely to be worth illustrating.

Example (c)
Going a further year with this account R. Brown suffers serious bad debts due to an economic slump. The total bad debts are £440 and his roll of debtors totals £8 900. Brown decides to increase the provision to 10 per cent of the debtors figure. This time the bad debts transferred to the Provision for Bad Debts Account use up the entire provision of £290 and leave an unsatisfied loss of £150. This will have to be written off the Profit and Loss Account. As we also need a new provision of £890 (10 per cent of the debtors) we have to write off £1 040 from the Profit and Loss Account into the Provision for Bad Debts Account. This will then have exactly the right balance for the new provision.

PROVISION FOR BAD DEBTS ACCOUNT   L199

19. .			£	19. .			£
Dec. 31	Bad debts		132	Jan. 1	Balance	b/d	213
31	Balance	c/d	290	Dec. 31	Profit and Loss Account		209
			£422				£422
Year 2			£	Year 2			£
Dec. 31	Bad Debts		440	Jan. 1	Balance	b/d	290
31	Balance	c/d	890	Dec. 31	Profit and Loss Account		1 040
			£1 330				£1 330
				Year 3			£
				Jan. 1	Balance	b/d	890

Figure 22.19 The old provision changed to the new provision figure (case (c))

Method 2
An alternative way to deal with the bad debts next year is to keep the Bad Debts Account and the Provision for Bad Debts Account

quite separate. At the end of the year the total of the Bad Debts
Account is written off to the Profit and Loss Account by a closing
Journal Entry.

Thus the £132 in Figure 22.18 would not be entered in the
Provision for Bad Debts Account but would be taken direct to the
Profit and Loss Account.

The Provision for Bad Debts Account is now adjusted to the
new provision. In Figure 22.20 the old provision is changed from
£213 to £290. Since Bad Debts are being treated separately from
the Provision for Bad Debts, and we have already dealt with them,
all we have to worry about is the new provision. This is to be £290
instead of £213, so all we need to do is to go to the Profit and Loss
Account and take another £77 of the owner's profits to tuckaway
in the Provision Account. The owner cannot have them, for we
suspect they will be lost by bad debts in the present unfavourable
business climate. We debit the Profit and Loss Account and credit
Provision for Bad Debts Account as in Figure 22.20.

				£					£
PROVISION FOR BAD DEBTS ACCOUNT									L199
19. .				£	19. .				£
Dec. 31	Balance		c/d	290	Jan.	1	Balance		213
					Dec.	31	Profit and Loss Account		77
				£290					£290
					19. .				£
					Jan.	1	Balance	b/d	290

Figure 22.20   The old provision changed to the new figure (case (a))

Note that the Profit and Loss Account will suffer the same
burden as before, but in a different way.

			£		
METHOD 1: PROFIT AND LOSS ACCOUNT					L175
19. .			£		
Dec. 31	Provision for Bad Debts		209		
METHOD 2: PROFIT AND LOSS ACCOUNT					L175
19. .			£		
Dec. 31	Bad Debts		132		
31	Provision for Bad Debts		77		

Figure 22.21   The effect on the Profit and Loss Account

22.12 Exercises set 22.4 – Bad debts and provision for bad debts

1.

(a) At January 1, 19. ., the balance of the Provision for Bad Debts Account of J. Moore stood at £1 250. During that year bad debts amounting to £480 were incurred and at December 31 a balance of £1 400 was carried forward. In the next year £175 was received in respect of a debt previously written off and a loss of £610 for bad debts was suffered. Moore decided to reduce his provision to £1 350.

You are to prepare the Provision for Bad Debts Account for years 1 and 2.

(b) Assuming that at the end of the second year Moore's debtors amounted to £27 000 give the entry in the Balance Sheet of that date in respect of them.

(RSA – Adapted)

2. The Balance Sheet of J. Wilson, dated January 1, 19. ., gave his total debtors as £32 500 and there was a provision of 8 per cent against bad debts. During the year the bad debts written off amounted to £2 430 but a debt of £630 written off in a previous year was paid in full.

At December 31, a year later, Wilson's debtors were £35 000 and he decided to increase his provision to 10 per cent of that amount.

You are to prepare the Bad Debts Account and the Provision for Bad Debts Account 19. ., and to show the relevant entries in the Profit and Loss Account and in the Balance Sheet dated December 31, 19. ..

(RSA – Adapted)

3. The following information relates to the wholesale business of Tupman. Show the account or accounts which you would expect to find in his Nominal Ledger to record the information for the year ended December 31, 19. .

(*Note*: Personal accounts are not required.)

January 1, 19. .. The provision for bad and doubtful debts amounts to £2 125. The following debts were written off as irrecoverable on December 31, 19. .:

	£
T. Wardle	1 137.50
W. Jingle	116.20
K. Trotter	293.75

On September 18, 19. . £54 was received in respect of a debt previously written off as irrecoverable. When the Final Accounts were being prepared it was decided to increase the provision for bad and doubtful debts to £2 400.

(RSA – Adapted)

4. At December 31, 19. ., a firm's debtors totalled £13 000 and its Provision for Bad Debts Account amounted to £650. It was decided to write off as irrecoverable debts of £800 and to carry forward a provision of 5 per cent of the remaining debtors.

Prepare the Provision Account for bad and doubtful debts, the entries in the Profit and Loss Account, and the entry for debtors on the Balance Sheet at December 31, 19. ..

(RSA – Adapted)

5. On January 1, 19. ., the Sales Ledger of T. & Co. showed the following debtors:

	£
Smith	1 250
Brown	640
Jones	110
Robinson	1 150
Williams	700

T. & Co. had a Bad Debts Provision equal to 10 per cent of the total debts outstanding. Trading continued during the year 19. . with these and other customers, except that there were no sales to Jones and Robinson; the former made no payment in respect of the amount due from him, while Robinson paid only £1 000 during the year. On December 31, 19. ., (a) it was found that the Sales Ledger debit balances, including those due from Jones and Robinson, totalled £4 760; (b) it was decided to write off as bad debts the amounts then due from Jones and Robinson; and (c) it was decided to adjust the Bad Debts Provision to 8 per cent of the remaining debts.

You are asked to show the entries recording the above in the appropriate *impersonal* Ledger Accounts for the financial year ended December 31, 19. ., including the entries in the firm's Profit and Loss Account for the year.

6. On January 1, 19. ., the Sales Ledger of Barber & Co. showed the following debtors:

	£
White	2 000
Grey	800
Brown	160
Green	330
Pink	125

A Bad Debts Provision of 10 per cent of these debts was set up (worked out to the nearest £1). Trading continued with these and other debtors during the year, but Brown and Green were not dealt with again, nor did they pay any money. Pink paid £60 off his debt and was sold further goods, value £40.

On December 31, 19. .:

(a) The total debtors figure including Brown and Green was £3 490.
(b) It was decided to write off Brown and Green as bad debts.
(c) Pink's debt was written down as a partially bad debt – to half the present value.
(d) A new provision of 8 per cent of the bad debts still outstanding was to be made (calculated to the nearest £1).

Show the Impersonal Accounts affected, including the Profit and Loss Account.

(RSA – Adapted)

7. Alexander Skeen, a merchant, has the following arrangements in respect of bad debts: the balances in his Sales Ledger of all debtors who fail, during any trading year, to discharge their indebtedness are charged to the Bad Debts Account as soon as Skeen is sure that recovery is unlikely. As a result of experience he also maintains a Provision for Bad Debts Account at 5 per cent of his total of sundry debtors at the date of his Final Accounts. This provision is varied upwards or downwards at the end of each trading year in accordance with changes in the sundry debtors total.

In his Balance Sheet as at January 1, 19. ., the gross total of his sundry debtors was £8 500 and the balance of his Provision for Bad Debts Account corresponded with this. During 19. ., the following events occurred:

Feb. 10 Skeen received from the trustee in bankruptcy of J. Wilcox, who owed him £270 (still standing as a debit in the Sales Ledger), a first and final dividend of £0.50 in the £1.

Apr. 8 On January 1, 19. ., H. Watkins owed Skeen £435. Skeen is now advised by his own solicitor that Watkins has emigrated and that there is no hope of receiving anything from him.

July 22 During 19. ., the account of T. Norie had been written off as a bad debt. Norie's solicitor now sends in a cheque for £390 being payment in full of the debt itself, £375 plus £15 as interest by way of compensation.

Dec. 15 Preparatory to drawing up his Final Accounts for the year, Skeen writes off the following small debts: A. Chivers £30, W. Hartley £40 and F. Bickersdyke £60.

Dec. 19 Skeen receives from his own solicitor an account for £142 charges in connection with debt recovery during the year.

On December 31, 19. ., the total of sundry debtors' balances still open in the Sales Ledger was £15 000.

You are required to write up the Bad Debts, Provision for Bad Debts, Interest and Legal Charges Accounts in Skeen's Ledger for the year 19. ., and to show the relevant entries in his Profit and Loss Account for the year.

(RSA – Adapted)

8. The books of Francis McCarthy, a wholesale dealer in toys showed the following balances at the close of business on December 31, 19. .:

	Dr. £	Cr. £
Capital at January 1, 19. .		43 805.00
Stock at January 1, 19. .	13 975.00	
Purchases	121 648.75	
Sales		216 187.50
Warehouse Wages	18 125.00	

Office Salaries	19 635.00	
Travellers' Salaries and Commission	17 125.00	
Customs Duty on Imported Purchases	1 585.00	
Carriage Outwards	2 150.00	
Returns Inwards	1 092.50	
Returns Outwards		373.75
Rent, Rates, and Insurance	10 850.00	
Fixtures and Fittings	14 500.00	
Discount Allowed	1 578.75	
Discount Received		1 423.75
Sundry Debtors	25 660.00	
Sundry Creditors		11 950.00
Drawings	16 000.00	
General Expenses	2 480.00	
Balance at Bank	6 605.00	
Cash in Hand	575.00	
Carriage Inwards	2 340.00	
Provision for Bad Debts		2 185.00
	£275 925.00	275 925.00

You are required to draw up McCarthy's Trading and Profit and Loss Accounts for the year ended December 31, 19. ., and his Balance Sheet as at that date, taking into account the following:

(a) On December 31, 19. ., his unsold stock was valued at £18 925.
(b) During the year bad debts, as they occurred, had been debited to the Provision for Bad Debts Account. Additional provision should be made, to bring the balance of this account up to £2 566.
(c) The rent of the offices is £5 000 a year, and the quarterly instalment due on December 24, 19. ., has not been paid.

(RSA – Adapted)

9. Here is B. Irving's Trial Balance on March 31, 19. .. You are asked to prepare, in good style, the Trading Account, Profit and Loss Account, and Balance Sheet of his business:

	Dr.	Cr.
	£	£
Cash in Hand	625	
Cash at Bank	6 175	
Purchases and Sales	79 950	173 632
Stock at April 1, 19. .	11 810	
Debtors and Creditors	28 900	21 842
Returns – In and Out	2 135	2 700
Bad Debts	2 180	
Carriage Out	3 240	
Plant and Machinery	21 500	
Power for Plant and Machinery	3 620	

Factory Light and Heat	4 182	
Factory Rent and Rates	4 903	
Office Light and Heat	3 143	
Office Rent and Rates	3 502	
Wages (Trading A/c)	10 130	
Salaries	16 840	
Factory Manager's Wages	15 750	
Drawings	16 250	
Commissions Received		15 803
Provision for Bad Debts		2 353
Capital		48 505
Factory Premises	30 000	
	£264 835	264 835

Closing Stock = £15 100. You are to restore the bad debts provision to £2 890.

(RSA – Adapted)

10. Here is M. Milwaukee's Trial Balance at December 31, 19. .. Prepare his Trading Account, Profit and Loss Account, and Balance Sheet, taking into account the adjustments below:

	Dr.	Cr.
	£	£
Stock at Start	7 700	
Rent and Rates	4 083	
Purchases and Sales	40 655	93 680
Packing Materials	2 770	
Debtors and Creditors	4 970	5 371
Plant and Tools (at cost)	25 000	
Cash at Bank	9 298	
Capital Account		38 104
Interest Received		888
Provision for Bad Debts		996
Office Salaries	16 042	
Light and Heat	2 520	
Power for Machines	3 386	
Wages (Trading A/c)	10 100	
Drawings	12 490	
Returns In and Out	1 680	1 655
	£140 694	140 694

(a) Closing stock was valued at £8 590.
(b) Of the debts £420 is reckoned to be definitely bad. After writing these off the provision is to be reduced to 10% of the outstanding debts.
(c) Office salaries due are £158.

22.13 Provisions for discounts

Another source of possible misconception about debtors arises from the discounts that may be taken by our debtors if they pay promptly. If we are allowing debtors to deduct discount, the valuation placed on debtors will be misleading if we do not provide for this discount.

The provision for discount is very similar indeed to the provision for bad debts, but when calculating the amount to be provided we use the **net debtors figure**, that is **debtors less provision for bad debts**. Since we have provided for the bad debts these debtors will not qualify for discount, since they are not going to pay promptly.

Example
R. Brown's debtors total £21 300 on December 31, 19. .. He provided for 5 per cent of possible bad debts and a further 2½ per cent of discount to be allowed to debtors.

Calculation
5 per cent of bad debts = £1065
This figure give a net figure of £21 300 − £1065 =£20 235.
2½ per cent of £20 235 = £505.90
The Journal Entry will be:

19. . Dec. 31	Profit and Loss Account Dr. Provision for Discount Being 2½% of Net Debtors pro- vided to cover discounts	L17 L25	£ 505.90	£ 505.90

Figure 22.22 Providing for discount

and the Balance Sheet entry for debtors now reads:

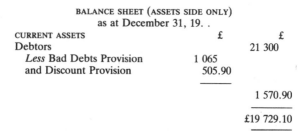

BALANCE SHEET (ASSETS SIDE ONLY)
as at December 31, 19. .

CURRENT ASSETS	£	£
Debtors		21 300
Less Bad Debts Provision	1 065	
and Discount Provision	505.90	
		1 570.90
		£19 729.10

Figure 22.23 Providing a true debtors figure

Similar but opposite entries could be devised so that the businessman reduces the creditors figure. If he intends to pay promptly it seems only sensible that he should offset the losses he is taking into account on his debtors with a little profit on his creditors' accounts. Unfortunately this offends against that book-keeping principle *never anticipate a profit, always anticipate a loss*. The cautious businessman will therefore not accept this profit because it is unrealized, and this is why provisions for profit on discount receivable are rarely seen.

22.14   Depreciation of assets

The entries for depreciation have already been dealt with fully in Chapter 14. These entries are often required as adjustments, since the normal time for depreciating assets is at the end of the year when the Final Accounts are being prepared. The student should note that if asked, in a note at the foot of a Trial Balance, to adjust for depreciation on an asset, he should deduct the depreciation entry from the profits in the Profit and Loss Account and from the stated value of the asset in the Trial Balance. If depreciation is merely included in the Trial Balance, and not in the footnotes, he should write the depreciation off in the Profit and Loss Account, but there is no need to reduce the book value of the asset; it will already have been reduced.

22.15   Goodwill, and Depreciation of Goodwill

Goodwill is a valuation placed upon a going concern over and above the value of the assets forming it. It is paid by the buyer to the seller in expectation of profits to be made, which result directly from the hard work of the former owner. It is sensible that the buyer should pay for the assets, premises, stock, etc., which he takes over. Why should he pay an extra sum for goodwill?

Imagine that Mr Jones buys Smith's business and opens shop on January 1. The doorbell rings as Roberts, a regular customer of Smith's enters the shop. 'Twenty cigarettes please, Joe – Hullo – where *is* Joe?' Mr Jones will explain that Joe has retired from business but that he will be very happy to serve him in future. The profit on that packet of cigarettes came from Smith's hard work and the goodwill borne him by the people in the area.

Goodwill – an intangible asset
Goodwill is often called an intangible asset. You cannot actually touch this asset, but it really does exist. The people who have had business relations with Smith will continue to deal with Jones

because they are used to the idea that this shop is efficiently run. It is for this intangible benefit that Jones pays a lump sum of money as compensation to the previous owner. The value of goodwill is a matter for negotiation between the parties when a business changes hands. The seller will demand a good price for the goodwill, the buyer will offer less, and by a process of haggling the bargain will finally be struck.

Depreciation of goodwill
Since goodwill is not a real asset in the normal meaning of the word 'real', it is frequently written off over the first few years of the business's new lease of life. There is no *necessity* to write off goodwill if the business is making steady profits, since steady profits are a sign of public goodwill. The goodwill must therefore still be as valuable as, or more valuable perhaps than, the original purchase value.

   If goodwill is to be written down, then it cannot be written off the Profit and Loss Account, because it is not a revenue loss. It is a decision by the proprietor to reduce the stated value of his assets. This must be met out of his own pocket by a capital loss, in other words the amount written off is taxable for Income Tax purposes. It is what we call an appropriation of profit, not a charge against the profits and will therefore be debited either to the Capital Account or to the Appropriation Account (see page 316), and not to the Profit and Loss Account.

   The Journal Entry will be as in Figure 22.24.

19. . Dec. 31	Capital Account Dr. Goodwill Account Being Goodwill reduced at this date	L17	£ 500.00	£ 500.00

Figure 22.24   Writing down the value of goodwill

The paradox of goodwill
Accountants sometimes speak of the paradox of gooodwill. A paradox is an apparent contradiction. We have on our books, when we take over a business, an asset at a high valuation called goodwill. In fact the public bears us no goodwill at all, for they do not even know that we exist. As the years go by, if we adopt the policy of writing off the intangible asset by a series of appropriations of profit, our goodwill gradually reduces until it is written off completely. At the same time, the public have now learned to know us; they realize our goods or services are reliable and they

now bear us some goodwill. Here is the paradox of goodwill: it is valued at a high figure on the books when it is worthless, and at nothing on the books when it is very valuable.

22.16 Exercises set 22.5 – Final accounts with all types of adjustment

1. From the following abridged Trial Balance of M. Montgomery dated December 31, 19. ., prepare his Profit and Loss Account for the year, and his Balance Sheet at that date. You should note that:

(a) Rates £140 were prepaid, and £250 was owing by Montgomery's tenant.
(b) The machinery balance is to be depreciated by 10 per cent and the additions by 5 per cent.
(c) £500 is to be written off the goodwill. (Debit to Capital Account.)

TRIAL BALANCE
at December 31, 19. .

	Dr. £	Cr. £
Rates	1 000	
Salaries	11 420	
Heating, Lighting, etc.	2 880	
Insurance	1 245	
Advertising	2 300	
General Expenses	3 685	
Drawings	12 050	
Cash in Hand	380	
Trade Debtors	5 520	
Stock at December 31, 19. .	13 090	
Machinery	10 000	
Machinery Additions	2 500	
Land and Buildings	35 000	
Goodwill	2 500	
Gross Profit		47 430
Discount Received		1 675
Rent Received		2 750
Bank Loan		4 750
Trade Creditors		1 965
Capital Account (January 1, 19. .)		45 000
	£103 570	103 570

(*RSA – Adapted*)

2. After his Trading Account has been prepared for the year ended December 31, 19. ., a manufacturer's position is as follows:

	Dr. £	Cr. £
Trading Account, Gross Profit		47 253.75
Plant and Machinery	16 450.00	
Stock at December 31, 19. .	6 052.50	
Debtors	8 128.75	
Creditors		5 901.25
Capital at January 1, 19. .		19 827.50
Discount Allowed	1 116.25	
Discount Received		917.50
Salaries and Office Expenses	15 800.00	
Rent, Rates, and Insurance	4 327.50	
Carriage Outwards	600.00	
Bad Debts	425.00	
Goodwill	2 175.00	
Drawings	14 250.00	
Cash at Bank	4 475.00	
Petty Cash	100.00	
	£73 900.00	73 900.00

Draw up the manufacturer's Profit and Loss Account for the year, and a Balance Sheet as at December 31, 19. ., taking into consideration:

(a) Depreciation on Plant and Machinery which is to be provided for at 10 per cent of its original cost, £20 000
(b) Rent is £2 000 a year, of which the quarterly instalment due December 25, 19. ., is unpaid.
(c) £1 087.50 is to be appropriated for the reduction of goodwill. (Debit to Capital Account.)
(d) A provision for bad debts of £500 is to be established.

3. The following Trial Balance was extracted from the books of Donald Haig. You are required to draw up the Trading Account and Profit and Loss Account of the business for the year ending September 30, 19. ., and a Balance Sheet as at that date.

TRIAL BALANCE
at September 30, 19. .

	Dr. £	Cr. £
Stock at start on October 1	21 000	
Purchases and Sales	41 935	111 430
Returns In and Out	930	3 413
Wages (Trading A/c)	27 683	
Carriage on Purchases	2 901	

Salaries	22 850	
Advertising	3 532	
Carriage on Sales	1 600	
Rates	2 642	
Heating and Lighting	3 095	
Bad Debts	2 995	
Insurance	1 390	
Debtors and Creditors	7 500	3 752
Capital		55 250
Drawings	8 000	
Cash in Hand	142	
Cash at Bank	6 650	
Goodwill	6 000	
Land and Buildings	40 000	
Fees Received		27 000
	£200 845	200 845

You should take the following into account:

(a) The stock in hand on September 30, 19. ., was valued at £26 105.
(b) The lands and buildings are to be depreciated by 5 per cent.
(c) Salaries £150 are owing.
(d) Rates have been pre-paid to the extent of £180.
(e) Goodwill is to be reduced by 25% (Debit to Capital Account.)

(RSA – Adapted)

4. M. Martindale carries on business as a retailer. On December 31, 19. ., the following Trial Balance was extracted from his books:

TRIAL BALANCE
at December 31, 19. .

	Dr. £	Cr. £
Goodwill	1 715	
Premises	50 000	
Debtors and Creditors	8 520	3 775
Wages	16 470	
Rent Received		850
General Expenses	6 540	
Bad Debts	1 030	
Discount Allowed	875	
Commission Paid	1 380	
Purchases and Sales	87 195	137 265
Capital at January 1, 19. .		97 500
Drawings	13 375	
Cash in hand	630	
Bank	6 050	
Stock at January 1, 19. .	12 000	

Carriage Outwards	2 362	
Salaries	21 627	
Loan Interest	400	
Loan (Midland Bank Ltd)		10 000
Advertising	3 486	
Returns Inwards and Outwards	1 825	1 380
Carriage Inwards	790	
Fixtures and Fittings	7 000	
Motor Vehicles	7 500	
	£250 770	250 770

(a) On December 31, 19. ., the value of stock in hand was estimated at £11 850.

(b) Two-thirds of the wages is to be charged to the Trading Account and one-third to the Profit and Loss Account.

(c) The goodwill is to be written off in full. (Debit to Capital Account.)

(d) A provision for bad debts of 5 per cent of the debtors figure is to be made.

(e) A provision for discount of $2\frac{1}{2}$ per cent of the net debtors is to be made (correct to the nearest £1).

You are to prepare the Trading Account and Profit and Loss Account for the year ending December 31, 19. ., and the Balance Sheet as at that date.

23
Partnership Accounts

23.1 Introduction – why take a partner?

There are several reasons why sole traders combine together to form partnerships. The chief advantages are:

(a) Increased capital, permitting the business to expand more rapidly than is possible by the 'ploughing back' of profits earned.

(b) The responsibility of control no longer rests with one person. This makes possible holidays and free week-ends, and reduces the worry the sole trader experiences at times of ill-health.

(c) Wider experience is brought to the firm and some degree of specialization is possible; this is particularly true of professional partnerships. A physician and a surgeon may form a partnership; or lawyers with experience in different fields – divorce, criminal law, commercial law – may combine to offer a more comprehensive service to the public.

(d) Very often a young man teams up with an older man. The young man has his health and strength; his partner has the capital and the experience. Together they make a satisfactory team.

23.2 The Partnership Act of 1890

Even when the partners agree now, the possiblity always exists that they will disagree later. This has led to a very complicated and ancient case law on partnership matters which was finally codified by the Partnership Act of 1890. This Act is very short, containing only fifty sections, but it is a very good example of an Act of Parliament. Any British student who is not familiar with the layout of an Act of Parliament is strongly advised to buy a copy of this one from his local book-seller and study it. Naturally it covers the entire range of possible dispute between partners, but the main book-keeping features are contained in Section 24 and are briefly as follows:

(a) All the partners are entitled to contribute equally to the capital. They must share equally the profits of the business, and must contribute equally to the losses.
(b) No partner is entitled to a salary for his part in the activities of the firm.
(c) No partner is entitled to interest on his capital.
(d) Where a partner loans money to the firm over and above his capital he shall be entitled to interest at 5 per cent per annum. This rate is raised to a more realistic figure today.
(e) Any partner may see and copy the books of the partnership which must be kept at the ordinary place of business.
(f) No new partner may be introduced without the general consent of all the partners.

These rules, and others, apply in any dispute where there is no clear evidence of what agreement the partners originally made. This evidence does not have to be written evidence; it can be implied from a course of conduct over the years. For instance, if two partners had for many years divided their profits two-thirds and one-third, this would imply that they had originally agreed to share the profits in this way. This fact would go against a partner who now claimed that profits should be shared equally.

23.3   The Partnership Deed

To avoid the ruling of the Partnership Act, partners must agree among themselves and should preferably draw up an agreement in writing. The partnership Deed should cover most of the following points:

(a) The amount of capital to be provided by each partner.
(b) The ratio of sharing profits and losses.
(c) The date at which the partnership shall begin, and the duration of the partnership.
(d) The amount of any salaries payable to partners.
(e) How much each partner shall be allowed to draw in anticipation of profits.
(f) Whether interest shall be allowed on capital and if so, whether it shall also be charged on drawings.
(g) What arrangements shall be made in the event of the death of a partner.
(h) How disputes shall be settled, i.e. by arbitration or some other method.

(i) What arangements shall be made in the event of the admission of a new partner.

23.4 The capital of the partnership

Since the capital of a partnership business forms an important part of the original agreement, it is desirable to preserve the original capital on the books as evidence of the capital position at the start. This means that the original capital shall not be varied, as sole trader capital varies, by the addition of profits to the Capital Account or the subtraction of losses from the Capital Account. Instead, each partner has a new account opened called a Current Account, to which profits can be credited and from which losses and drawings can be subtracted. It follows that each partner now has three accounts opened in his name:

(a) A Capital Account, which records the original capital.
(b) A Current Account, which records changes in the original capital as a result of the activities of the firm.
(c) A Drawings Account, which records the amounts drawn out.

Since the Capital Accounts are fixed, they will appear on the Balance Sheet every year, and will be added together to show the total initial capital. The Balance Sheet on the liabilities side, in the order of permanence, therefore begins:

BALANCE SHEET
as at December 31, 19. .

CAPITAL AT START	£	£
H. Brown	20 000	
R. Brown	10 000	
		30 000

Figure 23.1 The original capital of a partnership

23.5 The Final Accounts of a partnership business

The Trading Account and Profit and Loss Account of a partnership business are exactly the same as those of a sole trader's business. Perhaps the only point worth noting here is that, where a partner loans the business sums of money over and above his capital, the interest on this loan will be charged to the Profit and Loss Account exactly like any other type of interest, but instead of actually being paid out it will be credited to the partner's Current Account, which is discussed on page 320.

The main changes in Partnership Accounts begin when the

partners start to appropriate the profits. We now have a much more complex appropriation which requires an Appropriation Account.

23.6   The Appropriation Account of a partnership

The Appropriation Account will be opened as in Figure 23.2 by the transfer of the net profit to the credit side of the Appropriation Account. The following entries, in the order shown, may be required on the debit side, to authorize various appropriations to the partners' Current Accounts, or to implement agreed policies of the partners.

(a) *Goodwill.* If the partners have agreed to write down the value of goodwill, then the Appropriation Account will be debited and goodwill credited.

(b) *Partnership salaries.* If either partner is authorized by the Partnership Deed to draw a salary for his efforts in the business, this will have a first claim on the profits after goodwill. This requires a debit to the Appropriation Account, the amount being credited to the partner's Current Account.

(c) *Interest on capital.* Partners who have agreed to allow interest on capital are really withdrawing their profits in a slightly different way from the agreed ratio for sharing profits. The idea is to give some bias to favour the partner who has contributed the greater share of capital. Where partners have contributed equal capital sums, and share profits equally, there will be no point in deciding to give each other interest on capital at some agreed percentage. Where the capital contributed is unequal, the partners may well feel that interest on capital is desirable. The partner who has invested £20 000 will receive, at 10 per cent, interest amounting to £2 000. The partner who has invested only £10 000 will receive interest amounting to £1 000. The unequal payments represent fair rewards for the unequal services rendered.

(d) *Sharing the residue of the profit.* Whatever the Net Profit, considerable inroads into it may have been made by these earlier appropriations, leaving a residue to be shared in the agreed proportions. If there is no agreement, then the Partnership Act of 1890 states that these profits must be shared equally.

A typical Appropriation Account might look as follows:

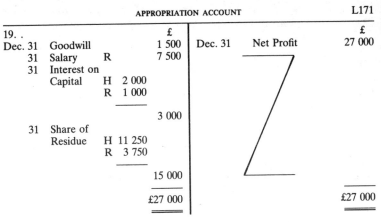

Figure 23.2   An Appropriation Account for a partnership business

Interest on drawings

The reward earned by partners is a share of the profits of the firm. Since profits are not calculated until the end of the year the partners may withdraw moneys in expectation of profits, in the same way as sole traders do. An element of unfairness creeps in here if these drawings are unequal. One partner may withdraw large sums early in the year, or throughout the year. The other may withdraw smaller sums, or not draw anything until later in the year. To equalize the position between the two partners some firms charge interest on drawings. This interest is usually calculated in a second money column on the Drawings Account, and then sub-totalled into the main column on the Account as shown below:

DRAWINGS ACCOUNT   L188
MR H

19. .			Interest	£	19. .			£
Mar. 31	Bank	CB1	225	3 000	Dec. 31	Transfer to Current Account	L172	12 450
June 30	Bank	CB9	150	3 000				
Sept. 30	Bank	CB12	75	3 000				
Dec. 31	Bank	CB18	—	3 000				
31	Bank Interest to Appropriation Account	L171		450				
			£	12 450			£	12 450

Figure 23.3   A Drawings Account with interest charged at 10 per cent

Notice that the interest is charged for the period when the funds were *not* available to the business i.e. 9 months, 6 months and 3 months respectively. The last £3 000 was only withdrawn on the last day of the year, so no interest is deducted.

The interest which is being entered in the main column for the year is the total interest the business is entitled to recoup from Mr H. As this interest is recouped it must be credited to the Appropriation Account, to enable the partners to share it out in the same ratio as that in which they agreed to share profits.

An Appropriation Account might therefore look like this:

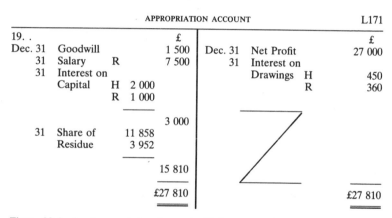

APPROPRIATION ACCOUNT						L171
19. .			£			£
Dec. 31	Goodwill		1 500	Dec. 31	Net Profit	27 000
31	Salary	R	7 500	31	Interest on	
31	Interest on				Drawings H	450
	Capital	H 2 000			R	360
		R 1 000				
			3 000			
31	Share of	11 858				
	Residue	3 952				
			15 810			
			£27 810			£27 810

Figure 23.4   **An Appropriation Account with interest on drawings**

What happens when there is only a loss to appropriate?

When a business is running at a loss, the loss will have to be appropriated to the partners. It makes no difference to the Appropriation Account. We still write off goodwill if this is agreed, and there is a very strong case for doing so. If we are making a loss, then we have lost public goodwill and should not have goodwill as an asset on the books. We still give the partners their salaries and interest on capital. Each of these appropriations increases the loss to be suffered, which is then shared between the partners in the way that they share profits or losses.

The Appropriation Account might therefore look like this:

APPROPRIATION ACCOUNT   L171

19. .			£				£
Dec. 31	Net Loss		5 760	Dec. 31	Interest on		
31	Goodwill		1 500		Drawings H		450
31	Salary	R	7 500		R		360
	Interest on						
	Capital	H 2 000			Share of		
		R 1 000			Loss	H 12 712	
			3 000			R 4 238	
							16 950
			£17 760				£17 760

Figure 23.5 Appropriating a loss

23.7 Exercises set 23.1 – the Appropriation Account

1. Hayes and Harlington are in partnership. On June 30, 19. ., their Capital Accounts (unchanged since July 1 in the previous year) are: Hayes £75 000 Harlington £50 000. Their deed of partnership provides that, after the net profit for any year has been ascertained, the balance available will be applied as follows:

(a) Harlington will receive a salary of £6 000.
(b) Each partner will be credited with interest on capital at 10 per cent per annum.
(c) After providing for (a) and (b), the remaining balance is to be divided equally between the partners.

You are required to draw up the partnership Appropriation Account for the year ended June 30, 19. . The Net Profit, as shown by the Trading and Profit and Loss Account, was £31 250.

2. Arthur and Brian Buckley are in partnership, sharing profits and losses in the ratio of three to two. It has been agreed that interest on capital at 8 per cent per annum should be allowed. Some years ago Brian had loaned the business £5 000 but agreed that as from January 1, 19. ., this should be converted to capital. It will carry the same interest at 8 per cent per annum. At the same date Arthur introduced £3 000 new capital. Before appropriating the interest and allowing Brian a salary of £4 800, the divisible profit for the year was £34 600. From the following details prepare the appropriation section of their Profit and Loss Account for the year ending December 31, 19. .:

	Arthur	Brian
Capital Account balances (At end of previous year)	£15 000	£10 000

(*RSA – Adapted*)

3. Sybrandt and Cornelis are in partnership. They have a written agreement which says:

(a) Partnership capitals shall carry interest at 10 per cent per annum.
(b) Cornelis shall have a salary of £4 500 per annum.
(c) Goodwill shall be reduced each year by 20 per cent.
(d) Profits over and above those required for the first three clauses shall be shared, two-thirds to Sybrandt and one-third to Cornelis.

Capitals are: Sybrandt £25 000 Cornelis £10 000. Goodwill is valued at £3 600. Show the Appropriation Account (i.e. the Appropriation Section of the Profit and Loss Account) if the profits at December 31, 19. ., were £33 410.

(East Anglian Examination – Adapted)

4. Nelson, Blake, and Hardy are partners in carrying on a business under an agreement which provides that, after allowing interest on capital (but not on Current Accounts) at 8 per cent per annum, and partnership salaries of £6 000 to Nelson and £5 000 to Blake, the remaining profit is to be shared one half to Nelson and one quarter each to Blake and Hardy.

The Net Profit for the year ended 31 March 19. ., was £38 600 before providing partnership salaries or interest on capital. The balances on the partners' capital accounts on April 1, 19. ., were: Nelson £40 000, Blake £10 000 and Hardy £8 000 and there was no further contribution of capital during the year.

(a) You are required to prepare the appropriation section of the firm's Profit and Loss Account for the year ended March 31, 19. ..
(b) Why do partnership agreements sometimes direct, as in this case, that interest on capital shall be provided before ascertaining divisible profits?

(RSA – Adapted)

5. At January 1, 19. ., G. Wilson owned a business in which he had £50 000 capital. As from July, 19. ., W. Gibbs came in as a partner on the following terms:

(a) Wilson's capital was to remain unchanged and Gibbs was to bring in £10 000
(b) Interest at 8 per cent *per annum* was to be allowed on both capitals from the start of the partnership.
(c) Gibbs was to be credited with a salary of £7 000 *per annum*.
(d) Profits, after charging interest and salary, were to be divided: Wilson two-thirds, and Gibbs one-third.

At December 31, 19. ., the Net Profit available for division before charging the partnership interest and salary was £33 782. You are required to prepare the partnership's Appropriation Account.

(RSA – Adapted)

23.8   The Current Accounts of the partners

On page 315 we saw that the Capital Accounts in a partnership business are not varied every year by the addition of profits or the deduction of losses. Instead, these fluctuations in capital are recorded in a Current Account for each partner. A Current Account, as its name implies, is one that varies from day to day, although in fact entries are few in the partners' Current Accounts.

At the beginning of the year a Current Account will either be clear, or have a balance on it. This balance may be a debit balance or a credit balance, according to the policy pursued the previous year by the partner. If the partner has been prudent, withdrawing only such sums as he feels sure will be covered by the profits, then at the year's end the profits appropriated to him will exceed his drawings, and leave him with a credit balance. If the partner has been rash, withdrawing more heavily than the business justifies in expectation of profits, the sums appropriated to him will leave him with a deficit on his Current Account, that is, a debit balance. Here are two such Current Accounts:

CURRENT ACCOUNT
(B. CAREFUL)   L165

19. .			£	19. .			£
Dec. 31	Sales		55	Dec. 31	Balance	b/d	840
31	Drawings		8 000	31	Salary		5 750
31	Balance	c/d	3 860	31	Interest		525
				31	Share of Residue		4 800
			£11 915				£11 915
				19. .			£
				Jan. 1	By Balance	b/d	3 860

CURRENT ACCOUNT
(A. RECKLESS)   L166

19. .			£	19. .			£
Dec. 31	Drawings		16 500	Dec. 31	Balance	b/d	420
				31	Interest		1 350
				31	Share of Residue		13 600
				31	Balance	c/d	1 130
			£16 500				£16 500
19. .			£				
Jan. 1	Balance	b/d	1 130				

Figure 23.6 Two Current Accounts

On these two accounts the student can follow the normal entries in a Current Account. They include the following:

(a) An opening balance, which may be either a debit or credit balance.
(b) Various appropriations of profit on the credit side. These include salaries, interest on capital, and shares of the residue of the profit. One that is not shown in either of these Current

Accounts is interest on a loan. This would be credited in the Current Account after being debited in the Profit and Loss Account as explained on page 315.

(c) Various drawings, *in cash* or *in kind*, on the debit side. These have not been dealt with before, so a word of explanation is required.

We know that *drawings in cash* are taken, either in cash from the till, or by cheque from the bank. They therefore appear on the credit side of the Cash Book, either in the Cash Account or the Bank Account, and are posted into the proprietors' Drawings Accounts. These accounts are closed off into the partners' Current Accounts at the end of the financial year. The Closing Entry will be as follows:

19. .				£	£
Dec. 31	Curent Account B. Careful	L165	8 000		
	Drawings Account B. Careful	L150			8 000
	Being drawings for year transferred				

Figure 23.7   Closing off the Drawings Account

When posted to the Drawings Account this will clear the account and the debit entry in the Current Account as shown in Figure 23.6 will set off the money already drawn out against the profits appropriated to the partner.

Drawings in kind means drawings in goods, or perhaps even drawings of assets out of the business. Businessmen often take home stock or surplus assets for their own use, and without payment. The goods are simply charged to the debit side of Current Account and set off against the profits earned. If we debit the Current Account in this way we must credit some other account. If the item taken home is an asset we shall treat it in the same way as the disposal of any other worn-out asset, removing it at its book value from the books, and adjusting depreciation if necessary.

If the item taken home is goods for resale, a difficulty arises. At what price should the partner pay for these goods. In a legal decision in the case of Sharkey *v* Wernher it was held that where a person takes goods from stock for own consumption this must be treated as a transfer at current market value. Had this decision not been made the trader taking goods for his own consumption would not have taken them at selling price but at cost price. In the first place, it is well recognized in law that a 'sale' involves the transfer of property from one person to another, and clearly there has been no such transfer in this case. Secondly, it is well recognized in accounting that a person cannot make profits on himself. It is therefore most unfair for the Inland Revenue to demand tax on profits that have never been made. The House of Lords decision was made 'per incuriam' which means that the points were not properly put to their lordships, so that they were unaware of some aspects of the point being decided. The fact that the Inland Revenue themselves, in the case of hotel and restaurant owners, allow goods taken for 'own consumption' to be on the basis of disallowing cost shows how weak the rule is. Also the Customs and Excise Authorities, in the VAT regulations for retailers (Notice No. 727, Paragraph 34) allows goods taken for own consumption to be deducted at cost price. The Inland Revenue authorities have in fact said that if a person feels particularly aggrieved by the ruling they will look at the facts of the case sympathetically. In the meantime, obeying the rule in Sharkey *v* Wernher, in Figure 23.6 B. Careful's drawings in kind have been credited to Sales Account, at selling price.

(d) A closing balance on the Current Account, which may be either a debit or credit balance.

The nature of the Current Account balance is something which needs a little further explanation. The Current Account is that part of the partner's capital which has accumulated since the business began and which is permitted to fluctuate.

What does Careful's Current Account balance of £3 860 represent? It is a credit balance, a liability of the business, and represents accumulated profit which the business owes to Careful.

What does Reckless's Current Account balance of £1 130 represent? It is a debit balance, an asset of the business, and represents an overdraft of profits by Reckless which he owes to the business. For the present we will show it as a Current Asset of the business.

CURRENT ACCOUNTS (B. CAREFUL AND A. RECKLESS)   L165

19. .		B. Careful £	A. Reckless £	19. .			B. Careful £	A. Reckless £
Dec. 31	Sales	55	—	Dec. 31	Balance b/d		840	420
31	Drawings	8 000	16 500	31	Salary		5 750	—
31	Balance c/d	3 860	—	31	Interest		525	1 350
				31	Share of Residue		4 800	13 600
				31	Balance c/d		—	1 130
		£11 915	16 500				£11 915	16 500
19. .		£	£	19. .			£	£
Jan. 1	Balance b/d	—	1 130	Jan. 1	Balance b/d		3 860	

Figure 23.8   An alternative presentation of Current Accounts

An alternative presentation of the Current Accounts is shown in Figure 23.8.

23.9 Exercises set 23.2 – Current Accounts of partners

Note: Since the partner's Current Accounts receive appropriations from the Appropriation Account it is not usually possible to decide what figures to enter without doing a rough Appropriation Account in the exercises below.

1. Messrs. Wilson and Brown are in partnership, sharing profits and losses: Wilson three-fifths, Brown two-fifths. Their fixed capitals are: Wilson £40 000, Brown £25 000. The partnership agreement provides that interest of 8 per cent per annum shall be paid on fixed capital and that Brown is to receive a salary of £5 000 per annum and 2 per cent commission on the balance of trading profit *after* charging his salary, but *before* charging interest on capital.

The balances on the Current Accounts at January 1, 19. ., are: Wilson credit £2 100, Brown credit £1 750.

Drawings during the year: Wilson £25 000, Brown £20 000.

The trading profit for the year ended December 31, 19. ., was £38 500.

Prepare the Current Account of each partner for the year ended December 31, 19. ..

(RSA – Adapted)

2. Hebron and Haifa are in partnership with capitals of £25 000 and £5 000 respectively. The partnership deed provides that:

(a) Haifa is entitled to a salary of £8 000 per annum.
(b) Each gets 10 per cent interest on capital per annum.
(c) The remaining profits are shared three-quarters to Hebron, one-quarter to Haifa.

Each partner has a Current Account to which all items of personal income arising from the firm are posted, and against which any drawings, either of cash or goods, are charged.

Show Haifa's Current Account for the year 19. .. On January 1, 19. ., he had a credit balance of £910. During the year he drew £9 800 in cash and took home goods valued at £420. Profits for the year were £26 000.

(East Anglian Examination Board – Adapted)

3. The partnership agreement between L. Hemp, T. Wool, and M. Cotton contains the following provisions:

(a) The partners' fixed capitals shall be: Hemp £60 000, Wool £50 000 and Cotton £40 000.
(b) Wool and Cotton are to receive salaries of £8 000 and £7 500 respectively.
(c) Interest on capital is to be calculated at 8 per cent per annum.

(d) Hemp, Wool, and Cotton are to share profits and losses in the ratios 3:2:1.
(e) No interest is to be charged on drawings or Current Accounts.

On January 1, 19. ., the balances on Current Accounts were: Hemp Cr. £3 500, Wool Cr. £2 000 and Cotton Dr. £500.

During the year the drawings were: Hemp £22 500, Wool £19 000 and Cotton £17 500.

The Profit and Loss Account for the year showed a profit of £63 284 before charging interest on capital or on partners' salaries.

Show the Capital and Current Accounts of Hemp, Wool, and Cotton, as at December 31, 19. ., after division of the profit.

(RSA – Adapted)

4. At January 1, 19. ., G. Watson owned a business in which he had £50 000 capital. As from July 1, 19. ., S. Holmes came in as a partner on the following terms:

(a) Watson's capital was to remain unchanged and Holmes was to bring in £12 500 of which £2 500 was to be credited to his current account.
(b) Interest at 9 per cent *per annum* was to be allowed on both capitals from the beginning of the partnership.
(c) Holmes was to be credited with a salary of £7 500 *per annum*.
(d) Profits, after charging interest and salary, were to be divided between Watson and Holmes in the ratio 2:1.

Holmes withdrew £850 on August 1, £1 650 on September 30, and £2 000 on November 30. At December 31, 19. ., the Net Profit available for division before charging the partnership interest and salary was £27 282.

You are required to prepare the Current Account of S. Holmes.

5. David and Peter Fitch are in partnership, sharing profits and losses in the ratio of three to two. It has been agreed that interest on capital at 8 per cent per annum should be allowed. Some years earlier Peter loaned the business £5 000 but agreed that as from July 1, 19. ., this should be converted to capital, though it was still to carry interest at 8 per cent per annum. The interest on this sum for the whole year is to be charged to Appropriation Account. At the same date David introduced £8 000 new capital. The divisible profit for the year, before charging loan and capital interest, and before allowing Peter a salary of £7 800 was £31 050. From the following details prepare the Appropriation Section of their Profit and Loss Account and the Current Accounts of the brothers for the year ending December 31, 19. .:

	David £	Peter £
Capital Account balances (January 1, 19. .)	15 000	10 000
Current Account balances (January 1, 19. .)	Cr. 1 180	Dr. 240
Drawings	12 850	11 250

No interest is to be charged on drawings.

(RSA – Adapted)

23.10   The Balance sheet of a partnership

It has already been said that Partnership Accounts differ from Sole Trader Accounts in that the Capital Accounts do not vary, Current Accounts being used instead to record fluctuations in the partners' holdings in the firm.

It follows that the Capital Accounts, as shown in Figure 23.9, are merely added together as a sub-total on the Balance Sheet. The Current Accounts will perhaps both have credit balances, in which case they can be shown added together as a second sub-total. If one is a debit balance, or if both are, the debit balances will appear on the asset side of the Balance Sheet. The partner is overdrawn on Current Account, and appears as a debtor of the business.

Here is a typical Partnership Balance Sheet, arranged in the order of permanence:

G. GOLD AND S. SILVER
BALANCE SHEET
as at December 31, 19. .

CAPITALS		£	FIXED ASSETS		£
Gold		100 000	Land and Buildings		135 000
Silver		40 000	Plant and Machinery		65 000
		140 000	Furniture and Fittings		15 000
CURRENT ACCOUNTS	£				
Gold	5 000				215 000
Silver	4 000				
		9 000	CURRENT ASSETS	£	
			Stock	14 280	
LONG-TERM LIABILITY			Debtors 25 000		
Mortgage		100 000	*Less* Prov. 2 500		
CURRENT LIABILITIES	£				22 500
Creditors	8 750		Cash at Bank	7 720	
Wages Due	2 250		Cash in Hand	500	
		11 000			
					45 000
		£260 000			£260 000

Figure 23.9   A partnership Balance Sheet

23.11   Exercises set 23.3 – the Final Accounts of partnerships

Note: In working Final Accounts exercises for partnerships, it is always advisable to do the Appropriation Account and the Current Accounts so that the Balance Sheet figures can easily be derived from the available information, even though the question may not ask for them.

1. Arthur and Brian Woods are in partnership sharing profits and losses in the proportions three-fifths and two-fifths respectively. The following is their abridged Trial Balance as at June 30, 19. . :

	Dr. £	Cr. £
Gross Profit		55 100
Carriage Outwards	1 952	
Bank Charges	155	
Rates	2 050	
Salaries	15 250	
Insurance	1 400	
Heating and Lighting	2 303	
Car Expenses	2 000	
Debtors and Creditors	5 000	3 505
Provision for Bad Debts		500
Bank Overdraft		2 503
Capital Accounts:		
Arthur		45 000
Brian		30 000
Drawings:		
Arthur	14 250	
Brian	14 500	
Current Accounts: July 1		
Brian	179	
Arthur		382
Cash in hand	251	
Stock	17 700	
Machinery	20 000	
Premises	40 000	
	£136 990	136 990

You are required to prepare the firm's Profit and Loss Account for the year ended June 30, 19. ., and the Balance Sheet as at that date, paying attention to the following:

(a) Depreciation is to be written off the machinery at the rate of 10 per cent.
(b) The premises have to be depreciated by 5 per cent.
(c) Of the car expenses £500 is to be charged to each of the partners.
(d) The provision for bad debts is to be increased by £250.
(e) £150 is due in respect of salaries.
(f) A salary of £5 000 is to be credited to Brian.
(g) The partners are to be credited with interest on the above capital balances at the rate of 8 per cent per annum.

(RSA – Adapted)

2. The following trial balance was extracted from the books of the partnership of Bath and Wells at December 31, 19. ., after the profit for the year had been ascertained:

	Dr. £	Cr. £
Capital Accounts (January 1, 19. .):		
Bath		12 500
Wells		7 200
Current Accounts (January 1, 19. .)		
Bath		2 600
Wells		150
Drawings during year:		
Bath	10 000	
Wells	9 500	
Profit and Loss Account		39 300
Cash in Hand	375	
Balance at Bank	8 300	
Goodwill	2 000	
Furniture and Fittings	13 700	
Sundry Debtors and Creditors	4 550	3 950
Rent due		400
Stock at close	18 020	
Provision for Bad Debts		470
Insurance Prepaid	125	
	£66 570	66 570

You are required to draw up the Appropriation Account, Current Accounts and Balance Sheet of the partnership as at December 31, 19. ., having regard to the following notes:

(a) The furniture and fittings have been depreciated by £1 300 during the year.

(b) Wells is entitled to be credited with a salary of £7 500 before the division of the profit, and both capitals are to earn interest at 8%.

(c) The balance of the profit or loss is to be divided between Bath and Wells in the proportion of three-quarters and one-quarter respectively.

(d) In preparing the Balance Sheet, you are to group the assets and liabilities so that the totals can be clearly seen of (i) the fixed assets, (ii) the current assets, and (iii) the current liabilities.

(RSA – Adapted)

3. Peele and Mellis conduct a merchanting business in partnership on the following terms:

(a) Interest is to be allowed on partners' Capital Accounts at 10 per cent per annum.

(b) Peele is to be credited with a partnership salary of £8 750 per annum.

(c) The balance of profit in any year is to be shared equally by the partners.

After preparing their Trading and Profit and Loss Account for the year ended March 31, 19. ., but before making any provision for interest on capital or for Peele's partnership salary, the following balances remained on the books:

	Dr. £	Cr. £
Capital Accounts:		
Peele (as on April 1 previous year)		5 000
Mellis (as on April 1 previous year)		30 000
Current Accounts:		
Peele		1 102
Mellis		504
Drawings Accounts:		
Peele	14 453	
Mellis	12 502	
Profit and Loss Account – Net Profit for year		42 500
Stock at March 31, 19. .	17 000	
Goodwill Account	5 000	
Plant and Machinery, at cost	25 000	
Plant and Machinery, depreciation		3 000
Fixtures and Fittings, at cost	9 000	
Fixtures and Fittings, Depreciation		4 740
Trade Debtors and Creditors	17 500	4 252
Loan from H. Oldcastle, and accrued interest		10 602
Rent accrued due at March 31, 19. .		750
Insurance unexpired at March 31, 19. .	470	
Cash at Bank, Current Account	1 525	
	£102 450	102 450

It is agreed by the partners to reduce the book value of goodwill by writing off £1 250 at March 31, 19. . (to be charged to the Appropriation section of the Profit and Loss Account).

You are asked to prepare the Appropriation section of the firm's Profit and Loss Account and the partners' Current Accounts for the year ended March 31, 19. ., together with the Balance Sheet as on that date.

(RSA – Adapted)

4. The following Trial Balance was extracted from the books of the partnership of Haig and Grant who share profits and losses: Haig three-fifths and Grant two-fifths.

TRIAL BALANCE
at September 30, 19. .

	Dr. £	Cr. £
Stock (at start of financial year)	21 010	
Purchases and Sales	61 930	181 430
Returns In and Out	1 860	4 415
Wages (Trading Account)	27 752	
Carriage on Purchases	2 902	
Salaries	22 854	
Advertising	3 532	
Carriage on Sales	1 600	
Rates	2 640	
Heating and Lighting	3 095	
Bad Debts	2 995	
Insurance	380	
Debtors and Creditors	16 250	16 800
Capital:		
Haig		52 800
Grant		35 200
Drawings:		
Haig	14 500	
Grant	13 500	
Cash in Hand	142	
Cash at Bank	16 653	
Motor Vans	16 000	
Land and Buildings	60 000	
Current Accounts:		
Haig		200
Grant	1 250	
	£290 845	290 845

You are required to draw up the Trading and Profit and Loss Account of the partnership for the year ending September 30, 19. ., and a Balance Sheet as at that date.

You should take the following into account:

(a) The stock in hand on September 30 was valued at £23 050.
(b) The vans are to be depreciated by 20 per cent of the book value.
(c) Salaries, £245 are owing.
(d) Rates have been pre-paid to the extent of £340.
(e) Grant is entitled to a salary of £8 500.
(f) Capital earns interest at 8% per annum on the balance at the start of the year.

5. Messrs. King and Snagsby are in business as retailers and on December 31, 19. ., the balances on their books were as shown below:

	Dr. £	Cr. £
Capital Accounts:		
King		16 000.00
Snagsby		8 000.00
Current Accounts:		
King (as on December 31 previous year)	752.00	
Snagsby (as on December 31 previous year)		1 252.50
Drawings Account:		
King	14 000.00	
Snagsby	12 500.00	
Carriage Inwards	601.25	
Discounts Received		1 056.75
Fixtures and Fittings (as on December 31 previous year)	10 500.00	
General Expenses	12 980.00	
Interest on Loan	400.00	
Lighting and Heating	2 403.75	
Loan, A. Horden		10 000.00
Motor Vehicles (as on December 31 previous year)	14 750.00	
Motor Expenses	7 634.00	
Purchases	34 803.75	
Rent, Rates, and Insurance	7 700.00	
Returns Inwards and Outwards	2 820.00	1 781.50
Sales		95 500.00
Stock (as on December 31 previous year)	15 300.00	
Debtors and Creditors	6 380.00	7 950.00
Bank Overdraft		1 984.00
	£143 524.75	143 524.75

Notes:

(a) On December 31, 19. ., stock was valued at £18 270.50.

(b) Motor vehicle expenses in advance on December 31, 19. ., amounted to £85.

(c) Fixtures and fittings to be depreciated by 8 per cent on original cost (£12 000) and motor vehicles by 20% on original cost £16 000.

(d) Snagsby is to be credited with a commission of 2 per cent on sales for the year. The capital of both partners is to earn 10% interest and the balance of profits (or losses) is to be shared equally between the partners.

From the foregoing information you are asked to prepare the firm's Trading and Profit and Loss Account for the year ended December 31, 19. ., the Appropriation Account, the partners' Current Accounts and the Balance Sheet as at that date.

(*RSA – Adapted*)

6. A. Forsyth and B. Gordon are in partnership as manufacturers and on December 31, 19. ., the balances in their books were as follows:

	Dr.	Cr.
	£	£
Capital Accounts:		
A. Forsyth		70 000
B. Gordon		35 000
Current Accounts:		
A. Forsyth (January 1, 19. .)		352
B. Gordon (January 1, 19. .)		503
Drawings Accounts:		
A. Forsyth	13 945	
B. Gordon	15 250	
Bank Overdraft		3 254
Debtors and Creditors	5 000	9 580
Stock at January 1, 19. .	19 725	
Purchases and Sales	94 762	172 481
Wages (Trading Account)	31 110	
Carriage Inwards	3 141	
Discounts Allowed and Received	658	453
Rent Received		1 500
Heating and Lighting	2 275	
Rates	3 392	
Salaries	12 112	
Insurance	748	
Bad Debts	1 165	
Carriage on Sales	2 050	
Cash in Hand	290	
Fixtures	13 500	
Motor Vehicles	15 000	
Machinery	17 500	
Land and Buildings	40 000	
Returns Inwards	1 500	
	£293 123	293 123

Notes: On December 31, 19. ., the unsold stock was valued at £21 380. The fixtures and motor vehicles are each to be depreciated by 20 per cent.

The firms tenant owes one-quarter's rent, £500

Insurance is paid in advance, £148.

A bad debts provision of 10% of the debts outstanding is to be created.

Gordon is to be credited with a salary of £7 500, the capital is to earn 8% interest on the opening balance, and the balance of profits (or losses) is to be divided equally.

From the above information you are asked to prepare the firm's Trading and Profit and Loss Account for the year ended December 31, 19. ., and the Appropriation Account, the partners' Current accounts and the Balance Sheet as on that date.

(RSA – Adapted)

7. The following Trial Balance was extracted from the books of Messrs. Tree and Branch, wholesalers, who share profits and losses three-quarters and one-quarter respectively. Prepare the Trading Account and Profit and Loss Account for the year ending December 31, 19. ., the Appropriation Account, the Current Accounts of the partners and the Balance Sheet as at that date.

TRIAL BALANCE
(at September 30, 19. .)

	Dr. £	Cr. £
Capital Accounts, January 1, 19. .:		
Tree		50 000
Branch		25 000
Drawings:		
Tree	8 750	
Branch	6 250	
Current Accounts, January 1, 19. .:		
Tree		2 500
Branch		4 500
Trade Debtors and Creditors	2 600	7 006
Warehouse Wages	16 000	
Office Salaries	17 500	
Stock at January 1, 19. .	21 670	
Purchases and Sales	52 360	131 165
Returns In and Out	1 805	2 736
Bank Balance	3 206	
Cash in Hand	701	
Lighting and Heating:		
Warehouse (¾) Office (¼)	2 360	
Rates:		
Warehouse (¾) Office (¼)	1 240	
Freehold Premises	42 500	
Fixtures and Fittings	17 200	
Vehicles	18 000	
Stationery	1 783	
Sundry Expenses	2 320	
Postage and Telephone	1 680	
Insurance	1 302	
Discounts allowed and received	1 241	2 133
Provision for Bad Debts		625
Bad Debts incurred during 19. .	265	
Vehicle Expenses	4 932	
	£225 665	225 665

In preparing the accounts provide for the following items which have not yet been passed through the books:

(a) Stock at December 31, 19. ., was valued at £23 250.
(b) Fixtures and fittings are to be depreciated by 10 per cent and vehicles by 20 per cent.
(c) Rates prepaid amount to £240.
(d) Insurance unexpired amounts to £225.
(e) Provision for bad debts at December 31, 19. ., to be 10 per cent of trade debtors total. (Take the balance as profit to Profit and Loss Account.)
(f) 8 per cent interest on the partners' capital and a salary of £6 500 for Branch are to be charged to the appropriation section of the Profit and Loss Account.

24
The accounts of clubs and non-profit-making organizations

24.1 Non-profit-making organizations

People join together for a multitude of reasons in voluntary organizations: for mutual entertainment, for protection, or for professional reasons. There are sports clubs, trade unions, consumer co-operatives, political associations, automobile associations, and many more. The richness of any society lies partly in the variety of the voluntary organizations it promotes.

From the book-keeping point of view the aim of such organizations is the pursuit of some interest other than financial gain, so that they may all be termed non-profit-making organizations. Yet associations of this sort must have funds to promote their activities, and these funds must be honestly accounted for. The official elected for this purpose is called the Treasurer, one of the key figures on the committee which is elected to run the club. The others are the Secretary, responsible for organizing the club's activities, and the Chairperson, or President, who controls the meetings.

The Treasurer's functions are to collect subscriptions, disburse such funds as are needed in the course of the activities, and report to the members when required, but especially at the Annual General Meeting – an important occasion in the club's life. At this meeting the activities of the club are reviewed, criticisms are voiced, or praise is accorded the Committee. The Treasurer submits suitable Final Accounts to the members, supported by an audited statement approved by two members who were elected as auditors at the previous Annual General Meeting. In this chapter we shall clarify the form of Final Accounts suitable for clubs. Before we do so we must first consider the ordinary records of club receipts and payments.

24.2   The Cash Book of a club

Clubs rarely keep a full set of Ledger Accounts, but some clubs are very large indeed and need just as huge an organization as any other large scale business. For example, the Automobile Association of Great Britain has an annual budget in excess of £35 million. It employs patrolmen, inspection staff, legal advisers, and operates a chain of regional headquarters. The Co-operative Movement is one of the greatest voluntary organizations in the world. In Great Britain trade exceeds one billion pounds a year. Such huge organizations can hardly conduct their affairs with a simple notebook, yet many club treasurers in small clubs do exactly that, while bigger clubs usually have just a Cash Book with analysis columns. We shall see that even very small clubs must analyse their receipts and payments once a year for the Annual General Meeting, so that we may say the analytical Cash Book is the basic club record, or book of original entry. Such a book is shown in Figure 24.1.

In this type of book the Treasurer keeps a record of all sums received and paid, and analyses them into various sub-headings as he goes along. He can add up the columns and cross-tot each page of the book to check that he is doing the work correctly and at any given time the balance in hand can be easily found.

A Treasurer who has no such book but merely keeps a record of the cash received and paid in an ordinary cash notebook will have to analyse the notebook at the end of the year, to find the totals spent under various headings. In this way he arrives at the same result as the Treasurer with a more sophisticated ruled book. From either method the Treasurer can prepare the Receipts and Payments Account.

24.3   The Receipts and Payments Account

Definition. The Receipts and Payments Account is the simplest way a Treasurer can account for the funds of a non-profit-making organization. It is a statement of receipts and payments, drawn up from an analysis of the club's Cash Book.

The Receipts and Payments Account for the club whose Cash Book is shown in Figure 24.1 is shown in Figure 24.2.

Notice that the sundry receipts and sundry expenses totals are not quite the same as those in the Cash Book. On the receipts side the opening balance, shown as a receipt to help the cross-tots to come right in the Cash Book, is shown separately. On the payments side the closing balance is similarly shown separately.

Receipts

Date	Details	Subscriptions £	Competitions £	Refreshments £	Sundries £	Total £
Jan. 1	Balance				187.25	187.25
7	Subscriptions	70.00				70.00
7	Raffle Proceeds		18.00			18.00
7	Refreshment Sales			17.30		17.30
7	Fine (broken cups)				0.50	0.50
14	Subscriptions	110.00				110.00
14	Raffle Proceeds		16.75			16.75
	And so on throughout year					
Dec. 28	Subscriptions	10.00				10.00
28	Raffle Proceeds		8.90			8.90
28	Children's Party Tickets				22.75	22.75
	£	395.00	275.00	138.00	381.25	1 189.25
Jan. 1	Balance				231.00	231.00

Payments

Date	Details	Equipment £	Competitions £	Refreshments £	Sundries £	Total £
Jan. 7	Raffle Prize		8.75			8.75
7	Postage				1.20	1.20
7	Prizes for Children's Party		23.25			23.25
14	Raffle Prize		7.75			7.75
14	Refreshment costs			3.75		3.75
14	Catering (Party)			90.65		90.65
	And so on throughout year					
Dec. 28	Table Tennis Equipment	38.75				38.75
28	Balance in Hand				231.00	231.00
	£	138.75	75.50	280.00	695.00	1 189.25

Figure 24.1 The analysis Cash Book of a club

RECEIPTS AND PAYMENTS ACCOUNT
QUEENSWOOD COMMUNITY ASSOCIATION
(year ending December 31, 19. .)

RECEIPTS		£	PAYMENTS		£
Jan.	1 Cash in hand	187.25		Purchase of equipment	138.75
	Subscriptions	395.00		Competition expenses	75.50
	Competition proceeds	275.00		Refreshment expenses	280.00
	Refreshment sales	138.00		Sundry expenses	464.00
	Sundry receipts	194.00	Dec. 31	Cash in hand	231.00
		£1 189.25			£1 189.25

		£			
Jan.	1 Cash in hand	231.00			

Figure 24.2   Final Accounts for the AGM

The Sundry Receipts and Sundry Expenses have therefore been reduced by these amounts.

Membership appraisal of the Receipts and Payments Account

The Treasurer will stand up at the Annual General Meeting and go through the points that are of interest. Firstly, the club has a better balance at the end of the year than it had at the start. He will offer to produce the £231 in hand, but as probably most of it will be in the bank he will perhaps produce the bank book and the odd cash in hand. The club has purchased equipment valued at £138.75 during the year. There are eighty-five members of whom seventy-two have paid their £5.00 subscriptions and seven have paid for next year in advance.

It will then be up to the members to criticize the accounts. There are serious drawbacks to this type of account from the accounting point of view, but before we discuss these let us see what an astute member might notice from this report.

(a) The club paid £280 for refreshment materials – loaves of bread, sandwich fillings, etc. – yet they only sold £138 worth of refreshments. Where did the rest go? Are there a lot of members who eat refreshments but don't pay? Do the committee take home refreshments not consumed? Perhaps these extra refreshments are eaten by visiting teams? (A reasonable enough explanation.)
(b) Who are the thirteen members who enjoy club facilities but do not pay subscriptions?
(c) The club spent only £138.75 on new equipment but £464 on Sundry Expenses. What were these expenses and how were they incurred?

These and similar questions will be explained by the Treasurer, no doubt to the satisfaction of the members. (Note: The Simplex *Accounts Book for Club Treasurers* is available from George Vyner Ltd., Holmfirth, Huddersfield.)

24.4 Exercises set 24.1 – Receipts and Payments Accounts

1. The following sums of money were received and paid by the Treasurer of the Coronation Croquet Club during the season April–September, 19. . . On April 1 the club had a Cash Balance of £203.25 brought forward from the year before.

Moneys received: Subscriptions £630; Visitors' fees £80; Refreshment sales £247.75; Sales of ties and blazer badges £111.75; Lottery receipts £194.75.

Money spent: Postage £23.25; Refreshment expenses £155.75; Gift to groundsman £52.50; New hoops, mallets, and balls £94.50; Secretary's honorarium £52.50; Treasurer's honorarium £26.25; Prizes and trophies £162.75; Lottery printing £13.25; Lottery prize £125.

Draw up the Receipts and Payments Accounts for the year, for submission to the Annual General Meeting on September 30, 19. . . Bring out clearly the Cash Balance on September 30.

2. The following particulars relate to the Hole in The Road Club for the year ended December 31, 19. . . The treasurer presents the information to the members in the form of a Receipts and Payments Account. You are required to draw up this account.

	£
Cash Balance:	
January 1	52.50
December 31	46.30
Bank Balance:	
January 1	300.00
December 31	143.60
Payments:	
Refreshments	705.50
New Games Equipment	95.00
Rent to September 30	450.00
Rates	125.00
Printing	77.90
Stationery	140.60
Postage	85.00
Repairs to Games Equipment	60.50
Lighting and Heating	257.50
Wages	603.00
Dance Expenses	268.00
Competition Prizes	71.50
Receipts:	
Subscriptions	1 660.50
Sale of Dance Tickets	365.90
Competition Fees	100.00
Sale of Refreshments	650.00

(*RSA – Adapted*)

3. The Arthurian England Archaeological Society has the following Receipts and Expenses during the summer season 19. .:

Receipts: Subscriptions £880; Donations £1 250; Collections at 'digs' £636.50; Sale of refreshments £187.50; Raffle (surplus artifacts) £139;

Payments: Rights to dig on land £250; Hire of barrows, etc., £125; Small tools £62.50; Refreshment purchases £142.50; Report printing £375; Wages of student labour £127.50; Transport costs £362.50; Carbon 14 test charges £181.

Draw up the Receipts and Payments Account and calculate the balance in hand.

4. The New University Mountaineering Club has the following Receipts and Expenses during the summer season 19. .:

Receipts: Student membership fees £432.50; Grant from College £2 500; Collection for Alpine trip £893.75; Dance proceeds £192.50; Annual Dinner tickets £727.50.

Payment: Use of Alpine huts and equipment £375; Camping fees £162.50; Transport £632.50; Purchase of ropes, etc., £282.50; Guide books £12.75; Refreshments £284; Dance expenses £91.25; Dinner expenses £492.50.

Draw up the Receipts and Payments Account and calculate the balance in hand.

24.5   Limitations of the Receipts and Payments Account

For a variety of reasons the Receipts and Payments Account is unsatisfactory as a record of the club's activities, and only very small clubs would produce their accounts in this way at the Annual General Meeting. The chief objections are:

(a) There is no record of the club's initial assets apart from cash in hand. Where a club had at the start of the year premises or equipment of value it is unsatisfactory to have no mention of this at the Annual General Meeting.

(b) Similarly, and more importantly, there is no record of the assets owned by the club at the end of the year. If a club has equipment it should be shown as a list of assets on a Balance Sheet.

(c) There is no mention of liabilities outstanding. The members must ask the Treasurer about outstanding bills, and payments in advance to the club.

(d) The members cannot see whether a profit or loss was made on the year's activities. In club accounts it is not usual to call profits and losses by these names. It is not the business of clubs to make profits out of the membership, the aim is rather to provide amenities with funds mutually subscribed, whether by subscription or by lotteries and similar harmless fund-raising techniques. We therefore use the phrase 'surplus' for profits, and 'deficiency' for losses. Members have either contributed more than necessary, leaving a surplus, or less than necessary, leaving a deficiency of funds.

We are therefore faced with the usual Final Accounts problems – how to present a 'true and fair view' of the club's affairs. The solution is to present a more sophisticated set of Final Accounts than the Receipts and Payments Account. These are the Income and Expenditure Account and a Balance Sheet as at the date of the Annual General Meeting. Sometimes a Trading Account is also produced if sales of drinks, etc., are considerable.

24.6 The Accumulated Fund of a club

Just as the phrase 'Profits and Losses' is not an appropriate one for non-profit-making organizations, so the word 'capital' is not really appropriate either. 'Capital' has acquired implications that are distasteful to many societies, co-operative societies, for example. So the gentler phrase 'accumulated fund' has come to be used for the capital fund of a club. It describes exactly how the fund is collected over the years.

The calculation of the accumulated fund is one that gives many students difficulty, yet it is quite simple. The accumulated fund, like the capital fund of a sole trader, can be calculated by the formula: **total assets less external liabilities.**

What the club owned at the beginning of the year, less what it *owed* at the start of the year, gives the accumulated (or capital) fund at the beginning. It is exactly like doing the arithmetic for an opening Journal Entry. The accumulated fund occupies the same position as the capital on the Balance Sheet. Like the Capital Account it is increased by the surplus (profit) which is added to it, or decreased by the deficiency (loss) which is deducted from it.

Example
The Space Exploration Society was set up some years ago to promote an interest in astronomy and space research. On January 1, 19. ., it had assets as follows: Premises £24 000; Telescopes, etc., £9 000; Furniture and Fittings £2 500; Cash at bank £1 902: Cash in hand £118; Subscriptions were due from fifteen members at £25 each, and seventeen members had paid next year's subscriptions in advance at £25 each; A printer's bill for £79 was due. Find the accumulated fund.

The calculation would be set out as follows:

TOTAL ASSETS	£	
Premises		24 000
Telescopes		9 000
Furniture and Fittings		2 500
Cash at Bank		1 902
Cash in Hand		118
Subscriptions due		375
		37 895
LESS LIABILITIES	£	
Subscriptions in Advance	425	
Printing Bill	79	
		504
Accumulated Fund		£37 391

24.7   Trading Accounts of clubs

It is quite common to prepare a number of Trading Accounts to show the results of a particular aspect of the club's activities. For instance, a Bar Trading Account for clubs with licensed premises is very common, especially since stocks would enter into the calculations. Similarly, a Trading Account on refreshments or on dances and socials might be presented as a preliminary account for Final Accounts.

24.8   The Income and Expenditure Account

This is the main account for the Final Accounts of a club. It is exactly like the Profit and Loss Account of a sole trader except that the final result is called a **surplus,** or a **deficiency,** not a net profit or net loss. Once again we must state the period 'for year ending, etc' and we must be careful to do adjustments so that the revenue expenses and revenue receipts are only those for the period concerned. Capital items do not enter into a Revenue Account, so any equipment purchased does not appear in the Income and Expenditure Account but goes straight to the Balance Sheet.

We see, therefore, that to prepare a full set of Final Accounts for a club we need:

(a) The figures for assets and liabilities at the start of the year.
(b) The Receipts and Payments Account for the year. Sometimes we are not given this in its final form, but are given the cash and cheque book details for the year, from which, we can draw up the Receipts and Payments Account.

We then use these figures:

(i) To find the Accumulated Fund at the start of the year.
(ii) To prepare a Trading Account if the club did any trading (for example if it ran a bar, or sold refreshments).
(iii) To prepare an Income and Expenditure Account to show the surplus (profit) or deficit (loss) for the year.
(iv) Finally we prepare the closing Balance Sheet, adding any surplus to the Accumulated Fund (we have accumulated a bit more over the year), or deducting any deficit from the Accumulated Fund (the members have been living off their capital a bit this year).

Example

The Woodlands Old Girls' Association was formed some years ago, and at January 1, 19. ., had assets and liabilities as follows: premises £11 250; games apparatus £250; cash at bank £550; cash in hand £210; Subscriptions were due from three members at £10 each and were paid in advance for next year by seven members, at £10 each. The treasurer produces the following Receipts and Payments Account for 19. . on December 31.

RECEIPTS AND PAYMENTS ACCOUNT
for year ending December 31, 19. .

RECEIPTS	£	PAYMENTS	£
Balance of Cash in Hand	210	Rent of Ground	150
Subscriptions	1 250	Groundsmen's Tips	125
Profit on Dances	200	Purchase of Equipment	300
Hire of Pitches	25	Donation to School Funds	500
		Banked in Deposit Account	500
		Balance in Hand	110
	£1 685		£1 685

You are asked to prepare the Income and Expenditure Account and the Balance Sheet at December 31, 19. ., bearing in mind that (a) subscriptions in advance were £125 and (b) the groundsman was owed £25 for preparing new hockey posts.

The solution is given in Figures 24.3 and 24.4, but the calculation of the Accumulated Fund at start is as follows:

	£
TOTAL ASSETS	
Premises	11 250
Games Apparatus	250
Cash at Bank	550
Cash in Hand	210
Subscriptions Due	30
	12 290
LESS LIABILITIES	
Subscriptions in Advance	70
Accumulated Fund at Start	£12 220

344   *Book-keeping Made Simple*

Notice particularly that subscriptions in advance are a liability, since we owe the members one year's entertainment, etc., in return for their subscriptions.

WOODLANDS OLD GIRLS' ASSOCIATION
INCOME AND EXPENDITURE ACCOUNT
for year ended December 31, 19. .

	£		£
Rent	150	Subscriptions	1 250
Groundsman's Tips 125		*Less* Subscriptions in Arrear	
Add amount due 25		on January 1	30
	150		1 220
Donation to School Funds	500	*Add* Subscriptions in	
Surplus (transferred to		Advance on January 1	70
Accumulated Fund)	590		1 290
		Less Subscriptions in	
		Advance on December 31	125
			1 165
		Profit on Dances	200
		Hire of Pitches	25
	£1 390		£1 390

Figure 24.3   An Income and Expenditure Account

BALANCE SHEET
as at December 31, 19. .

	£	£		£	£
ACCUMULATED FUND			FIXES ASSETS		
At Start		12 220	Premises		11 250
Add Surplus		590	Games Apparatus	250	
		12 810	*Add* New Apparatus	300	
					550
					11 800
CURRENT LIABILITIES			CURRENT ASSETS		
Subscriptions in Advance	125		Cash at Bank	1 050	
Groundsman's Tip	25		Cash in Hand	110	
		150			1 160
		£12 960			£12 960

Figure 24.4   A club's Balance Sheet

The task is now to prepare the Income and Expenditure Account and the Balance Sheet, from the receipts and payments we have been given. Since the Receipts and Payments Account is an analysed Cash Book, and this Cash Book has never been posted to any Ledger Accounts, it follows that the profits are on the debit side. They have never been posted over to the credit side of the profit accounts as in an ordinary business. Similarly the losses are on the credit side, having never been posted to the debit side of expense accounts. The resulting Income and Expenditure Account and Balance Sheet are as shown on page 344. The figures for the Balance Sheet come from three places: (a) the opening Accumulated Fund calculation, (b) the capital expenditure in the Receipts and Payments Account, and (c) the surplus of the Income and Expenditure Account.

The student should note carefully how this improved set of Final Accounts clarifies the position to the members. We now have a clear picture of the surplus collected during the year. We can also see what the assets are, and whether there are any outstanding liabilities. We have adjusted the receipts and payments to the exact figures for the year, and have carried our surplus to the Accumulated Fund.

24.9 Exercises set 24.2 – Club Final Accounts

Note: In these exercises if the question refers to a club beginning its activities in the year under discussion it means there could be no Accumulated Fund at the start of the year. If the year referred to is one dealing with an established club you will need to work out the Accumulated Fund at the start – using the formula: Accumulated Fund = assets at start – external liabilities at start.

1. The New Town Association began activities on January 1, 19. ., and the following is a summary of its transactions for that year:

	£	
Receipts:		
Subscriptions	1 752.50	
Net Income from Dances and Whist Drives, etc.	602.50	
Deposit Interest	25.00	
	2 380.00	

	£	
Payments:		
Rent of Premises	757.50	
Rates	202.50	
Lighting, Heating, etc.	262.50	
Purchase of Savings Certificates	600.00	
		1 822.50
Balance in Hand at December 31, 19. . (including £430 in the National Savings Bank)		£557.50

One quarter's rent, £252.50 is due at December 31, 19. ., and £50 for a fuel bill is not paid; Subscriptions received include £125 in advance for next year; Rates in advance at December 31, 19. ., were £75.

You are asked to prepare the Association's Income and Expenditure Account for the year and its Balance Sheet on December 31, 19. . .

(RSA – Adapted)

2. The Willesden Green Retired Teachers' Association began its activities on January 1, 19. . . On December 31, 19. . ., the Treasurer, Miss Sandon, prepared a list of receipts and payments as follows:

	£	£
Receipts:		
Subscriptions	2 125	
Net Income from Dances, etc.	1 175	
Deposit Interest	50	
		3 350
Payments:		
Rent of Club-house	1 050	
Rates Paid in Year	250	
Lighting and Heating	425	
Purchase of Savings Certificates	500	
		2 225
Balance in Hand (of which £1 000 is in the National Savings Bank)		£1 125

The following points were given in a report:

One quarter's rent £350 was due on December 31 but not paid; £85 was due for an electricity bill; Subscriptions received included £75 for the coming year which had been paid in advance; Rates in advance were £75. You are asked to assist Miss Sandon to prepare the club's Income and Expenditure Account and a Balance Sheet at that date.

3. The following is the Receipts and Payments Account of a social club for the year ended December 31, 19. . .

RECEIPTS AND PAYMENTS ACCOUNT

RECEIPTS	£	PAYMENTS	£
Balance (January 1, 19. .)	155	Games Equipment	120
Subscriptions:		Printing, Postages, and	
Current Year	2 560	Stationery	68
Previous Year	60	Periodicals	92
Profit on Refreshments	175	Competition Prizes	61
Competition Fees	90	Sundry Expenses	104
		Wages	1 390
		Rent	600
		Rates	185
		Balance c/d	420
	£3 040		£3 040

	£		
Balance b/d	420		

(a) Prepare the club's Income and Expenditure Account and Balance Sheet having regard to the following:

(i) Subscriptions due but unpaid for current year amounted to £90.
(ii) The club had furniture and games equipment at the beginning of the year valued at £1 400, and this is to be depreciated by 20 per cent. (No depreciation is to be written off additions made during the year.)
(iii) Of the rates payment, £65 was in respect of next year.

(b) State the amount of the society's Accumulated Fund as at December 31, 19. ..

(*RSA – Adapted*)

4. The Treasurer of the sports club of your firm provided the following analysis of his receipts and payments during the year ended December 31, 19. .. From it, and the notes given below, draw up the club's Income and Expenditure Account as it should have been presented to the members on December 31.

	£
Balance in hand at 1 January 19. .	372.50
Receipts:	
Subscriptions:	
Current Year	3 075.00
Previous Year	70.00
Profit on Refreshments	230.00
Competition Fees	87.50
Payments:	
New Games Equipment	94.50
Printing, Postage, and Stationery	72.50
Periodicals	81.50
Competition Prizes	52.50
Sundry Expenses	125.00
Wages for part-time staff	1 353.75
Rent	700.00
Rates	230.00
Banked in Deposit Account	400.00

Notes:

(a) Subscriptions due but unpaid for the current year amount to £112.50.
(b) The club furniture and games equipment at the beginning of the year was valued at £2 525. It is to be written down – ignoring additions during the year – by 20 per cent.
(c) At January 1, 19. ., rates paid in advance amounted to £60, and of the rates payment made during the year £65 was in respect of the following year.

5. (a) Distinguish briefly between (i) a Receipts and Payments Account, (ii) an Income and Expenditure Account, and (iii) a Profit and Loss Account.
   (b) The following is a summary of the receipts and payments of the West End Cricket Club for the period from the date of formation on January 1, 19. ., to December 31, 19. ..

	£		£
Subscriptions	3 170.00	Purchase of Land	8 500.00
Gate Money	1 620.50	Purchase of Refreshments	613.25
Sales of Refreshments	810.75	Equipment	1 310.00
Loan secured on Land	8 000.00	Printing, Stationery, etc.	305.75
		Travelling Expenses	90.70
		Sundry Expenses	210.80
		Club-house – paid on account	2 450.00
		Balance c/d	120.75
	£13 601.25		£13 601.25

	£
Balance b/d	120.75

Prepare the Income and Expenditure Account of the club for the year ended December 31, 19. ., and the Balance Sheet at that date, taking into consideration the following:

(a) There is an unpaid account for provisions amounting to £64.
(b) Subscriptions received included £170 paid in advance.
(c) The Stock of provisions on hand at December 31, was valued at £40.

The preparation of a Trading Account on refreshments is advisable.

(RSA – Adapted)

6. After the passing of certain entries for the calculation of the profits or losses on the restaurant and bar, the Trial Balance of the Bluewater Sailing club on December 31, 19. ., is as follows:

	Dr.	Cr.
	£	£
Club Motor Launch	14 250.00	
Members' Subscriptions Received		25 700.00
Accumulated Fund at January 1, 19. .		42 150.00
Club Sailing Boats	6 000.00	
Hiring Fees Received for Club Boats		3 102.50
Leasehold Premises	25 000.00	
Maintenance Expenses of Launch and Club Boats	4 202.50	
Furniture and Equipment	4 000.00	
Cash in Hand	125.00	
Balance at Bank	8 000.00	
Stock of Wines and Spirits	2 527.50	
Racing Entrance Fees Received		1 677.50
Cost of Racing Prizes	517.50	
Salaries of Secretary and Office Assistant	8 253.75	
Sundry Creditors		2 470.00
Printing and Stationery	453.75	
Wages of Club Boatman	6 600.00	
General Expenses	3 115.00	
Rates	1 627.50	
Loss on Restaurant Catering	927.50	

Profit on Bar		11 900.00
Office Expenses, Postages and Telephone	1 400.00	
	£87 000.00	87 000.00

You are required to draw up the club's Income and Expenditure Account for the year, and a Balance Sheet as at December 31, 19. ., taking the following into account:

(a) The motor launch, the fleet of club boats, and the furniture and equipment should all be depreciated by 10 per cent.
(b) On January 1, 19. ., the club's lease had twenty years to run, and a proportionate amount for the current year should be written off the Leasehold Premises Account.
(c) Members' subscriptions for the current year, amounting to £300 were in arrear and unpaid on December 31, 19. ..

7. The following is the Trial Balance of the Greensward Cricket and Social Club on December 31, 19. ..

	Dr. £	Cr. £
Accumulated Fund at January 1, 19. .		20 680.00
Club-house	20 000.00	
Club-room Equipment	2 100.00	
Sports Equipment	1 350.00	
Sale of Refreshments		1 415.00
Purchase of Refreshments	927.50	
Interest Free Loan from a Member		2 500.00
Subscriptions Received for Current Year		11 850.00
Subscriptions Outstanding for Previous Year	25.00	
Receipts from Club-room Games		912.50
Maintenance of Games and Sports Equipment	1 212.50	
Postages	382.50	
Insurance	193.75	
Sundry Expenses	2 241.25	
Printing and Stationery	402.50	
Wages	7 042.50	
Cash at Bank	1 311.25	
Cash in Hand	168.75	
	£37 357.50	37 357.50

Prepare:

(a) An account to show the profit or loss on sale of refreshments, and
(b) The Income and Expenditure Account for the year ended December 31, 19. ., and a Balance Sheet at that date.

The following notes are to be taken into consideration:

(a) Sports equipment is to be depreciated at 20 per cent per annum and club-room equipment at 10 per cent per annum.
(b) Subscriptions, £75, are due for the current year and not yet paid.
(c) There is an unpaid account for provisions (refreshments) amounting to £60.
(d) The stock of provisions (refreshments) on hand at December 31, 19. ., was £70.
(e) Subscriptions from the previous year still outstanding are now to be written off as a bad debt.

(RSA – Adapted)

8. Last year the Treasurer of an archery club received £1 625 on account of subscriptions, of which £200 represented subscriptions in advance for this year. This year £1 700 was received on account of subscriptions. Of this sum £125 represented subscriptions for the previous year which, on January 1, were in arrear, and £100 represented subscriptions in advance for the coming year. Subscriptions in arrear for this year 19. . at December 31 were £75. It may be assumed that none of the subscribers in arrear this year will fail to pay in due course, but subscriptions regarded as still owing from last year are unlikely to be collected.

Give a statement showing the amount that should be credited in the club's Income and Expenditure Account for the current year, on account of subscription income, and how this amount is arrived at.

(RSA – Adapted)

9. The following figures were taken from the records of the Riverside Club for the year 19. . .

Prepare:

(a) A Trading Account for Refreshments.
(b) The Receipts and Payments Account.
(c) The Income and Expenditure Account of the club for the year ended December 31, 19. . .

Receipts and Payments figures were as follows. They were all paid through the club's Bank Account.

		£
Receipts:		
	Members' Subscriptions	3 450
	Sale of Refreshments	10 105
	Sundry Receipts	700
Payments:		
	Suppliers of Refreshments	7 170
	Wages of part-time staff	3 250
	Rent, Rates, and Insurance	1 250
	Repairs and Renewals	1 065
	Purchase of New Furniture for Lounge	1 025
	Sundry Expenses	630
		£
Members' Subscriptions in Arrear at January 1, 19. ., and paid during 19. .		300

Members' Subscriptions in Arrear at	
December 31, 19. .	175
Cash at Bank, January 1, 19. .	655
Rates Paid in Advance at December 31, 19. .	130
Estimated depreciation on Club Furniture and	
Fixtures for the year 19. .	360
Purchases of Refreshments during the year	7 700
Stocks of Refreshments at January 1, 19. .	690
Stocks of Refreshments at December 31, 19. .	780

Note: Necessary calculations must be shown clearly either above or below the accounts.

(University of London – Adapted)

10. The assets and liabilities of the Happy Venturers' Football Club on January 1, 19. ., were: Cash in hand £100, Cash at bank £650, Bar stocks £1 550, Furniture and fittings £2 800, Subscriptions due for the previous year £100.

On December 31, 19. ., the office cash record showed:

	£
Cash drawn out from Bank	4 500
Wages paid to part-time staff	
Cleaners	2 000
Barman	1 750
Postage and Sundry Expenses	375

The bank paying-in slips showed:

Subscriptions received £2 450 (this includes the amount owing for the previous year)

Receipts from Dances and Socials	£632.50
Receipts from Bar	£14 252.50

Cheque-book counterfoils showed:

	£
Rent	682.50
Rates and Insurance	823.75
Lighting and Heating	432.50
Expenses of Dances and Socials	375.00
Cash for Office Use	4 500.00
Purchase of Stocks for Bar	7 200.00

The annual subscriptions to the club were £10 per member.
Twelve members were in arrears for one year's subscriptions.
Insurance £70 was prepaid.
It was decided to depreciate furniture and fittings by 10 per cent.
Stock in the bar at December 31 was valued at £1 230.00.

Prepare the Income and Expenditure Account of the club for the year ended December 31, 19. ., and a Balance Sheet as at that date. Calculations must be shown in the accounts or immediately below them.

Note: In preparing the accounts show the profit made on the bar and on the dances and socials.

(University of London – Adapted)

25
The increased net-worth method of finding profits: single entry or incomplete records

25.1 Introduction

We have now learned how to calculate the profits of the three simple types of business organization: the sole trader, the partnership, and the non-profit-making club. We have assumed that the sole trader and the partnership keep proper book-keeping records, and that the club treasurer keeps a Cash Book which can be analysed. We have not yet dealt with the Final Accounts of a limited liability company, since these are more complex, and will be dealt with in Chapter 28 page 388. But before we proceed we must pick up a loose thread we have ignored until now. This is the calculation of the profits of a small business whose owner keeps either no record of transactions at all, or incomplete records. This type of book-keeping is called **single entry,** to distinguish it from double entry book-keeping. This system amounts to no system at all, for the proprietor cannot keep more than a rough check on his financial affairs.

Many small business are run successfully by relatively untrained people. One does not need higher education to succeed in business – a tough character and a capacity for hard work are more important. Establishing the right business in the right place is even more vital. The ideal thing is to discover some bottle-neck situation in a commercial or industrial activity which can be relieved by the type of service you can supply.

How does the self-made man, who conducts his entire affairs without written records, face up to the problem of discovering the profitability of his business? Years ago he would not have bothered; he would judge it by the gradual increase in worldly goods with which he was endowed. Today the Revenue Authorities of whatever country he lives in will require an annual assessment of his affairs, so that they can decide the government's share of that income.

25.2   Profit as an increase in net worth

The businessman who does not keep written records can see, as the years go by, a gradual increase in the assets of his business. An airline operating in the South of England began forty years ago with a single Puss Moth aircraft, and now has a capital of £16 million pounds. Where did this increased wealth come from? It was accumulated over the years by the profitable activities of the sole pilot who founded it. He did not withdraw all the profits he made, but he clearly must have lived on these profits by drawing some of them. The rest were retained in the business – for buying new aircraft and premises, building booking offices, and so on.

Profit can therefore be measured as an increase in the **net worth** of a business. The net worth of a business is the value of the business to the owner of the business. Consider this example:

Example 1

John Trader sets up in business on January 1, 19. ., as a hawker. He has a van, value £1 800, weighing machines and shelving worth £480, and he buys stock valued at £800. He keeps no records, but on December 31 he has two vans, value £3 650 and £1 200, scales and other equipment worth £850, and stock valued at £3 000. He has £2 350 in the bank, and a cash float of £200. He owes A. Supplier £320 for goods supplied in the last month. He has during the year given his wife housekeeping money of £70 per week and has used £30 per week for personal expenses. During the year an aunt left him a legacy of £2 000 which he put into the business. How do we calculate the profits of the business?

First we have to discover the net worth of the business at the beginning and end of the year, and see whether there has been an increase. To do this we need a Balance Sheet for each of the days mentioned, but the term 'Balance sheet' is not a satisfactory one

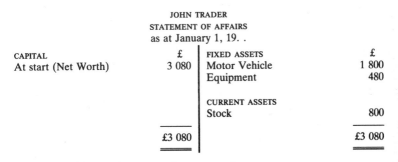

JOHN TRADER
STATEMENT OF AFFAIRS
as at January 1, 19. .

CAPITAL	£	FIXED ASSETS	£
At start (Net Worth)	3 080	Motor Vehicle	1 800
		Equipment	480
		CURRENT ASSETS	
		Stock	800
	£3 080		£3 080

Figure 25.1   The opening net worth

354 Book-keeping Made Simple

here, for it implies that there are Ledger Accounts, with balances on them. It is better to call such a Balance Sheet by another name: **Statement of Affairs.** Figure 25.1 shows the Statement of Affairs for January 1, 19. .:

From this statement of affairs we can see that on January 1 the net worth of the business to John Trader was £3 080.

The second statement of affairs is as follows:

JOHN TRADER
STATEMENT OF AFFAIRS
as at December 31, 19. .

CAPITAL	£	FIXED ASSETS		£
At Close (Net Worth)	10 930	Motor Vehicle		4 850
		Equipment		850
				———
		CURRENT ASSETS	£	5 700
		Stock	3 000	
CURRENT LIABILITIES		Cash at Bank	2 350	
Creditors	320	Cash in Hand	200	
			———	
				5 550
	———			———
	£11 250			£11 250

Figure 25.2 The closing net worth

It is clear that the net worth of John Trader's business to him has increased from £3 080 to £10 930. This increase in net worth has come partly from the profits made during the year and partly from the legacy left to him by his aunt. He is now surrounded by more worldly goods than he had before, for these two reasons.

25.3 Calculating the profits by the increased net-worth method

The calculations are as follows:

(a) Calculate the increase in net worth by drawing up two statements of Affairs as shown above, and subtracting the opening net worth from the closing net worth. In our example:

$$Closing\ net\ worth - opening\ net\ worth = £10\ 930 - £3\ 080$$
$$\therefore\ Increase\ in\ net\ worth = £7\ 850$$

(b) Adjust this figure to take account of drawings.
Trader gave his wife £70 per week and also drew £30 per week himself.

$$\therefore\ Drawings = £100 \times 52$$
$$= £5\ 200$$

If Trader had not withdrawn this money it would still have been in the business, so that the increase in net worth would have been more noticeable.

$$\therefore \text{ True increase in net worth} = £7\ 850\ +\ £5\ 200$$
$$= £13\ 050$$

(c) Adjust this figure for any increases or decreases of net worth that can be explained by something other than profits.

In this case a legacy of £2 000 explains some of the increase in net worth. This £2 000 did not come from profits but from a source outside the business. Therefore we have:

$$\text{Profit for year} = \text{True increase in net worth} - legacy$$
$$= £13\ 050\ -£2\ 000$$
$$= £11\ 050$$

This is the profit on which John Trader should pay tax.

The student will see that such a calculation depends upon the honest valuation of the assets and an honest revelation of the sums drawn. Clearly it is easy for Trader to falsify the figures in the hope of evading tax, but the Tax Authorities of all countries are able to compare the profits earned in all similar businesses, and a trader who appears to be making less than normal profits is subjected to careful investigation of his affairs. A common method of dealing with the type of trader who will not give reasonably honest figures is to assess him at a very high tax figure. When he protests that he is quite unable to pay such a high tax the Revenue Authorities point out politely that they are only too willing to be more reasonable with him, provided that he will be more reasonable with them, and give them the true figures.

25.4   Adjustments with the increased net-worth method

Just as in all other Final Accounts there may be adjustments to consider here. Before drawing up the two statements of affairs we would question the proprietor on the valuations he is placing on his assets. For instance, if the motor vehicle was valued at the end of the year at the same value as at the beginning, we would point out that it must have depreciated. The adjustments tend to be taken into account directly, by reducing the value of the asset on the statement of affairs. This particularly affects the asset, debtors, since it will be necessary to ensure that the proprietor is not including debts he knows to be bad. We would also point out to him that he should take into account some provision for bad debts that may arise.

25.5   Exercises set 25.1 – Finding profits by the increased net-worth method

1. The following statements of affairs have been drawn up to give the financial position as on January 1, 19. ., and December 31, 19. ., respectively, of A. Brogan, who keeps his books on a single entry basis:

STATEMENT OF AFFAIRS
as at January 1, 19. .

CAPITAL		£	FIXED ASSETS		£
At start		22 350.00	Fixtures		2 350.00
CURRENT LIABILITIES			CURRENT ASSETS		
Creditors		2 655.00	Stock	12 600.00	
			Debtors	8 777.50	
			Cash	1 277.50	
					22 655.00
		£25 005.00			£25 005.00

STATEMENT OF AFFAIRS
as at December 31, 19. .

CAPITAL		£	FIXED ASSETS		£
At close		30 035.00	Fixtures		2 200.00
CURRENT LIABILITIES			CURRENT ASSETS		
Creditors	3 390.50		Stock	14 000.00	
Wages Due	124.50		Debtors	11 500.00	
		3 515.00	Cash at Bank	4 250.00	
			Cash in Hand	1 600.00	
					31 350.00
		£33 550.00			£33 550.00

Brogan has transferred £600 a month regularly from his business Bank Account to his private Bank Account by way of drawings, and has taken £125 of stock for his private use. Calculate Brogan's profits for the year.
(RSA – Adapted)

2. A. Rover is in the entertainments profession. He has little time to keep books and relies solely on his memory for receiving fees and paying his way. Once a year he consults his accountant on his financial position. They draw up the following figures for 19. .:

	January 1	December 31
	£	£
Cash in Hand	137.50	813.75
Cash at Bank	2 137.50	11 901.25
Instruments and Electronic Equipment	8 000.00	13 000.00
Motor Vehicles	5 400.00	4 600.00
Debts Due by A. Rover	313.75	1 602.75
Fees Due to A. Rover	61.25	1 152.50

Capital contributed during year (and partly responsible for his extra assets) as a result of a legacy and prize award, £5 000.

Drawings for personal support during year, £8 200.

You are asked to draw up a statement of affairs as at December 31, and to show your calculations of the profit made during the year.

3. On January 1, 19. ., T. J. Wise began business by paying £4 000 into a Bank Account. He did not keep complete books of account, and used the Bank Account for both his private and business expenses. On March 31, 19. ., Wise wished to ascertain his profit or loss for the quarter. On that date his cash in hand was £50 and the balance at the bank £1 375. Stock-in-trade was valued at £8 400 and a motor van at £2 850. Trade creditors were £2 480 and trade debtors £1 945. Rent, £125, was prepaid, and an account for electricity, £250, was outstanding.

An examination of bank withdrawals disclosed that £1 290 of these were for private expenses. Wise had also taken £2 600 for private expenses out of the business takings before paying them into the bank. The motor van was brought into the business during the quarter at the same figure as its valuation on March 31, 19. . .

Prepare a statement to show the profit or loss of the business for the quarter ended March 31, 19. . .

(*University of London – Adapted*)

4. On January 1, 19. ., A. Singleton decided to go into business. His only asset was a bank balance of £5 000. For the next six months he kept no books except a Cash Book.

At June 30, 19. ., his cash balance was £225 and his bank balance £2 875. Singleton estimated his debtors at £3 200, stock-in-hand at £28 000 and he had a van worth £2 550. His creditors amounted to £4 750. During the half-year he had drawn £4 650 for his personal expenses.

(a) Draw up a statement showing the profit or loss Singleton had made by June 30, 19. . .
(b) State two items of information, which you consider important, that Singleton cannot ascertain from the statement you have prepared.

(*RSA – Adapted*)

5. A trader began business on January 1, 19. ., his position then being – Assets: Land and buildings £37 500; Fixtures and fittings £2 750; Balance at bank £8 750. Liabilities: Loan on mortgage of land and buildings £22 000.

He traded for a year, drawing nothing out of the business for his personal use, and paying in no additional capital. His position on December 31, 19. ., was – Assets: Land and buildings £37 500; Fixtures and fittings £2 750; Delivery van £3 250; Sundry debtors £2 250; Stock £14 850; Balance at bank £7 225; Cash in hand £575. Liabilities: Loan on mortgage of land and buildings £25 000; Sundry creditors £4 375.

You are required to calculate his profit or loss for the year.

(*RSA – Adapted*)

6. On January 1, 19. ., A. Alexander began business in premises valued at £27 500 and with a bank balance of £2 500. On December 31, 19. ., his financial position was as follows: Creditors £1 250, Debtors £1 800, Cash in hand £200, Stock £5 950. His rates were prepaid by £120 and during the year he had withdrawn for his private use £8 250. The bank balance stood at £3 195.

Calculate the profit made by Alexander after he had depreciated his premises by 10 per cent.

(RSA – Adapted)

25.6   Unsatisfactory aspects of the increased net worth method

Although the profits of a business may be estimated in this way, as described in Sections 25.1–25.5 above, there are several unsatisfactory aspects of the increased net worth method. If we know the position of a business at the start of a trading period and at the end of a trading period, but nothing about what went on in the time in between it is clearly not very satisfactory. In particular many of the **accounting control ratios,** which are examined in Chapter 29 cannot be determined. For example the following things are not known about a business whose profits are calculated in this way:

(a) We do not know the sales for the period – which is called the **turnover** of the business.
(b) We do not know the purchases of the business stock in the same time, so it is not possible to calculate a Trading Account, or find a gross profit on trading.
(c) We do not know anything about the individual expenses, or have any way of checking whether they were excessive on any particular heading.

If a business is not keeping proper books of account the affairs of the business, and therefore the profits calculated, must always be to some extent suspect. The Inland Revenue has a long memory, and if in subsequent years hidden assets are discovered and it is found that a trader has property which cannot be explained from the profits declared in earlier years, substantial back taxes, and fines, may be imposed.

25.7   Producing a full set of Final Accounts from incomplete records

In Section 25.6 above we referred to the unsatisfactory nature of the 'increased net worth method' of finding profits. It is usually possible to obtain enough information to prepare a full set of final accounts even if proper accounts have not been kept. Provided there is a record of cash received and paid, and cheques received and paid, by a certain amount of investigative work we can build up enough of a picture to prepare a set of final accounts. These exercises are called by the names 'single entry' or 'incomplete records'. They form an area which makes a lot of problems for accountants and one often sees advertisements for staff who are experienced in the preparation of accounts from incomplete records. The following elements come into the calculations:

(a) Prepare an opening statement of affairs as already discussed in Section 25.2 above.
(b) Use the cash records to prepare a Receipts and Payments Account for cash items. This will tell us a good deal about the purchases paid for in cash, the cash takings (sales) and the expenses paid in cash. It will also tell us of any cash drawings.
(c) Use the cheque book record and the bank statements to prepare a Receipts and Payments Account for bank items. This will help us find the credit purchases paid for, the credit sales made, any expenses paid by cheque, any drawings from the bank and any capital items purchased.
(d) Use the debtors and cheques received figures to prepare a Total Debtors' Account and hence find the sales for the period.
(e) Similarly the creditors' figures and cheques paid can be used to prepare a Total Creditors' Account which will give the purchases for the period.
(f) Prepare a closing statement of Affairs as in Section 25.2 above.

From all these figures we can then build up a Trading Account, Profit and Loss Account and Balance Sheet.

These exercises are some of the most difficult activities in accounting. We are using the increased net worth method to find the profits but are analysing the receipts and payments to discover exactly how those profits arose. The student is urged to persevere with these difficult exercises; practice makes perfect.

Example
Ian Faulkener does not keep a complete set of books but is able to provide the following information relating to his cash and bank transactions which are summarized below:

SUMMARY OF CASH RECEIPTS AND PAYMENTS
for the year ending 31 December 19. .

	£		£
Cash sales	47 850	Cash purchases	12 895
Cash withdrawn from bank	6 350	Sundry expenses	8 825
Cash from credit customers	1 256	Cash paid into bank	30 000

SUMMARY OF BANK STATEMENTS
for the year to 31 December 19. .

	£		£
Balance, 1 January	5 680	Private payments (drawings)	2 384
Cheques from credit customers	59 874	Cash withdrawn from bank	6 350
Cash paid into bank	30 000	Cheque drawn for rent	3 750
Rate refund	194	Cheques for sundry	
		business expenses	4 925
		Cheques for salaries	14 359
		Cheque for rates	2 294
		Cheque to trade suppliers	26 258
		Drawings from bank	4 000
		Purchase of van	3 500
		Purchase of fixtures	4 180
		Balance c/d	23 748
	£95 748		£95 748

19. .		£
Jan. 1 Balance	b/d	23 748

The other available information regarding the business is as follows:

	1 Jan. 19. .	31 Dec. 19. .
	£	£
Cash in hand	225	375
Stock	9 785	14 325
Trade debtors	1 686	1 343
Trade creditors	2 594	3 605
Creditors for expenses	217	350
Motor vehicles	1 254	3 950
Fixtures and fittings	2 300	5 760

(*continues opposite*)

STATEMENT OF AFFAIRS
as at 1 January 19. .

CAPITAL		£	FIXED ASSETS		£
At Start		18 119	Furniture and Fittings		2 300
			Motor Vehicles		1 254
CURRENT LIABILITIES	£		CURRENT ASSETS	£	3 554
Trade Creditors	2 594		Stock	9 785	
Expense Creditors	217		Debtors	1 686	
			Cash at bank	5 680	
		2 811	Cash in hand	225	
					17 376
		£20 930			£20 930

Figure 25.3   The statement of affairs at start
Note: The only figure not in the list given for 1 January was the opening Bank Balance given in the summary of bank statements.

The fixtures and fittings have been depreciated by £720, and the motor vehicles by £804. Any difference on Cash Account is to be treated as unrecorded drawings.

Prepare Trading and Profit and Loss Accounts for the year ended 31 December, 19. . and a Balance Sheet as at that date.

(a) First, we prepare the opening statement of affairs as in Figure 25.3

(b) Next the Receipts and Payment Account for cash, as in Figure 25.4. Note that as the figures do not balance the rest is to be treated as unrecorded drawings in cash.

CASH RECEIPTS AND PAYMENT ACCOUNT

19. .		£	19. .		£
Balance in hand		225	Purchases		12 895
Sales		47 850	Sundry Expenses		8 825
Drawn from Bank		6 350	Paid into bank		30 000
Cash from credit customers		1 256	Unrecorded drawings		3 586
			Balance	c/d	375
		£55 681			£55 681
19. .		£			
Jan. 1 Balance	b/d	375			

Figure 25.4   The Receipts and Payments Account for cash

(c) The Receipts and Payments Account for the bank is complete in the question and does not need to be calculated.

(d) We must now prepare a Total Debtors Account. The items used are debtors at start, cash and cheques received from credit customers and debtors at close. This will enable us to calculate the credit sales in the following way:

Credit sales = Receipts from customers
 − debts at start
 + debts at close

Here were are assuming that all the original debtors paid up and their payments are included in the receipts. The rest of the receipts plus the debts still outstanding gives the credit sales figure. As we can see in Figure 25.5 the credit sales are £60 787.

(e) We must now prepare a Total Creditors' Account to find the credit purchases for the year. Credit purchases will be found by the formula:

Credit purchases = Amounts paid to trade creditors
 − trade creditors at start
 + trade creditors at end

As we see in Figure 25.6 the credit purchases were therefore £27 269.

TOTAL DEBTORS' ACCOUNT

19. .		£	19. .			£
Jan. 1	Opening Balance	1 686	Jan.–Dec.	Cash from customers		1 256
Jan.–Dec.	Credit Sales	60 787	Jan.–Dec.	Cheques from customers		59 874
			Dec. 31	Balance	c/d	1 343
		£62 473				£62 473
19.1		£				
Dec. 31	Balance	b/d 1 343				

Figure 25.5   The Total Debtors' Account

TOTAL CREDITORS' ACCOUNT

19. .			£	19. .		£
Jan.–Dec.	Payments to Creditors		26 258	Jan. 1	Creditors	2 594
Dec. 31	Balance	c/d	3 605	Jan.–Dec.	Credit Purchases	27 269
			£29 863			£29 863
				19. .		£
				Jan. 1	Balance b/d	3 605

Figure 25.6   The Total Creditors' Account

(f) The closing statement of affairs need not be prepared at this stage as it will become the Balance Sheet at the end of the year, which we are now about to prepare, as part of completing the final accounts.

TRADING ACCOUNT
for year ending 31 December 19. .

		£		£
Opening Stock		9 785	Cash Sales	47 850
Cash Purchases	12 895		Credit Sales	60 787
Credit Purchases	27 269			
		40 164	Net Turnover	108 637
		49 949		
Less Closing Stock		14 325		
		35 624		
Gross Profit		73 013		
		£108 637		£108 637

PROFIT AND LOSS ACCOUNT
for year ending 31 December 19. .

	£		£
Expenses in Cash	8 825	Gross Profit	73 013
Expenses by cheque (see note)	5 058		
Rent	3 750		
Salaries	14 359		
Rates 2 294			
Less refund 194			
	2 100		
Depreciation			
Fixtures 720			
Motor vehicles 804			
	1 524		
Total Expenses	35 616		
Net Profit	37 397		
	£73 013		£73 013

BALANCE SHEET
as at 31 December 19. .

Capital	£	*Fixed Assets*	At Cost	Less Depr.	Value
At Start	18 119	Furniture and			
Add Net Profit 37 397		Fittings	6 480	720	5 760
Less Drawings		Motor Vehicles	4 754	804	3 950
3 586			11 234	1 524	9 710
+ 4 000					
+ 2 384 9 970					
	27 427				
	45 546				
CURRENT LIABILITIES		CURRENT ASSETS		£	
Trade Creditors 3 605		Stock		14 325	
Expense Creditors 350		Debtors		1 343	
		Cash at Bank		23 748	
		Cash in Hand		375	
	3 955			39 791	
	£49 501			£49 501	

Figure 25.7 The Final Accounts of the business
Note: Expenses by cheque £4 925 − £217 owing at start + £350 owing at end = £5 058.

You should now try some of the exercises which follow.

25.8   Exercises set 25.2 – Producing a full set of Final Accounts from incomplete records

1. R. Michelmore, a retailer, keeps only an incomplete set of books and asks that you produce from them a Trading and Profit and Loss Account for the year ended 31 March 19. ., and a Balance Sheet at that date. You ascertain the following:

His assets and liabilities:

	1 Apr. 19. .	31 Mar. 19. .
	£	£
Premises	30 000	42 500
Debtors	1 196	1 974
Creditors	492	875
Wages owing	436	565
Insurance in advance	124	165
Stock	12 274	15 385
Shop fittings	2 384	3 360
Vans	2 560	4 370
Mortgage	20 000	28 500

A summary of his cash records show:

	£		£
Balance, 1 April, 19. .	95	Sundry expenses	894
Rent from sub-tenant	1 040	Cash purchases	1 325
Cash sales	27 258	Drawings	1 850
		Wages	12 650
		Payments to bank	10 000
		Van expenses	1 275
		Balance c/d	399
	£28 393		£28 393
	£		
Balance b/d	399		

His cheque book records show:

	£		£
Balance	2 374	Paid to trade suppliers	24 758
Received from trade debtors	92 254	Extension of premises	12 500
Increased mortgage	10 000	Salaries	13 155
Payments from cash	10 000	Mortgage repayments	1 500
		Mortgage interest	1 600
		Insurance	328
		Repairs and renewals	268
		Purchase of van	1 810
		Drawings	12 000
		Shopfittings	976
		Balance c/d	45 733
	£114 628		£114 628
	£		
Balance b/d	45 733		

Michelmore has taken for his own use goods which cost £448. These have not been included in the books at present. He wants vans depreciated by 20% of the closing figure, and the shopfittings by 10% on the closing figure. Prepare (a) Trading and Profit and Loss Accounts for the year, and (b) the Balance Sheet as at 31 March 19. ...

2. The figures below relate to the business affairs of M. Deal, who keeps a chicken farm. You are required to prepare a Trading and Profit and Loss Account for the year ended 31 December, 19. ., and a Balance Sheet as at that date.

	1 Jan. 19. .	31 Dec. 19. .
	£	£
Trade Creditors	3 854	5 684
Wages due	275	865
Stock	19 256	22 656
Trade Debtors	32 754	26 254
Poultry Houses	20 000	60 000
Fixtures and fittings	3 600	5 400

A summary of Deal's cash book for 19. . appeared as follows:

	£		£
Balance in hand 1 Jan.	185	Cash paid to credit suppliers	1 652
Cash Sales	4 250	Cash purchases	2 362
Cash received from		Cash drawings	585
(credit) customers	2 250	Balance 31 Dec. c/d	2 086
	£6 685		£6 685

19. .	£
Dec. 31 Balance in	
hand b/d	2 086

His cheque books revealed the following situation:

	£		£
Balance at bank 1 Jan.	5 284	Payments to Credit suppliers	17 824
Receipts from Credit		Rent	3 000
Customers	82 564	Rates	1 400
Mortgage on Premises	20 000	Wages (Trading a/c)	16 054
		Salaries	11 275
		Drawings	8 000
		New poultry houses	40 000
		Fixtures and fittings	1 800
		Balance c/d	8 495
	£107 848		£107 848
	£		
Balance b/d	8 495		

In preparing the final accounts you should consider the following:

(a) Depreciation of fixtures and fittings at 10 per cent on the final value at the end of the year.
(b) Provision of 5 per cent on trade debtors (correct to the nearest £).
(c) Goods withdrawn for private use £480.
(d) Discounts allowed during the year were estimated at £540 and discounts received £620.

3. R. Morgan does not keep a complete set of books but provides you with information about his cash and bank transactions which are summarized below:

CASH RECEIPTS AND PAYMENTS
for year ending 31 December 19. .

	£		£
Cash sales	19 249	Cash purchases	8 347
Cash withdrawn from bank	5 400	Sundry expenses	2 158
Cash from credit customers	427	Cash paid into bank	14 000

BANK RECORDS FOR YEAR

	£		£
Balance, 1 January 19. .	4 519	Private payments	2 864
Receipts from credit customers	58 256	Cash withdrawn from bank	5 400
Cash paid into bank	14 000	Motor vehicle	4 040
		Wages (Trading Account)	17 250
		Salaries	11 752
		General expenses	8 254
		Drawings	6 500
		Payments to suppliers	8 500
		Balance c/d	12 215
	£76 775		£76 775

	£
Balance c/d	12 215

The other available information regarding the business is as follows:

	£	£
Cash in hand	126	194
Stock in trade	11 216	15 684
Trade debtors	2 512	4 386
Trade creditors	1 845	15 632
Motor vehicles	5 680	9 720
Fixtures and fittings	3 250	3 250

The fixtures and fittings are to be depreciated at the rate of 10 per cent per annum, and the motor cars by £1 720. Any difference on cash account is to be treated as unrecorded drawings.

Prepare Trading and Profit and Loss Accounts for the year ended 31 December, 19. ., and a Balance Sheet as at that date.

26
Departmental Accounts

26.1 Introduction

Where a business has several departments, the proprietor, as explained in Chapter 12, may prefer to take out Departmental Trading and Profit and Loss Accounts, which throw up the profitability of each department as well as the profitability of the whole business. Even a firm with only two departments, which is making profits as a whole, might find that one department was running at a loss while the other department was making all the profit. If a firm has ten or more departments the chance is increased that one of them is not contributing to the profits. It is a basic principle of modern accounts that every section or department must contribute in a reasonable way to the profits of the enterprise, or be closed down.

26.2 Departmental Accounts – the basic figures

In order to prepare departmental accounts we must have the basic figures that we need in departmental form. This will involve having Departmental Purchases Day Books and Sales Day Books, Departmental Returns Books and Departmental Expense Accounts.

This might seem a big reorganization of the book-keeping arrangements, but if a system is decided upon and then strictly adhered to it will cost very little more in the way of new rulings of paper, etc., and the figures available will give the proprietor a much clearer view of his business. Alternatively, if computerized accounting is being used the various departments can be coded in such a way that the computer will collect the departmental records.

Consider some of the basic figures for the Final Accounts in a firm which has two Departments, A and B. The Stock Account will be recording the opening stock at the start of the year and the closing stock at the end of the year. To provide the necessary figures all we need do at stock-taking is to calculate the stocks for each department and then record them in a Stock Account that has extra columns ruled on it, as shown in Figure 26.1.

			Dept. A	Dept. B	Total	L137
			£	£	£	
19. .						
Jan. 1	To Opening		4 360.00	2 240.00	6 600.00	
	Stock					

STOCK ACCOUNT

Figure 26.1   A Departmental Stock Account

Similarly, the Purchases Account and the Sales Account will be ruled up to show both the departmental and total Purchases and Sales.

Expenses of the business would need to be allocated either directly to the departments or in some fair way. For instance, with wages we can allocate the wages of the workers in Department A to be charged against that department, and similarly for the wages of workers in Department B. Where the expense is not directly separable into two parts in this way, we must adopt some agreed policy. For instance, rates are often apportioned according to the floor space occupied by each department, and advertising costs might be allocated in proportion to their turnover.

26.3   A set of Departmental Final Accounts

Once the basic figures are available, a set of Departmental Accounts is exactly the same as ordinary Final Accounts. In Figure 26.2 the student will see that the layout has not changed except that extra columns are used and the proprietor can now see clearly how much of the profit is being contributed by each department.

26.4   Exercises set 26.1 – Departmental Accounts

1. Prepare a Departmental Trading Account from the following, so that the gross profit is discovered on each department and on the business as a whole:

	Dept. A	Dept. B
	£	£
Opening Stocks	12 760.50	13 820.50
Purchases	34 250.75	26 380.50
Sales	79 204.25	92 000.50

Figure 26.2 Departmental Trading and Profit and Loss Accounts for year ending 31 December 19. .

Debit side

	Dept. A £	Dept. A £	Dept. B £	Dept. B £	Total £
Dec. 31					
Opening Stock		4 360.00		2 240.00	6 600.00
Purchases	14 162.00		13 236.00		27 398.00
Add Carriage In	48.50		24.25		72.75
	14 210.50		13 260.25		27 470.75
Less Returns Out	10.50		160.25		170.75
		14 200.00		13 100.00	27 300.00
Total Stock Available		18 560.00		15 340.00	33 900.00
Less Closing Stock		2 560.00		1 340.00	3 900.00
		16 000.00		14 000.00	30 000.00
Wages		2 000.00		7 000.00	9 000.00
Cost of Sales		18 000.00		21 000.00	39 000.00
Gross Profit		11 164.00		6 100.00	17 264.00
		£29 164.00		£27 100.00	£56 264.00
19. . Dec. 31	£		£		£
Light and Heat		140.00		120.00	260.00
Salaries		980.00		740.00	1 720.00
Office Stationery		115.00		85.00	200.00
Sundry Expenses		79.50		70.50	150.00
		1 314.50		1 015.50	2 330.00
Net Profit		9 874.00		5 096.00	14 970.00
		£11 188.50		£6 111.50	£17 300.00

Credit side

	Dept. A £	Dept. B £	Total
19. . Dec. 31 Sales	29 206.50	27 384.25	56 590.75
Less Returns	42.50	284.25	326.75
	29 164.00	27 100.00	56 264.00
	£29 164.00	£27 100.00	£56 264.00
19. . Dec. 31 Gross Profit	£ 11 164.00	£ 6 100.00	£ 17 264.00
Commission Received	24.50	11.50	36.00
	11 188.50	6 111.50	17 300.00
	£11 188.50	£6 111.50	£17 300.00

Carriage In	1 106.50	2 102.70
Returns In	1 260.25	1 360.75
Returns Out	1 420.50	2 240.75
Closing Stock	11 800.50	21 500.75
Wages	22 000.00	23 000.00

2. Prepare a Departmental Trading Account and a Departmental Profit and Loss Account from the following information:

	Dept. A £	Dept. B £
Opening Stocks	12 400.50	13 400.65
Purchases	24 260.75	37 000.75
Sales	99 890.75	83 050.80
Returns Out	4 240.50	3 380.10
Returns In	2 160.25	1 220.95
Closing Stocks	15 800.20	12 160.75
Salaries	23 400.65	26 650.45
Wages (Trading Account)	12 400.75	12 900.25
Light and Heat for Office	940.45	960.65
Sundry Expenses	2 240.80	4 640.35

3. (a) W. Wellesley manufactures two products, 'Junior' and 'Senior'. From the following information prepare a Departmental Trading Account for the year ending December 31, 19. .:

	Junior £	Senior £
Stocks of Raw Materials at December 31	5 500	3 975
Stocks of Raw Materials at January 1	5 000	4 500
Purchases of Raw Materials	17 500	13 500
Carriage Inwards	600	475
Wages	14 000	15 500
Allowances Received in Respect of Defective Raw Materials	100	250

Wellesley's sales during the period were: 4 200 'Juniors' at £10 each, and 1 120 'Seniors' at £25 each.

(b) What advice would you give Wellesley on the future conduct of his business?

(RSA – Adapted)

4. A. New and J. Castle are in partnership in a retail business dealing in groceries and fruit, and the balances on the books of the firm at December 31, 19. ., are:

	Dr. £	Cr. £
Capital Account:		
New		40 000
Castle		20 000
Drawings Account:		
New	16 000	
Castle	14 000	

Fixtures and Fittings	3 570	
Bank Balance	18 700	
Sales:		
Groceries		162 480
Fruit		82 690
Motor Vehicles	20 000	
Light, Heat, and General Expenses	13 045	
Purchases:		
Groceries	91 425	
Fruit	19 380	
Carriage Inwards: Groceries only	1 190	
Discounts Received		950
Wages (Dealt with in Profit and Loss Account)	39 350	
Rent	5 000	
Debtors:		
Groceries	22 615	
Fruit	4 100	
Creditors:		
Groceries		3 000
Fruit		1 050
Stocks at January 1, 19. .		
Groceries	36 120	
Fruit	1 870	
Bad Debts	255	
Carriage Outwards	1 550	
Rates	2 000	
	£310 170	310 170

Prepare Departmental Trading Accounts and the General Profit and Loss Account for the year ending December 31, 19. ., an Appropriation Account, two Current Accounts and a Balance Sheet at that date, taking into consideration the following:

(a) The values of the stocks at December 31, 19. ., were: groceries £28 390, fruit £2 550.
(b) A provision of £225 for further bad debts is required.
(c) Fixtures and fittings are to be depreciated at the rate of 12½ per cent *per annum* on the cost £4 080 and the motor vehicles by 20%. They were purchased on 1 January.
(d) An account for the supply of electricity to December 31, 19. ., amounting to £130 was received after the completion of the Trial Balance.
(e) The partnership agreement provides for interest on the partners' Capital Accounts (which are fixed) but not on drawings, at the rate of 8 per cent *per annum*, and for the balance of profit to be divided equally between New and Castle.

5. A business is to be carried on in two departments, A and B. From the Trial Balance given below prepare Trading and Profit and Loss Accounts in departmental form so as to bring out clearly the profit on each department as well as on the business as a whole. Where not specifically given, expenses are to be allocated to the departments in the same ratio as their sales.

TRIAL BALANCE
(as at December 31, 19. .)

	Dr. £	Cr. £
Cash at Bank	5 170	
Capital		58 000
Fixtures and Fittings	12 500	
Debtors	25 080	
Creditors		23 255
Stock at 1 January:		
Department A	22 000	
Department B	15 000	
Purchases:		
Department A	26 300	
Department B	24 000	
Salaries	26 250	
Sales:		
Department A		63 000
Department B		42 000
Motor Vehicles	8 000	
Rents, Rates, and Insurance	2 325	
Water and Electricity	530	
Discounts Allowed	430	
Stationery	795	
Carriage In	180	
Carriage Out	4 250	
Telephone Expenses	200	
Cash at Bank (Deposit Account)	8 500	
General Expenses	4 745	
	£186 255	186 255

Value of Closing Stock December 31, Department A: £19 250; Department B: £19 875.

27
Manufacturing Accounts

27.1 Introduction

A manufacturer does not buy goods to sell again, but buys raw materials which he processes to yield some more sophisticated product. He then sells the finished goods at such a price as to yield him a profit on the total enterprise. Such manufacturing processes may be very long and complicated, requiring skilled scientists and engineers to control them, and the accounts recording the expenditure and apportioning costs are fairly complex too.

In *Book-keeping Made Simple* we cannot go over the entire field of Manufacturing Accounts and Costing Accounts, but we can take a first look at them. First we must consider some of the important terms used in this type of accounting.

27.2 The vocabulary of Manufacturing Accounts

(a) *Stocks and work in progress*
Since a manufacturer buys raw materials and makes them up into finished goods, he must, at any stock-taking time, have stocks of both raw materials and finished goods in hand. In addition he is bound to have a stock of items which are neither in the raw material state, nor the finished goods state. Such partly-finished goods are called **work in progress.** The book-keeper must therefore expect to have three classes of Opening Stock and three classes of Closing Stock:

  (i) Stock of raw materials.
 (ii) Stock of work in progress or partly finished goods.
(iii) Stock of finished goods.

Naturally, like all Closing Stocks, these three classes of stock will appear on the Balance Sheet as assets of the business. Like all stocks it is essential to value them as fairly as possible. This is straightforward with stocks of raw materials and stocks of finished goods. With stocks of partly finished goods it is a little more difficult. Some firms value them at Prime Cost, but the more usual method is to value them at Factory Cost. Some explanation of these terms is given below in section (d). For a factory cost valuation you add in a share of the overhead costs to the prime costs already expended on the Work in Progress.

(b) *Variable (or direct) expenses*
In Manufacturing Accounts there is an important distinction of expenses into two groups. The first group is called **variable expenses,** or **direct expenses.** Both these words are applied to the type of expense that alters in relation to the volume of output of the factory. To take a particular example – a furniture factory. The raw materials are wood, cloth, plastic, or latex foam and an assortment of metal fixing materials, nuts, bolts, etc.

Suppose we double the output of furniture; would we expect to use double the wood, double the cloth, double the number of bolts? Clearly, we *would* expect to do so; the amount used of these materials would vary with output, and 'raw materials' is therefore a variable expense. 'Direct expense' refers to expenses which are attributable to a particular product, rather than to the business as a whole. Raw materials are direct expenses, rent and rates are not.

Another variable expense is the wages of the operators. If we double our output, would we expect to pay more wages? We certainly would if the workers were on 'piece work', and even if they were paid by the hour we would need to pay overtime or take on more workers to get a larger volume of production through the factory.

The commonest variable expenses, or direct expenses, are therefore:

 (i) Raw materials.
(ii) Labour costs – wages.

There are a number of doubtful cases, for instance Depreciation on Machines. Is it variable, or is it an overhead expense? It is up to the accountant to lay down how he will treat it for his own system of book-keeping.

(c) *Overhead (invariable, or indirect) expenses*
Overhead expenses are expenses that do not necessarily vary with output. If we double the output of our factory we shall not have to pay double the rent, or double the rates. We shall not need to redecorate twice as often, or to employ two General Managers. Such expenses are **fixed,** at least in the short run. The phrase

'overhead costs' refers to this type of expense precisely because these costs have to be borne, irrespective of the actual output of the factory. Even if the factory shuts down production altogether it will still be necessary to pay the rent, and the salaries of top executives. These are not involved directly with the product, but form the overhead framework of the enterprise, which must be established before production can begin.

The chief overhead costs are:

(i) Rent, rates, and insurance.
(ii) Salaries of administrative staff.
(iii) Repairs and depreciation of machines, etc.
(iv) Office expenses of all kinds, connected with the manufacturing side of the business.

(d) *Prime costs and overhead costs*

In preparing a Manufacturing Account we usually prepare it in two sections, a **prime cost section** and a **cost of manufactured goods section.** 'Prime cost' means first cost, and refers to the variable, or direct, expenses. The phrase 'cost of manufactured goods' refers in addition to the second set of costs, the overhead, or invariable, or indirect, or fixed costs. Four names for the same costs – all the terms are widely used.

27.3 The preparation of Manufacturing Accounts

When preparing the final accounts of a manufacturing business, the accountant would need to produce the following accounts:

(a) A Manufacturing Account in two parts, the prime cost section and the cost of manufactured goods section.
(b) A Trading Account.
(c) A Profit and Loss Account.
(d) In the case of partnerships or limited companies an appropriation section of the Profit and Loss Account.
(e) A Final Balance Sheet.

This makes a lengthy piece of work, most of which the student can do already. It is not necessary to take a whole Trial Balance, but only the matter that is needed for the Manufacturing and Trading Accounts. The Profit and Loss Account, etc., are no different from usual.

There are two ways of preparing these accounts:

(a) Disregarding the profit on manufacture, the profits all appearing in the Trading Account as gross profits.
(b) So as to bring out a profit on manufacture.

The example given below is dealt with under method (a) and later is treated under method (b) to show how the manufacturing profit can be obtained if desired.

Example 1
T. Jones is a manufacturer. Prepare his Manufacturing Account and Trading Account for year ending December 31, 19. . He does *not* extract a manufacturing profit but leaves all profits to accumulate as gross profit in the Trading Account.

	£
Stocks at January 1, 19. .:	
Raw Materials	12 400.50
Work in Progress (valued at	
Factory Cost)	13 800.75
Finished Goods	37 200.25
Purchases of Raw Materials	128 750.00
Sales	366 300.00
Returns In	5 300.00
Factory:	
Wages (variable)	47 800.50
Power (fixed)	5 600.50
Salaries (fixed)	32 800.00
Rent and Rates (fixed)	8 300.00
Factory:	
Lighting (fixed)	4 400.75
Repairs (fixed)	4 600.25
Depreciation (fixed)	12 300.00
Warehouse:	
Wages	23 600.50
Rates	2 600.00
Stocks at December 31, 19. .:	
Raw Materials	12 800.50
Work in Progress (valued at	
Factory Cost)	16 000.25
Finished Goods	53 000.50

Method (a)
The manufacturing Account is prepared first, as shown in Figure 27.1, with its two sections: the prime cost section and the cost of manufactured goods section. Then the Trading Account is prepared in the usual way as in Figure 27.2, but its purchases, as explained in (v) below, are replaced by manufactures. Points worth noting are:

(i) *Raw materials*. This is similar to the opening of a normal Trading Account, with the opening stock, purchases less returns and closing stock. If there is any carriage in or duty on imported purchases they would go in the usual place, added to the purchases figure before deducting returns.

(ii) *Labour and other prime costs*. These are now added to the cost of materials used, to give us the total prime costs of the goods produced. Just which costs are considered prime costs depends upon the type of manufacturing concerned. For example in certain industries power might be considered a prime cost, or components built into the product.

(iii) *Cost of manufactured goods section*. In this section we add the overheads to the prime costs and also adjust for the work in progress. We thus get the total cost of manufactured goods. This is carried to the Trading Account.

(iv) *Work in progress*. This simply consists of an opening stock, which has all been pushed through the manufacturing process at the start of the year, and a closing stock which has not gone through, but is in suspense until the next year begins. The effect can be either a positive or negative one. If the opening figure is greater than the closing figure it means that more work in progress was pushed through the manufacturing process at the start of the year than has been held back at the end of the year. This results in an increased cost of materials used.

In this example the closing figure was larger than the opening figure, so that the extra balance, £2 199.50, has to be deducted from the factory costs, since this amount of extra partly finished goods is being held back and will not now become finished goods until next year.

(v) *The Trading Account*. This is exactly the same as the ordinary Trading Account except that there are no purchases, since the manufacturer does not purchase any goods to sell, he manufactures them. Instead of a purchase figure we have the cost of manufactured goods figure, coming from the Manufacturing Account. The gross profit is then calculated in the usual way.

T. JONES

MANUFACTURING ACCOUNT

for year ending December 31, 19. .

PRIME COST SECTION

RAW MATERIALS		£	Prime Costs (carried to	£
Stock at Start		12 400.50	Cost of Manufactured	
Purchases	128 750.00		Goods Section)	176 150.50
Less Returns	—			
		128 750.00		
		141 150.50		
Less Closing Stock		12 800.50		
Cost of Raw Materials used		128 350.00		
LABOUR				
Wages		47 800.50		
		£176 150.50		£176 150.50

COST OF MANUFACTURED GOODS SECTION

	£		£
Prime Costs	176 150.50	Cost of Manufactured	
OVERHEADS		Goods (transferred to	
Power	5 600.50	Trading Account)	241 952.50
Salaries	32 800.00		
Rent and Rates	8 300.00		
Lighting	4 400.75		
Repairs	4 600.25		
Depreciation	12 300.00		
	68 001.50		
	244 152.00		
WORK IN PROGRESS			
Stock at Start	13 800.75		
Less Closing Stock 16 000.25			
	−2 199.50		
	£241 952.50		£241 952.50

Figure 27.1   A Manufacturing Account

TRADING ACCOUNT
for year ending December 31, 19. .

	£		£
Opening Stock of		Sales	366 300.00
Finished Goods	37 200.25	*Less* Returns In	5 300.50
Cost of Manufactured			
Goods	241 952.50	Net Turnover	360 999.50
	279 152.75		
Less Closing Stock	53 000.50		
Cost of Stock Sold	226 152.25		
Warehouse			
Wages	23 600.50		
Warehouse			
Rates	2 600.00		
	26 200.50		
Cost of Sales	252 352.75		
Gross Profit	108 646.75		
	£360 999.50		£360 999.50

	PROFIT AND LOSS ACCOUNT		
	(for year ending December 31, 19. .)		£
		Gross Profit	108 646.75

Figure 27.2   A Manufacturer's Trading Account

27.4 Taking manufacturing profit into Account

The type of Manufacturing Account shown in the last section has one disadvantage. It does not reveal how profitable the factory was, compared with other factories. For instance, the cost of manufactured goods was £241 952.50. Suppose we made 20 000 articles for this money, and that these articles could have been purchased from another manufacturer for £280 000.00? Was it worth while running the factory? Yes, because we made the goods for £38 047.50 less than the price for which we could have bought them.

On the other hand, supposing we could have bought them from someone else for £235 000.00? In that case we might as well close down the factory, and leave the manufacturing to our more efficient competitor. We are losing £6 952.50 by trying to make them in our own inefficient way.

How can we bring out the extent of the manufacturing profit, or loss? It is very simple. All we need do is to transfer the goods manufactured not at cost price to the Trading Account but at **current market price.** Suppose the Current Market Price is £280 000.00, as suggested above? The second half of our Manufacturing Account, and the Trading Account and the Profit and Loss Account will now read as shown in Figure 27.3.

COST OF MANUFACTURED GOODS SECTION

	£			£
Prime Costs		176 150.50	Market Value of	
OVERHEADS			Manufactured Goods	280 000.00
Power	5 600.50			
Salaries	32 800.00			
Rent and Rates	8 300.00			
Lighting	4 400.75			
Repairs	4 600.25			
Depreciation	12 300.00			
		68 001.50		
		244 152.00		
WORK IN PROGRESS				
Stock at Start	13 800.75			
Less Closing Stock	16 000.25			
		−2 199.50		
Cost of Manufactured				
Goods		241 952.50		
Manufacturing Profit		38 047.50		
		£280 000.00		£280 000.00

TRADING ACCOUNT
(for year ended December 31, 19. .)

	£		£
Opening Stock of		Sales	366 300.00
Finished Goods	37 200.25	*Less* Returns In	5 300.50
Market Value of			
Manufactured Goods	280 000.00	Net Turnover	360 999.50
	317 200.25		
Less Closing Stock	53 000.50		
	264 199.75		
Cost of Goods sold			
Warehouse			
Wages 23 600.50			
Warehouse			
Rates 2 600.00			
	26 200.50		
	290 400.25		
Gross Profit	70 599.25		
	£360 999.50		£360 999.50

PROFIT AND LOSS ACCOUNT
(for year ending December 31, 19. .)

Manufacturing Profit	38 047.50
Gross Profit	70 599.25

Figure 27.3   Bringing out the manufacturing profit

Notice that the profit still comes to £108 646.75, but it has now been divided into the two components: the profit on manufacture and the profit on trading.

Where should work in progress appear?
If work in progress is valued at prime cost only it should appear as an adjustment in the prime cost section of the Manufacturing Account. If it is valued at factory cost it should appear, as in Figure 27.1, as an adjustment to the cost of manufactured goods section of the Manufacturing Account.

27.5   Break-even analysis

Break-even analysis is an activity we can engage in when we are planning a manufacturing project. We can estimate the various costs of the product we are about to make and the receipts we can expect to achieve when it goes on sale. We would like to know at what point the receipts will cover the costs incurred and we can hope to begin making profits on the product. The point where receipts cover costs is called the **break-even point.**

We have seen that every manufacturing activity includes two major types of cost – the fixed costs and the variable costs (the ones that vary with output). Suppose we take a factory set up to manufacture a particular component, such as the windscreen wiper of a car. Suppose the component will sell for £8, but the costs of the actual materials are £1 and a further £1.50 for labour. Suppose the fixed costs – the overheads – are £30 000. Now imagine we make 1 unit. We have variable costs of £2.50 and a selling price of £8. The difference is a surplus of £5.50 – which is called the **contribution.** It is the contribution made by each unit towards the fixed costs of £30 000. Clearly we are not in profit yet, because even with that £5.50 we have still £29 994.50 to recover from our fixed costs.

Now imagine we increase the output to 1 000 units. We now have sales revenue of £8 000 and variable costs of 1 000 × £2.50 = £2 500. We have a surplus of £5 500 towards the fixed costs of £30 000. Increasing output to 10 000 units we find as follows:

Sales revenue = 10 000 × £8   = £80 000
Variable costs = 10 000 × £2.50 = £25 000

Contribution   = £55 000

We can see that the contribution completely covers the £30 000 fixed costs and we have passed the break-even point. We are now in profit, with a profit of £25 000.

A break-even chart such as the one shown in Figure 27.4 shows the break-even point very clearly. It is based upon an activity in which an engineering component selling for £25 has variable costs for materials and labour of £10 and overhead costs of £60 000.

The margin of safety

The horizontal distance from the break-even point to the output level selected by management is called the margin of safety. This is the extent to which we are safe from financial difficulties, because we are making profits. If costs rise the break-even point will move to the right (reducing the margin of safety) which we can resist by passing the increased prices on to our customers – thus increasing the sales revenue. If competition increases we shall have to reduce prices and the break-even point will move to the right, reducing the margin of safety. We can meet this by lowering costs by remonstrating with our suppliers, our workers, our landlord, etc.

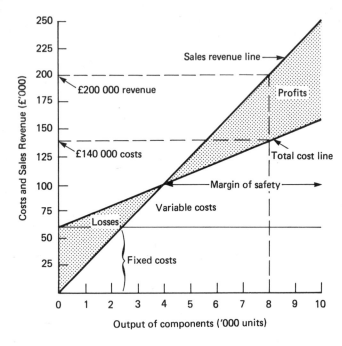

Figure 27.4   A break-even chart

Notes:
  (i) The fixed costs of £60 000 are shown as a horizontal line, they do not vary whatever the output.
 (ii) The variable costs are featured above the fixed costs and increase by £10 per unit manufactured.
(iii) The total costs (made up of the fixed and variable costs) are shown by the total cost line.
 (iv) Sales revenue rises from zero to £250 000 – i.e. £25 per unit.
  (v) The break-even point is at 4 000 units, where fixed costs of £60 000 and variable costs of £40 000 exactly equal sales revenue of 4 000 × £25 = £100 000.
 (vi) At that point we move into profit. We can find the profit at any level of output by reading off the figures from the Y axis – for example at 8 000 units costs are £140 000 and revenues £200 000. Therefore profits are £60 000.
(vii) The margin of safety is explained in the main text.

Limitations of break-even analysis

Although break-even charts are certainly helpful in planning a manufacturing activity and in preparing such things as a case to present to our bankers to borrow money to get started, they are just a little over-simplified. For example the straight-line example in Figure 27.4 has the following defects:

(a) It shows the cost as straight lines, but they may not increase in direct proportion as output rises. We could get better terms if we place larger orders for materials. We might have to pay overtime rates to turn out the extra units.

(b) It shows the sales revenue as a straight line, but we may not be able to get the same price for our product if we are trying to sell more. We may need bigger discounts to wholesalers etc. The slope of the graph may fall away as we have to lower our profit margins to get the extra sales.

(c) Fixed costs may also vary – more supervisory staff may be needed as output rises, etc.

27.6 Exercises set 27.1 – Manufacturing Accounts

1. F. Wayman is a manufacturer. From the following information prepare his Manufacturing Account and Trading Account, and open his Profit and Loss Account for the year ended December 31, 19. . :

	£
Sales	234 690
Stocks at January 1, 19. .	
Raw Materials	18 510
Work in Progress (valued at Factory Cost)	5 810
Finished Goods	53 120
Purchases of Raw Materials	85 298
Stocks at December 31, 19. . :	
Raw Materials	16 490
Work in Progress (valued at Factory Cost)	6 670
Finished Goods	72 980
Factory:	
Wages Paid	44 340
Wages Due at December 31, 19. .	450
Factory and Machinery Maintenance	5 520
Depreciation on Plant and Machinery	11 140
Factory Power (not a Prime Cost)	3 490
Factory Salaries	21 830
Factory Expenses:	
Rent, Rates, and Insurance	4 570
Lighting and Heating	2 472

(*University of London – Adapted*)

2. T. Jones is a manufacturer. Prepare his Manufacturing Account and Trading Account. He does *not* extract a manufacturing profit but leaves all profits to accumulate as gross profits in the Trading Account. Carry down the gross profit to open the Profit and Loss Account.

	£
Stocks at January 1, 19. . :	
Raw Materials	21 850
Work in Progress (at Factory Cost)	13 250
Finished Goods	46 800
Purchase of Raw Materials	127 500
Sales	346 295
Returns In	1 255
Factory:	
Wages (variable)	37 860
Power (fixed)	3 660
Salaries (fixed)	22 899
Rent and Rates (fixed)	8 300
Factory:	
Lighting (fixed)	2 350
Repairs (fixed)	11 550
Depreciation (fixed)	12 225
Warehouse:	
Wages	13 660
Rates	5 660
Stocks at December 31:	
Raw Materials	22 550
Work in Progress (at Factory Cost)	5 500
Finished Goods	32 326

3. L. Langton is a manufacturer of children's toys. It is his custom to work out a Manufacturing Account which tells him (a) the prime cost, and (b) the cost of manufactured goods. He then transfers these goods to the Trading Account not at the cost price, but at the price it would cost him to buy them on the market. This price gives him a manufacturing profit before he works out a Gross Profit on the Trading Account. Prepare his Manufacturing and Trading Account for the year ended December 31, 19. ., and carry the respective profits to the Profit and Loss Account.

	£
Stocks at Start:	
Raw materials	12 040.00
Work in Progress (at Factory Cost)	13 240.50
Finished Goods	42 480.50
Purchase of Raw materials	121 192.75
Sales of Finished Goods	338 760.50
Stocks at Close of Year:	
Raw Materials	19 960.00
Work in Progress (at Factory Cost)	12 680.50
Finished Goods	61 920.50

Factory:	
Wages Paid	57 360.75
Wages Due at End of Year	600.25
Factory and Machine Repairs	12 000.00
Depreciation of Plant and Machinery	14 640.00
Power for Machines (prime cost)	4 960.50
Factory:	
Salaries	37 320.75
Rent, Rates, and Insurance	6 280.50
Light and Heat	2 288.50
Warehouse Wages and other Costs	24 720.50

The value of the manufactured goods on the market is considered to be £270 000.00.

4. Metalmakers Ltd, produce a component which sells for £20. The fixed costs of productions are £42 000 and the variable costs are £6 per unit. Draw a break-even chart to show the profitability of the product for outputs up to 10 000 units.

(a) Where is the break-even point?
(b) At an output of 7 000 units, what will be (i) the total costs and (ii) the manufacturing profits achieved?

5. R. Lawson is a manufacturer of household utensils. It is usual for him to work out a Manufacturing Account in the usual two sections, prime cost section and cost of manufactured goods section. He then 'sells' the articles made at current market value to the Trading Account, thus taking a separate manufacturing profit. Prepare his Manufacturing Account and Trading Account for 19. . and open his Profit and Loss Account, given these figures:

	£
Stocks at January 1:	
Raw Materials	22 800.65
Work in Progress	33 600.55
Finished Goods	73 060.35
Purchases of Raw Materials	122 035.50
Sales of Finished Goods	448 200.50
Stocks at December 31:	
Raw Materials	12 300.35
Work in Progress	43 100.55
Finished Goods	52 680.65
Factory Wages Paid	54 000.50
Repairs to Machines	11 800.00
Depreciation on Machines	13 600.00
Power for Factory (prime cost)	4 400.00
Depreciation of Patent Rights	2 250.00

Factory Salaries	26 000.00
Warehouse Rates	3 800.50
Factory Rates	12 200.50
Warehouse Wages	23 500.50
Warehouse Salaries	11 600.50

The value of the manufactured goods on the open market at trade price was £288 500.00.

6. Special Steels Ltd, manufacture a surgical instrument which sells for £40, and has direct costs of £15 for materials and £7 for labour. The fixed costs are £90 000. Draw a break-even chart for sales up to 15 000 units. (a) Where does the break-even point occur? (b) At an output of 12 500 units read off from your graph (a) the total costs and (b) the profit.

7. M. Leman is a manufacturer. Every year he does the usual type of Manufacturing Account and Trading Account but he charges the Trading Account with the costs of the manufactured goods at *market price*. Prepare his Manufacturing Account, Trading Account, and begin his Profit and Loss Account.

	£
Stocks at January 1, 19. .	
Raw Materials	12 000.00
Work in Progress (at Factory Cost)	15 000.00
Finished Goods	33 000.00
Stocks at December 31, 19. . :	
Raw Materials	11 650.50
Work in Progress (at Factory Cost)	22 500.50
Finished Goods	42 860.50
Purchases	98 900.75
Sales	242 314.50
Returns In	2 865.50
Factory:	
Wages	27 000.25
Power (Prime Cost)	3 600.75
Depreciation	12 300.00
Salaries	12 000.00
Rent and Rates	4 800.00
Warehouse Wages	23 000.75
Market price of manufactured goods estimated at	150 000.00

8. Riding Tack Ltd, make saddles and other leatherware. Their main product is a saddle which sells for £230. The materials for each saddle cost £30 and the labour costs £65. The fixed costs are £27 000. Draw a break-even chart for sales of up to 800 units. (a) Where does the break-even point come? (b) What will be the total revenue at sales of 700 units, and the net profit at that output?

9. From the following figures prepare a Manufacturing Account and Trading Account in such a way as to show (a) the cost of raw materials used, (b) the prime cost, (c) the total cost of manufacture and the manufacturing profit, (d) the cost of goods sold, and (e) the cost of sales and gross profit. Carry both profits to the Profit and Loss Account.

	£
Stocks at January 1, 19. .:	
Raw Materials	11 600
Work in Progress (at Factory Cost)	23 850
Finished Goods	35 250
Stocks at December 31, 19. .:	
Raw Materials	18 800
Work in Progress (at Factory Cost)	24 250
Finished Goods	34 600
Purchases of Raw Materials	132 500
Factory:	
Wages (Prime)	42 800
Wages (Indirect)	12 560
Carriage In on Raw Materials	1 225
Power (Prime)	8 000
Rent and Rates of Factory	14 300
Depreciation of Machinery	13 600
Warehouse:	
Expenses	11 400
Wages	32 300
Factory Expenses	21 650
Sales during Year	342 650

The trade price of manufactured goods charged to Trading Account was estimated at £250 000.

28
The accounts of limited companies

28.1 Introduction – what is a limited company?

A limited liability company is a type of business organization authorized by Act of Parliament, whose capital is contributed by members who are accorded the privilege of limited liability. This means that they are liable for the debts of the company to the extent of the shareholding that they have contributed, or have agreed to contribute. Beyond that sum they are not liable for the company's debts.

The limited company is the only practicable way of collecting the vast sums of capital required for the complex industrial projects of the modern world, at a time when taxation is high. High taxation is a feature of most national finances these days, because the services supplied by governments are so far-reaching and expensive. If you tax people heavily it is natural to tax the rich more than the poor; and if you tax the rich heavily you cannot collect capital from them for industrial purposes. Even if there were no taxation at all it seems likely that no single rich family could afford to run the giant enterprises that we need today to take full advantage of mass-production methods. We have to rely instead on collecting small sums from a multitude of shareholders. These shareholders can have little voice in the conduct of the company's affairs, and it would be unfair to hold them liable for the actions of directors whom they are unable to control. In the early years of the industrialization of Great Britain such shareholders were considered partners in the firm, and were held fully liable for the firm's debts. The bankruptcies of some of the early railway companies resulted in many poor persons being arrested for debt, and their homes and property being sold to pay the debts of the firms concerned. This was obviously unfair, and the limited liability company solved the problem by limiting the shareholders' losses to the amount of money they had actually contributed, or promised to contribute.

The result of this is that persons who deal with a limited liability company on credit, supplying it with goods or services, run a certain risk; they may never be paid. Every person who engages in trade with a company ought to know he is running such a risk, and for this reason the Companies Act 1985 (like all earlier Acts) requires the company to include in its name the word 'limited'. For the smaller type of company (private companies) the name of the company must end with the word Limited. For companies large enough to be quoted on the Stock Exchange the name must end in Public Limited Company (PLC), or the Welsh equivalent. These endings are warnings to all who deal with them; this firm has limited liability. Many people think a limited company is safer and more reliable to deal with than a sole trader or partnership, but this is not necessarily so. A few basic points about the accounts of limited companies are dealt with in the next secion.

28.2 Special features of Company Accounts

There are many features of company accounts which the advanced student needs to know, particularly as the requirements of the law become more onerous each year. For British students the requirements of the Companies Act 1985, which consolidated into one statute the Acts of 1948, 1967, 1976, 1980 and 1981 are important.

Other students should discover their own law on the matter. It is not within the scope of *Book-keeping Made Simple* to make a full study of these accounting requirements, but students who wish to consider them in detail should consult a copy of the Act. However, the following points are important and give a basic introduction to the subject.

(a) *The capital of a limited company*
The capital that a public company may invite the public to subscribe is authorized by the Registrar. It is a requirement of Schedule of the Company Act of 1985 that the amount so authorized must be stated on the Balance Sheet even though it has not yet been collected from the members. The capital is subscribed by investors who become shareholders. They may be private persons or institutional investors. These are organizations which collect funds from small savers for a variety of reasons, and invest it in industrial and commercial firms. The commonest examples are banks, insurance companies, unit trusts and trade unions.

The shares which shareholders hold may be of about a dozen different types of which the most common are **Ordinary Shares** and **Preference Shares.** Ordinary Shares are often called **Equity**

Shares because they divide up the available profits equally among the shareholders, according to the size of their shareholding. They are also called **Risk Shares,** since they suffer the losses of the company equally fairly. Preference Shares, as their name implies, have a preferential right to some reasonable level of profit. At the time of writing this is about 7 per cent, but it varies with the supply of, and demand for, available funds. When the Preference Shareholders have had their 7 per cent profit the Ordinary Shareholders divide up the rest of the profits equally. Preference Shareholders usually have a prior right to the refund of their capital should the company get into difficulties, but this is not always so. Where it is so, it is clear that the Preference Shares are less risky than Equities.

(b) *Loans to a company*
Where a company borrows money from people other than the shareholders who are actually taking an active interest in its affairs by becoming members, it does so by means of a bond called a **Debenture.** A Debenture is a loan to a company secured on the assets of the firm. There are two main kinds, **Fixed Debentures** and **Floating Debentures.** Fixed Debentures are secured on the fixed assets, and if the interest is not paid regularly, the Debenture holders may seize the fixed assets and sell them to regain their money. This naturally winds up the company. A Floating Debenture is secured on the circulating assets of the company, chiefly the stock, which can be seized if the interest is not paid.

(c) *Investing in a company – who buys what?*
Consider the case of a timid, elderly lady with a few pounds to invest. Should she buy Ordinary Shares, Preference Shares, or Debentures? If she buys Ordinary Shares she runs the chance of losing her money, but she may get very good profits when the dividend is announced. If she buys Preference Shares she will earn a fixed rate, say a 9 per cent dividend, but she runs less risk of losing her money. If she buys Debentures she will be absolutely sure she will not lose her money, but she will earn a smaller return, say 7 per cent. She will probably choose the debentures.

(d) *The Final Accounts of a limited company*
Under the 1985 Companies Act every company must specify to the Registrar of Companies on a special form a date called an **accounting reference date.** This date will be the date at which an **accounting reference period** comes to an end. Final accounts for the period will then be prepared and submitted to the Registrar, and of course to the members. Accounts for public companies

must be published. These published accounts differ from the accounts used for internal accounting so that the accountant must modify his ordinary accounts to comply with the regulations. A Manufacturing Account (for manufacturing companies), a Trading Account, a Profit and Loss Account, an appropriation section of the Profit and Loss Account, and a Balance Sheet will be required in a full set of Final Accounts. At this stage students should observe the following points about the Appropriation Account and Balance Sheet.

28.3   The Appropriation Account of a limited company

A company is in some ways like a very large partnership, except that the shareholders have limited liability. Each shareholder hopes to receive an appropriation of profit, but the directors will decide this, and not even the Preference Shareholders can insist on being paid a dividend. The directors have the right to keep profits in reserve for a variety of purposes, and to be niggardly with their dividends – provided they are prepared to risk being dismissed at the Annual General Meeting of the shareholders.

One way in which the Appropriation Account of a company differs from the Appropriation Account of a partnership is that the shareholders cannot be given every last penny of the profits. If you have 27 213 shareholders and you make £100 000 profit, it is impossible to give away the last penny. You cannot divide the profit equally. There must always be a balance left over and carried down to next year. An Appropriation Account for a

THE X CO. LTD.
APPROPRIATION ACCOUNT
for year ended December 31, 19. .

19. .		£	19. .		£
Dec. 31	Goodwill	2 500.00	Jan. 1	Balance b/d	17 427.50
	Plant and Machinery		Dec. 31	Net Profit	117 256.75
	Reserve	24 000.00			
	General Reserve	25 000.00			
	Preference Dividend	14 000.00			
	Ordinary Dividend	20 000.00			
	Balance c/d	49 184.25			
		£134 684.25			£134 684.25
			19. .		£
			Jan. 1	Balance c/d	49 184.25

Figure 28.1   A company's Appropriation Account

company therefore usually starts with an opening balance on the credit side. Then the net profit is transferred from the Profit and Loss Account to the credit side, under the balance.

Figure 28.1 shows a typical Appropriation Account for a limited company.

The appropriation of the profit

The directors here have followed a middle-of-the-road policy. They have put a good deal of the profit away as reserves, and have given a generous share of it as profits to the shareholder. Without knowing how many shareholders there are we cannot say how generous they have been.

First they have reduced the value of goodwill by £2 500. Goodwill was fully explained in Chapter 22 and this is the same cautious reduction of an intangible asset whose value is not certain. Secondly, they have put away in reserve £24 000 for plant and machinery, and £25 000 in the **general reserve.** Remember that this only retains the profit in the business, but it may not be in cash form. If they want money to be available from a source outside the business they should use the sinking fund method referred to in Chapter 14, page 204.

The general reserve is a reserve set aside for any purpose the directors may decide, but the chief one is the equalization of the dividend, as between good and bad years. It is a fact that shareholders who are paid fluctuating dividends get restless, because their expectations are disappointed in a bad year. A group of shareholders who are paid a 40 per cent dividend one year and a 2 per cent dividend the next year will be much more restive and unsettled than if they had been paid 20 per cent each year. In fact they have done better by the first method, but their natural feeling of disappointment the second year overrides a sensible appraisal of the results. If the directors create a general reserve from which the above-average profits of good years can be recouped to help the less-than-average profits of bad years, the shareholders will be spared this feeling of frustration.

Each of these debit entries in the Appropriation Account will be credited to the account named. The credit in the Goodwill Account reduces the value of this asset. The credit in each of the Reserve Accounts means that this is outstanding profit, which has been put away for the reasons stated, and may not be enjoyed by the shareholders this year. In many ways it is just like a provision for bad debts. The distinction between *provisions* and *reserves* is explained carefully below. Finally the dividends will be credited in the Preference Share Dividend Account and the Ordinary Share Dividend Account. These dividends will become current liabilities to the shareholders until the Annual General Meeting authorizes their payment to the members. As the shareholders' **Dividend Warrants** are paid, the money credited in the Bank Account will be debited to the Dividend Account, to close it off.

The difference between provisions and reserves

Both provisions and reserves are sums taken from the profits and put away where the owners or shareholders of a business cannot have them. They are both credit items, since they are like extra capital retained in the business and belonging to the proprietor.

A provision is a *charge against the profits*, to provide for some anticipated loss the amount of which cannot be accurately determined. Provisions for bad debts and provisions for discounts are the two best known. *Reserves are not a charge against the profits but an appropriation of profit.* They may be **Reserves for Corporation Tax, Specific Reserves** like **Plant Replacement Reserve,** or **General Reserves** to equalize dividends from year to year or expand the enterprise. Apart from Tax Reserves these are voluntary decisions by the members to reduce dividends temporarily.

28.4 The Balance Sheet of a limited company

Schedule 4 of the Companies Act 1985 lays down Parliament's rules for British companies with regard to the published Balance Sheet. The legislature rightly held that since companies appeal to the public for funds the published Balance Sheet should reveal as much information as possible to potential investors. It is not possible in *Book-keeping Made Simple* to go into all the detail that is necessary to prepare the final accounts of a company in good style. What we can do is deal with sufficient points to enable a reasonable Appropriation Section of the Profit and Loss Account to be prepared, and a Balance Sheet. The formats given in the Act are in two styles, the traditional horizontal style and a vertical style. The latter, although widely adopted because it is easily set out in printed form, is not as satisfactory as the horizontal style. There is something ridiculous about striking a Balance Sheet vertically. Any balance must logically be achieved by a horizontal equality.

The more important requirements of this section will be made clear in the following example, which is typical of the type of examination question set about Limited Company Accounts at the elementary level. (The one feature that is usually completely disregarded at this level is the requirement to show last year's figures as well, for comparison purposes.)

Example

After taking out the Trading and Profit and Loss Accounts at December 31, 19. ., the revised Trial Balance of Enterprise Ltd is as follows:

	Dr. £	Cr. £
Cash	2 751	
Bank	29 250	
Stock at End of Year	27 500	
Balance from January 1 on Appropriation Account		3 894
Preliminary Expenses	3 000	
Net Profit for Year		126 106
Furniture and Fittings (cost £14 000)	12 500	
Patent Rights Owned (cost £2 000)	1 000	
Premium on Preference Shares		11 000
Ordinary Capital (authorized 100 000 shares of £1)		60 000
9% Preference Share Capital (authorized £40 000)		20 000
8% Debentures of £100 each		10 000
General Reserve		20 000
Land and Buildings (at cost)	48 000	
Plant and Machinery (cost £65 000)	58 000	
Quoted Investments held (market value £34 750)	33 000	
Unquoted Trade Investments (valued by directors at £22 450)	22 000	
Motor Vehicles and Spares (cost £24 500)	22 999	
Debtors and Creditors	4 700	13 700
	£264 700	264 700

You are to show the Appropriation Account and Balance Sheet after taking into account the following decisions of the Directors:

(a) A dividend of 9 per cent on the Preference Shares is to be paid (*continues on page 396.*)

ENTERPRISE LTD. APPROPRIATION ACCOUNT
(for year ending December 31, 19. .)

	£		£
Reserve for Corporation Tax	40 000	Balance at Start	3 894
Preliminary Expenses	3 000	Net Profit	126 106
General Reserve	10 000		
Preference Dividend	1 800		
Ordinary Dividend	12 000		
Balance c/d	63 200		
	£130 000		£130 000
			£
		Balance b/d	63 200

Figure 28.2   The Appropriation Account of Enterprise Ltd

BALANCE SHEET
as at December 31, 19. .

FIXED ASSETS

INTANGIBLE ASSETS

	At Cost (£)	*Less* Depreciation (£)	Value (£)
Patent rights	2 000	1 000	1 000

TANGIBLE ASSETS

Land and Buildings	48 000	—	48 000
Plant and Machinery	65 000	7 000	58 000
Furniture etc.	14 000	1 500	12 500
Motor Vehicles	24 500	1 501	22 999
	151 500	10 001	141 499

TRADE INVESTMENTS
(valued by directors at £22 450)   22 000

Total Fixed Assets   164 499

CURRENT ASSETS	£	
Stock	27 500	
Debtors	4 700	
Investments (Market value £34 750)	33 000	
Cash at Bank	29 250	
Cash in Hand	2 751	
	97 201	

Less

CURRENT LIABILITIES		
Trade creditors	13 700	
Dividends:		
Preference	1 800	
Ordinary	12 000	27 500

Net Working Capital   69 701

Net Value of Assets   £234 200

ORDINARY SHAREHOLDERS' INTEREST IN THE CO. (capital and reserves)

	Authorized £	Issued £
Ordinary Shares of £1 fully paid	100 000	60 000

Capital Reserves		
Share Premium Account		11 000
Revenue Reserves		
General Reserves (at start)	20 000	
Add New Appropriation	10 000	
	30 000	
Balance on Profit and Loss Account	63 200	
		93 200

Ordinary Shareholders' Equity 164 200

PREFERENCE SHAREHOLDERS' INTEREST IN THE COMPANY

	Authorized	
9% Preference shares of £1 fully paid	£40 000	20 000

DEBENTURES

8% Debentures of £100 each		10 000
Reserve for Corporation Tax		40 000

£234 200

Figure 28.3 The Balance Sheet of a limited company

(b) A dividend of 20 per cent is recommended on the Ordinary Shares.
(c) £10 000 is to be put to General Reserve Account.
(d) Preliminary Expenses are to be written off completely.
(e) £40 000 is to be appropriated as a Reserve for Corporation Tax.

A solution to this question is given in Figures 28.2 and 28.3. It incorporates the main requirements of Schedule 4. Note particularly that the Companies Act 1985 requires the assets to be shown on the left-hand side and the liabilities on the right-hand side – and thus at last corrects the error made in the 1856 Companies Act (see page 252).

The preparation of a full set of company final accounts is inappropriate for *Book-keeping Made Simple*. The following points will explain why the Balance Sheet of Enterprise Ltd has been displayed in the ways shown on page 394–5.

Assets side
The Act lays down a sequence in which the assets should be displayed but permits accountants to leave out any items which are irrelevant to their particular company. The order is generally speaking the **Order of Permanence,** though Parliament got in a bit of a muddle in one or two places in this respect.

First, it splits the **Fixed Assets** up into three parts, **Intangible Assets** (like goodwill and other legal rights), **Tangible Assets** (like premises, plant and machinery, etc.), and **Trade Investments.** These are investments in subsidiaries. Of course investments can always be sold, so these might appear to be outside the heading of *fixed* assets. In fact of course we cannot sell them without losing control of our subsidiary company, so strictly speaking they are fixed assets. This is all therefore in excellent style.

Then come the **Current Assets,** in the order stock, debtors, other investments (held for reasons other than to control subsidiaries – such as 'sinking fund' investments referred to in Chapter 14). If these are quoted on the Stock Exchange their market value must be shown. If they are unquoted the directors must reveal the value they place upon the investment. Finally the cash at bank, and cash in hand and any accrued receipts or payments in advance appear (though in our exercise there were none).

It is permitted if desired to bring the **current liabilities** over to the assets side and show them as a deduction from the current assets. This brings out the net working capital, and when added to the fixed assets it brings out the 'net value of assets' situation. These terms are explained in more detail in Chapter 29.

Liabilities side
The Act specifies that the capital and reserves shall be shown first, but it is a great help to distinguish between the Ordinary Shareholders' Interest in the company and the Preference Shareholders' Interest. So often on Company Balance Sheets the Ordinary and Preference Capitals are added together, and Capital and Revenue Reserves are shown below. This is not at all helpful, because it does not make clear who owns what. The presentation shown here makes absolutely clear that the Capital Reserves and Revenue Reserves belong to the Ordinary Shareholders and form part of their interest in the company. Capital Reserves are profits made in an unusual way, for example in this Balance Sheet the Share Premium Account is a sum of capital contributed by the Preference Shareholders as a premium on entry to the company. By paying more than the face value of the shares the Preference Shareholders are compensating the Ordinary Shareholders for their efforts in building up the company. A Debenture Premium Account is similar. These Capital Reserves therefore belong to Ordinary Shareholders, not to the people who actually contributed the money. However such profits may not be withdrawn by the Ordinary Shareholders, they must be left in the business as permanent capital: sometimes they are issued as bonus shares to the Ordinary Shareholders. Other Capital Reserves are Profits Prior to Incorporation and written-up appreciations on fixed assets like Revaluation of Premises Account.

Revenue Reserves are reserves set aside out of profits, like the General Reserve used for equalizing dividend over good and bad years. Such reserves may be taken out and distributed to the Ordinary Shareholders. Why do such reserves still belong to the Ordinary Shareholders only? Because the Preference Shareholders never leave any profits in the firm but always take their full fixed dividend out and enjoy it. It follows that the Ordinary Shareholders' interest in the company includes all the reserves.

We can now see that the 60 000 Ordinary Shares in Enterprise Ltd are worth £164 200, or about £2.74 per share (because of the reserves ploughed back into the business).

Before leaving the rules in the Act we must just mention one more point – fictitious assets.

Fictitious Assets
The Act makes it quite clear that fictitious assets may not appear as assets on the Balance Sheet of a company. What exactly are fictitious assets? The best example is Preliminary Expenses Account. When we set up a company we incur certain legal expenses, registration charges, etc., and if it is a public company

we probably pay to underwrite the new issue of shares. All this costs money, and as we credit the Bank Account with these payments we must debit Preliminary Expenses Account – an Asset Account. Actually we have nothing to show for this expenditure except a Certificate of Incorporation and one or two other pieces of paper. The asset is therefore fictitious and since it may not appear on the Balance Sheet it must be written off the profits at the end of the year. This reduces the balance on the Appropriation Account (or some people prefer to say the Appropriation Section of the Profit and Loss Account) and consequently reduces the Ordinary Shareholders Equity.

The vertical style of Balance Sheet

The Balance Sheet of Enterprise Ltd can be rearranged in vertical style. The advantage of this method is that it is easy to print. It also gives plenty of room to print the depreciation, etc. Many companies have adopted this style, which is also given in Schedule 4 of the Act, and the student should compare it with the more traditional style in Figure 28.3. Despite this popularity in the United Kingdom our European partners reject a *vertical* Balance Sheet as a contradiction in terms. The horizontal Balance Sheet *is* the only true Balance Sheet.

ENTERPRISE LIMITED
BALANCE SHEET IN VERTICAL STYLE
as at December 31, 19. .

ORDINARY SHAREHOLDERS' INTEREST IN THE COMPANY		Authorized	Issued
Capital and Reserves		£	£
Ordinary Shares of £1 each, fully paid		100 000	60 000
Capital Reserves			
Share Premium Account		11 000	
Revenue Reserves			
General Reserves (at start)	20 000		
Add New Appropriation	10 000		
	30 000		
Balance on Profit and Loss Account	63 200		
		93 200	
			104 200
			164 200
Ordinary Shareholders' Equity			
PREFERENCE SHAREHOLDERS' INTEREST IN THE COMPANY			
		Authorized	
9% Preference Shares of 1.00 each, fully paid		40 000	20 000
		(*Carried forward*)	184 200

(*Note: The Balance Sheet has been deliberately broken at this point to emphasize that it is a vertical presentation and continues opposite.*)

		£
(brought forward)		184 200

DEBENTURES
8% Debentures of £100 each		10 000
Reserve for Corporation Tax		40 000
		£234 200

REPRESENTED BY | | *Less* | |

FIXED ASSETS	AT COST	DEPRECIATION TO DATE	
Intangible Assets	£	£	£
Patent Rights Owned	2 000	1 000	1 000
Tangible Assets			
Land and Buildings	48 000	—	48 000
Plant and Machinery	65 000	7 000	58 000
Furniture and Fittings	14 000	1 500	12 500
Motor Vehicles	24 500	1 501	22 999
	151 500	10 001	141 499
Trade Investments (valued by Directors at £22 450)			22 000
Total Fixed Assets			164 499

CURRENT ASSETS
Stock	27 500	
Other Investments (Market Value £34 750)	33 000	
Debtors	4 700	
Cash at Bank	29 250	
Cash in Hand	2 751	
	97 201	

Less CURRENT LIABILITIES
Trade creditors	13 700	
Preference dividend	1 800	
Ordinary dividend	12 000	
	27 500	

| Net Working Capital | 69 701 |
| Net Value of Assets | £234 200 |

Figure 28.4   A Balance Sheet in vertical style

Contingent Liabilities
Another requirement of the 1985 Act is that **contingent liabilities** should be stated as notes on the Balance Sheet. These are liabilities that may arise in certain contingencies. The commonest one is where **Bills of Exchange** are dishonoured by our debtors. In such cases we may become liable for them. Lawsuits pending also give rise to a possibility that the Court will find against us. A note on the bottom of the Balance Sheet stating the directors' valuation

of likely contingent liabilities ensures that investors are aware of such possibilities, but we do not need to specify the matter because this would tell the Court we expected to lose the case.

28.5   Exercises set 28.1 – Limited Company Accounts

1. A limited liability company has an Authorized Capital of £100 000, divided into 20 000 9 per cent Preference Shares of £1 each and 80 000 Ordinary Shares of £1 each. All the Preference shares and 60 000 of the Ordinary Shares are issued and fully paid. On December 31, 19. ., it was ascertained that the company had made a Net Profit of £37 250. There was a balance of £4 350 brought forward from the previous year. The directors decided to transfer £18 500 to General Reserve and to pay the year's dividend on the Preference Shares. They proposed a dividend of 15 per cent on the Ordinary Shares.

Show how the above information would appear on the Appropriation Account and draw up the liabilities side only of the Balance Sheet as at December 31, 19. .. Ignore Corporation Tax.

(University of London – Adapted)

2. A limited liability company has an Authorized Capital of £200 000 divided into 20 000 8 per cent Preference Shares of £1 each and 180 000 Ordinary Shares of £1 each. All the Preference Shares are issued and fully paid: 100 000 Ordinary Shares were issued with £0.75 per share paid on each share.

On December 31, 19. ., the company's Revenue Reserves were £30 000; Current Liabilities £7 500; Current Assets £62 750; Fixed Assets (at cost) £90 000 and Provisions for Depreciation on Fixed Assets £20 250.

Make a summarized Balance Sheet as at December 31, 19. ., to display this information. Set out the Balance Sheet in such a way as to show clearly the Net Value of Current Assets.

(University of London – Adapted)

3. A limited company has authorized capital of 200 000 Ordinary Shares of which 100 000 shares of £1 are issued, and 50 000 9% Preference Shares of £1 of which 30 000 are issued. On March 31, 19. ., it was found that the Net Profit was £73 420 for the year. There was also a balance on the Appropriation Account of £4 150 from the previous year.

The directors resolved:

(a) To put £25 000 to General Reserve and £8 500 to Plant Replacement Reserve.
(b) To reserve £22 000 for Corporation Tax.
(c) To pay the 9 per cent Preference Dividend.
(d) To recommend a 16 per cent dividend on the Ordinary shares.

Show the Appropriation Account and the liabilities side of the Balance Sheet. There are no current liabilities other than any resulting from the appropriation.

4. From the following data and information you are asked to prepare a Balance Sheet for Brown and Jones Ltd, which brings out the separate classes of shareholders' funds and the net working capital.

BROWN AND JONES LTD.
BALANCE SHEET
as at December 31, 19. .

	£		£
Ordinary Share Capital	80 000	Stocks:	
Creditors	18 212	Raw Materials	12 500
7% Debentures	44 000	Finished Goods	35 100
Proposed Ordinary dividend	24 000	Work in Progress	5 400
Balance on Appropriation		Preliminary Expenses	4 000
Account	22 658	Land and Buildings	112 000
General Reserve	44 500	Plant and Machinery	49 520
Plant Replacement Reserve	22 500	Motor Vehicles	21 480
Premium on Debentures		Cash	5 500
Account	4 000	Debtors	14 500
Bad Debts Provision	1 450	Trade Investments	26 000
Expenses Accrued	2 280	Other Investments	13 400
Preference Shares	20 000		
Proposed preference dividend	1 600		
Bank overdraft	14 200		
	£299 400		£299 400

Notes:

(a) The Authorized Capital is £120 000 of which £20 000 is in the form of 8% Preference Shares of £1. Of the Ordinary Share Capital 80 pence per share has been paid.
(b) The work in progress is valued at factory cost.
(c) The Debentures are secured on the plant and machinery.
(d) The preliminary expenses are not to appear on the Balance Sheet, but are to be written off Appropriation Account.
(e) The original costs of the following assets are:

Land and Buildings	£112 000.00
Plant and Machinery	£95 000.00
Motor Vehicles	£31 600.00

(f) The present value of the Trade Investments according to the directors' estimates is £35 900.
(g) The other investments are all quoted shares, current market value £12 900.
(h) Contingent liabilities exist on Bills of Exchange for £530.

5. Draw up the Appropriation Account and Balance Sheet of Trihard Ltd, whose authorized capital is £100 000, made up of 80 000 £1 Ordinary Shares and 20 000 9 per cent Preference Shares of £1. Details are:

	£
Balance on Appropriation Account, January 1, 19. .	3 725
Profits for Year	71 206
Ordinary Share Capital Fully Paid	60 000
Preference Share Capital Fully Paid	20 000
Profits prior to Incorporation	18 260
Revenue Reserves – General Reserve	20 000
8% Debentures 600 at £100 each, secured on Land and Buildings of the company.	
Land and Buildings (at cost)	82 000
Plant and Machinery (at cost)	44 000
Provision for Depreciation on Plant and Machinery	6 000
Provision for Bad Debts	2 000
Motor Vehicles (at cost)	18 450
Stock	17 561
Investments (Market Value £25 000)	22 890
Cash at Bank	57 250
Debtors	18 500
Creditors	11 860
Cash in Hand	550
Trade Investments (valued by Directors at £19 500)	18 000
Provision for Depreciation on Motor Vehicles	6 150

The directors decide:

(a) To pay the Preference Dividend for the year.
(b) To put £25 000 into the General Reserve.
(c) To recommend a dividend of 20 per cent on the Ordinary Shares.
(d) To put £22 000 into a Reserve for Corporation Tax.

(*Note*: The debenture interest has already been paid in full).

6. The following Trial Balance was extracted from the books of Strangford, Ltd., at December 31, 19. .:

TRIAL BALANCE
as at December 31, 19. .

Share Capital: Authorized and Issued 150 000 shares of £1 each		150 000
Carriage In	400	
Provision for Bad Debts, January 1		1 200
Stock-in-Trade, January 1	27 350	
Purchases	121 400	
Sales		238 840
Trade Debtors	19 500	
Trade Creditors		13 800
Freehold Property at Cost	106 000	
General Expenses	17 240	
Wages and Salaries	26 130	
Rates	2 250	
Directors' Fees (Profit and Loss Account)	8 000	
Furniture and Fittings at Cost	14 000	

Provision for Depreciation of Furniture etc. Jan. 1		3 600
Motor Vehicles (purchased Jan. 1)	30 000	
Bad Debts Written Off	1 630	
Profit and Loss Appropriation Account Balance, January 1		12 050
Balance at Bank	45 590	
	£419 490	419 490

The following matters are to be taken into account:

(a) Wages and salaries outstanding at December 31 £1 460. Half the expenses under this heading are to go to the Trading Account.
(b) The Provision for Bad Debts required at December 31 is £1 950.
(c) Rates paid in advance at December 31 amounted to £450.
(d) Stock-in-Trade December 31 was valued at £23 425.
(e) Provide for depreciation of furniture and fittings at the rate of 5 per cent of cost, and on Motor Vehicles at 20% on cost.
(f) The directors propose to pay a dividend of 15 per cent for 19. . on the issued capital as at December 31, 19. ., to put £12 000 into a Reserve for Corporation Tax and to put £20 000 into General Reserve Account.

You are required to prepare a Trading and Profit and Loss Account (including an Appropriation Section) for 19. . and a Balance Sheet as at December 31, 19. ... Bring out the net value of current assets on your Balance Sheet.

(RSA – Adapted)

7. The following Trial Balance was extracted from the books of Pembroke, Ltd as on December 31, 19. .:

TRIAL BALANCE

	£	£
Share Capital, Authorized and Issued, 100 000 Ordinary Shares of £1 each		100 000
8% Debentures		25 000
Purchases	150 430	
Sales		288 590
Stock-in-Trade at January 1	45 325	
Provision for Bad Debts		1 225
Freehold Properties (at cost)	115 000	
Furniture and Equipment (at cost)	23 400	
Motor Vehicles (at cost)	45 000	
Provision for Depreciation of Furniture		5 360
Provision for Depreciation on Motor Vehicles		5 000
Debenture Interest to June 30, 19. .	1 000	
Bank Overdraft		515
Trade Debtors	16 440	
Trade Creditors		9 870

Preliminary Expenses	1 800	
Wages and Salaries (Profit and Loss Account)	19 200	
Rent and Rates	2 850	
General Expenses	23 950	
Bad Debts	1 360	

Appropriation Account: Balance at January 1, 19. .		10 195
	£445 755	445 755

You are given the following information:

(a) Stock-in-Trade at December 31, 19. ., £48 220.
(b) The Provision for Bad Debts is to be increased to £1 644.
(c) Rates paid in advance at December 31 were £450.
(d) Provision is to be made for depreciation of furniture and equipment at the rate of 10 per cent per annum (on cost) and at 20% on Motor Vehicles (on cost).
(e) The whole of the balance on the Preliminary Expenses Account is to be written off. The rest of the debenture interest is to be paid.
(f) The directors have decided to recommend a dividend of 15 per cent, and to put away £60 000 in General Reserve Account and £8 000 in Motor Vehicle Replacement Reserve Account.

You are required to prepare a Trading and Profit and Loss Account, a Profit and Loss Appropriation Account for the year 19. ., and a Balance Sheet as on December 31, 19. ., in vertical style.

(RSA – Adapted)

29
The interpretation
of Final Accounts:
statistical control figures

29.1 Introduction – controlling a business

The businessman who has successfully prepared a set of Final Accounts from an accurate set of records has completed the routine book-keeping functions; but if he is astute enough to pursue his accounting a little further he can discover many useful facts about the trends of his business affairs. Is the business expanding or contracting? Is it more profitable than last year or less profitable? Has the manager been stealing the cash? Do the shop assistants take home the stock? Do they give it away free to relations and friends? Are some lines more profitable than others?

The chief matters to be dealt with in this chapter are:

(a) **The gross profit percentage** and its significance to the proprietor.
(b) **The net profit percentage** and its significance to the proprietor, including **expense ratios to turnover**.
(c) **The rate of stock turnover** and its significance to the proprietor.
(d) **The interpretation of a Balance Sheet** including the significance of the following to the proprietor:

  (i) Capital owned
  (ii) Capital employed
  (iii) Fixed capital
  (iv) Floating capital
  (v) Liquid capital
  (vi) Net working capital
  (vii) Solvency and insolvency
  (viii) Overtrading
  (ix) The return on capital invested.

The student should particularly note the control of his business that can be achieved by a proprietor who understands what is happening to these control ratios and percentages. By indicating that something is wrong with his business they can lead him to discover what is wrong, and apply the remedy before the business has suffered irreparable damage.

29.2   The gross profit percentage

This is the percentage of gross profit that we make upon sales, or a better phrase is net turnover. The term net turnover means *sales less returns*, and the net turnover of the business is itself an important statistic about any enterprise. The formula for the gross profit percentage is therefore:

$$Gross\ profit\ percentage = \frac{Gross\ profit}{Net\ turnover} \times 100$$

Consider the Trading Account show in in Figure 29.1.

TRADING ACCOUNT
for year ending December 31, 19. .

	£		£
Opening Stock	7 250	Sales	139 500
Purchases	69 000	*Less* Returns	2 000
Add Carriage In	2 250		
		Net Turnover	137 500
	71 250		
Less Returns	3 500		
Net Purchases	67 750		
Total Stock Available	75 000		
Less Closing Stock	10 000		
Cost of Stock Sold	65 000		
Warehouse Expenses	12 500		
Cost of Sales	77 500		
Gross Profit	60 000		
	£137 500		£137 500

Figure 29.1   A Trading Account for interpretation

The gross profit percentage on this Trading Account is:

$$\frac{Gross\ profit}{Net\ turnover} \times 100$$

$$= \frac{£60\ 000}{£137\ 500} \times 100$$

$$= \frac{60\ 000}{1\ 375}$$

$$= \frac{480}{11} \qquad \text{(cancelling by 125)}$$

$$= \underline{\underline{43.6\%}}$$

Supposing that next year the firm does twice as much business? Would it need to purchase twice as many purchases? Would it expect to pay out twice as many expenses? Would it expect to make twice as much profit? Of course we cannot answer a 'yes' with absolute confidence to all these questions, but generally speaking the answer will be 'roughly yes'. If we sell twice as many goods we would expect to buy twice as many goods. For the sake of this argument we will assume that everything simply doubles. Next year the gross profit percentage works out as follows:

$$\frac{Gross\ profit}{Net\ turnover} \times 100$$

$$= \frac{£120\ 000}{£275\ 000} \times 100$$

$$= \frac{480}{11}$$

$$= \underline{\underline{43.6\%}}$$

You will see that it is the same answer as we had before, and this is the vital thing about the gross profit percentage: it is a constant. It ought to come out the same every year providing our business is running in the same way. We say, in a scientific way:

Gross profit percentage = K (constant)

(Scientists can't say C for constant; it already stands for Celsius.)

It is important to work your Trading Account out the same way from year to year. If it is not prepared in a similar manner each year, the different items introduced will prevent you comparing the gross profit percentages.

What can be wrong when the gross profit percentage falls?

Remember, year by year, the gross profit percentage should be more or less constant. Supposing we find that it has fallen? There could be many possible explanations.

(a) The manager, or the staff, are stealing the cash takings. This will reduce the sales figure and the profits will fall. The cash is being diverted into the manager's pocket, or someone else's pocket. What can we do about it? We can query the matter with the manager, let him know we are watching the situation. This may be enough. We might point out that it must be very expensive driving that huge car. How does he do it on his money? If it appears unlikely that he is responsible we can watch the assistants. Who has the luxurious handbag or the expensive new clothes? How does she do it on her money?

(b) Perhaps someone is stealing the stock? One of the good things about stock-taking is that it discovers losses of stock. A low stock figure means a high cost of sales figure and a lower gross profit. Who takes the stock home? Two pounds of sugar and a quarter of tea every night for a year makes quite a big hole in the stock. A very common practice of dishonest shop assistants is to help their friends to free goods. A packet of cigarettes to each boy friend soon stops the gross profit percentage being K.

(c) If neither (a) nor (b) is the cause, stock might be getting lost in other ways. For instance, breakages due to clumsiness in the crockery department transfer some of the stock to the dustbin. Bad buying of perishables has the same effect – we throw away the tomatoes that go bad, the cheese that gets stale, the cakes that go dry. If we don't actually throw them away we have to sell them cheaply and that still means the profit on them is lost.

(d) Another type of bad buying, in the clothing and footwear trades especially, concerns the out-of-touch buyer who is behind the times and *will* buy lines that have to be reduced in the sales because we can't get rid of them in any other way. We have to keep our fashion buyers young in heart or their work will adversely affect the gross profit percentage.

(e) A quite legitimate explanation for the falling gross profit percentage may be that the cost of goods to us has risen and we have been slow to pass this on to the public. It may be because we have poor control in our pricing department, or because competition from more efficient traders prevents us from raising prices. Sometimes governments regulate prices by law and force the trader to accept lower profit margins. A government tax may be levied but because of the demand in our particular market we are unable to pass the tax on and must suffer it ourselves. The astute businessman will at least be ready with his plans to recoup these losses as soon as the law, or the market situation, changes.

(f) The expense items on the Trading Account may be the cause of the trouble. Is the manager taking on more staff than he needs? Perhaps the light and heat bill has risen violently. Is it a hard winter? If it is, there is nothing we can do about it. If it is not, perhaps the staff have brought in electrical appliances without our knowledge and are eating hot buttered toast with our electricity.

In this case we will order the bright fellow who thought of the idea to take his toaster home again.

(g) It may be that the stock is wrongly valued. As explained in chapter 21, an error in stock valuation affects the gross profit. If we overvalue our closing stock we overvalue the gross profit; but the next year, when that closing stock has become the opening stock, we undervalue our gross profit. This double action produces a drop in the gross profit percentage compared with the previous year.

(h) Sometimes assets are purchased and wrongly included in Purchases Account, instead of being posted to the debit side of the asset account concerned. This is going to increase the cost of goods sold, and reduce the gross profit, and hence the gross profit percentage.

What can cause a rise in gross profit percentage?

If the types of inefficiency described in the last section cause a fall in gross profit percentage, then an improved efficiency in these directions will cause a rise in gross profit percentage. Honesty over the cash takings will keep the cash sales figure up, and hence the gross profit percentage will improve. A manager who takes over and at once detects sharp practice by assistants with cash takings or stock, will similarly improve the percentage. If he improves the buying, or eliminates breakages, or is quick to pass on increased prices to the customer, he will keep up the gross profit percentage.

What action should we take in this event? Clearly we should reward him. That is what a bonus is all about; it is a reward for efficiency in the line of duty.

29.3 Gross profit percentage on cost

A very similar figure to the gross profit percentage on turnover is the gross profit percentage on cost. This is calculated as follows:

$$\textit{Gross profit percentage on cost} = \frac{\textit{Gross profit}}{\textit{Cost of stock sold}} \times 100$$

In the Trading Account shown in Figure 29.1 we would get:

$$\frac{£60\ 000}{£65\ 000} \times 100$$

$$= 92\%$$

The Trader concerned is actually making a 92 per cent profit on the goods he buys to sell again, but some of this profit is being eroded by expenses and overheads.

A common example of this sort of things is where a shopkeeper sells you something for £10 that cost him £5. He may say to you, 'I get £5 of the sales price, i.e. 50 per cent.' In fact, of course, he is making a profit of £5 on an original outlay of £5 which is not 50 per cent but 100 per cent. In this way he hides the true profit from the simple customer.

29.4   Absolute and relative changes

It is important to understand the difference between absolute and relative changes. Absolute changes mislead many proprietors into thinking that their businesses are doing quite well when in fact serious weaknesses have begun to creep in. Relative changes, that is to say ratio, or percentage, changes, throw up quite clearly the true picture of what is happening. Consider the following case:

Mr A. owns a business and gives the following figures for two successive years:

	Year 1 £	Year 2 £
Turnover	100 000	200 000
Gross Profit	25 000	40 000

He speaks very highly of his manager who has increased the profits from £25 000 to £40 000 and describes him as 'dynamically successful'. Criticize this assessment of the manager.

Mr A. is looking at the absolute changes in gross profits, that is, at the actual figures themselves. It is true that profits have risen from £25 000 to £40 000. But in fact the turnover has doubled. When we work out the relative changes we find:

Year 1   *Gross profit percentage* $= \dfrac{£25\ 000}{£100\ 000} \times 100 = 25\%$

Year 2   *Gross profit percentage* $= \dfrac{£40\ 000}{£200\ 000} \times 100 = 20\%$

In fact these extra profits have been made at a greater cost than the earlier profits, and diminishing returns have begun to set in. This does not mean that the manager is necessarily incapable, but he is not quite as brilliant as Mr A. thinks. As we expand any business we often have to accept lower rates of profit on the new business, so this type of decline in gross profit percentage may be experienced by the expanding firm. If Mr A lets the manager go ahead and expand the business still further he may get to the point fairly quickly where he is overtrading and profits will begin to fall back. The relative figure, the gross profit percentage, sounds a note of early warning about the trend of the business, and could save Mr A.'s business if he paid attention to it and restrained the enthusiasm of his manager with a word of warning about the dangers ahead.

29.5 Exercises set 29.1 – gross profit percentage

1. (a) State, briefly and clearly, what you understand by the term Net Turnover in relation to the business of a retailer.

  (b) A trader had in stock on 1 February 300 articles costing £20 each. During the month he bought 900 more of these articles at the same price and sold 860 at £30 each, of which 10 were returned. Draw up a statement showing the gross profit earned and express the gross profit as a percentage of the turnover.

(RSA – Adapted)

2. (a) Describe the method of calculation and explain the significance of the ratio of gross profit to sales in a retail business.

  (b) A retailer sells only three types of commodity which should give him, respectively, Gross profit ratios of $22\frac{1}{2}$ per cent, 20 per cent, and $17\frac{1}{2}$ per cent on sales, i.e. an average of 20 per cent.

  On preparing a Trading Account at the end of his latest financial year, he finds that the ratio of gross profit to sales is only 18 per cent.

  You are asked to give three possible circumstances, any of which would account for the apparent shortage as compared with the expected result, and explain why each would operate to reduce the ratio.

(RSA – Adapted)

3. On preparing the Trading Account of T. Weave, a retailer, for the financial year ended March 31, 19. ., it was found that the ratio of gross profit to sales was 15 per cent, whereas for the previous financial year the corresponding ratio had been 25 per cent. State, with your reasons, whether or not the following may have contributed to cause the decline:

(a) The stock at March 31, 19. ., was under-valued.

(b) The cost of a new delivery van had been included in the purchases for the year ended March 31, 19. ., and charged to Trading Account.

(c) The sales for the year ended March 31, 19. ., showed a decline compared with the previous year.

(d) In both years T. Weave and his family had been supplied with goods from the shop but the value of these goods had not been recorded in the books of the business.

(e) The stock at March 31, 19. ., included a number of items which were soiled and at this stock-taking had been written down in value by one-half of their cost.

4. H. Anderson is a wholesale dealer in British and imported toys. His Trial Balance on June 30, 19. ., was as follows:

	Dr. £	Cr. £
Capital at Start		27 900
Motor Vehicles	19 500	
Balance at Bank	23 100	
Drawings	12 400	
Motor Vehicles Expenses	1 840	
Rates	2 000	
Warehouse Wages	13 750	
Fixtures and Fittings	13 250	
Purchases (Dr.) and Sales (Cr.)	94 900	220 830
Cash in Hand	650	
Carriage Outwards	730	
Returns Outwards		875
Stock at Start	19 325	
General Wages and Salaries	28 325	
Carriage and Freight Inwards	1 105	
Discounts Allowed	2 380	
Discounts Received		2 610
General Expenses	5 895	
Customs Duty on Imported Purchases	2 945	
Returns Inwards	2 830	
Insurance	1 115	
Debtors (Dr.) and Creditors (Cr.)	9 000	8 300
Bad Debts	975	
Rent	4 500	
	£260 515	260 515

Taking note of the facts that Anderson's unsold stock at June 30, 19. ., was valued at £31 500 and that the item 'warehouse wages' should be dealt with in the Trading Account, you are required:

(a) To choose from the above figures those that would appear in Anderson's Trading Account for the year ended June 30, 19. ., and to draw up this account.
(b) To state the amount of Anderson's turnover for the year.
(c) To state the amount of Anderson's gross profit.
(d) To express the gross profit as a percentage of this turnover (correct to 1 decimal place.

Note: *No Profit and Loss Account or Balance Sheet is required.*

(*RSA – Adapted*)

29.6   The net profit percentage

The net profit is the clear profit left after the office and selling expenses have been deducted from the gross profit. If we wish to check on the efficiency of the office and sales sides of our business, the ratio that gives us a clear picture of the trends shown is the net profit percentage. This is found by the formula:

$$\text{Net profit percentage} = \frac{\text{Net profit}}{\text{Turnover}} \times 100$$

Consider Figure 29.2 a Profit and Loss Account which follows from the Trading Account, Figure 29.1.

PROFIT AND LOSS ACCOUNT
for year ending December 31, 19. .

	£		£
Salaries	23 750	Gross Profit	60 000
Light and Heat	2 350	Commission Received	2 540
Insurance	1 450	Rent Received	1 860
Advertising	860		
Depreciation	1 505		64 400
Bad Debts	635		
	30 550		
Net profit	33 850		
	£64 400		£64 400

Figure 29.2   A Profit and Loss Account

The net profit percentage here is calculated as follows:

$$
\begin{aligned}
\text{Net profit percentage} &= \frac{£33\ 850}{£137\ 500} \times 100 \\
&= \frac{33\ 850}{1\ 375} \\
&= \frac{1\ 354}{55} \quad \text{(cancelling by 25)} \\
&= 24.6\%
\end{aligned}
$$

Once again we would expect the net profit percentage to be fairly constant, that is to remain roughly the same from year to year providing we always prepare our Profit and Loss Account in the same way. It follows that any significant change in net profit percentage, say 2 per cent or more, would be investigated to discover the cause.

Suppose that last year the net profit percentage was 26.5 per cent and this year it has fallen to 4.6 per cent. This is a significant fall and we must find the reason.

What can have caused a fall in the net profit percentage?
If the gross profit percentage is steady, but the net profit percentage has fallen the fault must lie in the expenses or profits shown on the Profit and Loss Account. We should examine each expense item carefully, working out an **expense ratio to turnover**, for this year and the previous year. This is quite simple and involves a calculation:

$$\frac{Expense}{Turnover} \times 100$$

So for salaries it would be:

$$\frac{Salaries}{Turnover} \times 100$$

$$= \frac{£23\ 750}{£137\ 500} \times 100$$

$$= \frac{23\ 750}{1\ 375}$$

$$= \underline{\underline{17.3\%}}$$

By comparing this with the similar figure for the previous year we may discover some increase in expense. Perhaps the manager has taken on more staff than are really necessary? Similar expense ratios may reveal other causes of the change. Perhaps the advertising has been excessive? An increased advertising budget did not yield proportionately higher sales. Perhaps insurance rates have risen, and have not been passed on to the consumer in higher prices? The profits on the credit side may show some falling off from the previous year. Have we received less commission than previously, or less rent? These will also affect net profit percentage.

When we discover the cause of the fall in net profit percentage we must take the necessary action to correct the profitability of the business. This means we must reduce the expenses that are soaring, or increase the receipts that have been declining. If such action is impossible, we must pass the increased cost on to the final consumer.

One final point here. Although the idea of these ratios is to look for possible trouble it is a fact that they may also indicate an improved position. It is also true to say that we cannot expect net profit percentages to stay as constant as gross profit percentage because some of our expenses do not vary with turnover directly and consequently an increased turnover would not mean increased expenses and the net profit percentage should rise with increased turnover and fall with decreased turnover.

Interim Final Accounts

Some firms find the annual check-up on gross profit and net profit percentage too long a period to wait before correcting undesirable trends. The quicker we can discover adverse variations, the quicker we can take steps to put them right. For this reason many firms prepare interim Final Accounts, say at three-monthly intervals. A quick check every three months on gross and net profit percentages keeps management and staff informed of the dynamic trends of the business.

29.7   Exercises set 29.2 – gross and net profit percentages

1. In making a comparison between two successive years of his business, N. Peters notices the following matters:

	Year 1	Year 2
	£	£
Turnover	65 000	95 000
Gross Profit	28 000	42 560
Net Profit	13 500	26 600

Present these two sets of results in such a way as to make a comparison, and state any conclusions you can draw.

2. At January 1, 19. ., D. Dickinson valued his stock in hand at £16 000. For the ensuing year he made the following estimates: Sales £86 000, Returns inwards £2 000, Carriage inwards £1 500, Manufacturing wages £14 000, Purchases £38 000, Returns outwards £3 500, Dickinson's Gross Profit ratio on all his sales was 33⅓ per cent.

(a) Prepare Dickinson's Estimated Trading Account, showing the value of his stock at December 31, 19. ..
(b) To what amount must Dickinson limit his revenue expenditure to ensure at least a 20 per cent return on his capital of £75 000? You may assume he has no miscellaneous profits on his Profit and Loss Account.

(*RSA – Adapted*)

3. T. is proposing to set up in business as a retailer and is negotiating for a shop, the rent of which is £2 500 per annum and rates £1 800 per annum. He expects that he will need to employ an assistant at a salary of £60 per week, and that the incidental expenses of the business will be £5 000 per annum. The rate of gross profit he expects is 50 per cent on sales. Assuming that T. will make a net profit of £12 500 and that at the end of the year he will have a stock of £5 650 draft a *pro-forma* Trading and Profit and Loss Account for the first year.

(*RSA – Adapted*)

4. The statement below summarizes the trading results of B. Barnaby, a wholesaler, for the year ended December 31, 19. .:

		£
Sales (*less* returns)		100 000
Less Cost of Goods Sold		55 000
Gross Profit		45 000
Less Assistants' Wages	18 500	
Less Other Expenses	12 500	
		31 000
Net Profit for the year		£140 000

During the next year Barnaby hopes to expand his business, and estimates that he will be able to increase his sales to £140 000, maintaining the rate of gross profit.

To handle the additional trade, he expects to have to employ two more assistants costing £4 000 each in wages. Of his other expenses those costing £8 500 would not increase, but he estimates that the others would increase in proportion to the increase in sales.

Prepare for B. Barnaby a statement, similar in form to the summary given above, showing the estimated results for the next year.

(*RSA – Adapted*)

5. Two friends, Guppy and Jobling, are engaged in preliminary discussions with a view to setting up in business as retailers. It is agreed that net profits and losses are to be shared between them in the ratio of two-thirds to Guppy and one-third to Jobling. They further estimate that:

(a) The net profit for the first year will be sufficient for Jobling to get £8 500 as his share of it.
(b) Rent, assistant's wages, and other expenses will amount to £17 300 for the first year.
(c) The ratio of gross profit will be 40 per cent of the sales.
(d) The stock at the end of the first year will be £4 000.

You are asked to show (giving your calculations):

(a) The value of sales necessary to produce the required net profit.
(b) The amount of purchases for the year.

(*RSA – Adapted*)

6. For the trading year ended December 31, 19. ., the figures in a merchant's Trading Account are: Stocks, January 1, £21 775, and December 31, £6 825; Sales £402 025; Purchases £236 650; Returns inwards £2 025; Returns outwards £1 600. In his Profit and Loss Account the summarized net debits for general, administrative, and distributive expenses are £100 000.

(a) You are required:
    (i) To draw up the merchant's abridged Trading and Profit and Loss Account for the year ended December 31, 19. .:
    (ii) To state the cost price of the goods sold.
    (iii) To state the amount of the merchant's turnover for the year.
    (iv) To state the percentage rate of *gross profit* on cost (correct to 1 decimal place).
    (v) To state the percentage rate of *gross profit* on turnover.
    (vi) To state the percentage rate of *net profit* on turnover (correct to 1 decimal place)

(b) On the assumption that during the following year turnover will increase by 25 per cent, that the percentage rate of gross profit will remain unchanged, and that overhead charges (i.e. general, administrative, and distributive expenses) will increase by 4 per cent for every increase of £10 000 in turnover over the 19. . figure, you are required to draw up an estimated Trading and Profit and Loss Account for the year ended December 31 of the next year.

                                                    (RSA – Adapted)

7. A firm has two branches selling the same range of goods; one in Sheffield, the other in Manchester. The following figures are drawn from the records of these branches:

		Year 1 £	Year 2 £
Gross profits	Sheffield	135 000	145 000
	Manchester	420 000	400 000
Net profits	Sheffield	90 000	96 667
	Manchester	185 000	210 000
Turnover	Sheffield	540 000	580 000
	Manchester	1 260 000	1 000 000

You are asked to draw up the gross profit percentage and net profit percentage for each branch for the two years and hence criticize their performances and those of their managers. The Trading and Profit and Loss Accounts may be assumed to have been prepared in a consistent manner. Answers correct to 1 decimal place.

8. In making a comparison between two successive years of trading F. Taylor, a trader, has the following information:

	Year 1	Year 2
Turnover	230 000	270 000
Gross Profit	75 900	81 000
Net Profit	27 600	33 800

Present these results in such a way as to make a comparison between the two years and state the conclusions you draw from the comparison.
                              (London University 'O' Level – Adapted)

9. What conclusions do you draw from the following statements relating to the accounts of W. Ames, a sole trader, after the books have been closed and the Final Accounts prepared?

(a) F. James's Account in the Sales Ledger has a debit balance.
(b) The Capital Account has a debit balance.
(c) There is a credit balance on the Rates Account.
(d) There is a debit balance on the Packing Materials Account.
(e) There is a debit balance on the Insurance Account.
(f) The Bank Account in the Cash Book has a credit balance.
(g) There is a debit balance on the advertising Account.

10. What conclusions do you draw from the following information about R. Lord's business?

(a) R. Coombe's Account in the Purchases Ledger has a credit balance.
(b) T. Low's Account in the Sales Ledger also has a credit balance.
(c) There is a debit balance on the Advertising Account on January 1st, the first day of his financial year.
(d) There is a credit balance on the Rent Payable Account on the same day.
(e) The Bank Account in the Cash Book has a credit balance.

29.8 Turnover and rate of turnover, or rate of stock turnover

We have already defined turnover as the net sales of a business, i.e. *sales less returns*. Another figure that can easily be confused with turnover is the **rate of turnover**, sometimes called the **rate of stock turnover**. This is quite a different idea from turnover, but it is a most important concept which every student should understand.

Stock turnover is a very important thing, because it is at the point where stock turns over that the profits are made. We say that stock has turned over when it has been sold and replaced with new stock. In Chapter 1 we learned about **circulating assets**, which revolve from stock to debtors to cash and back to new stock again. Every revolution of this circle yields a profit. If we want to double our profits, one way is to double the rate of stock turnover.

The rate of stock turnover is always expressed as a number. To say that the rate of stock turn is six means that the stock turns over six times in a year. Is this a good rate of stock turn? Or is it a poor rate of stock turn? We can't possibly say until we know the product we are discussing. If a grocer turned over his stock of eggs six times a year they would be in stock for an average of two months each. This hardly makes them new-laid eggs by the time they are consumed. On the other hand, grand pianos tend to be a slow-moving line and do not deteriorate if kept in stock two months. Some classes of goods are very 'perishable', like newspapers, which must be turned over every day if they are to be sold at all.

Calculating the rate of stock turnover

Two formulae which give the same answer are:

1. *Rate of stock turn* $= \dfrac{\text{Cost of stock sold}}{\text{Average stock at cost price}}$

2. *Rate of stock turn* $= \dfrac{\text{Net turnover}}{\text{Average stock at sales price}}$

Use formula 1 for the moment. If you find the average stock, and divide it into the amount of stock sold at cost price, you will find out how often the stock turns over in each trading period.

The average stock is found by taking opening stock + closing stock and dividing by two. If quarterly stock figures are available we can add up the four quarterly figures and divide by four.

Using the Trading Account of Figure 29.1 we find the average stock comes out to £8 625.

$$\frac{£7\ 250 + £10\ 000}{2} = \frac{£17\ 250}{2} = £8\ 625$$

As the cost of stock sold is £65 000 it follows that

$$\begin{aligned}
\textit{Rate of stock turn} &= \frac{£65\ 000}{£8\ 625} \\
&= \frac{520}{69} \text{ (cancelling by 125)} \\
&= 7.5 \textit{ times per year}
\end{aligned}$$

Whether this is a good rate of stock turnover we cannot say, but it means that goods are in stock for roughly seven weeks on average. For some classes of goods this might be a good rate of stock turn. For fresh fish, or spring flowers, it would hardly do.

To find how long goods are in stock we divide the number of times the stock turns over in the year into either 12 months (to give an answer in months) or 52 weeks (to give an answer in weeks). Using the illustration given above we have:

$$\textit{Average life of stock} = \frac{12}{7.5} \text{ months} = \underline{1.6 \text{ months}}$$

$$\textit{Average life of stock} = \frac{52}{7.5} \text{ weeks} = \underline{6.9 \text{ weeks}}$$

29.9   Exercises set 29.3 – rate of stock turnover

1. A trader carries an average stock valued at cost price, of £10 000, and turns this over five times per year. If he marks his stock up by 50 per cent on cost price, what is his gross profit for the year?

2. A trader carries an average stock valued at cost price of £31 250 and turns this over six times a year. If his mark-up is 20 per cent on cost, and his overheads came to £18 000, what is the net profit for the year?

3. A retailer carries an average stock valued at cost price of £3 000. His rate of stock turn is 150, his gross profit is 20 per cent on cost, and his overheads and running expenses come to £52 500. What is his net profit for the year?

4. H.J. is in business as a retailer and during the year ended December 31, 19. ., the average value of his stock at cost price was £40 000. He turned this over six times per year, at an average mark-up of 25 per cent. His fixed expenses were £12 000 and his variable expenses 10 per cent of the turnover. Calculate H.J.'s profit or loss for the year. If he had turned over his stock only five times during the year, by how much would his profit or loss have been affected?

(RSA – Adapted)

5. L.P. & Co. Ltd are a firm of wholesalers. Their average stock is valued at £60 000 at cost, and is turned over eight times in each trading year at an average mark-up of 50 per cent on cost. The firm's fixed, or standing charges are £40 000 and their variable expenses are 20 per cent of the turnover. Calculate (a) the firm's profit for the year, and (b) the profit if the stock is turned over nine times in a year. What conclusion would you draw from the difference in the amount of profit?

(RSA – Adapted)

6. During the year 19. ., J. W. Hardman made a gross profit of 25 per cent on a turnover of £108 000 and a net profit of 12 per cent on turnover. His rate of turnover of stock for the year was 10.

For the following year Hardman estimates that he can increase his rate of turnover of stock to 14, while carrying the same average stock, by reducing his prices by 5 per cent on selling price. If he does this, his ratio of expenses to turnover will be reduced by 2 per cent.

Calculate:

(a) Hardman's gross profit for 19. ..
(b) Hardman's expenses for 19. ..
(c) Hardman's net profit for 19. ..

and then calculate to the nearest £1

(d) Hardman's estimated sales for the following year.
(e) Hardman's estimated gross profit for the following year.
(f) Hardman's estimated expenses for the following year.
(g) Hardman's estimated net profit for the following year.

(London University – Adapted)

7. During 19. . Harper made a gross profit of 20 per cent on sales. His total turnover was £210 000. His net profit was 12½ per cent on turnover, and his rate of stock turn was 6.

During the next year Harper estimates that he can increase his rate of stock turn to 10, while carrying the same average stock, if he reduces his prices by 10 per cent, and this should also bring him a reduction in expenses of 2½ per cent on turnover.

Calculate:

(a) Gross profit for 19. ..
(b) Net profit for 19. ..
(c) Expenses for 19. ..

and then calculate, to the nearest £1, for the following year:

(d) His estimated sales.
(e) His estimated gross profit.
(f) His estimated expenses.
(g) His estimated net profit.

Would it be worth his while to carry out this policy?

8. The following details relate to J.B.'s busines for the year ended December 31, 19. .:

	£
Sales	169 920
Sales returns and allowances	1 900
Stock (January 1st, 19. .) valued at cost price	6 890
Stock (December 31, 19. .) valued at cost price	9 070
Gross profit for the year	40 340

Calculate:

(a) The turnover for the year.
(b) The cost of goods sold during the year.
(c) The amount of purchases for the year.
(d) The rate of turnover of stock for the year.
(e) The percentage of gross profit to turnover (to nearest whole number).

29.10 Terminology used in the interpretation of the Balance Sheet

Balance Sheets are not always well presented and the first task of any investor wishing to decide whether a business is sound or not is to arrange the Balance Sheet in good style. Good style for a Balance Sheet involves grouping the assets in the way shown in Chapter 1 of this book, either in the *Order of Liquidity* or the *Order of Permanence*. The groups are as shown in the following example, so that we bring out clearly the Current Assets, Fixed Assets, Current Liabilities, Long-term Liabilities, and Capital or Net Worth

For the purpose of recapitulation these groups are defined as:

Current Assets. Those assets which are held in the business with a view to their conversion into cash in the ordinary course of the firm's profit-making activities.

Fixed Assets. Those assets which are retained in the firm for use by the proprietor and his employees, because they permanently increase the profit-making capacity of the business.

Current Liabilities. Those liabilities which fall due for payment fairly quickly, and certainly within less than one year.

Long-term Liabilities. Those liabilities which will not fall due immediately, but which will gradually be repaid over an agreed period greater than one year.

Capital. The net worth of the business to the owner of the business; that portion of the owner's wealth which he has invested in the business either originally or by leaving past profits to accumulate in the service of the firm.

Figure 29.3 shows a typical Balance Sheet which will serve as a basis for discussion.

M. ERASMUS
BALANCE SHEET
as at December 31, 19. .

CAPITAL			FIXED ASSETS		£
At Start		120 000	Premises		37 000
Add Net Profit	22 500		Plant and Machinery		70 000
Less Drawings	20 000		Motor Vehicles		19 000
		2 500			126 000
		122 500	CURRENT ASSETS		
LONG-TERM LIABILITIES			Stock	44 490	
			Debtors	18 520	
Bank Loan		50 000	Bank Moneys	13 250	
CURRENT LIABILITIES			Cash in Hand	240	
Creditors		30 000			76 500
		£202 500			£202 500

Figure 29.3   A Balance Sheet for appraisal

By careful consideration of this Balance Sheet the reader may learn more phrases which are commonly used in business to help in the interpretation of Final Accounts. A mastery of these terms enables an investor to make sound judgements about the business whose affairs are being considered.

The new terms are:

(a) **Fixed Capital**. This is capital tied up in fixed assets, and in the case of M. Erasmus the fixed capital is £126 000. The significance of fixed capital is that it is sunk into the business and cannot be regained without seriously affecting the conduct of the business. If Erasmus tries to realize this fixed capital by selling motor vehicles or plant and machinery, the distribution or production of the firm's products will be hampered. If he tries to sell the premises he will be out in the street.

(b) **Floating capital** or **circulating capital**. This is capital tied up in current assets, which can be realized more easily and without interfering with the conduct of the business; indeed that is what we are in business for – to turn over stock and make profits as the stock turns into cash. In this case the circulating capital is £76 500.

(c) **Liquid Capital**. The term 'liquid' in economic matters means 'in cash form'. The liquid capital is that portion of the assets that are available as cash, or near cash. In this case it is £32 010; the total of cash, bank moneys and debtors.

(d) **Working capital**. This is the most important of these four terms – one of the most vital concepts in business. It is that portion of the capital invested in the business which is left to run the business *after providing the fixed capital*. Once a firm has bought its premises, plant and machinery, etc., it still needs working capital to run the business, to pay wages and sundry expenses. One might really say that having expended all the capital expenditure one still needs funds for revenue expenditure. The £76 500 that Erasmus has left after paying for his fixed assets is clearly something to do with working capital, but the real way to find working capital is as follows:

$$Working\ capital = Current\ assets - Current\ liabilities$$
$$= £76\ 500 - £30\ 000$$
$$= £46\ 500$$

A firm should never allow itself to run short of working capital. This is a very common reason for failure in business. If you allow your firm to buy too many fixed assets (called **over-capitalization**), then you are forced to borrow from the bank to find your working capital and this will probably cost you 2 per cent more than the bank's base rate; say 11 or 12 per cent interest. This means that the bank is creaming off most of your profits, and in fairly competitive trades this may leave you unable to earn a fair reward for yourself. A wise investor never buys shares in a firm that is short of working capital.

What is a reasonably safe working capital? It is generally agreed that 2:1 is a minimum working capital ratio, that is, the ratio of current assets to current liabilities. This is found by:

$$Working\ capital\ ratio = \frac{Current\ assets}{Current\ liabilities}$$

and in this case comes to

$$\frac{£76\ 500}{£30\ 000} = 2.55 \text{ times}$$

This is perfectly satisfactory. So important is the working capital figure considered to be that many limited companies publish their Balance Sheets with the current liabilities taken over and deducted from the assets side. This is illustrated in the section on Company Accounts, page 395.

Here is another ratio: the liquid capital ratio or **acid test ratio**.

$$Liquid\ capital\ ratio = \frac{Current\ assets - stock}{Current\ liabilities}$$

$$= \frac{£76\ 500 - £44\ 490}{£30\ 000} = \frac{£32\ 010}{£30\ 000} = 1.07 \text{ times}$$

The name 'acid-test ratio' is used to show that this is the critical test of solvency. Can the firm, with its present cash and debtors (due to pay within the month) meet its current liabilities (due for payment within the month)? An acid test ratio should be at least 1. In this case it is only just over 1, and it shows how weak this firm is as far as liquid assets go. Most of its current assets are stock.

(e) **External liabilities**. These are the liabilities owed to persons outside the business, and that means both current liabilities and long-term liabilities, in this case £80 000.

(f) **Capital owned**. This is the net worth of the business, the value of the business to the owner of the business. In this case it is £122 500.

(g) **Capital employed**. This is a very important figure. It can be defined in different ways, but the most commonly used method is to define it as the long-term capital employed, whether by the proprietor or other people outside the business. The outsiders may be debenture holders, or mortgagors who have provided capital to finance the purchase of buildings, or bankers and others who have provided long-term loans. Current liabilities are not counted in capital employed.

In this case therefore, the figure is made up of:

	£
Capital (including profits ploughed back)	122 500
Long-term liabilities: Bank Loan	50 000
Capital employed	£172 500

29.11   Appraising a Balance Sheet

We are now ready to discuss the Balance Sheet. Is the business whose Balance Sheet we are considering in a healthy or an unhealthy state?

Is Erasmus solvent? This means can he pay his debts, or at any rate such debts as are likely to be presented to him in the near future? The answer is that he has £30 000 of such debts likely to be presented to him and he has £76 500 of current assets. He will therefore probably be able to pay his debts as they fall due, but there is just a little worry over liquidity. He should really sell some of that stock to improve his liquidity position. He is solvent: the business is reasonably reliable.

Is he overtrading? Overtrading is a term used to describe a situation where the trader is tending to run short of working capital. He has over-capitalized, bought too many fixed items and left himself short of cash for revenue expenses. Here again Erasmus is just a little shaky. That stock figure is the worry, but he is probably safe enough. That bank loan is a long-term liability so that it isn't likely to be repaid in less than three years. If we say that £17 000 of it is due this year then that makes £47 000 Erasmus might have to pay back this year. He has only £32 010 in cash or near cash so unless he can dispose of a good deal of that stock fairly quickly he could be in difficulties. Certainly he should not, on any account, invest in any more fixed assets until his bank loan is substantially reduced. This means he must pay particular attention to his **cash flow**. This is the last item we need to discuss in this chapter about interpretation of Final Accounts. (See Section 29.12 below.)

Before doing so we must consider two items, the return on capital employed and the return on capital invested.

The return on capital employed. This calculation enables us to compare the profits earned with the capital employed to earn them, to see whether the return is adequate. In this particular case the profits were £22 500, and the capital employed was £172 500. The formula for the calculation is:

$$Return\ on\ capital\ employed = \frac{Net\ profit}{Capital\ employed} \times 100$$

$$= \frac{£\ 22\ 500}{£172\ 500} \times 100$$

$$= \frac{22\ 500}{1\ 725}\ \%$$

$$= 13.04\%$$

This is not a particularly brilliant result – most capital invested today in a safe investment such as gilt-edged securities earns about 9%. We would expect an investment in a risky business (and to some extent all businesses are risky) to earn much more than 9%.

The return on capital invested. The calculation above for the return on capital employed considers what the return was over-all on the capital used. The return on capital invested considers the results from the point of view of the proprietor only.

Here we have one or two points to consider. They are:

(a) The point we wish to investigate is the results for the year, and the figure 'capital invested' implies 'invested at the start of the year'. In this case the figure is £120 000.

(b) The return earned is the net profit figure, but we cannot include it all. We must take account of one further point. This is that by working in the business Erasmus has lost the opportunity of earning an income by working for someone else – perhaps as the manager of a similar firm. This lost opportunity is called the **'opportunity cost'** of being self-employed. Suppose Erasmus could have earned £8 000 working for someone else. The true earnings from the business are found by the formula:

$$True\ earnings\ =\ Net\ profit\ -\ Opportunity\ cost$$

Therefore the return on capital invested is:

$$Return\ on\ capital\ invested\ =\ \frac{(Net\ profit-opportunity\ cost)}{Capital\ invested\ at\ start}\times 100$$

$$=\frac{(£22\ 500\ -\ £8\ 000)}{£120\ 000}\ \times\ 100$$

$$=\frac{£14\ 500}{£120\ 000}\ \times\ 100$$

$$=\frac{145}{12}\ \%$$

$$=12.08\%$$

This again is not a very satisfactory return on capital – only a little more than Erasmus could have earned by a secure investment, without all the worry and work as a self-employed person.

Conclusions about Erasmus's Business. We can conclude by saying these things about Erasmus's business:

(a) The results are not poor, but they are not brilliant either.
(b) The working capital is adequate, but the liquid capital is barely adequate, as revealed by the acid-test ratio.

(c) This could have been improved if Erasmus had not drawn out so much cash. £20 000 was too much drawings out of £22 500 net profit, because he has a large bank loan to repay. He is really living beyond his means and this explains his rather illiquid position.

29.12 Cash flow

One problem which worries accountants at all times of the year is the problem of cash flow. Flows of funds in and out of a business are not regular, but change with the pattern of business trade, the seasons etc. Some companies have very uneven flows – perhaps the most spectacular example would be a manufacturer of fireworks in the United Kingdom. The majority of its products are consumed in a single evening's activities, the celebrations on Guy Fawkes' night. While making its products steadily all through the year, and paying wages and other expenses in the same way, its sales are largely made in the month before November 5, and payment arrives in November. The rest of the year, apart from export trade, it has few cash flows in and must budget its finances carefully so that it can survive until the next November 5 celebrations.

Budgeting for cash flow. A budget is a forecast which looks ahead to the future and envisages the likely income and expenditure. The usual arrangement as shown in Figure 29.4 is to draw up a spread-sheet with two columns per month, one for the **budget** and one for the **actual** figures. We cannot fill in the 'actual' figures until the month actually arrives and we find the true cash flows in and out. We can then set these figures against the budget (made several months before) and analyse any differences between them. This is called **variance analysis** – which is explained later.

It is usual to draw up a budget for at least three months ahead (six months is even better) and roll it forward into the future for a further period at regular intervals.

For the moment let us look at Figure 29.4 and notice how the budget for these three months has been built up. The following points are of interest:

(a) *The cash balance.* This is the figure carried forward from the previous month. If the budget leads us to expect a shortage of finance in a particular month we make plans about how to meet it and write them in the budget column. When the actual month arrives we shall then take action to solve the problem along the lines planned.

(b) Sales in cash will be cash flows in during the month concerned but sales on credit may not bring in funds until the following month, or the one after, according to the period of credit allowed. These will then come on the 'debts collected' line.

(c) Other receipts might include rent from a sub-tenant, commission expected, etc.

Cash Flow	July Budget (£)	July Actual (£)	August Budget (£)	August Actual (£)	September Budget (£)	September Actual (£)
1 Cash Balance (cash & bank)	2 346		2 239		−3 791	
Receipts:						
2 Sales in cash	4 592		5 210		6 500	
3 Debts collected	2 310		3 450		3 000	
4 Other receipts	160		160		160	
5 Extra capital contributed	—		—		2 500	
6 Total receipts (add 2–5)	7 062		8 820		12 160	
7 Total cash available (1+6)	9 408		11 059		8 369	
Payments:						
8 Payments for business stock	3 750		4 500		3 250	
9 Wages	2 354		2 500		2 350	
10 Other Payments	465		1 250		450	
11 Capital items	—		6 000		—	
12 External payments (add 8–11)	6 569		14 250		6 050	
13 Drawings	600		600		600	
14 Total payments	7 169		14 850		6 650	
15 Final Cash Balance (7–14)	2 239		Deficit −3 791 *Note*: Bring in new capital £2 500 Ask for £1 500 overdraft		1 719	

Figure 29.4   Budgeting for cash flow

Cash Flow Smoothing. Once we know how our pattern of cash flows varies we may be able to do a little **cash flow smoothing**. For example if we can see ahead a period of considerable cash flows into the business we might plan to purchase capital items that we know will be needed in the next few month at this time – when we are in funds. We might arrange for payments from people who owe us royalties for the use of patents etc., to pay us at times when other cash flows are at a reduced rate, and so on.

Variance analysis is the analysis of actual figures to see why they varied from budgeted figures. For example if the price of materials has risen there may be little we can do to correct the variance but we must pass on the higher costs to our customers by raising prices for our products. If the variance is caused by wasteful use of resources we must deal with the problem to eliminate the waste, and so on. Variance analysis is quite advanced work and we cannot do more than mention it in *Book-keeping Made Simple*.

29.13 Exercises set 29.4 – Balance Sheet interpretation and general questions on the interpretation of Final Accounts

1. Here is F. Clement's Balance Sheet. You are to answer the questions below (with calculations if needed).

BALANCE SHEET
as at December 31, 19. .

CURRENT LIABILITIES		£	CURRENT ASSETS		£
Creditors		15 000	Cash		120
LONG-TERM LIABILITIES			Bank		1 630
Bank Loan		25 000	Debtors		9 250
CAPITAL			Stock		22 250
At Start	80 000				
Add					33 250
Profit	11 250		FIXED ASSETS		
Less			Motor Vehicles	7 000	
Drawings	15 000		Plant and Machinery	36 000	
			Premises	40 000	
		−3 750			
		76 250			83 000
		£116 250			£116 250

(a) What is the capital owned by the proprietor?
(b) What is the capital employed in the business?
(c) What is the working capital?
(d) Express the profit as a percentage of the capital invested by the proprietor at the start of the year. (Answer correct to 1 decimal place).

(East Anglian Examination Board – Adapted)

2. Castle and Cary are in partnership as retail traders, and the following is their Balance Sheet:

BALANCE SHEET
(as at December 31, 19. .)

LIABILITIES	£	ASSETS	£
Capital:		Premises	37 500
Castle	20 000	Transport Vehicles, *less*	
Cary	16 000	Depreciation	16 000
Current Account: Castle	3 750	Fixtures and Fittings, *less*	
Loan, secured by mortgage		Depreciation	4 250
of Premises	20 000	Stock	9 000
Sundry Creditors	14 250	Sundry Debtors	1 750
Expenses Due, but not yet		Bank Balance on Current	
paid	500	Account	4 375
		Current Account: Cary	
		(overdrawn)	1 625
	£74 500		£74 500

You are required to state:

(a) The amount of the capital owned by the partnership.
(b) The total capital employed in the business.
(c) Whether the business has sufficient working capital.

For (a) and (b) the bais of your calculations should be stated; for (c) your reasons should be given; both very briefly.

(RSA – Adapted)

3. (a) From the following details find D. Jones's capital and show his Balance Sheet at March 31, 19. .:

Debtors £21 870; Stock £17 930; Creditors £22 360; Loan from K. Hind £15 000; Accrued expenses £370; Motor vans £6 700; Furniture and fittings £7 500; Premises £40 000; Payments in advance £620; Bank overdraft £10 000; Cash in hand £240.

(b) In relation to your completed Balance Sheet answer the following questions:

(i) What is the total of fixed assets?
(ii) How would you find the working capital, and what is its amount?
(iii) Was Jones solvent or insolvent? Give your reasons.

(RSA – Adapted)

4. The following Trial Balance was extracted from the partnership books of Grouse and Moor after the Trading and Profit and Loss Account for the year had been prepared.

TRIAL BALANCE
(as at December 31, 19. .)

	£	£
Profit and Loss Account (net profit)		40 040
Cash in Hand	480	
Balance at Bank	16 750	
Trade Debtors and Creditors	4 665	2 595
Provision for Bad Debts		390

Insurance Prepaid	120	
Rent Owing		200
Furniture, Fittings, and Equipment (cost)	4 400	
Stock-in-Trade	23 200	
Motor Van	2 400	
Loan (Grouse)		3 000
Capital Accounts (January 1):		
Grouse		11 890
Moor		7 050
Drawings Accounts:		
Grouse	7 550	
Moor	5 600	
	£65 165	65 165

Notes: 1 The motor van had been purchased for £3 000 on January 1, 19. ..

2 Grouse's loan – made for the purchase of the van – bears interest at 10 per cent per annum, and this has not been provided for.

3 Moor is entitled to be credited with a partnership salary of £7 500.

4 The partners share profits and losses in the proportions: Grouse, three-quarters; Moor, one-quarter.

(a) From the above information, prepare the Profit and Loss Appropriation Account, the Current Accounts of the partners and the Balance Sheet of the partnership.

(b) State the amount of:

(i) The current assets.
(ii) The fixed assets.
(iii) The liquid assets.
(iv) The current liabilities.
(v) The working capital.

5. From the following balances prepare the Balance Sheet of B. Hopeful as at December 31, 19. .:

		£
Trade Debtors		6 000
Insurance Paid in Advance		200
Stock at December 31, 19. .		23 125
Wages Outstanding		425
Trade Creditors		18 600
Profit and Loss Account to December 31, 19. .	Dr.	1 200
Bank Overdraft		6 250
Motor Van at Cost *less* Depreciation		4 000
Premises at Cost		42 500
B. Hopeful's Capital		60 000
Drawings Account		8 250

Comment briefly on the financial position disclosed by the Balance Sheet.

(RSA – Adapted)

6. Given below in abridged form is the Balance Sheet of C. Cantone:

C. CANTONE
BALANCE SHEET
as at March 1, 19. .

	£		£
Creditors	9 450	Cash	100
Capital Account	11 775	Debtors	3 125
		Stock	10 500
		Machinery	7 500
	£21 225		£21 225

The following transactions took place on March 2, 19. .:

(a) Cantone receives a loan of £2 500 which he used to pay £1 000 to a creditor and £1 500 for the purchase of new machinery.
(b) A debtor pays £600 on account, in cash.
(c) Cantone purchases on credit goods for resale (stock) costing £375.
(d) Old machinery is sold for £500 in cash; the book value was £1 250
(e) It is decided to correct the valuation of stock on March 1, 19. ., reducing it by £1 600.
(f) Goods were sold on credit for £950 (cost price £725).

Show Cantone's Balance Sheet as it would appear on March 2, 19. ., after the transactions, as noted, had been recorded.

(RSA – Adapted)

7. The following is the Balance Sheet of Dee and Jaye, who share profits and losses equally:

DEE AND JAYE
BALANCE SHEET
(as at March 31, 19. .)

	£		£
Capital:		Freehold Premises	42 500
Dee	32 500	Machinery	16 000
Jaye	25 000	Stock-in-Trade	17 500
Loan on Mortgage	19 000	Debtors	4 500
Trade Creditors	6 500	Cash at Bank and In Hand	2 500
	£83 000		£83 000

(a) From the above you are asked to state, showing your caluculations, the amount of (i) the current assets, and (ii) the working capital of the partnership.
(b) Suppose that the value of the stock at March 31, 19. ., had been £16 000 and the freehold premises had been written up, as the result of a revaluation, to £45 000, state the effect on the amount of working capital and on the Capital Accounts of Dee and Jaye respectively.

(RSA – Adapted)

8. (a) State what you understand by the term 'working capital' and say how you would ascertain the working capital of A. Bunn (a sole trader) from his Balance Sheet.

Giving your reasons, indicate whether or not the following transactions would tend to increase or decrease Bunn's working capital: If there would be no change write 'no effect'.

(b) (i) Bunn receives a loan of £5 000 in cash for business purposes repayable at the end of five years.
   (ii) A delivery truck, no longer required, is sold for £800 in cash.
   (iii) £240 is paid for goods purchased for resale, by cheque.
   (iv) £560 is received from a trade debtor in cash.
   (v) An old machine is traded in for an up-to-date model at a further cost of £4 800, by cheque.

(*RSA – Adapted*)

9. (a) The following statement, which is incomplete, sets out information regarding the position, at a particular date, of five different businesses identified in the statement as A, B, C, D and E. Copy it and insert the missing amount in whichever space is appropriate (Note: A deficiency means an 'overdrawn' Capital Account).

	Liabilities £	Capital £	Assets £	Deficiency £
A	11 550	?	40 000	?
B	?	60 000	80 550	?
C	17 500	23 500	?	?
D	72 500	?	60 500	?
E	?	?	95 000	5 000

(b) What book-keeping terms are used to indicate the following?
 (i) Assets held not for resale but merely to increase the profit-earning capacity of the business.
 (ii) Loans to the business of a semi-permanent nature.
 (iii) Debts falling due to be settled by the business in the immediate future.
 (iv) Assets which fluctuate in the ordinary course of trading.

(c) Which of the above items would you use in determining the amount of the working capital?

(*RSA – Adapted*)

10. Each of the following transactions of a sole trader affects either the Balance Sheet only, or the Trading Profit and Loss Account only, or, in some cases, both:

(a) The trader settles an account for £250 due to a creditor, by sending the creditor a cheque for £237.50 the balance being allowed as a discount.
(b) The trader withdraws £150 from his business account at the bank for his personal expenses.
(c) A debtor's account for £130 is irrecoverable and written off as a bad debt.
(d) A second-hand motor van, costing £500 and standing in the books at that figure, is sold on credit for exactly that sum.

(e)   A debtor, who owes £360 settles his indebtedness in full, by cheque.

(f)   At the close of the trading year an entry is passed for Bank Charges, £28.50.

(g)   The trader moves into new rented premises. In consequence, his old premises, which he owned freehold and which stand in the books at £42 500 are sold for £65 000, which is paid into the bank.

You are required to write down the words 'Balance Sheet' or 'Profit and Loss Account', as may be appropriate, against each of the items (a) to (g). If in your judgement the correct answer should be 'both', write 'both'.

11. Give the effect of each of the following transactions on the capital of a business, stating exactly by how much the capital would be increased or decreased. If you think there would be no change write 'no change'.

(a)   A sale of goods on credit for £1 000, their purchase price having been £725.

(b)   The purchase of a motor vehicle for £5 750, by cheque.

(c)   The payment of an insurance premium, £175.

(d)   The increase of a Provision for Bad Debts from £1 000 to £1 250.

(e)   The receipt of £475 from a debtor, in settlement of his account of £500.

12. From a trader's Final Accounts for the year his net profit was £18 750, but he had made the following errors:

(a)   Fixtures and fittings had been over-depreciated by £500.

(b)   Of the amount charged to his Profit and Loss Account for insurance, £250 represented a prepayment for the following year.

(c)   £125 interest allowed on his Bank Deposit Account had been left out of his calculations.

(d)   Bank charges, £50, had similarly been omitted.

(e)   £250, the debit balance of a hopelessly insolvent customer, had been left out of his Bad Debts Account.

(f)   Final stock had been over-valued by £750.

(g)   £1 250 rent for the final quarter, had been neither paid nor allowed for in his Profit and Loss Account.

Considering each of the above items entirely separately from the others, write down against (a) to (g) the corrected amount of the net profit as altered from the original £18 750.

13. The following estimates of Peter Markham's cash flows are available for the month of March. Work out a cash flow budget for the month and hence find the probable balance at the end of the month.

Cash in hand £420; Cash at bank £6 160; Cash sales £9 418; Credit sales £7 260; Debts to be settled by customers during March from previous periods £7 214; One third of this month's credit sales are also expected to be settled during the month; refund from VAT office £464; Cash purchases £7 250; payments to suppliers for business stock in earlier periods £3 426; Wages £1 542; Capital expenses (buying assets for cash) £3 260; Rates £440; Drawings £500.

14. The following estimates of B. Casual's cash flows are available for the month of September. (a) Work out the cash flow budget for the month and determine the balance at the end. (b) What advice would you offer Casual about cash flows in September?

Cash in hand £484; Cash at bank £2 384; Cash sales £7 590; Credit sales £4 960; Debts settled by customers in September from previous periods £3 214; one quarter of this month's credit sales is also expected to be paid in the month; rent received £260. Cash purchases £5 865; payment to creditors £2 956 for business stock; Wages £1 626; Capital expenses £4 400; Rates £385; Drawings £650.

30
Control Accounts

30.1 Introduction

With very large firms, handling thousands of accounts, the work involved in a Trial Balance used to be very laborious. These days we have almost magical aids in the form of computerized systems which pick up, read off, and print out, the balances on Ledger Accounts electronically. This chapter explains how we can take some of the trial out of a Trial Balance even if we are not provided with a computerized system. The student who hopes eventually to work with advanced accounting systems will learn here the fundamental ideas behind their control activities.

30.2 The sub-division of the Ledger

Figure 30.1 illustrates how the Ledger has been sub-divided over the years as businesses have increased in size. We have to progress from the idea of a bound Ledger to one where at least the personal accounts are kept in a loose-leaf system, or on a computerized system. Such systems are operated by junior book-keepers each of whom cannot take care of more than about 1 000 accounts. Suppose we have 5 000 debtors; we shall need five book-keepers to handle them.

If we make a rule that no one may go home until the Trial Balance is correct, our five book-keepers will become more and more depressed as the hours go by. Pity the luckless one who has made the mistake when they all catch the last bus home.

What is needed to avoid such trouble is a system of **Control Accounts** which enable a section of the work to be balanced off by itself, and the clerk who has prepared it will know whether he/she is correct or not. Those members of staff whose section balances will go off to catch their trains and keep their evening appointments. Those less fortunate, or less efficient, stay behind and look

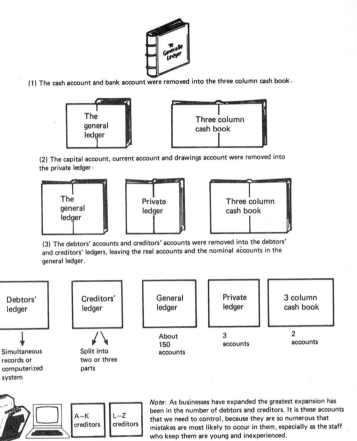

(1) The cash account and bank account were removed into the three column cash book.

(2) The capital account, current account and drawings account were removed into the private ledger.

(3) The debtors' accounts and creditors' accounts were removed into the debtors' and creditors' ledgers, leaving the real accounts and the nominal accounts in the general ledger.

Note: As businesses have expanded the greatest expansion has been in the number of debtors and creditors. It is these accounts that we need to control, because they are so numerous that mistakes are most likely to occur in them, especially as the staff who keep them are young and inexperienced.

Figure 30. 1 How the Ledger has been sub-divided

for the mistake with the help of the supervisor. Some offices call this work **sectional balancing**.

30.3   Control Accounts – the basic idea

Consider a typical section of the Debtors' Ledger – say the A–E section. Figure 30.2 depicts it in its filing cabinet tray. At the back one more account, the Control Account, has been added. This account is only a **Memorandum Account**, that is to say an account which is not a part of the double entry system, but simply a useful 'memo' or note. This book is kept by Miss Wright, one of our best posting clerks. How can we help Miss Wright to prove that she has done her work correctly, and deserves to go home at the normal time?

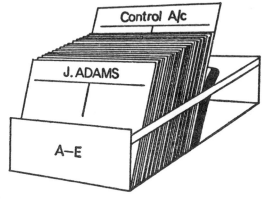

J. ADAMS				
19..		£	19..	£
Jan 1	Balance	100·00	Jan 5 Cash	98·00
13	Sales	272·00	5 Discount	2·00
13	Carriage	6·30	14 Returns	12·00
27	Sales	146·50	15 Allowance	5·30
27	Insurance	7·20	16 Cash	258·00
			16 Discount	3·00
			31 Balance	153·70
		£ 532·00		£ 532·00
19..		£		
Feb 1	Balance	153·70		

Figure 30.2   A section of the Ledger

A careful consideration of Miss Wright's tray of accounts shows the following matters:

(a) Nearly all these accounts have opening debit balances (after all – these people are debtors).

(b) Just the odd one or two have opening credit balances, usually because they have returned goods after paying for them. They are therefore debtors who are, just for a week or so, creditors instead.

(c) Nearly every account has a debit item 'Sales', because goods were bought during the month.

(d) Some of them have debit items, 'Carriage', 'Insurance', etc., for small items we have charged up to the accounts.

(e) Nearly all the accounts have credit items 'Cash', 'Discount', because goods purchased last month have been paid for this month.

(f) Some people's accounts will have 'Returns', 'Allowance', etc., entered on the credit side, because they have returned goods or been given allowances this month.

If we now record on the Control Account the total opening balances, the total sales, the total returns, the total cash, and the total discounts, etc., we shall be able to see whether the tray of accounts agrees with the **total figures**. If it does, then Miss Wright's section of the work is correct and she may go home. Her section has balanced.

This simple type of Control Account is all that we need to consider for *Book-keeping Made Simple*, but more advanced systems that are fully integrated with the double entry system are also used.

30.4 Where do we get the total figures for the Control Accounts?

The ideal thing is to get the total figures for the Sales, the Returns, the Cash and Discount, and the remaining items from a source separate from the source of Miss Wright's information. This involves a little extra organization.

First we must institute departmental systems (see Chapter 26) into all the major books of original entry, so that the Sales, the Purchases, the Sales Returns, and the Purchases Returns can be analysed into the various sections we need. Miss Wright keeps the A–E Sales Ledger so that the Sales Day Book will need analysis columns, as shown in Chapter 12, for A–E, F–K, L–S, and T–Z, or whatever the sections are called. From this analysis column we can collect the total sales figure for Miss Wright's Ledger without any difficulty whenever we want it – usually on the last day of the month. The Sales Returns Book will need similar analysis columns to give the total returns figure for the A–E book. The Three-column Cash Book will need a similar set of analysis columns to give us the total cash and discount figures for the A–E book.

The Journal Proper cannot have analysis columns in it, but the entries are so few that we can easily analyse them off when required. We simply open the Journal Proper at the beginning of the month we want and run our eye down it for any items concerning debtors whose names begin with A–E. We find one – a bad debt – and make a note of it. Are there any more? None on the next three pages, but on the last page there are two more, another bad debt and a dishonoured cheque. We make a note of the details and put them in the Control Account.

30.5 A simple Control Account

A typical control account is shown in Figure 30.3. It is the type of Memorandum Control Account which is not part of the double entry system.

SALES LEDGER A–E CONTROL ACCOUNT   L175

19. .				£	19. .				£
Jan.	1	Balances	b/d	22 762.50	Jan.	1	Balances	b/d	25.50
	31	Total Sales		69 578.75		31	Cash		44 726.75
	31	Interest Charged		105.65		31	Discounts		2 175.55
	31	Carriage Charged		497.65		31	Returns		1 476.50
	31	Dishonoured				31	Bad Debts		
		Cheques		214.60			Written Off		146.60
	31	Balances	c/d	117.20		31	Balances	c/d	44 725.45
				£93 276.35					£93 276.35
19. .				£	19. .				£
Feb.	1	Balances	b/d	44 725.45	Feb.	1	Balances	b/d	117.20

Figure 30.3   A simple Control Account

The account shown in Figure 30.3 is exactly like that of any ordinary debtor, except that it has balances on both sides. A debtor cannot be both a debtor and a creditor on the first day of the month, but as our Control Account, or Total Account, gives us the total figures for the whole of the A–E Ledger there may be some debtors who are creditors for a short while. Apart from this, the usual transactions are recorded. These are:

(a) Many of the debtors have bought goods during the month, and the total sales are debited in the Control Account.
(b) Many of the debtors have paid cash, and have been allowed discount. These total payments and discounts have been credited on the Control Account.
(c) Many of the debtors have returned goods, and the total returns have been credited to the Control Account.
(d) Finally a number of other items have been analysed out from the Journal Proper: interest charged, dishonoured cheques and bad debts.

Miss Wright can now compare the Control Account with her own ledger tray. She will balance off each of the accounts in her tray (they may already be kept on a 'running balance' method – see page 33.) She will then list the balances, and should find that the total debit balances agree with the Control Account above; and that the total credit balances of those debtors who are temporarily creditors also agree with the credit items shown above. If the tray fails to agree with the Control Account she must look for an error in her month's work.

30.6 The accountant who is wrong

An accountant may prefer to keep the Control Account in the General Ledger where the junior book-keeper cannot see it. He prepares it himself. The junior must come to the manager and tell him what the tray totals. 'I'm sorry,' he says, 'You've made a slip somewhere. Will you check it please? The junior must go back and look for a mistake.

Supposing the section does not balance? Is it necessarily the junior's fault? Could the manager be wrong? Well of course he could, because if he prepares the Control Account incorrectly the tray will not agree with it. The manager must make absolutely sure he gets the Control Account right, because if he keeps the junior in until late in the evening looking for the mistake and they then discover it is his fault, the junior will take great pleasure in letting the whole office know. The aim for a good manager should be (a) to get his Control Account right, and (b) to approach the problem of correcting the junior's work in a sympathetic and co-operative way. If it turns out to be his fault he can then apologize gracefully and save face. He can never know until that section of the ledger balances whose fault it is that the tray won't agree with the control.

30.7 Exercises set 30.1 – simple Control Accounts

1. Thomas is in business in only a small way, but he works out each month a Sales Ledger Control Account which is kept at the back of the Sales Ledger. Prepare it for the month of July given these figures:

			£
19. . July	1	Opening Balances	1 300
	31	Sales for Month	4 210
	31	Cash Received	1 280
	31	Discount Allowed	64
	31	Bad Debt	25
	31	Returns	28
	31	Allowance for Damaged Goods	50

Bring down the balance.

2. B. Irving keeps a Control Account as a control on her Creditors' Ledger. It is kept in the back of the Creditor's Ledger. Prepare it from these figures:

			£
19. .	Jan. 1	Amounts owed to Creditors	14 030
	31	Purchases for Month	13 015
	31	Payments to Creditors	15 880
	31	Discount Received	780
	31	Returns to Creditors	705
	31	Interest Charged by a Creditor	30
	31	Carriage Charged by a Creditor	25
	31	Outstanding Balance Owed by a Creditor to Irving	135

3. (a) Why do we draw up a Sales Ledger Control Account? (b) Set out the following items in an account of this kind appearing in the back of the Sales Ledger A–C tray.

	£
Credit Sales for January	213 780
Cash Received from Debtors during Month	162 505
Discount Allowed to Debtors during Month	8 135
Opening Balances on January 1	168 645
Dishonoured Cheques	735
Bad Debts Written Off	256
Sales Returns for the Month	6 730

4. (a) Prepare a Sales Ledger Control Account from the following information which relates to the month of October, 19. .:

	£
Balances on Debtors' Accounts at October 1	30 877
Receipts from Debtors	22 983
Sales on Credit	26 278
Sales Returns	2 323
Discounts Allowed	522

(b) This account is in the back of the Sales Ledger, but on taking out a balance of the book it proves not to be correct. What possible explanations are there?

30.8   Contra entries in Control Accounts

We usually connect Contra Entries with the Three-column Cash Book – that type of entry which is done when we take cash out of the bank for office use, or take cash out of the till to put it in the bank. A quite different kind of Contra Entry occurs with Control Accounts. These entries arise in the following way:

We usually have one Leger Account for each person with whom we deal, but this becomes very awkward in a sophisticated book-keeping system where we have split the Ledger up into several pieces as shown in Figure 30.1. If we have a single person with whom we deal in two capacities, as a debtor and as a creditor, it will be impossible to have all our transactions with him recorded on one page in the Ledger, because the debtors are split away from the creditors. Our debtors' accounts will perhaps be in a computerized system, while our creditors' accounts may be hundreds of yards away in another office, or on different floors perhaps.

The solution is for our client to have two accounts, one in the Debtors' Ledger and one in the Creditors' Ledger, and as these accounts are opposite in character we call them Contra Accounts.

Consider the case of M. Grenfell, a trader with whom we deal in both capacities. He is a wholesale druggist who buys considerable quantities of drugs from our firm, which manufactures pharmaceutical products. He also allows us to purchase, on behalf of staff, any chemist's sundries they wish to buy, at specially favourable terms. In any given month Grenfell buys from us about £5 000 of pharmaceutical goods, while we buy for our staff about £200 of chemist's sundries from Grenfell. On our books Grenfell has two Contra Accounts, a debtor's account for his large purchases from us, and a creditor's account for the small purchases we make from him.

Here are these two accounts:

DEBTORS' LEDGER
M. GRENFELL   L67

19. .		£			
Jan. 31	Sales	5 126.55			

CREDITORS' LEDGER
M. GRENFELL   L73

			19. .		£
			Jan. 31	Purchases	195.15

Figure 30.4 Two Contra Accounts

What shall we do about these accounts at the end of the month? Is there any point in sending Grenfell a cheque for the £195.15 we owe him when he owes us £5 126.55? Clearly there is not. The sensible thing is to contra the small item off against the big item, and let M. Grenfell pay us the outstanding balance, i.e. £4 931.40. A simple Journal Entry will settle the matter. Here it is:

19. .			£	£
Jan. 31	M. Grenfell (Creditors' Ledger) Dr.	L73	195.15	
	M. Grenfell (Debtors' Ledger)	L67		195.15
	Being contra entry against outstand-			
	ing debtor's balance			

Figure 30.5   Journalizing a contra entry

When posted into the Ledger Accounts this will clear off the Creditor's Ledger Account completely, and leave the Debtors' Ledger Account at a lower figure. This lower figure represents what Grenfell owes us for pharmaceutical goods supplied. He has paid for some of them by giving us the goods for our staff who use this opportunity to purchase cheap goods.

How does this affect the Control Accounts? The Journal Entry, Figure 30.5 is one of the Journal Entries we shall pick up when we analyse the Journal for Control Account items. It is going to affect two Control Accounts, the Debtors' Ledger Control Account and the Creditors' Ledger Control Account. In each case it affects the Control Account just like cash paid, the entry 'Contra' will come in on each Control Account just like cash paid, to reduce both the debtors' debts to us and our debts to our creditors.

30.9   Exercises set 30.2 – more difficult Control Accounts

1. (a) What accounts would you expect to find in a Sales Ledger?
(b) R. Blenkinsop checks his Sales Ledger monthly by means of a Control Account. Name the sources from which he is likely to ascertain the figures to prepare this Control Account.
(c) What should the balance of the Control Account represent and with what amount should it agree?

2. A firm keeps a Purchases Ledger which is checked by a Control Account. For the month of May the following figures are available for the Control Account:

	£
Credit Balance at May 1, 19. .	
(agreeing with total balances in Purchases Ledger)	23 045
Purchases for Month	27 010
Purchases Returns for Month	550
Cash Paid to Creditors	24 375
Discount Received	1 285
Transfers of Debit Balances in Sales Ledger to Purchases	
Ledger (Contra Entries)	400

(a) Construct the Control Account for May 19. ..

(b) State the source from which each of the above figures would be ascertained.
(c) State what the balance of the Control Account represents.

(London University – Adapted)

3. Goldbourn Ltd keep a separate Sales Ledger and Purchases Ledger, with special Memorandum Control Accounts, kept in the back of these two Ledgers.

You are asked to draw up the Sales Ledger Control Account and the Purchases Ledger Control Account.

			£
Jan.	1	Balances on Debit Side of Sales Ledger Accounts	217 648
	1	Balances on Credit Side of Sales Ledger Accounts	368
	1	Balances on Credit Side of Purchases Ledger Accounts	47 572
	1	Balances on Debit Side of Purchases Ledger Accounts	196
	31	Cash Received from Customers	388 896
	31	Sales to Customers	769 732
	31	Cash Paid to Creditors	39 680
	31	Goods Purchased	153 648
	31	Returns Inwards	3 606
	31	Returns Outwards	5 362
	31	Amounts Charged to Customers for Carriage	384
	31	Bad Debts Written Off	604
	31	Sales Ledger Debits Written Off to Creditors Accounts	1 480
	31	Interest Charged to A. Debtor (overdue account)	40

(London University – Adapted)

4. (a) From the following particulars prepare the Sales Ledger Control Account of T. Thompson:

	£
Amounts Owing by Customers on January	40 000
Amounts Due to Customers on January 1	384
Sales in January	393 600
Bought Ledger Contras (Credits on the Bought Ledger transferred)	4 016
Goods taken by Landlord in Lieu of Cash for Rent Due	400
Discounts Allowed	5 600
Bad Debts	6 400

On January 10 A. Brown, who owed £1 040 since the previous August, paid in full. Thompson had already reduced this Account to £560 as a doubtful debt.
Cash Received (excluding A. Brown above)   360 000
An Invoice of £3 840 had been issued in duplicate and charged twice to A. Debtor's Account. This had been corrected by a Journal entry.

(b) You are now told that the total balances on Thompson's Sales Ledger are £52 400 and that there is an error of £100 in the Trial Balance. What conclusion do you draw?

5. (a) Prepare the Bought Ledger Control Account and Sold Ledger Control Account from the information given below.

	£
Debtors on Sold Ledger at January 1, 19. .	189 325
Creditors on Bought Ledger at January 1, 19. .	143 651
Goods Purchased on Credit during Month	536 911
Goods Sold on Credit during Month	924 614
Sundry Credit Balances on Sold Ledger, January 31	932
Cash Payments by Debtors during Month	854 718
Bills Receivable Received during Month	9 275
Bills Payable Issued during Month	9 307
Cheques Paid to Creditors during Month	501 498
Discounts Received	7 612
Discounts Allowed	8 374
Bad Debts	433
Goods Returned Outwards during Month	8 362
Interest Charged on Overdue Sales Ledger Accounts	791

(b) You are now told that there is a £10 error on the Trial Balance, which shows total debtors of £241 930 and total creditors of £153 773. What do you conclude?

31
The amalgamation of businesses

31.1 Introduction

When two sole traders amalgamate their businesses a variety of arrangements are possible, but it usually means some adjustment to the existing firms. For instance, they may not need both sets of premises, or both sets of plant and machinery, or both sets of motor vehicles. The terms of the agreement drawn up will set out what assets and liabilities each partner is bringing in. It may also be agreed that either or both partners shall open a Goodwill Account to value the goodwill of the businesses being merged. This will be included as one of the assets of the new business. Any adjustment in this way to the Balance Sheets of the old businesses alters the Capital Account of the trader concerned, which will form his capital in the new partnership being established.

31.2 Drawing up the Statements of Affairs on amalgamation

Consider the following example:

R. Elder and T. Younger are in business separately as sole traders. They decide to set up a partnership from January 1, 19. ., using Elder's premises and fixtures and fittings. Younger is to sell his premises and fittings privately, but is to bring in £15 000 as capital in addition to his existing bank balance. Elder's motor vehicles consist of one new and one old vehicle. The latter is valued at £1 500 on his books, and as it is surplus to the needs of the new business he will sell it privately. Elder will be allowed to open a Goodwill Account for £5 000 to compensate him for the hard work done in the past, since Younger will now share the benefits of this. Their existing Balance Sheets are shown on page 448. Carry out the amalgamation and show the Balance Sheet of the new business after the books have been opened.

The first thing to do is to reconstruct these Balance Sheets in the

R. ELDER
BALANCE SHEET
as at December 31, 19. .

LIABILITIES	£	ASSETS	£
Creditors	11 500	Cash	1 000
Capital	100 000	Cash at Bank	19 000
		Stock	23 500
		Motor Vehicles	9 000
		Furniture and Fittings	4 000
		Land and Buildings	55 000
	£111 500		£111 500

T. YOUNGER
BALANCE SHEET
as at December 31, 19. .

LIABILITIES	£	ASSETS	£
Creditors	9 500	Bank Balance	2 000
Capital	57 500	Debtors	13 000
		Stock	15 000
		Motor Vehicles	9 000
		Furniture and Fittings	8 000
		Land and Buildings	20 000
	£67 000		£67 000

light of the information given, so that the new statements of affairs leave out any items not being brought into the new business. The result will be the following statements of affairs, which on this occasion are given in the order of liquidity.

R. ELDER
STATEMENT OF AFFAIRS
on amalgamation with T. Younger on January 1, 19. .

CURRENT LIABILITIES	£	CURRENT ASSETS		£
Creditors	11 500	Cash		1 000
		Cash at Bank		19 000
		Stock		23 500
				43 500
CAPITAL				
At Start	103 500	FIXED ASSETS		
		Motor Vehicles	7 500	
		Furniture and Fittings	4 000	
		Land and Buildings	55 000	
		Goodwill	5 000	71 500
	£115 000			£115 000

T. YOUNGER
STATEMENT OF AFFAIRS
on amalgamation with R. Elder on January 1, 19. .

CURRENT LIABILITIES	£	CURRENT ASSETS	£
Creditors	9 500	Balance at Bank	17 000
		Debtors	13 000
		Stock	15 000
			45 000
CAPITAL		FIXED ASSETS	
At Start	44 500	Motor Vehicles	9 000
	£54 000		£54 000

Note: In each case the capital of the two proprietors is changed. Elder's increases because of the Goodwill Account opened. Younger's decreases because he retains some of the proceeds of the sale of his premises and fittings.

31.1 Amalgamating the two businesses

All that is now required on amalgamation is to put these two statements together into one Opening Journal Entry, post it to the Ledger Accounts and the Cash Book, and extract a Balance Sheet. The Opening Journal Entry will be as show in Figure 31.1

19. .				£	£
Jan.	1	Cash in Hand	Dr. CB1	1 000	
		Cash at Bank	Dr. CB1	36 000	
		Debtors	Dr. L1	13 000	
		Stock	Dr. L2	38 500	
		Motor Vehicles	Dr. L3	16 500	
		Furniture and Fittings	Dr. L4	4 000	
		Land and Buildings	Dr. L5	55 000	
		Goodwill	Dr. L6	5 000	
		Creditors	L7 etc.		21 000
		Capital E	L99		103 500
		Capital Y	L100		44 500
			£	169 000	169 000
		Being assets and liabilities at this date			

Figure 31.1   Opening the books of the new business

The amalgamated Balance Sheet is given in Figure 31.2.

R. ELDER AND T. YOUNGER
BALANCE SHEET
as at January 1, 19. .

CURRENT LIABILITIES	£		CURRENT ASSETS		£
Creditors		21 000	Cash in Hand		1 000
			Cash at Bank		36 000
CAPITAL			Debtors		13 000
At Start E	103 500		Stock		38 500
Y	44 500				————
	————				88 500
		148 000	FIXED ASSETS		
			Motor Vehicles	16 500	
			Furniture and		
			Fittings	4 000	
			Land and Buildings	55 000	
			Goodwill	5 000	
					————
					80 500
		————			————
		£169 000			£169 000

Figure 31.2   An amalgamation completed

31.4   Exercises set 31.1 – amalgamations

1. Flower agreed to take Rose into partnership as from July 1 19. .. On that day the following balances were extracted from their books:

	Flower £	Rose £
Freehold Premises	30 000	23 000
Machinery and Tools	10 300	7 000
Stock of Materials	4 250	2 250
Cash at Bank	3 000	—
Stock of Finished Goods	7 250	4 750
Bank Overdraft	—	3 825
Cash in Hand	150	125
Sundry Creditors	12 700	6 350
Rates and Insurance Prepaid	250	200
Sundry Debtors	8 150	4 850
Provision for Bad Debts	650	—

Rose was to pay off the amount of his bank overdraft out of his private funds and to make a Provision for Bad Debts of £825.

The terms of the partnership were:

(a) Interest on capital to be allowed at 8 per cent per annum.
(b) Rose was to act as manager of the business and receive a bonus of 20 per cent of profits *after* charging interest on capital. The remainder of the profits was to be divided equally between Flower and Rose.

(i) Draft the opening Balance Sheet of the new firm as at 1 July, 19. ..

(ii) On December 31, 19. ., the Net Trading Profit for the half-year, before charging interest on capital and Rose's bonus, was £24 150. Draft the Profit and Loss Appropriation Account for the half year.

(*University of London – Adapted*)

2. Miss P. Whitehead agrees to enter into partnership with Miss D. Poole as from January 1, 19. .. On that day their records showed the following situation:

	P. Whitehead £	D. Poole £
Land and Buildings	35 000	25 000
Machinery	14 000	20 000
Furniture and Fittings	3 000	2 000
Stocks:		
Raw Materials	2 750	2 250
Work in Progress	6 750	6 250
Finished Goods	10 000	9 000
Cash	400	2 375
Bank	12 500	10 780
Creditors	770	1 670
Rent Due	250	300
Debtors	9 000	5 000
Bad Debts Provisions	750	600

Miss Whitehead will not bring in her machinery and Miss Poole will not bring in her Land and Buildings or her Furniture and Fittings.

Draw up the Amalgamated Balance Sheet.

3. R. Brown and B. Jones are in business separately as sole traders. They decide to set up a partnership business with effect from January 1, 19. .. Brown's premises, furniture and fittings, and motor vehicles are to be sold separately by Brown and not brought into the partnership business. He will bring in, instead, a further £5 000.00 cash, as well as all his stock-in-trade and book debts. Jones brought in all his assets and liabilities. Here are their two business Balance Sheets. Draw up the Amalgamated Balance Sheet as at January 1, 19. ..

	R. Brown £	B. Jones £
ASSETS		
Cash	1 000	2 500
Debtors	15 000	12 000
Stock	22 500	28 000
Motor Vehicles	9 000	14 000
Furniture and Fittings	3 000	6 000
Land and Buildings	17 500	25 000
LIABILITIES		
Creditors	8 000	7 500
Capital	60 000	80 000

4. A. and B. are independent traders in the same line of business, their respective Balance Sheets on December 31, 19. ., being as follows:

Balance Sheet details at 31 December

ASSETS	A.	B.
Goodwill	5 000	—
Property and Land	42 000	—
Fixtures and Fittings	2 950	2 000
Motor Vehicles	—	5 500
Stock	49 300	20 000
Debtors	42 950	15 000
Cash at Bank	5 350	—
LIABILITIES		
Capital	137 000	29 350
Creditors	10 485	11 990
Bank overdraft	—	1 160
Wages due	65	—

They decide to amalgamate on the following terms:

(a) All assets and liabilities to be taken over at their agreed values except B.'s fixtures and fittings which he will dispose of privately, and stocks, which will each be reduced by 10 per cent.
(b) B.'s goodwill to be valued at £4 000.
(c) B.'s overdraft to be cleared privately, and A. to pay the wages due out of his own pocket.

Draw up the Opening Entry for the new business and the Opening Balance Sheet as at January 1, 19. ..

32
The purchase of a business

32.1 Introduction

When one person purchases a business from another the buyer agrees to pay a sum, called the purchase price, to the seller – usually called the **vendor**. The purchase price nearly always includes a payment for goodwill over and above the value of the actual assets taken over. The signing of the agreement is the moment when the contract takes effect, unless a specific moment of time is embodied in the agreement. At that time the purchaser will open his books with the necessary opening Journal Entries, and will assume control of the business.

32.2 The purchase price and the goodwill figure

Consider the following example:

Example
On January 1, 19. ., T. Brown's Balance Sheet is as follows:

T. BROWN

BALANCE SHEET

as at January 1, 19. .

LIABILITIES	£	ASSETS	£
Capital	35 000	Shop premises	26 000
Trade Creditors	7 500	Furniture and Fittings	4 000
		Motor Vehicle	2 500
		Stock	8 750
		Cash at Bank	1 250
	£42 500		£42 500

At this date Brown agrees to sell his business to R. Gray for £46,000. Gray will take over all the assets except the bank balance and will also pay the trade creditors. Gray decides to value the shop premises at £40 000 the furniture and fittings at £2 800 the motor vehicle at £1 500 and the stock at £7 250. Show the records for the purchase of the business in Gray's books, his capital contribution being £50 000 placed in a current account at his local bank.

The important point to remember in recording these matters is that the valuations of the purchaser, Gray, are the important ones in the calculations. The purchase price is agreed at £46 000. What does Gray expect for his money? The list of assets reads:

	£
Assets taken over:	
Premises	40 000
Furniture and Fittings	2 800
Motor Vehicle	1 500
Stock	7 250
	51 550
The liability to the trade creditors must be deducted from this:	7 500
Net Value of Assets	44 050

Gray is receiving assets valued at the net figure of £44 050, yet he is prepared to pay £46 000. This extra sum must be Gray's valuation of the goodwill, i.e. £1 950.

When listing the assets in the Opening Entries we shall include goodwill, £1 950.

32.3   Opening the accounts of the new business

The stages of this series of entries are most easily understood if we number them in the correct order of events.

(a) At the moment of purchase Gray agrees to pay the vendor the purchase price. The vendor therefore becomes a creditor, and to enable us to credit him at once we open up a special account called the Purchase of Business Account which can be debited. The Journal Entry is as shown in Figure 32.1 and the accounts are as shown in Figure 32.2.

19. .				£	£
Jan.	1	Purchase of Business Account Dr.	L1	46 000	
		T. Brown	L2		46 000
		Being agreed price of business taken over			

Figure 32.1   The vendor becomes a creditor

PURCHASE OF BUSINESS ACCOUNT   L1

19. .			£		
Jan.	1	T. Brown	J1	46 000	

T. BROWN ACCOUNT   L2

			19. .		£
			Jan.	1	Purchase of
					Business J1 46 000

Figure 32.2   The accounts of the new business are opened

(b) The next thing Gray needs to do is to take on the assets, including goodwill, at his own valuations. The Journal Entry is shown in Figure 32.3, and the accounts in Figure 32.4. Note that the assets are all debited and Purchase of Business Account is credited.

19. .					£	£
Jan.	1	Premises Account	Dr.	L3	40 000	
		Furniture and Fittings Account	Dr.	L4	2 800	
		Motor Vehicle Account	Dr.	L5	1 500	
		Stock Account	Dr.	L6	7 250	
		Goodwill Account	Dr.	L7	1 950	
		Purchase of Business Account		L1		53 500
		Being assets taken over at this date				

Figure 32.3   Opening the Asset Accounts

(c) Gray now has to take on the liability. The effect of this will be to clear the Purchase of Business Account, which has served its purposes and is closed off. The Journal Entry will be as shown in Figure 32.5.

In fact this is not a very sensible Journal Entry because each creditor would have an account opened in his name and a large number of accounts would really be credited with sums of money which in total would come to £7 500. The Purchase of Business Account would now read as shown in Figure 32.6

(d) The last thing for Gray to do is to pay the vendor, Brown, his purchase price. He contributes his capital £50 000 paying Brown by cheque. The relevant Journal Entries are as shown in Figure 32.7.

Note: It is not strictly necessary to Journalize cash entries, but on occasions like this a full record of the day to day events is desirable.

When posted to the Cash Book and the Ledger the vendor's

account is cleared and the Opening Balance Sheet of the new business is as shown in Figure 32.8.

PURCHASE OF BUSINESS ACCOUNT   L1

19. .			£	19. .			£
Jan.	1	T. Brown	J1	46 000	Jan.	1	Sundry Assets J1	53 500

PREMISES ACCOUNT   L3

19. .				£
Jan.	1	Purchase of Business	J1	40 000

FURNITURE AND FITTINGS ACCOUNT   L4

19. .				£
Jan.	1	Purchase of Business	J1	2 800

MOTOR VEHICLES   L5

19. .				£
Jan.	1	Purchase of Business	J1	1 500

STOCK ACCOUNT   L6

19. .				£
Jan.	1	Purchase of Business	J1	7 250

GOODWILL ACCOUNT   L7

19. .				£
Jan.	1	Purchase of Business	J1	1 950

Figure 32.4 The Asset Accounts

19. .					£	£
Jan.	1	Purchase of Business Dr.	L1		7 500	
		Trade Creditors	L8, etc.			7 500
		Being liabilities taken over on purchase				

Figure 32.5 Taking over the creditors (but actually each creditor would need a separate account)

PURCHASE OF BUSINESS ACCOUNT   L1

19. .			£	19. .			£
Jan. 1	T. Brown	J1	46 000	Jan. 1	Sundry Assets J1		53 500
1	Creditors	J1	7 500				
			£53 500				£53 500

Figure 32.6   The Purchase of Business Account cleared

19. .				£	£
Jan. 1	Bank Account Dr.	CB1	50 000	
	Capital Account	L100		50 000
	Being Capital contributed by R. Gray at this date			
1	T. Brown Account Dr.	L2	46 000	
	Bank Account	CB1		46 000
	Being cheque in settlement			

Figure 32.7   Paying the vendor

R. GRAY
BALANCE SHEET
as at January 1, 19. .

CAPITAL	£	FIXED ASSETS		£
At Start	50 000	Goodwill		1 950
		Premises		40 000
		Furniture and Fittings		2 800
CURRENT LIABILITIES		Motor Vehicles		1 500
Creditors	7 500			46 250
		CURRENT ASSETS		
		Stock	7 250	
		Cash at Bank	4 000	
				11 250
	£57 500			£57 500

Figure 32.8   The Balance Sheet of the new business

32.4   Exercises set 32.1 – purchase of a business

1. On December 31, 19. ., A. Brownjohn purchases for £66 000 all the assets of A. Rowntree, a trader, with the exception of the debtors. At that date the assets shown in A. Rowntree's Balance Sheet were:

	£
Freehold Property	40 000
Furniture and Fittings	5 500
Stock-in-Trade	13 250

It was agreed that these figures represented fair valuations. Brownjohn contributed £70 000 as capital to a Bank Account for the business, and Rowntree was paid by cheque.

Show the Journal Entries in Brownjohn's books for the purchase of this business – including the Cash Book entries, and the new firm's Balance Sheet.

2. The following is the Balance Sheet of J. Whitty on April 30, 19. .:

	£			£
Capital	25 000	Fixtures and Fittings		8 750
Creditors	5 854	Motor Van	6 800	
		Less Owing on Hire		
		Purchase	1 800	
				5 000
		Stock		12 854
		Debtors		4 250
	£30 854			£30 854

On this date. A. Walsall purchased the business for £29 500, taking over all the assets and liabilities at the values shown. He contributes £32 000 as capital to a business Bank Account and pays by cheque.

Draft entries in the Journal of the purchaser to open his books, and the Balance Sheet of the new business.

(*RSA – Adapted*)

3. On October 31, 19. ., A. Coughlan arranged to take over the business carried on by J. Frost.

The assets were taken over at the following valuations: Goodwill £5 000; Fixtures and fittings £7 250; Stock £17 750 and Debtors £3 275. The creditors totalled £4 562 and it was found that:

(a) Rent was owing for one month at the rate of £2 400 per annum.
(b) Rates amounting to £420 had been paid for the half-year to March 31, next.
(c) The Telephone Account owing amounted to £320.
(d) The Electricity Account owing amounted to £125, against which the suppliers held a permanent deposit for £50 which was taken over by the purchasers.
(e) On October 15, 19. ., A. Coughlan had paid a deposit of £2 500.

Prepare a statement showing the amount due to the vendor at the completion of the transaction.

(*RSA – Adapted*)

4. On January 1, 19. ., A-B purchased for £95 000 the business of Smith, a trader. At that date the assets appearing in the books of Smith were:

		£
Buildings		36 500
Plant		24 700
Motor Vans		9 800
Stock-in-Trade		14 300
Debtors		3 750

There were liabilities to trade creditors of £4 475. These valuations were accepted as fair by A-B and the assets and liabilities were entered in his books at those figures. The purchase price was paid by cheque after A-B had contributed capital of £100 000 to a business Bank Account.

Show the Journal Entries in the books of the new business and its Balance Sheet.

33
Accounting for Bills of Exchange

33.1 What is a Bill of Exchange?

A bill of exchange is a method of payment used between
businessmen which has certain advantages over other methods of
payment. It has a very precise definition which is given below,
from the Bills of Exchange Act 1882. An illustration is given in
Figure 33.1, and explained in the notes below it. It is best to read
the definition first, and then look at Figure 33.1 and notice how it
fits the definition. This is:

> 'A bill of exchange is an unconditional order in writing,
> addressed by one person to another, signed by the person
> giving it, requiring the person to whom it is addressed to pay
> on demand or at a fixed or determinable future time a sum
> certain in money to or to the order of a specified person, or to
> bearer.'

(Bills of Exchange Act 1882)

The following points will help your understanding:

(a) The one who writes out the order to pay is called the
drawer.

(b) The one who is drawn upon (i.e. ordered to pay) is called
the **drawee**.

(c) Later this person (the drawee) may 'accept' the bill. This is
a special use of the word 'accept' because it means 'accepts the
obligation to pay expressed in the bill'. If I accept the duty to
pay I write 'accepted' across the face of the bill and sign it (even
just signing my name on it will do). From that time on I am
known as the **acceptor** of the bill and have absolute liability on it
– I must honour the bill on the due date. If I dishonour it that is
an utterly disgraceful act and may lead to bankruptcy (unless I
make other arrangements).

(d) The amount of money must be absolutely clear. 'A sum

certain' – this is not the same as 'a certain sum'. For example, I cannot make out a bill requiring someone to pay the value of my horse Dobbin. That is an uncertain sum. It must say 'Three thousand pounds' or 'Four hundred pounds'.

(e) The time must either be fixed or at least determinable. For example, '90 days after date' is determinable if the bill is dated 1 July. It is 29 September.

(f) The person who is entitled to be paid is called the 'payee', but it is usually the same person as the drawer, since – as we shall see – it is usually the drawer who is supplying goods to the value of the bill, and wants to be paid for them. If the drawer decides he wants the acceptor to pay someone else he can always order him to pay that person by endorsing the bill (writing on the back of it) 'Pay J. Smith' or whoever it is. That is why the definition says 'to pay . . . to, or to the order of, a specified person'.

(g) A bill can be made payable to bearer, but this is risky, since any finder of the bill, or any thief, could claim the money and the acceptor would be free of debt if he paid the wrong person, even if that person had no right to the bill.

Now read the defintion again and study Figure 33.1 carefully.

33.2 The use of Bills of Exhange

It is very important to understand how bills of exchange work. The process is illustrated in Figure 33.2(a) and (b), but first notice the following points.

(a) A person who wishes to buy goods but has no money may agree to accept a Bill of Exchange drawn at some future date for the full value of the order he wishes to place. Let us suppose this is £3 500 of furniture from a furniture manufacturer, Peter Laidlaw (Cambridge) Ltd, and that 90 days credit is agreed.

(b) The drawer draws a bill for £3 500 on the customer (the drawee) who accepts it (thus becoming the acceptor of the bill) and returns it to the drawer. The drawer delivers the goods and has a 90 day bill for £3 500 instead. He can either keep the bill and present it on the due date or he can cash it straight away, as explained below.

(c) When a drawee 'accepts' a bill and acknowledges the obligation in it he is bound by law – in the most solemn way – to honour the bill on the due date. If he is a reputable person the bill is as good as money, and any bank will discount it. There is a special kind of bank that does little else but discount bills of exchange – they are called discount houses. What they will do is cash the bill by giving the drawer the *present value* of the bill. This

No. 1.

EXCHANGE FOR £3 500 =   1st July   19..

At 90 days after data pay this   first   Bill of Exchange
to, or   to the Order of
Peter Laidlaw (Cambridge) Ltd
three thousand five hundred pounds only

Value Received   which place to Account

To Belbridge, Jones and Co. Ltd   Peter Laidlaw (Cambridge) Ltd
    2173. One Tree Hill,   4932 Comberton Rd
    Stanford-le-Hope,   Cambridge
    Essex.   Peter Laidlaw. (Director)

P.S.100 Foreign B/X. Published & Sold by Formecon Services Ltd., Douglas House, Gateway, Crewe, Cheshire, CW1 1YN, England.

Figure 33.1   An inland bill of exchange

Notes:

(i) The drawer of the bill is Peter Laidlaw, a director of Peter Laidlaw (Cambridge) Ltd.

(ii) The drawees are Beleridge, Jones and Co. Ltd. They have not yet accepted the bill, and so have no liability on it at all at present.

(iii) The bill is an unconditional order in writing. It says 'Pay three thousand five hundred pounds to Peter Laidlaw (Cambridge) Ltd. It does not say 'provided you are in funds at the time' or any condition. It just says 'Pay!'.

(iv) It is addressed by one person (Peter Laidlaw) to another (Beleridge, Jones and Co. Ltd) and is signed by the person giving it (Peter Laidlaw).

(v) The date is determinable, it is 90 days after 1 July, which is 29 September, 19. ..

(vi) The sum of money is certain, three thousand five hundred pounds.

(vii) The bill is payable to, or to the order of, Peter Laidlaw (Cambridge) Ltd.

is the face value less interest at an agreed rate for the number of days it has to run. So the drawer who discounts the bill with the bank gets less than the face value – in other words a discount is deducted by the Discount House.

(d) The bill is endorsed by the drawer with a signed and dated order to pay the bank. The bank is now a 'holder in due course' of the bill, and owns it, having given value for it.

(e) On the due date the bank will present the bill to the acceptor, who honours it by paying the full value. The bank has earned the amount of interest it deducted when it discounted the bill, and the 'loan' it made to the drawer had been paid in full. Where does the acceptor get the money to honour the bill? The answer is that he has had 90 days to sell the furniture at a profit, and can therefore honour the bill and have something left over for himself.

We can now follow what is happening in the two diagrams, Figure 33.2(a) and Figure 33.2(b).

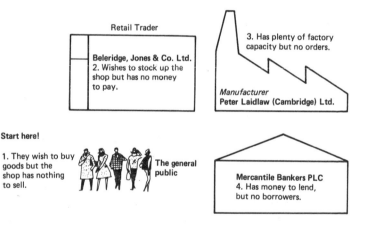

Figure 33.2(a)   Trading inactivity before the use of a Bill of Exchange

Notes:
  (i) Business cannot proceed because the retail trader has nothing to sell and no money to buy stock.
 (ii) What is needed is a mechanism by which the retailer can order supplies without paying for them at once, but which enables the manufacturer to be paid immediately.
(iii) Since a Bill of Exchange from a reputable trader is almost as good as money it will be as acceptable to a bank as money. They have plenty of money to lend out to reliable customers, so they do not mind oiling the wheels of commerce by advancing money to the holder of a Bill of Exchange.

Now look at Figure 33.2(b).

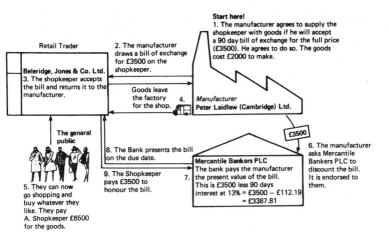

Figure 33.2(b) Active trading under the influence of a Bill of Exchange

Notes:

(i) How did everyone do out of the various activities sparked off by the drawing of this Bill of Exchange?

(ii) The manufacturer sold goods costing £2 000 for £3 500, but actually only realized £3 387.81 after discounting charges. Profit = £1 387.81.

(iii) Beleridge, Jones & Co Ltd sold goods costing £3 500 for £6 500 Profit £3 000.

(iv) Mercantile Bankers PLC loaned £3 387.81 for 90 days and earned £112.19. This is actually 13.4% interest.

(v) The general public enjoyed the pleasures of the consumer society; comfortable furniture costing £6 500.

The conclusion is that Bills of Exchange are a useful instrument to encourage business activity, and are mutually beneficial to all parties so long as no difficulties arise and the bill is honoured on the due date.

33.3 Recording Bills of Exchange 1 – recording bills payable

Every bill has two different aspects. To the drawer, who has supplied goods and wants to be paid for them it is a **bill receivable**, he hopes to receive the money in due course. To the acceptor of the bill, who has agreed to honour it on the due date, it is a **bill payable**, and he must arrange in due course to have funds available to honour the bill when it falls due. On the due date, someone – we have no idea who – will present the bill for payment, either in person or through the banking system. We must have the money ready on the due date. Let us consider bills payable first of all.

A bill is rather special, because it is as good as money. When Beleridge, Jones & Co. Ltd accept the Bill of Exchange from Peter Laidlaw (Cambridge) Ltd, as shown in Figure 33.1 they have

BILLS PAYABLE BOOK (BOOKS OF BELERIDGE, JONES & CO. LTD)

BPB1

No.	Date of Entry	Drawer	Acceptor	Payee	Where payable	Date of Bill	Tenor	Due Date	F.	Amount £	p	Presented by
1	19. . July 1	Peter Laidlaw (Cambridge) Ltd	Self	Peter Laidlaw (Cambridge) Ltd	4932 Comberton Rd Cambridge	19. . 1 July	90 days	29 Sept	L17	3 500	=	
2	15	John Smith Ltd	Self	John Smith Ltd	2743 High St. Oxford	19. . 14 July	6 months	19.1 14 Jan	L39	2 350	=	
3	31	R. Petersen & Co.	Self	R. Petersen & Co.	94 The Leys Cambridge	19. . 30 July	2 months	30 Sept	L182	3 840	=	
									£	9 690	=	
										L56		

Figure 33.3   The Bills Payable Book

settled their debt to Peter Laidlaw who has been paid with something as good as money. Therefore when we accept a bill we debit the creditor's account (debit the receiver). However, we cannot credit Bank Account, because we have not paid the money yet. What account shall we credit? The answer is Bills Payable Account. Instead of paying Peter Laidlaw we must pay the holder of the bill on the due date – whoever that turns out to be.

Actually we enter the bill payable in a Bills Payable Book, which is ruled up as shown in Figure 33.3. It is a special type of day book; with any bills payable that we have accepted recorded in it. The work 'tenor' means the period of credit given on the bill. In this case it is 90 days. Notice that one part of the book cannot be completed yet. It is the section which reads 'Presented by'. We do not yet know who will present the bill on the due date. Usually contact will be made through the banking system and when we are approached for payment we will record the closing of the entry by honouring the bill and completing the 'Presented by' column. Once entered in the Bills Payable Book the bill is posted into the creditor's account to clear the debt to the creditor, who has been paid with the Bill of Exchange. The other half of the double entry is posted to the Bills Payable Account on the last day of the month, along with all other bills payable. The liability to the known creditor, Peter Laidlaw (Cambridge) Ltd, has been changed into a liability to some unknown holder in due course of the Bill of Exchange. The ledger accounts would therefore look as shown in Figure 33.4.

PETER LAIDLAW (CAMBRIDGE) LTD A/C   L17

19. .			£	19. .			£
July	2	Bills Payable BPB1	3 500.00	July	1	Purchases PDB17	3 500.00

BILLS PAYABLE A/C   L56

				19. .			£
				July	31	Sundry bills BPB1	9 690.00

Figure 33.4   Ledger entries for a bill payable

Honouring a bill payable
On the due date the bill will be presented for payment, and we shall honour it by payment – usually through the banking system. The entries will therefore be (a) to credit the Bank Account, so that it gives the money, and (b) to debit Bills Payable Account –

thus reducing the amount owing for outstanding bills of exchange. These entries are shown in Figure 33.5.

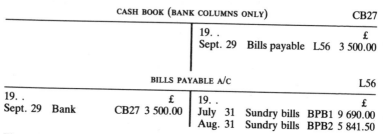

Figure 33.5   Honouring a bill payable

33.4   Recording Bills of Exchange 2 – recording bills receivable

For the drawer of a Bill of Exchange, who has supplied goods or services, the approach is the opposite of the acceptor, who is responsible for honouring the bill as a bill payable. The drawer is usually also the payee (though it is possible to name some other payee). The payee is expecting to be paid and the bill must be recorded in a Bills Receivable Book. This is illustrated in Figure 33.6, and is very similar in appearance to the Bills Payable Book.

Note that some of the bills have not yet been disposed of. We will discuss this below – but first let us follow the postings to the ledger from the Bills Receivable Book. Beleridge, Jones and Co., are debtors for £3 500 of goods which they have paid for with the bill receivable. We must therefore credit the entry for Bill no. 1 to their account (credit the giver). We cannot debit the Bank Account, as with an ordinary receipt because we have not yet received the money. Instead we shall debit Bills Receivable Account with the bill at the end of the month, as part of the total £7 998. The debt from Beleridge, Jones and Co., has become a debt on this Bills Receivable Account which will be settled by the bill in due course. However – we don't have long to wait, because we decide to discount the bill at once with Mercantile Bankers Ltd. They discount the bill for £3 387.81, charging £112.19 as discount charges. For convenience sake this is entered in the Cash Book in an unusual way. We enter the whole £3 500 as a debit on the Bank Account, as if we had received the whole value of the bill. This can then be credited to Bills Receivable Account to clear the bill off the account – we no longer have it. The £112.19 is credited in the Bank Account as 'Discount on Bills' and we post this to the debit side of the Discount on Bills Account – one of the losses of the business. At the same time we would complete the

BILLS RECEIVABLE BOOK (BOOKS OF PETER LAIDLAW (CAMBRIDGE) LTD)

BRB17

No.	Date of Entry	From whom Received	Drawer	Acceptor	First Endorser	Other Endorsers	Where Payable	Date of bill	Tenor	Due date	F	Amount £	p	How disposed of	Discount charges	
1 1	19. . July 1	Acceptor	Self	Beleridge, Jones and Co. Ltd.	Self	—	Stanford-le-Hope, Essex	1 July	90 days	29 Sept	L36	3 500	=	Discounted Mercantile Bankers Ltd.	112	19
2	20	Acceptor	Self	Mike Styles			Birmingham	19 July	3 mths	Oct 19	L51	1 814	=			
3	29	Acceptor	Self	Smith (Bolton) PLC			Bolton	23 July	2 mths	Sept 23	L72	2 684	=			
											£	7 998	=	£	112	19
												L13				

Figure 33.6   The Bills Receivable Book

'How disposed of' column in the Bills Receivable Book. The
ledger entries for all these items are shown in Figure 33.7

BELERIDGE JONES AND CO. LTD A/C   L36

19. .			£	19. .			£
July	2	Sales	SDB27 3 500.00	July	1	Bills Receivable	BRB17 3 500.00

BILLS RECEIVABLE A/C   L13

19. .			£	19. .			£
July 31		Sundry Bills BRB17 7 998.00		July	2	Bank	CB25 3 500.00

CASH BOOK (BANK COLUMNS ONLY)   CB25

19. .			£	19. .			£
July	2	Bills Receivable L13	3 500.00	July	2	Discount on Bills L14	112.19

DISCOUNT ON BILLS A/C   L14

19. .			£		
July	2	Bank	CB25	112.19	

Figure 33.7　Postings to the Ledger for bills receivable

33.5　More about bills receivable

The holder of a bill receivable has three alternative courses open
to him.

(a) He can keep the bill until the due date and present it for
    payment either in person or (more likely) through the
    banking system.
(b) He can discount the bill at once, as explained in Section 33.4
    above, to obtain its present value.
(c) He can pass the bill on to a third party in settlement of a debt
    he owes to the third party.

Let us consider (a) and (c) since (b) has already been explained.

Presenting the bill on maturity
If we keep a bill until maturity we shall be paid the full price for it
– on the due date it is worth its face value (say £3 500). The entries
are very simple – debit the Bank Account with £3 500 received.

Credit the Bills Receivable Account to remove the bill from the account – it is no longer receivable – it has been honoured by the acceptor on the due date. The entries are shown in Figure 33.8.

	CASH BOOK (BANK COLUMNS ONLY)			CB39
19. .			£	
Sept. 29	Bills Receivable	L13	3 500.00	

			BILLS RECEIVABLE A/C			L13
19. .			£	19. .		£
July 31	Sundry Bills	BRB17	7 998.00	Sept. 29 Bank	CB39	3 500.00
Aug. 31	Sundry Bills	BRB18	5 594.60			

Figure 33.8 A bill receivable honoured at maturity

Passing the bill on to a creditor

Suppose Peter Laidlaw (Cambridge) Ltd, who have a bill receivable for £3 500 owe a supplier, Timber Mills Ltd, the sum of £5 000 for materials provided. They could ask this creditor if he would be prepared to take the bill in payment. The agreed price would be the present value of the bill. Suppose they suggested doing this on 4 August when the bill has 56 days to run. The present value taking interest to be 13% is £3 500 – 56 days interest

$$= £3\ 500 - £69.81$$
$$= £3\ 430.19$$

The book keeping arrangements are:

(a) Credit Bills Receivable Account which is giving up the bill.
(b) Debit the creditor with the present value £3 430.19.
(c) Debit the Discount on Bills Account with the loss suffered.

The bill would be endorsed 'Pay Timber Mills Ltd' and signed by Peter Laidlaw on behalf of the company. The bill is said to have been **negotiated** to Timber Mills Ltd.

The Ledger entries are shown in Figure 33.9.

The 'How disposed of' column in the Bills Receivable Book would be completed 'Negotiated to Timber Mills Ltd'.

Contingent liabilities on bills receivable

We have seen that when we negotiate a bill to someone else, whether we discount it at the bank or pass it on to a creditor in payment of a debt the bill ceases to be our property and is written

BILLS RECEIVABLE A/C   L13

19. .			£	19. .			£
July	31	Sundry Bills BRB17	7 998.00	Aug.	4	Timber Mills Ltd etc.	3 500

TIMBER MILLS LTD A/C   L98

19. .				£	19. .				£
Aug.	4	Bills Receivable	L13	3 430.19	July	1	Purchases	PDB4	5 000

DISCOUNT ON BILLS A/C   L14

19. .				£	
Aug.	4	Bills Receivable	L13	69.81	

Figure 33.9   A bill passed on to a further holder in due course

off the Bills Receivable Account as it is no longer receivable. However, there is one way in which we could still be affected by this bill. The primary person liable on the bill is the acceptor, who has accepted the obligation on the bill. Suppose the acceptor gets into financial difficulty; who is going to honour the bill? The answer is that every one whose name is on a bill must honour it, but the person with the greatest liability is the drawer of the bill who became the first endorser when he endorsed the bill over to someone else. Why is it fair for the drawer to honour the bill? The reason is that, on the strength of the bill being a valid bill which would be honoured, the drawer took the present value from the bank, or paid up the money owed to a creditor who took the bill. Just because the acceptor gets into difficulties is that any reason why the drawer should not refund the bank's money, or pay for the goods he purchased? Of course not! The drawer must honour the bill and turn to the acceptor for his money. If he can't pay now perhaps we can renew the bill for a month or two while he sorts out his affairs. Perhaps we shall have to make him bankrupt and get what we can in the bankruptcy. Either way the bill must be honoured by the drawer.

We therefore see that until a bill is honoured on the due date there is always just a chance that we shall become liable on the bill. This is called a **contingent liability** – a liability that will only arise if a certain contingency occurs – the acceptor gets into difficulties.

At the end of the year we have to draw up final accounts and a Balance Sheet of the business. We know that the Balance Sheet

19. .
July 25
	Anne Acceptor A/c Dr.
	   Bank A/c
	Being restoration of debt to debtor
	   after dishonour of a bill of
	   exchange at this date
		L94
		CB43
			£
			5 000.00
				£
				
				5 000.00

BANK ACCOUNT (BANK COLUMNS ONLY)   LB3

		19. . July 25	Acceptor A/c L94	£ 5 000

ANNE ACCEPTOR A/c   L94

19. . May 4 Sales July 23 Bank	£ 5 000.00 ═════ 5 000.00	19. . May 7 Bills Receiv- able A/c	£ L12 5 000.00 ═════

Figure 33.10 Journal and Ledger entries for the dishonour of a Bill of Exchange

must give a 'true and fair view' of the affairs of the business. If we have outstanding contingent liabilites on bills receivable we should declare them on the Balance Sheet as a note:
Note: Contingent liabilities of £2 725 exist on bills of exchange discounted with the bank.

33.6 Dishonoured bills

What happens when a bill is dishonoured? Suppose M has a bill for £5 000 which he got from L, who got it from K, who got it from J, who got it from the original drawer I. L does not know I although his name is on the bill. When M is disappointed because the acceptor A does not honour the bill it is necessary for him to get official recognition that the bill has been dishonoured. He goes to an official called the notary public (there is one in every area) and gets him either to note, or to protest the bill. Noting is good enough for an inland bill, protesting is a more formal process in which a legal document (the protest) giving all the facts of the case is made out. Noting simply involves the notary public in presenting the bill again, and writing on the bill that it was presented and was dishonoured, and giving the reasons for the dishonour. M can now take action on the bill. The easiest thing for M to do is turn to L, who negotiated it to him and say 'This bill is no good – you must honour it for me'. L does so and takes the bill to K and says the same thing. The bill is said to move backwards to the drawer – but if the drawer is a famous name – like a merchant bank – we could approach the drawer directly. We can ask anyone higher up on the list of endorsers to honour the bill, for all are liable fully upon it.

What will be the drawer's book-keeping entries? First, the money will go out of the Bank Account as he honours the bill (credit the Bank Account). Second – this entry will be posted to the debit of A – the acceptor's – Account. We must restore the debt to the debtor for he paid us with a bill that proved to be 'not worth the paper it was written on'. We would probably do a Journal Entry for the dishonour of the bill – just as we do with a dishonoured cheque. The book-keeping entries are shown in Figure 33.10.

33.7   Exercises set 33.1 – accounting for Bills of Exchange

Note: In some of these exercises you will need to rule up paper similar to the Bills Payable Book and Bills Receivable Book shown in Figures 33.3 and 33.6.

1. On 1 November, R. Watson agrees to purchase goods value £9 500 for Ship Supplies Ltd, and to accept a bill of exchange for 60 days drawn on them by Ship Supplies Ltd, at this date. Show the Ledger entry in Watson's books to record the purchase of the goods. Show the entry in the Bills Payable Book to record the acceptance of the bill, its posting to the Ledger (supposing it was the only bill of exchange in the month), and its settlement on the due date.

2. On 20 May, M. Lincoln agrees to purchase goods value £3 800 from R. Todd & Co. Ltd, and to accept a bill of exchange at 90 days drawn on him at this date. Show the Ledger entries for the purchase of these goods; the entry in the Bills Payable Book for the bill (supposing it was the only Bill Payable that month) and the entries for settlement of the bill on the due date.

3. On 25 June Mothram & Co. Ltd, agree to purchase goods value £7 290 from Benson Brothers, PLC and to accept a bill of exchange for that amount at 180 days. Show the Ledger entries only for the original purchase, the entry in the Bills Payable Book (supposing it was the only entry that month) and the postings to the Ledger. Show also the entries for the final settlement on the due date.

4. Using the data given in Question 1 above, show the records in the books of Ship Supplies Ltd for the sale, the bill receivable and the final settlement if Ship Supplies Ltd, keep the bill to maturity. (For extra practice the same exercise can be done for Questions 2 and 3 above.)

5. Using the data given in Question 1 above, show the records in the books of Ship Supplies Ltd, if they discount the bill receivable with the bank the same day at 12% per annum. (For extra practice the same exercise can be done with Questions 2 and 3 above.)

6. Using the data given in Question 1 above, show the records in the books of Ship Supplies Ltd, supposing that they pass the bill on 7 days later to Navigational Components Ltd, with the discount on the bill calculated at 14% per annum. (For extra practice the same exercise can be done with Questions 2 and 3 above.)

7. R. Maxwell accepted a bill of exchange for £9 800 for B. Ltd, and his account is at present clear on B. Ltd's books. B. Ltd, are approached by D. Ltd, to whom they negotiated the bill. They complain that the bill has been dishonoured. (a) Why is it fair that B. Ltd, must pay D. Ltd? (b) What would be the book-keeping entries in B. Ltd's books when they pay the money and restore the debt to R. Maxwell's Account?

8. Z. Ltd accepted a bill of exchange for Q. Ltd, for £4 800, having been supplied with goods to that value on the day they accepted the bill. Q. Ltd discounted it with a bank, S. Ltd. On the due date Q. Ltd are approached by R. Ltd (the holders in due course) and told that the bill has been dishonoured by Z. Ltd. Q. Ltd are therefore liable, say R. Ltd. (a) Explain why Q. Ltd are liable. (b) Show the book-keeping entries in Q. Ltd's books for the dishonour of this bill, on the assumption they pay R. Ltd by cheque.

34
The concepts and principles of accounting

34.1   The philosophy of accounting

We are coming to the end of a long introduction to accounting in which we have tried to make the business of keeping books of account as simple as possible. In the process we have learned many things about the way business is run, about the way records are kept, about the accountability of managers to the owners of the business, the shareholders of companies and indeed to the whole nation. It is time to stand back from the detailed records we have been keeping and consider the whole philosophy of accounting – much of which we have assimilated incidentally in the course of our studies.

It might seem pretentious to talk about the philosophy of accounting though one philosopher of international repute did describe Double-entry Book-keeping as the 'sublimest creation of the human mind'. The fact is that accountancy does set standards by which the business activities of the whole world are judged and since economic life is an essential pre-requisite for life itself in our over-crowded planet we should be absolutely clear what principles guide us in the conduct of economic affairs. These principles may be listed as follows, and are then best discussed in detail, and by reference to the many aspects of accounting records we have already studied in depth. The list reads as follows:

(a) The concepts of business entity, and stewardship.
(b) The 'going concern' concept.
(c) The duality concept.
(d) The concepts of substance and materiality.
(e) The objectivity concept.
(f) The consistency concept.
(g) The prudence concept.

(h) The accruals concept.
(i) The stable money concept.
(j) The concepts of capital and revenue.
(k) The 'preservation of capital' concept.

We shall see that every one of these concepts has been fully discussed already in *Book-keeping Made Simple*. All we need to do is remind ourselves of the many things we have already learned which constitute the underlying philosophy of accounting, which we shall proceed to use throughout our lifetimes as a yardstick to judge the accuracy, honesty and fairness of all our future business activities.

34.2 The concept of business entity

Business activity is carried on by various types of business units, particularly by sole-traders, partnerships, limited companies and non-profit making bodies. It is a fundamental principle of accounting that we regard each business we meet as a separate entity, with its own receipts, payments, assets and liabilities. It is true that hovering in the background there will be some individual, or group of individuals, who are in fact the owners of the business unit we are dealing with, and who – at the end of any given accounting period are entitled to hold out their hands for, and receive, the proceeds of the enterprise, but they are separate (in accounting terms) from the enterprise itself. So the sole trader, the partners, the shareholders of a company and the members of a club are not the same as the business itself. Thus the business expenses of a sole-trader are not the same as the personal expenses of the sole-trader – and the business expenses of a limited company are certainly nothing to do with the shareholders of that company (and they cannot be made liable for them).

Linked closely to this concept of business entity is the **concept of stewardship**, for it often happens that the owner of a business entity is not personally involved in its operations and may even be forbidden by law to take an active part in it (like the sleeping partner in a partnership under the Limited Partnership Act of 1907). In such circumstances the persons actually running the business and keeping the accounts are in the position of stewards who are accountable to the true owners for the conduct of the business's affairs. Today this duty of stewardship extends to the whole nation, to some extent, in that accounts must be presented to the Inland Revenue and pay such taxes as are due. In preparing the accounts of any business the accountant must prepare them in such a way that they comply with national laws as well as with the requirements of the owners of the business – whoever they may be.

34.3 The 'going concern' concept

This concept holds that when the final accounts of a business are prepared the accountant will prepare them in the belief that the business entity will continue for the conceivable future. If he has reason to believe that this is not so, and that the business will cease to trade in the near future it will alter the basis on which the assets should be valued and it it would be wrong (and possibly fraudulent) to value them as if the business was a 'going concern'. To illustrate the problem consider as asset like a motor car. It may be 'worth' £3 500 on the books as a 'going concern' but if we decide to cease trading and sell the car for what we can get we may find the best price obtainable to be much less than £3 500. If this is true of a car, which can be widely used by many businesses and individuals how much more true is it of a **specific asset** like a cement kiln or a catalytic cracking tower for an oil refinery. Such production units cost hundreds of thousands of pounds to build, yet have very few potential buyers since they can only be used to roast cement, or refine crude oil. Their value to a going concern may be high, but if the cement works or the oil company closes down they are virtually unsaleable except at their scrap value.

When we prepare final accounts therefore we should enquire from the owners or managers whether there is any uncertainty about their intention to continue trading, and if reassured on this point we can proceed to prepare the final accounts as those of a 'going concern'.

34.4 The 'duality' concept

This concept holds that accounts should be based upon Double-entry Book-keeping, which recognizes that every transaction has a dual nature, in which one account is receiving value (debit the receiver) while another account is giving value (credit the giver). Having studied an entire book about Double-entry Book-keeping this concept is not likely to puzzle the reader, but it is a fact that in these days, when so much of our accounting is done by computers, there is a surprising shortage of people who really understand double-entry. Beneath the electronic wizardry of the computer lies a careful programming of its behaviour, to achieve perfect double-entries. A really good grounding in double-entry is essential for those programming computers.

34.5 Substance and materiality

These two concepts call for the accounts to be prepared in such a way that they do bring out the true substance of the firm's situation and the actual nature of the transaction engaged in, while at the same time ignoring any facts which are immaterial. For example, suppose the directors are empowered to make loans in the course of their business activities, we would expect to find a large figure for loans made on the Balance Sheet at the end of the year. However, suppose that 80 per cent of these loans had been made by the directors to one another, this would need to be declared separately since the true substance of the situation would not be revealed by the mere statement that loans had been made to an unspecified group of persons. Similarly at one time it was a common practice for directors who had been made loans to give a cheque in full settlement on the last day of the financial year (to extinguish the loan), borrowing back on the first day of the new year. Clearly the final accounts would not show the true substance of that situation (laughingly described as a 'bed and breakfast' arrangement).

On the other hand too detailed a set of final accounts would only confuse the issue. Where we have a relatively trivial amount – let us say the purchase of small capital items – we could include this under a general heading like Plant Machinery Account when in fact it was neither plant nor machinery, but, say, gardening tools for the groundsman. It would not make any material difference to anyone trying to understand the firm's accounts to have these items hidden in this way.

34.6 The objectivity concept

This concept aims to ensure that in making any decision about the state of affairs of any firm or company, and the value of its assets the accountant will view the matter from the standpoint of a disinterested outsider, taking an objective view (as distinct from the subjective view of the insider). This is an important concept because accountants are inside the organization, and often are in a subordinate position. They therefore might be pressured by more senior staff to do things which offend against the concepts and principles of accountancy. For example, suppose the managing director has got himself into financial difficulties due to gambling, and is being pressured by unsavoury elements to pay the full amount at once. A sympathetic board might order the accountant to meet the debt from company funds. The accountant is now faced with a dilemma. Viewed from an objective standpoint the debt has nothing to do with the company and the accountant should not pay it. The directors might then pass a resolution that the managing director be given a bonus to the amount of the debt. The accountant might then point out that such a bonus would be taxable and after paying tax the sum would be insufficient to meet the debt, quite apart from the fact that however it was paid the true substance of the matter would be hidden from the shareholders. This example might sound fanciful, but such situations do arise. The accountant has to stand his corner in all such confrontations.

Sometimes an objective view might be obtained free from any bias by using the services of an outsider altogether, for example valuers are often called in to value stock and assets like premises and plant. They may also be used in making insurance claims, to assess the loss suffered.

34.7   The consistency concept

One of the chief reasons for preparing final accounts is to appraise the state of a business and compare its present situation with its position in earlier years. This comparison will be spoiled if the accounts are not prepared on a consistent basis, with the same principles being applied year after year. For example if we depreciate by 5% in one year and 50% in the next the profits will be seriously distorted by the change in the rate of depreciation. Similarly changes in the basis of stock valuation, or in the way foreign exchange calculations are made, could affect the results. The Companies Act 1985 requires that any such changes should be drawn to the attention of the shareholders of companies in a special note to the accounts.

34.8   The prudence concept in accounting

This is one of the most ancient principles of accounting; sometimes called the 'conservative' principle (with a small 'c'). The principle is that a prudent businessman does not take a profit until it has actually been realized, but always takes a loss into account if there is a reasonable prospect of it occurring. For example – suppose I have a large stock of a particular component which I purchased at a certain price some time ago, but they are now in strong demand and are worth much more than their original cost price. I would not be able to take this appreciation in value into my accounts as a profit unless I actually sell these items and realize the profit. It would be imprudent to take this as a profit, since the value may fall again before I actually sell. The reader will recall that we sometimes break this rule and take appreciation into account in certain circumstances. For example increases in the value of premises are sometimes taken into account in case we attract a take-over bid from another company which wishes to sell our valuable premises and realize the profits on them. This is an example of one principle (the prudence principle) conflicting with another (the objectivity concept). The outsiders' view of our property might be such that it would be unwise **not** to take account of the increased value of our premises.

By contrast with our disregard of profits until they are actually realized we always take account of losses which are likely to occur. Thus the reader will recall that we always make a Provision for Bad Debts if these are likely to occur and even a Provision for Discount if debtors are likely to take a discount on settlement. By contrast, we do not take a profit in the form of a reduction in our creditors, even if we will be entitled to take discount when we pay the creditors, because *that* would be taking a profit before we had actually realized it, and we never do that, under the 'prudence' concept.

34.9 The accruals concept

We are already familiar with the accruals concept, sometimes called the **'matching' concept**, which holds that in preparing a set of final accounts we must match the income for the period against the expenditure of the period. Any liabilities that have accrued but not yet been paid, and any income to which we are entitled but which has not been received must be included in the figures to arrive at a 'true and fair view' of the profits for the period. This is the whole basis of 'adjustments' in accounting and has been thoroughly discussed in Chapter 22.

The basic principles stated in Chapter 22, and repeated here, are as follows:

(a) The Manufacturing, Trading and Profit and Loss Accounts should contain every penny of income received (or due to be received) in the period whether actually received or not. It should exclude any items relating to a previous accounting period or to a subsequent accounting period.

(b) Set against these revenues should be all the expenses incurred in earning those revenues, including any expenses which have accrued (accumulated) but have not yet been paid. Expenses of an earlier period, or relating to the next period should not be included.

(c) These adjustments will of course affect the Balance Sheet of the enterprise, since items accrued due to us will appear as assets and items accrued as payable by us will appear as liabilities. Therefore not only shall we achieve correct profit figures but the Balance Sheet will also give a 'true and fair view of the affairs of the business.

34.10   The stable-money concept

This concept holds that since accountancy can only be expressed in money terms it has to be assumed that money is stable in value, but the accountant knows very well that in fact it is not, and must 'read between the lines' when reading any accountancy statement to bear the value of money in mind.

In the United Kingdom for example between the years 1740 and 1940 there was practically no inflation – 200 years of stable money. By contrast between the years 1945 and 1985 money fell to about one-twentieth of its value. The average weekly wage of about £6 per week in 1945 had risen to £120 per week by 1985. These changes produced serious difficulties for accountants, and a wide-ranging debate on **'historical-cost' accounting** versus **'inflation' accounting** arose.

One example of this problem is in depreciation of assets. When we write off the value of assets over the years, basing the amount written off on the original (historical) cost we find at the end of the asset's life that the sums we have set aside are insufficient to purchase a replacement asset now that inflation has raised its price. We need to write off more each year than the amount of fair wear and tear on the old asset if we are to afford a new asset.

Another illustration is the replacement of stock sold in the normal course of trading. Suppose an accountant who normally adds 50% to cost prices to get his selling price takes a stock item costing £100 and sells it for £150. The profit is £50, which seems a fair profit. When he orders more stock the new price is £140 because of inflation. The effective profit on the item sold, now the stock has been replenished, is only £10 – so that the profit has been seriously overstated. When we overstate the profits in inflationary times by using 'historical cost' accounting, three things happen:

(a) The shareholders demand a 'fair' share of the profits, which in fact have not been made.
(b) Employees demand wage increases as a fair share in the 'profitable' company.
(c) The Inland Revenue Department demands tax on the high profits declared.

Countless persons have been driven into bankruptcy by these

demands in recent years. The answer – when money is unstable – is to use some form of 'inflation accounting'. A really good scheme of inflation accounting was agreed between the accountancy bodies in 1980, but its complexity (at a time when inflation was being brought under control by Government policies) led to its disregard by many companies. It may still be revised should the inflationary situation return.

34.11 The distinction between capital expenditure and revenue expenditure

This has already been fully explained in Chapter 20, but it is worth reminding ourselves here that these are basic concepts in accounting which enable us to make the decisions needed when matching income and expenditure as required by the accruals concept (see Section 34.7 above). Any item purchased which has a life of over one year may be regarded as the purchase of a capital asset – capital expenditure. If the life of the item is less than one year it is called a revenue item, and will be one of the expenses of the business to be written off the profits at the end of the year. Items of a revenue nature (such as redecorations) but which last several years, may be apportioned over a few years.

34.12 Exercises set 34.1 – the concepts and principles of accounting

1. (a) What is meant by the 'concept of business entity'? (b) A. Brown is a sole-trader who uses a single cheque book for both his personal and business affairs. What problems does this make when dealing with his business accounts?

2. (a) What is the concept of stewardship? (b) A is the accountant of the Magnificent Oil Co. PLC. For whom is he a steward, and who else might feel that the accountant owed them a duty as a steward?

3. (a) What is the 'going conern' concept? (b) M, a shareholder in Heavy Engineering PLC has just received her copy of the company's final account for the year. What assumption is she entitled to make about these accounts?

4. (a) What is Double-entry Book-keeping? (b) Why is the duality concept still an important part of accounting?

5. (a) What is meant by the twin concepts of substance and materiality? (b) Heavy Haulage (Camside) Ltd, have a fleet of very ancient road haulage vehicles which originally cost £250 000 but are now valued on the books at only £25 000. They also have a fleet of executive cars which cost £180 000 and are valued currently on the books at £165 000. Discuss whether the companies accounts which read Motor Vehicles: Cost £430 000; less depreciation £240 000; value £190 000 convey the true substance of the firm's affairs.

6. (a) What is meant by 'objectivity' in accounting? (b) What should be the attitude of the accountant to the valuation of plant and machinery after a fire which has caused considerable damage?

7. (a) Why should accounting be consistent from year to year? (b) If a change in arrangements is needed, how should it be drawn to the attention of interested parties?

8. 'Accounting is above all an exercise in prudence in business affairs.' Explain this statement illustrating it by reference to (a) stock valuation (b) debtors.

9. (a) What is the meaning of the term 'accruals'? (b) Give suitable illustrations of accrual procedures at both the beginning and the end of the accounting year.

10. (a) What problems does inflation present to accountants? (b) Illustrate your answer with references to (i) pricing policies for goods sold (ii) depreciation of assets.

34.13   Conclusion about Double-entry Book-keeping

We have come to the end of a long and detailed book about Double-entry Book-keeping. The author apologizes if the reader feels – at the end of *Book-keeping Made Simple* – that it was not as simple as all that. With ten thousand little pieces of knowledge to acquire and to fit together into the giant jig-saw that is modern accounting the student was bound to face many problems.

Unfortunately this is not the end of the story. Having raised his/her head above the level of elementary book-keeping the student only finds a wider horizon, with further areas to be studied. The author wishes you every success in your examinations, and best wishes for your further studies. There is an enormous need for qualified accountants and the sound grounding you should have obtained in double-entry from working conscientiously through *Book-keeping Made Simple* should help you to go on to a full, professional qualification.

Answer section

In this answer section one question in most of the sets has been fully worked to enable the student to see what a complete answer should look like.

The first question has not usually been chosen, since the questions are graded in difficulty. One of the more difficult questions in each main set has therefore been selected, as the working most likely to be of benefit to the student.

Other questions have been answered in abbreviated form.

Chapter 1, Exercises set 1.1 – opening Balance Sheets, page 12.

1. Total £187 500.00; Current assets £115 000.00; Fixed assets £72 500.00.
2. Totals £166 250.00; Current assets £88 750.00; Fixed assets £77 500.00.
3. Capital £90 505.00; Current assets £24 105.00; Fixed assets £66 400.00.
4. Capital £57 830.00; Current assets £30 030.00; Fixed assets £27 800.00.
5. Capital £25 000.00; Current assets £16 420.00; Fixed assets £31 817.50; Current liabilities £5 737.50; Long-term liabilities £17 500.
6. See page 486.

PETER CLEMENS
balance sheet
as at 1 January 19. .

CURRENT LIABILITIES	£	CURRENT ASSETS	£
Wages Due	247.50	Prepaid Expenses	86.25
Creditors	5 260.00	Cash in Hand	162.50
	5 507.50	Cash at Bank	3 632.50
		Trade Debtors	7 921.25
LONG-TERM LIABILITIES £		Stock	7 600.00
Bank Loan 5 000.00			19 402.50
Mortgage 15 000.00			
	20 000.00	FIXED ASSETS £	
		Motor Vehicles 8 277.50	
CAPITAL		Furniture 1 627.50	
At Start	60 000.00	Plant and	
		Machinery 36 200.00	
		Land and Buildings 20 000.00	
			66 105.00
	£85 507.50		£85 507.50

Chapter 2, Exercises set 2.1 – simple Debtors' Accounts, page 19.

1. Balance £1 277.65 Dr.; Account totals £2 235.80.
2. Balance £580.55 Dr.; Account totals £1 860.05.
3. Balance £1 265.35 Dr.; Account totals £1 482.55.
4. See below:

R. THOMAS A/C   DL37

19. .		£	19. .			£
Jan. 1	Balance	1 235.80	Jan. 3	Bank		1 174.01
2	Sales	275.00	3	Discount		61.79
14	Sales	240.00	19	Sales Returns		70.00
14	Carriage Out	12.50	31	Balance		683.75
29	Sales	226.25				
		£1 989.55				£1 989.55

19. .		£
Feb. 1	Balance	683.75

Chapter 2, Exercises set 2.2 – simple Creditors' Accounts, page 22.

1. Balance £1 830.35 Cr.; Account totals £3 094.60.
2. Balance £7 065.05 Cr.; Account totals £8 925.65.
3. Balance £1 126.35 Cr.; Account totals £2 407.30.
4. See opposite.

G. M. WHITESIDE A/C   CL59

19. .			£	19. .			£
Oct.	2	Bank	3 512.44	Oct.	1	Balance	3 602.50
	2	Discount	90.06		11	Purchases	2 132.50
	14	Returns	132.50		19	Purchases	1 122.50
	27	Motor Vehicles	3 750.00		20	Carriage In	125.50
					31	Balance	502.00
			£7 485.00				£7 485.00

19. .			£
Nov.	1	Balance	502.00

(a) On 27 October Whiteside became a debtor for a motor vehicle valued at £3 750.00. This can only mean that we supplied him with a vehicle which was surplus to our requirements.
(b) Whiteside owes the balance to us.
(c) In this example we have a creditor who was on October 31 temporarily a debtor

Chapter 2, Exercises set 2.3 – simple Cash Accounts, page 28.

1. See below:

CASH A/C   GL27

19. .				£	19. .				£
Dec.	1	Balance	b/d	85.50	Dec.	1	Wages		63.00
	1	Bank		100.00		1	Postage		5.75
	3	R. Jones		10.50		2	Sundry Expenses		1.50
	3	P. Brown		19.00		2	Stationery		15.50
	4	Sales		920.50		2	Stationery		11.25
						3	R. Lewis		5.75
						4	Sundry Expenses		11.25
						4	Gratuities		1.00
						4	Bank		750.00
						4	Balance	c/d	270.50
				£1 135.50					£1 135.50

19. .				£
Dec.	5	Balance	b/d	270.50

2. Balance £772.85; Totals £2 775.85.
3. Balance £435.30; Totals £2 648.80.
4. Balance £216.10; Totals £1 779.50.

Chapter 2, Exercises set 2.4 – simple Bank Accounts, page 29.

1.   Balance £2 076.25; Totals £3 409.25.
2.   Balance £790.05; Totals £1 170.05.
3.   Balance £5 079.65; Totals £5 918.90.
4.   Balance £1 648.20; Totals £1 906.45.

Chapter 2, Exercises set 2.5 – running Balance Accounts, page 33.

1.   See below:

Name R. Bird Address						A/c No. 135 Sheet No. 1
Date	Particulars	F	Debit	Credit		Balance
Jan. 1	Balance	b/d	160.00			160.00
14	Bank (cheque)			28.50		131.50
14	Discount Allowed			1.50		130.00
16	Sales		90.00			220.00
18	Furniture			200.00		20.00
21	Sales Returns			15.00		5.00
29	Furniture (Returns)		30.00			35.00

Bird is still a debtor and owes us money.
2.   Final running balance £441.20. Note that the return was only £28.80 (£36 less 20%). On Sheet 2 the balance would be a debit (Bagret is a debtor).
3.   Final running balance £258.85. Barnes owes Mace this £258.85 since Mace is a creditor.

Chapter 3, no exercises in this chapter.

Chapter 4, Exercise set 4.1 – the Purchases Day Book, page 52.

1. See below:

19. .		F	Details	VAT	PDB77
Apr. 1	G. Emerson				
	24 pictures at £2.65 each	L17	63.60	6.36	69.96
3	R. Longfellow				
	20 boxes envelopes at £1.25 box		250.00		
	100 writing pads at £0.65 each		65.00		
		L25	315.00	31.50	346.50
14	M. Twain				
	48 prints at £3.20 each		153.60		
	36 files at £1.50 each		54.00		
		L33	207.60	20.76	228.36
25	S. Clemens				
	24 sets paint and brushes at £2.30 each	L12	56.40	5.64	62.04
30	H. Melville				
	240 boxes sticky tape at £0.55 each		132.00		
	60 boxes paper clips at £0.18 each		10.80		
		L18	142.80	14.28	157.08
	£		785.40	78.54	863.94
			L42	L95	

Note: Be very careful in adding the details column. Only the totals of each invoice before VAT should be added in.

2. Total purchases £3 949.00; total VAT £67.50; grand total £4 016.50.

3. Total purchases £400.70; total VAT £40.07; grand total £440.77.

4. Total purchases £819.10; total VAT £81.91; grand total £901.01.

Chapter 4, Exercises set 4.2 – the Sales Day Book, page 58.

1. Total sales £295.05; total VAT £29.50; grand total £324.55.

2. Total sales £404.80; total VAT £40.48; grand total £445.28.

3. Total sales £4 440.36; total VAT £444.04; grand total £4 884.40.

4. See page 490.

19. .		F	Details	VAT	SDB197
Jan. 1	R. Harper				
	24 dozen tins Scrumptious meal at £0.65 per tin		187.20		
	12 dozen packets dog biscuits at £0.50 pkt		72.0		
			259.20		
	Less 25% Trade Discount		64.80		
		L19	194.40	19.44	213.84
3	T. Birchin				
	30 dozen tins Scrumptious meal at £2.50		900.00		
	Less 25% Trade Discount		225.00		
		L21	675.00	67.50	742.50
14	R. Harper				
	24 dozen tins Scrumptious meal at £0.65		187.20		
	6 dozen packets biscuits at £0.50 pkt		36.00		
			223.20		
	Less 25% Trade Discount		55.80		
		L19	167.40	16.74	184.14
25	M. Jones				
	3 dozen tins meal (large size) at £2.50		90.00		
	6 dozen packets meal at £0.65 per pkt		46.80		
			136.80		
	Less 25% Trade Discount		34.20		
		L33	102.60	10.26	112.86
		£	1 139.40	113.94	1 253.34
			L45	L46	

Chapter 4, Exercises set 4.3 – the Purchases Returns Book, page 65.

1.   Total returns £136.50; total VAT £13.65; grand total £150.15.
2.   Total returns £702.60; total VAT £70.26; grand total £772.86.
3.   Total returns £103.60; total VAT £10.36; grand total £113.96.
4.   See opposite.

19. . Oct. 3	M. Venables	F	Details	VAT	PRB94
	1 woollen jumper (seams not sewn properly)	L17	8.40	0.84	9.24
14	M. Spurgeon				
	2 table cloths (faded) at £12.25 each	L62	24.50	2.45	26.95
17	H. Morton				
	2 white woollen scarves (marked) at £3.60 each		7.20		
	1 Orlon jumper (wrong colour)		15.95		
		L15	23.15	2.32	25.47
		£	56.05	5.61	61.66
			L41	L55	

Chapter 4, Exercises set 4.4 – the Sales Returns Book, page 69.

1. See below:

19. . Jan. 4	M. Smith	F	Details	VAT	SRB5
	2 steam irons at £12.85 each (element faulty)	L24	25.70	2.57	28.27
15	R. Thompson				
	3 electric fires at £23.30 each (switches faulty)	L17	69.90	6.99	76.89
17	R. Leighton				
	1 Washette dishwasher (faulty motor)	L63	237.50	23.75	261.25
18	M. Kehu				
	Overcharge on invoice (typing error)	L15	10.00	1.00	11.00
		£	343.10	34.31	377.41
			L89	L59	

2. Total returns £437.75; total VAT £43.78; grand total £481.53.
3. Total returns £142.75; total VAT £14.27; grand total £157.02.
4. Total returns £181.70; total VAT £18.17; grand total £199.87.

Chapter 5, Exercises set 5.1 – saving work on the day books, page 83.

Numerical answers are not required. Re-read the text if in difficulties answering these questions.

Chapter 6, Exercises set 6.1 – the Three-column Cash Book, page 101.

Note: Question 8 has been selected as the answer to be fully displayed so that the reader may see how an overdraft is dealt with.

1. T. Brophy Cash balance £92.50; Bank balance £3 269.85; Discounts £2.65 and £6.25.
2. B. Jorgensen Cash balance £252.31; Bank balance £1 088.05; Discounts £14.99 and £102.78.
3. T. Charles Cash Balance £143.50; Bank balance £1 735.00; Discounts £16.25 and £28.16.
4. R. Jolliboy Cash balance £352.70; Bank balance £8 708.47; Discounts £40.34 and £12.33.
5. L. Lewis Cash balance £353.85; Bank balance £8 601.45; Discounts £1.50 and £10.00.
6. R. Jolson Cash balance £354.85; Bank balance £6 665.35; Discounts £4.65 and Nil.
7. R. Lunnis Cash balance £266.55; Bank Balance £1 609.60; Discounts £33.57 and £11.25.

			R. WICH A/C				L1
19. .			£	19. .			£
May 1	Balance	b/d	25.00	May 3	Cash	CB1	25.00

			SALES A/C				L2
				19. .			£
				May 4	Cash	CB1	438.50
				7	Cash	CB1	1 325.00

			R. LIBBEY A/C				L3
19. .			£	19. .			£
May 1	Balance	b/d	500.00	May 6	Bank	CB1	487.50
				6	Discount	CB1	12.50

			POSTAGE A/C		L4
19. .			£		
May 2	Cash	CB1	13.00		

			REPAIRS A/C		L5
19. .			£		
May 2	Cash	CB1	7.35		

8. Books of John Brown

Debit

Date 19..	Details	F	Discount Allowed	Cash £	Bank £
May 2	Balance	b/d		137.50	
3	R. Wich	L1		25.00	
4	Sales	L2		438.50	
4	Cash	C			250.00
6	R. Libbey	L3	12.50		487.50
7	Sales	L2		1 325.00	
7	Cash	C			1 000.00
7	Balance	c/d			479.25
		£	12.50	1 926.00	2 216.75
			L13		
May 8	Balance	b/d		488.90	

Credit

Date 19..	Details	F	Discount Received	Cash £	Bank £
May 2	Balance	b/d			1 353.25
2	Postage	L4		13.00	
2	Repairs	L5		7.35	
2	R. Jones	L6	7.25		137.75
3	Travelling Expenses	L7		11.75	
4	Bank	C		250.00	
5	Purchases	L8			465.00
5	Rent	L9			147.50
5	Wages	L10		80.00	
7	Rates	L11			113.25
7	Drawings	L12		75.00	
7	Bank	C		1 000.00	
7	Balance	c/d		488.90	
		£	7.25	1 926.00	2 216.75
			L14		
May 8	Balance	b/d			479.25

R. JONES A/C · L6

19. .				£	19. .				£
May	2	Bank	CB1	137.75	May	1	Balance	b/d	145.00
	2	Discount	CB1	7.25					

TRAVELLING EXPENSES · L7

19. .				£
May	3	Cash	CB1	11.75

PURCHASES · L8

19. .				£
May	5	Bank	CB1	465.00

RENT A/C · L9

19. .				£
May	5	Bank	CB1	147.50

WAGES A/C · L10

19. .				£
May	5	Cash	CB1	80.00

RATES A/C · L11

19. .				£
May	7	Bank	CB1	113.25

DRAWINGS A/C · L12

19. .				£
May	7	Cash	CB1	75.00

DISCOUNT ALLOWED A/C · L13

19. .				£
May	7	Sundry Discounts	CB1	12.50

DISCOUNT RECEIVED · L14

					19. .				£
					May	7	Sundry Discounts	CB1	7.25

Chapter 7, Exercises set 7.1 – opening Journal Entries, page 113.

1. Capital £800.00; total £800.00.
2. Capital £19 050.00; total £19 050.00.
3. Capital £54 720.00; total £55 620.00.
4. Capital £19 038.00; total £22 158.50.
5. Capital £266 815.80; total £270 539.10.
6. Books of A. Jordan and C. French

Note: As they are equal partners we will assume they have provided half the capital each:

19. .				£	£ J1
Apr. 1	Cash A/c	Dr.	CB1	1 350.00	
	Bank A/c	Dr.	CB1	21 500.00	
	Stock A/c	Dr.	L1	23 500.00	
	Computer A/c	Dr.	L2	2 150.00	
	Office Equipment A/c	Dr.	L3	1 400.00	
	Furniture and Fittings A/c	Dr.	L4	3 780.00	
	Premises A/c	Dr.	L5	27 000.00	
	Investments A/c	Dr.	L6	2 250.00	
	B. Trotman A/c	Dr.	L7	2 025.00	
	M. Wrenn A/c	Dr.	L8	3 300.00	
	R. Keen A/c		L9		1 380.00
	B. Bunyan A/c		L10		1 900.00
	Capital A/c Jordan		L11		42 487.50
	Capital A/c French		L12		42 487.50
			£	88 255.00	88 255.00
	Being assets and liabilities at this date				

Chapter 7, Exercises set 7.2 – Purchases of assets, page 116.

1. Debit Typewriters £375.00; Credit Cash £375.00.
2. Debit Machinery £825.00; Credit Bank £825.00.
3. Debit L. & B. Account £28 000.00; Credit Loamshire Property Ltd £28 000.00.
4. Yachts Account Debit £1 400.00; Credit Seaway Ltd £1 400.00.
5. See page 496.

19. . Aug. 1	Furniture and Fittings	Dr.	L1	£ 340.50	£
	Office Machinery	Dr.	L2	808.75	
	Business Supplies Ltd.		L3		1 149.25
	Being purchase of new equipment at this date				

6. Debit Pipelayer A/c £5 000.00; Trench Cutter A/c £9 250.00; Water Carrier A/c £7 250.00; General Equipment A/c £8 500.00; Credit Bank Account £30 000.00.
7. Debit Plant and Machinery £11 000.00; Motor Vehicles £2 250.00; Word Processor A/c £4 000.00; Furniture A/c £1 400.00. Credit Bank A/c £18 650.00.

Chapter 7, Exercises set 7.3 – Depreciation of assets, page 118.

1. Debit Depreciation £1 000.00; Credit Motor Vehicles £1 000.
2. Debit Depreciation £740.00; Credit Furniture and Fittings £740.00.
3. Debit Depreciation A/c £950.00; Credit Plant and Machinery £950.00.
4. Final balance on Computer A/c £16 000.00.
5. Books of A. Farmer:

19. . Dec. 31	Depreciation A/c	Dr.	L68	£ 7 470.00	£ J1
	Tractors A/c		L3		1 500.00
	Ploughs, harrows etc. A/c		L7		195.00
	Fencing and gates A/c		L9		625.00
	Barns A/c		L12		1 400.00
	Buildings A/c		L15		3 750.00
	Being depreciation for one year at the agreed rates per cent				

Chapter 7, Exercises set 7.4 – sale of worn-out assets, page 121.

1. Debit Cash A/c £50.00; Credit Typewriters A/c £50.00.
2. Debit R. Dealer A/c £500.00; Credit Machinery A/c £500.00.
3. Debit Cash A/c £12.50; Debit Sale of Typewriters A/c £7.50; Credit Typewriters A/c £20.00.
4. Debit A. Farmer A/c £4 000.00; Debit Sale of Machinery A/c £50.00; Credit Farm Plant A/c £4 050.00.
5. Debit Cash A/c £60.00; Credit Small Buildings A/c £40.00; Credit Sale of Assets A/c £20.00.

6. Debit R. Cooper £1 450.00; Credit Motor Vehicles A/c £1 250; Credit Sale of Motor Vehicle A/c £200.00.
7. See below:

19..
Dec. 12
	Cash A/c Dr.
	Office Equipment A/c Dr.
	  Machinery A/c
	  Sales of Machinery A/c
	Being sale of pile driver in exchange
	for 2 office machines and cash
		CB9
		L5
		L14
		L27
			£
			1 500.00
			1 000.00
				£ J5
				
				1 900.00
				600.00

CASH BOOK (CASH A/C ONLY)   CB9

19.. Dec. 12 Machinery etc. J5	£ 1 500.00	19..	£

OFFICE EQUIPMENT A/C   L5

19.. Dec. 12 Machinery etc. J5	£ 1 000.00	19..	£

MACHINERY A/C   L14

19..	£	19.. Dec. 12 Cash etc.	£ J5 1 900.00

SALE OF MACHINERY A/C   L27

		19.. Dec. 12 Cash etc. J5	£ 600.00

Chapter 7, Exercises set 7.5 – simple bad debts, page 125.

1. Debit Bad Debts Account £15.60; Credit A. Debtor £15.60.
2. Debit Bad Debts Account £250; Credit A. Borrower £250.
3. Debit Bank Account £250 and Bad Debts Account £250; Credit Anne Alien £500.
4. Debit Bank Account £60 and Bad Debts Account £1 140; Credit B. Henriques £1 200.
5. See page 498.

Y A/c   L21

19. .			£	19. .			£
June 17	Sales	SDB21	2 000.00	Nov. 30	Bank A/c and		
					Bad Debts J1		2 000.00
			£2 000.00				£2 000.00

Note: The words *bad debtor* would be written across Y's account.

19. .				£	£ J1
Nov. 30	Bank A/c	Dr.	CB31	1 400.00	
	Bad Debts A/c	Dr.	L49	600.00	
	Y A/c		L21		2 000.00
	Being bad debt written off at this date on receipt of £1 400 in settlement at 70p in the £1				

6. Debit Bank Account £1 475; Credit Interest Received A/c £75 and Bad Debt Recovered Account £1 400.
7. Same as 6 above but £1 575; £75 and £1 500.
8. Same as 6 above but £365.75; £65.75 and £300.
9. Debit Bank Account £500 and Motor Spares Account £400. Credit Bad Debt Recovered Account £775.00, Legal Charges Recovered Account £65 and Interest Received Account £60.

Chapter 7, Exercises set 7.6 – correction of errors, page 128.

1. (a) Debit Typewriters A/c £377.50; Credit Purchases A/c £377.50.
   (b) Debit R. Morton A/c with £225; Credit R. Morgan A/c £225.
2. (a) Debit Machinery A/c £2 500; Credit Purchases A/c £2 500.
   (b) Debit Discount Received A/c £25; Credit J. Johnson A/c £25.
   (c) Debit Fixtures and Fittings A/c £1 000; Credit Motor Vehicles A/c £1 000.
3. Debit Alan Gee A/c £1 150; Credit G. Allen A/c £1 150.
4. (a) Debit Machinery A/c £500; Credit Motor Vehicles A/c £500.
   (b) Debit Discount Received A/c £37.50; Credit S. Jones £37.50.
   (c) Debit Machinery A/c £5 000; Credit Purchases A/c £5 000.

(d) Debit Sales Account £360; Credit Derby & Co. £360.
5. (a) Debit M. Haji £100; Credit G. Haji £100.
   (b) This is a single sided entry. All we need to do is to debit the Purchases A/c with an extra £270.
   (c) Debit Typewriters A/c £327.50; Credit Purchases Account £327.50.
   (d) Debit Discount Allowed A/c with £271.50. There is no credit entry required – it is a single sided entry.
6. (a) Debit Cornish A/c with £63.00 and Credit Sales Returns A/c £63.00.
   (b) Debit Purchases A/c £750; Credit Stationery A/c £750.
   (c) Debit P. Robson A/c £275; Credit P. Robison A/c £275.
   (d) Debit Fixed Machinery A/c £5 000; Credit Purchases A/c £5 000.
7. (a) Debit E. Kemp £300; Credit E. Kempster £300.
   (b) Debit sale of Motor Vehicle A/c £200; Credit Motor Lorry A/c £200.
   (c) Debit L. Bates £198; Credit Sales A/c £198.
8. (a) Debit Discount Received A/c £317.80 (it is a single sided error only).
   (b) Debit R.J.'s A/c £180; Credit Bad Debts Recovered A/c £180.
   (c) Debit Sales A/c £212.50; Credit Machinery A/c £212.50.

Chapter 7, Exercises set 7.7 – dishonoured cheques, page 131.

1. Debit R. Thomas A/c £262.50; Credit Bank A/c £262.50.
2. Debit L. Jones A/c £254.75; Debit T. Peterson A/c £132.25; Credit Bank A/c £387.00.
4. See below:

19. .				£	£ J5
11 May	R. Jowett A/c Dr.			297.50	
	Bank A/c				282.75
	Discount Allowed A/c				14.75
	Being restoration in full of a debt paid earlier with a cheque which was dishonoured				

5. Debit M. Cole A/c £1 850.00; Credit Bank A/c £1 822.50 and Discount Allowed A/c £27.50.
6. Debit T. Cruiser A/c £920.00; Credit Bank A/c £904.00 and Discount Allowed A/c £16.00.

Chapter 7, Exercises set 7.8 – bank loans, interest and charges, page 134.

1. Debit Bank A/c £2 500.00; Credit Loan A/c (General Bank Ltd) £2 500.00
2. Debit Bank A/c £5 000.00; Credit Loan A/c (A. Friend) £5 000.00.
3. Debit Bank A/c £50 000.00; Credit Loan A/c (Steady Bank Ltd) £50 000.00
4. Debit Interest Payable A/c £3 000.00; Credit Loan A/c (Steady Bank Ltd) £3 000.00.
5. Debit Bank A/c £150.00; Credit Interest Received A/c £150.00.
6. Debit Bank Charges A/c £13.75; Credit Bank A/c £13.75.
7. Debit Building Society Savings A/c £138.25; Credit Interest Received A/c £138.25.

Chapter 7, Exercises set 7.9 – VAT on cash takings, page 136.

1. Debit Sales A/c with £3 217.20; Credit VAT A/c £3 217.20.
2. Debit Sales A/c with £5 105.25; Credit VAT A/c £5 105.25.
3. Debit Sales A/c with £1 762.50; Credit VAT A/c £1 762.50. Balance owing to Customs and Excise £5 311.15.

Chapter 8, Exercises set 8.1 – the Petty Cash Book, page 146.

1. Total disbursements £67.40; balance in hand £32.60; drawn from cashier £67.40.
2. Total disbursements £32.20; balance in hand £35.07; drawn from cashier £14.93.
3. Total disbursements £60.35; balance in hand £47.87; drawn from cashier £52.13.
4. Total disbursements £91.05; balance in hand £11.20; drawn from cashier £88.80.
5. Shown in displayed form, page 501.
6. (a) It means that a sum of money (the imprest) is set aside from the main cash book for the use of the petty cashier. At regular intervals the book is balanced off and a sufficient sum drawn from the cashier to restore the balance in hand to the agreed imprest.
    (b) See text for this section, page 138.
    (c) Total disbursements £36.80; balance in hand £28.55; drawn from cashier £21.45.
7. Total disbursements £61.00; balance in hand £49.00; drawn from cashier £51.00.

THE PETTY CASH BOOK

Dr. £ p	19..		Particulars	PCV	Total £ p	Postage	Trav. Expenses	Sundry Expenses	Wages	Repairs	Folio	Cr. Ledger A/cs
75.00	Jan.	1	Imprest	CB1								
		1	Postage	1	12.50	12.50						
		2	Repairs	2	12.25					12.25		
		2	Sundries	3	0.50			0.50				
		2	Postage	4	1.25	1.25						
8.75		2	R. Morgan	L27								
		3	Sundry Expenses	5	3.10			3.10				
		3	Cleaner's Wages	6	12.50				12.50			
		4	Postage	7	1.80	1.80						
		4	Travelling Expenses	8	1.25		1.25					
		5	Sundry Expenses	9	2.75			2.75				
		5	Stamps	10	7.25	7.25						
		6	Postage	11	7.15	7.15						
		6	M. Clark	12	18.25						L43	18.25
					80.55	29.95	1.25	6.35	12.50	12.25		18.25
			Balance	c/d	3.20	L1	L2	L3	L4	L5		
£83.75				£	83.75							
3.20			Balance	b/d								
71.80		1	Restored Imprest	CB9								

8. (a) Drawn from cashier £85.85.
    (b) Debit Carriage Inwards A/c £20.80, General Expenses
         A/c £10.75, Postage A/c £10.50, Stationery A/c £0.75,
         Travellings Expenses A/c £25.65, Clerys Ltd A/c £17.40.
    (c) Clerys Ltd A/c would have its folio number against
         £17.40.

**Chapter 9, Exercises set 9.1 – Book-keeping to the Trial Balance,
page 163.**

1.   Books of Peter Newman: Capital on Opening Journal Entry
     £38 630; Cash Book balances at end of month: Cash £726.25
     Bank £3 456.25; Trial Balance totals £44 407.75.
2.   Books of Alan Dawlish: Capital on Opening Journal Entry
     £32 650; Cash Book balances at end of month: Cash £470.25
     Bank £3 585.00; Trial Balance totals £38 350.75.
3.   Books of Derek Webster: Capital on Opening Journal Entry
     £12 609.35; Cash Book balances at end of month: Cash
     £209.40 Bank £3 892.50; Trial Balance totals £14 335.20.
4.   Books of R. Palmer: Capital on Opening Journal Entry
     £17 500; Cash Book balances at end of month: Cash £768.25
     Bank £14 780.00; Trial Balance totals £20 675.25.
5.   Book of George Dickens: Capital on Opening Journal Entry
     £13 390; Cash Book balances at end of month: Cash £177.50
     Bank £2 258.00; Trial Balance totals £18 722.50.

**Chapter 10, Exercises set 10.1 – Trial Balances and Suspense
Accounts, page 174.**

1.   Refer to Section 9.5, page 155, if in difficulty.
2.   Refer to Section 10.2, page 166, if in difficulty.
3.   Refer to Section 10.2, page 168, if necessary.
4.   Refer to Section 10.2, page 167, if necessary.
5.   Refer to Section 10.2, page 166, if necessary.
6.   Journal Entry to debit the Suspense Account with £500 and
     credit the Bank Account with £500. This clears the Suspense
     Account.
7.   Journal entry debits the Suspense Account with £138.00 and
     credits R. Lang's Account with £107.50 and Discount
     Received Account with £30.50.
8.   (i) (a) Error of commission – neither side affected.
              (b) Debit side – overstated by £38.25.
              (c) Debit side – understated by £100.
              (d) Debit side – understated by £46.35.
     (ii) The total effect on the debit side is that it is understated

by £108.10. The Suspense Account must be debited with £108.10.

9. The Journal Entries must:
   (a) Debit Suspense A/c with £57.75 (no credit entry required).
   (b) Debit Suspense A/c with £27.00 and credit Motor Lorry Account £27.00.
   (c) Debit Suspense A/c with £12.00 and credit Interest Received Account £12.00.

10. See below:

19. .				£	£ J21
Sept.	5	Suspense A/c Dr.	L21	50.00	
		Sales A/c	L32		50.00
		Being correction of under-cost Sales Day Book			
	19	A. Debtor A/c Dr.	L69	50.75	
		Suspense A/c	L21		50.75
		Being removal of item from debtor's account previously closed off			
	21	Dr.			
		Suspense A/c	L21		18.60
		Being correction of incorrect extraction from the Ledger – Ledger Accounts correct			
	24	Suspense A/c Dr.	L21	254.25	
		B. Debtor A/c	L72		254.25
		Being correction of error – debtor not credited with payment			

SUSPENSE ACCOUNT   L21

19. .			£	19. .			£
Sept. 5	Sales A/c	J21	50.00	Aug. 31	Difference on books		235.50
24	B. Debtor A/c	J21	254.25	Sept. 19	A. Debtor A/c	J21	50.75
				21	Extraction error	J21	18.00
			£304.25				£304.25

Note: The difficult entry to understand here is the £18. As the true figure extracted to the Trial Balance was £18 less than the figure actually put on the credit side, if this figure had been correct the difference on books would have been £18 greater. Therefore we have to credit the Suspense A/c with another £18.

11. (a) Debit Discount A/c with £243.00 and credit Suspense A/c.
     (b) Debit R. Lee and credit Suspense A/c (£50.00).
     (c) Debit Suspense A/c £90.00 and credit Heating A/c £90.00.
     (d) Debit F. Brown £74.70 and credit Suspense A/c £74.70.
     (e) Debit J. Place £91.00 and credit Suspense A/c £91.00.

Chapter 11, Exercises set 11.1 – Bank Reconciliation Statements, page 181.

---

1. Books of W. Evans. New Cash Book balance £1 788.25. Reconciles with Bank Statement £2 103.20.
2. Books of T. Fitt. New Cash Book balance £1 735.00. Reconciles with Bank Statement £780.00. (b) Brown's cheque.
3. Books of Woodlands Girls School. New Cash Book balance £225.05. Reconciles with Bank Statement £162.55.
4. Book of R. Heron. New Cash Book balance £1 279.65. Reconciles with Bank balance £1 645.55.
5. Books of J. Trueman. The two balances do reconcile.
6. Books of J. Cooper. New Cash Book balance £3 050.00. Reconciles with Bank Statement £4 000.
7. Books of R. Miller. New Cash Book balance £1 004.70. Reconciles with Bank Statement £1 018.30.
8. Books of F. Graham. New Cash Book balance £2 623.70. Reconciles with Bank Statement £2 629.80.
9. Books of R. Herd. New Cash Book balance £1 307.60. Reconciles with Bank Statement £1 730.70.
10. Books of R. Jones. New Cash Book balance £1 480.15. Reconciles with Bank Statement £2 394.20.
11. Books of R. Barnaby. New Cash Book balance £4 534.10. Reconciles with Bank Statement £4 711.90.
12. Books of J. Jones and Co. New Cash Book balance £911.70. Reconciles with Bank Statement £916.50.

Chapter 12, Exercises set 12.1 – Analysis Day Books, page 188.

---

1. See Figure 12.1 for guidance.
2. See Figure 12.1 for guidance.
3. Purchases: music centres £2 497.50, records £735.00, musical instruments £1 801.25. Total purchases £5 033.75, VAT £503.37, Grand total £5 537.12.
4. See fully displayed answer, opposite.
5. Purchases: stationery £235.00, confectionery £246.10, chem-

Date	Details	Seeds £	Bulbs £	Flowers £	Plants £	F	Details £	Sales £	VAT £	Total £
19.. Oct. 3	R. Mulligan									
	200 pkts flower seeds	23.75					23.75			
	200 pkts vegetable seeds	18.75					18.75			
	5 sacks bulk daffodils		61.25				61.25			
						L36		103.75	10.38	114.13
10	M. Bews									
	6 boxes cut Chrysanthemums			47.50			47.50			
	12 boxes cut roses			72.50			72.50			
	200 pkts Iris bulbs		52.00				52.00			
						L12		172.00	17.20	189.20
17	R. Peachey									
	40 boxes cut Scabious			182.50			182.50			
	2 000 pkts flower seeds	237.50					237.50			
	2 000 pkts vegetable seeds	187.50					187.50			
						L45		607.50	60.75	668.25
27	M. Lupin									
	6 boxes cut Chrysanthemums			47.50			47.50			
	100 pot plants (various)				80.00		80.00			
	200 pkts flower seeds	23.75					23.75			
						L44		151.25	15.12	166.37
		491.25	113.25	350.00	80.00			1'034.50	103.45	1 137.95
		L7	L7	L7	L7			L7	L95	

ist's sundries £330.00, toys £93.50. Total purchases £904.60, VAT £90.46, grand total £995.06.

Chapter 13, Exercises set 13.1 – the Bank Cash Book, page 194

1. Final balance at bank £4 988.24. Totals: Discount Allowed £13.54, Bank columns (both sides) £5 401.34.
2. Final balance at bank £4 308.85. Totals: Bank columns (both sides) £5 141.35, Discount Received £30.85.
3. Final balance at bank £3 064.90. Totals: Discount Allowed £23.45, Bank Account (both sides) £6 002.90, Discount Received £25.00.
4. Final balance at bank £7 917.32. Totals: Discount Allowed £127.88, Bank Account (both sides) £9 209.97, Discount Received £43.25.

Chapter 14, Exercises set 14.1 – Depreciation, page 205.

1. Depreciation £800.00 each year. Balance on January 1, Year 3 = £7 400.00.
2. (a) Journal Entry. Debit Depreciation A/c £1 150.00. Credit Provision for Depreciation on Machinery £1 150.00.
   (b) Machinery A/c. Debit entry in Year 1 £10 000.00. No other entry. Provision for Depreciation on Machinery A/c. Credit entry of £1 150.00 each year.
   (c) Value of Machinery = £10 000.00 −£2 300 = £7 700.00.
3. Final value = £11 543.00; Depreciation £750.00 Year 1; £1 425.00 Year 2; £1 282 Year 3.
4. (a) Machinery A/c at start. Debit entry of £12 000.
   (b) Provision for Depreciation Account: Credit entries of £1 200.00, £2 160.00 and £1 728.00.
   (c) Value of machine on 1 January Year 4 = £12 000 −£5 088.00 = £6 912.00.
5. Motor Vehicles A/c: Depreciation Year 1 £2 350.00, Year 2 £1 762.00. Value of car written off = £2 812.00. Final balance £2 476.00.

Calculation re car:	£
Cost Price	5 000.00
Less depreciation Year 1	1 250.00
	3 750.00
Less depreciation Year 2	938.00
Value on books	£2 812.00

Journal Entry. Debit Cash £2 000.00; Debit Loss on Sale of Motor Vehicle A/c £812.00; Credit Motor Vehicles A/c £2 812.00.

6. Books of R. Long:
The Motor Vehicles Account will appear as follows:

MOTOR VEHICLES ACCOUNT L11

Year 1			£	Year 2			£
Jan. 1	Cash	J1	3 600.00	Dec. 31	Bank A/c etc.	J19	3 600.00
Oct. 1	Cash	J17	5 700.00	31	Balance c/d		5 700.00
			£9 300.00				£9 300.00
Year 3			£				
Jan. 1	Balance b/d		5 700.00				

PROVISION FOR DEPRECIATION ON MOTOR VEHICLES ACCOUNT L12

Year 2			£	Year 1		£
Dec. 31	Motor Vehicles A/c	J19	1 296.00	Dec. 31	Depreciation	1 005.00
31	Balance c/d	J19	1 368.00	Year 2		
				Dec. 31	Depreciation	1 659.00
			£2 664.00			£2 664.00
				Year 3		£
				Jan. 1	Balance b/d	1 368.00

Calculation on disposal of the van:

	£
Original cost	3 600.00
Less first year's depreciation (20%)	720.00
	2 880.00
Less 2nd year's depreciation (20%)	576.00
Value on books	£2 304.00

To remove this value we must credit Motor Vehicles A/c with £3 600.00 and debit Provision for Depreciation A/c with £1 296.00. This removes both the asset and the depreciation. The £2 304 value of the asset is then taken into account by a £2 000 cheque and £304 loss on sale.

Year 2				£	£ J19
Dec. 31	Provision for Depreciation A/c	Dr.	L12	1 296.00	
	Bank A/c	Dr.	CB37	2 000.00	
	Loss on Sale of Vehicle A/c		L15	304.00	
	Motor Vehicles A/c		L11		3 600.00
	Being sale of van at this date				

CASH BOOK (BANK COLUMNS ONLY)   CB37

Year 2			£	
Dec. 31	Motor			
	Vehicles A/c	J19	2 000.00	

LOSS ON SALE OF VEHICLE A   L15

Year 2			£	
Dec. 31	Motor			
	Vehicles A/c	J19	304.00	

7. Debit Depreciation A/c £12 375.00; Credit Herd A/c £12 375.00. Balance on Herd A/c £66 375.00.
8. Debit Depreciation A/c £1 010.00; Credit Small Tools A/c £1 010.00.

Chapter 15, Exercises set 15.1 – simple wages calculations, page 209.

1. Gross pay £180; total deductions £59.60; take-home pay £120.40.
2. Gross pay £175; total deductions £30.25; add refund £28; take-home pay £172.75.
3. Gross pay £432.50; total deductions £153.29; bank giro credit £279.21.
4. Calculations are as follows:

		£
Salary		300.00
Commission $12\frac{1}{2} \times$ £40	=	500.00
Gross pay		800.00

Deductions:		£
Pension 6% × £800	=	48.00
Nat. Insur. 9% × £800	=	72.00
Income Tax	=	84.50
Trade Union	=	1.50
Savings	=	25.00
Charity	=	2.00
		233.00
		£567.00

Chapter 15, Exercises set 15.2 – simple Wages Books, page 211.

1.

	Taxable pay to date (£)	Total deductions (£)	Net pay (£)
A.B.	70.65	33.18	51.12
C.D.	77.85	32.29	79.81
E.P.	52.30	27.28	50.62
G.H.	48.00	20.07	45.43

Total net pay: £226.98
Total tax due: £74.10
Total national insurance (employees' + employer's): £72.33
Total trade union contributions: £2.00
Total charity: £0.40
Total SAYE: £10
Total superannuation: £17.80

2.

	Taxable pay to date (£)	Total deductions (£)	Net pay (£)
R.S.	86.78	34.06	60.97
T.U.	60.31	29.47	45.64
V.W.	116.94	52.05	97.59
Y.Z.	150.96	73.84	94.42

Total net pay: £298.62
Total tax due: £123.60
Total national insurance (employees' and employer's): £104.67
Total trade union contributions: £2.60
Total charity: £0.40
Total SAYE: £25.00
Total superannuation: £30.96

Chapter 15, Exercises set 15.3 – the Kalamzoo Wages System, page 218

	1 A.B £	2 C.D £	3 E.F. £	4 G.H. £
Gross pay	71.05	126.30	97.04	101.20
Gross pay for tax purposes	67.50	119.98	92.19	96.14
Gross pay to date for tax	67.50	As given	As given	As given
Taxable pay to date	41.35	646.80	604.70	1 028.90
Tax	12.30	9.10 (refund)	14.50	17.20
Total deductions	17.78	9.45	21.79	24.61
Net pay	49.72	110.53	70.40	71.53
Refunds	—	9.10	—	—
Total Payable	49.72	119.63	70.40	71.53
NI Employer's	9.25	16.44	12.63	13.17
NI Contributions	14.48	25.74	19.77	20.38

Chapter 16, Exercises set 16.1 – the Trial Balance, page 225.

1. Totals of Trial Balance = £448 375.00
2. Totals of Trial Balance = £189 670.00
3. Totals of Trial Balance = £600 550.00
4. Totals of Trial Balance = £264 299.50
5. Totals of Trial Balance = £2 329 600.00
6. (1) Dr. Column–Asset; (2) Cr. Column–Liability; (3) Cr. Column–Liability; (4) Dr. Column–Loss; (5) Cr. Column –Profit; (6) Dr. Column–Capital withdrawn.
7. Trial Balance totals = £88 125
8. Totals of Trial Balance = £232 000
9. See below:

TRIAL BALANCE OF R. JOINER'S BOOKS
as at 28 February 19. .

	Dr. £	Cr. £
Capital at start		33 000
Premises	27 000	
Drawings	4 750	
Plant and Machinery	14 850	
Stock at March 1	4 500	
Office Furniture, March 1	3 500	
Insurance	425	
Office Salaries	9 950	
Commission Received		800
Bank Loan		5 000
Cash at Bank	3 250	
Bad Debt	325	
Discount Allowed	450	
Debtors and Creditors	3 100	2 900
Returns Inwards	400	
Returns Outwards		200
Purchases and Sales	28 500	61 250
Rent Paid	2 150	
	£103 150	£103 150

10. Totals of Trial Balance = £276 161.25

Chapter 17, Exercises set 17.1 – Trading Accounts, page 239.

1. Gross Profit £59 444.50
2. Gross Profit £130 346.75
3. Gross Profit £22 847.75
4. Gross Profit £16 466.50

5.   See below:

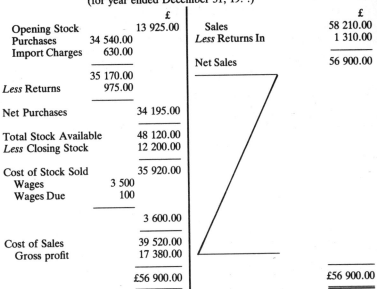

E. RANDALL
TRADING ACCOUNT
(for year ended December 31, 19. .)

	£		£
Opening Stock	13 925.00	Sales	58 210.00
Purchases	34 540.00	*Less* Returns In	1 310.00
Import Charges	630.00		
	35 170.00	Net Sales	56 900.00
Less Returns	975.00		
Net Purchases	34 195.00		
Total Stock Available	48 120.00		
Less Closing Stock	12 200.00		
Cost of Stock Sold	35 920.00		
Wages	3 500		
Wages Due	100		
	3 600.00		
Cost of Sales	39 520.00		
Gross profit	17 380.00		
	£56 900.00		£56 900.00

6.   Gross Profit £16 310.00
7.   Gross Profit £15 000.00 (b) it would have been £10 800.00
8.   (a) A decrease of £100.
     (b) An increase of £300.
     (c) None.
     (d) A decrease of £3 245.
     (e) A decrease of £450.
     (f) None.

Chapter 18, Exercises set 18.1 – Profit and Loss Accounts, page 248.

1.   Net profit £12 538.40.
2.   Net profit £14 215.00.
3.   Net profit £19 754.00.
4.   Gross profit £77 932.45; Net profit £33 781.30.
5.   Gross profit £94 000.00; Net profit £35 000.00.
6.   Gross profit £104 000.00; Net profit £65 500.00.

Chapter 19, Exercises set 19.1 – simple Final Accounts, page 255.

1. Gross profit £50 650; Net profit £44 930; Balance Sheet totals £121 880.
2. Gross profit £73 000; Net profit £45 850; Balance Sheet totals £194 453.
3. Gross profit £39 789.50; Net profit £25 208.25; Balance Sheet totals £79 262.00.
4. Gross profit £34 510.00; Net profit £10 626.25; Balance Sheet totals £81 553.75.
5. Gross profit £102 995; Net profit £73 920; Balance Sheet totals £113 420.
6. Gross profit £89 747.50; Net profit £57 157.50; Balance Sheet totals £100 923.75.
7. Gross profit £93 640; Net profit £36 780; Balance Sheet totals £236 740.
8. See below:

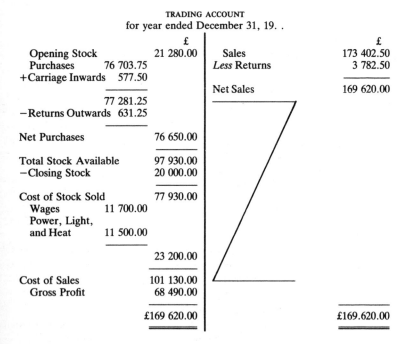

TRADING ACCOUNT
for year ended December 31, 19. .

	£		£
Opening Stock	21 280.00	Sales	173 402.50
Purchases 76 703.75		*Less* Returns	3 782.50
+Carriage Inwards 577.50			
		Net Sales	169 620.00
77 281.25			
−Returns Outwards 631.25			
Net Purchases	76 650.00		
Total Stock Available	97 930.00		
−Closing Stock	20 000.00		
Cost of Stock Sold	77 930.00		
Wages 11 700.00			
Power, Light, and Heat 11 500.00			
	23 200.00		
Cost of Sales	101 130.00		
Gross Profit	68 490.00		
	£169 620.00		£169.620.00

PROFIT AND LOSS ACCOUNT
for year ending December 31, 19. .

	£		£
Discount Allowed	3 653.75	Gross profit	68 490.00
Rent and Rates	6 250.00	Discount Received	1 141.25
Motor Vehicle Expenses	2 607.50	Interest Received	502.50
Salaries	23 650.00		
Office Expenses	3 150.00		70 133.75
Depreciation	2 000.00		
Total overheads	41 311.25		
Net profit	28 822.50		
	£70 133.75		£70 133.75

BALANCE SHEET
as at December 31, 19. .

	£	£		£	£
CAPITAL			FIXED ASSETS		
At Start		64 800.00	Freehold Premises		36 500.00
Add Profit	28 822.50		Motor Vehicles		11 500.00
Less Drawings	10 500.00		Fixtures and Fittings		8 800.00
		18 322.50			56 800.00
		83 122.50	CURRENT ASSETS		
LONG-TERM LIABILITIES		—	Stock	20 000.00	
			Debtors	31 502.50	
			Cash at Bank	16 050.00	
CURRENT LIABILITIES			Cash in Hand	11 272.50	
Creditors		52 502.50			
					78 825.00
		£135 625.00			£135 625.00

Chapter 20, Exercises set 20.1 – capital and revenue expenditure, page 267.

1. (a) Telephone expenses and office salaries would be revenue expenses. New weighing machines and new counters are capital expenses. Wages of men fitting counters are a revenue expense that has to be capitalized so they count as a capital expense.

   (b) Telephone expenses and office salaries would appear on the debit side of the Profit and Loss A/c as losses. The others would appear as an increase in the asset Fixtures and Fittings.

2. The Gorilla and the Monkey House are capital expenses and go in the Balance Sheet. The hire of equipment and repairs are revenue expenses and go in the Profit and Loss Account. Keepers' wages are a revenue expense and go in the Trading

Account, or some people might put them in the Profit and Loss Account.

3. The crockery loss is taken in as a reduction of stock.
4. Debit Plant and Machinery with £12 550. Credit Carriage Account £425; Wages Account £375 and Wormco Eng. Ltd £11 750.
5. Motor van and typewriter are capital expenses. Postage, stationery, goods for resale, repairs, and teas for staff are Revenue Expenses. The motor vehicle and typewriter will still be on his books – also possibly some of the goods for resale, and some of the stationery. These might require adjustments to be done (see Chapter 22).
6. The painting machine, the new canteen, and the wages of the building workers are capital items which appear in the Balance Sheet, the wages of the lino workers, and the pitch are revenue items appearing in the Trading Account, and the paper and string is a revenue item appearing in the Profit and Loss Account.
7. These losses appear as reduced stock.
8. Wages as attendants are a revenue expense appearing in the Trading Account, wages as repairers are a revenue expense appearing in the Profit and Loss Account, wages paid erecting the sideshow are a capital expense, and are capitalized as Sideshows Account in the Balance Sheet.
9. (a) See text; (b) Cooker and alterations to premises – capital expenses. Hire charges and redecorations revenue expenses – but some of the redecorations might be capitalized, because they last longer than a year.
10. See Text.
11. This loss appears as reduced stock.
12. (a) Adding listing machine and two typewriters for office use are capital expenditure – other items revenue expenditure; (b) Premises increase by £1 250; profits increase by £1 250, since only half the amount is now treated as a loss.
13. Premises are debited with £27 500 altogether, Repairs Account with £1 480; Painting and Decorating Account with £1 750 and Bank Account is credited with a total of £30 650.
14. (a) See text; (b) Debit Premises Account with £2 000 and Decorations in Suspense Account with £800. Debit Depreciation Account with £200. Credit Wages Account with £1 500 and Purchases Account with £1 500 to remove the amounts on these accounts which are not revenue expenses.

Chapter 21, Exercises set 21.1 – Stock valuation, page 278.

1. (a) Final balance 57 items; (b) value £510.15.
2. Final balance 1 200 hinges.
3. Final stock value £19 615.
4. (a) See text.
    (b) 3 000 units worth £11 755.
5. (a) See text.
    (b) Final stock value £46 900.
6. Gross profit £13 639 (closing stock = £3 409).
7. Gross profit £14 780 (closing stock = £15 600).
8. Closing stock £2 141; Gross profit £11 441.
9. Closing stock £17 855 (Cost of stock sold = £69 895).
10. Closing stock £27 100 (Sales cost £1 665, returns £45).
11. (a) See text.   £
    (b) Stock at April 2   14 310
        Less purchases delivered on 1 and 2 April
            (not in stock on March 31)   −2 130
                                                                             _____
                                                                              12 180
        Add Sales on 1 and 2 April at cost price
            (still in stock on 31 March)
            £1 825 −20% = £1 825 −£365   +1 460
                                                                             _____
                                                                              13 640
        Deduct returns at cost price (not in stock on
            March 31 – returned on April 1)
            £200 −£40 =   −160
                                                                             _____
                                                                             £13 480
                                                                             ════════

12. Closing Stock at 31 March = £19 385.
13. Loss due to burglary = £22 450.
14. Loss due to fire = £7 616.

Chapter 22, Exercises set 22.1 – payments in advance, page 287.

1. Debit Balance of £500; Transfer to Profit and Loss Account £2 000.
2. Debit Balance £245; Transfer to Profit and Loss Account £691.
3. Credit Balance of £1 425; Transfer to Income and Expenditure Account is £30 825.
4. Credit Balance £2 628; Transfer to Profit and Loss Account £27 932.

Chapter 22, Exercises set 22.2 – accrued expenses and accrued receipts, page 290.

1. Debit Balance £446; Profit carried to Profit and Loss Account = £1 784.
2. Credit Balance £413.50; carried to Manufacturing Account £756.00 and to Profit and Loss Account £378.00.
3. Credit Balance of £260; Balance Sheet entry, Rent due £260.
4. Debit Balance £5 104; Amount transferred to Profit and Loss Account £50 857; Balance Sheet entry, Repairs unpaid – asset side £5 104.

Chapter 22, Exercises set 22.3 – Final Accounts exercises with payments in advance and accrued expenses, page 291.

1. (a) Salaries Credit Balance £140; Rates Debit Balance £925; (b) The profits would have been £785 less.
2. Amount chargeable to Profit and Loss Account £1 539; Credit Balance £179 or can be shown as Debit Balance £171, and Credit Balance £350.
3. Amount charged to Profit and Loss Account = £2 758; Balances Debit side £192; Credit side £500.
4. Gross profit £45 600; Net profit £30 361.50; Balance Sheet totals £86 212.50.
5. Gross profit £52 585.00; Net profit £38 466.25; Balance Sheet totals £98 412.50.
6. Gross profit £81 341.75; Net profit £64 696.25; Balance Sheet totals £116 733.75.
7. Trial Balance totals £142 075. Gross profit £34 247; Net profit £17 619; Balance Sheet totals £73 252.

Chapter 22, Exercises set 22.4 – Bad debts and provisions for bad debts, page 301.

1. (a) Charge to Profit and Loss Account 1st year £630, 2nd year £385; (b) Debtors £27 000 −£1 390 = £25 650.
2. (a) Total charge to Profit and Loss Account £2 700; Final Value of Debtors after deducting Provision = £31 500.
3. Charge to Profit and Loss Account £1 768.45.
4. Charge to Profit and Loss Account £760; Final Value of Debtors after deducting Provision £11 590.
5. Charge to Profit and Loss Account £235; Final Provision £360.
6. Charge to Profit and Loss Account £436.50; Final Provision £236.

7. Charge to Profit and Loss Account for Provision £650; for Legal Charges £127.
8. Gross profit £76 720; Net profit £22 694; Balance Sheet totals £63 699.
9. Gross profit £58 952; Net profit £45 313; Balance Sheet totals £99 410.
10. Gross profit £40 404; Net profit £15 840; Balance Sheet totals £46 983.

Chapter 22, Exercises set 22.5 – Final Accounts with all types of adjustments, page 309.

1. Net profit £28 590; Balance Sheet totals £67 755.
2. Net profit £22 902.50; Balance Sheet totals £33 793.75.
3. Gross profit £46 499; Net profit £33 425; Balance Sheet totals £83 077.
4. Books of M. Martindale, see below.

TRADING ACCOUNT
for year ending 31 December 19. .

		£		£
Opening Stock		12 000	Sales	137 265
Purchases	87 195		*Less* Returns Inwards	1 825
Add Carriage In	790		Net turnover	135 440
	87 985			
Less Returns Outwards	1 380			
		86 650		
		98 605		
Less Closing Stock		11 850		
Cost of Stock sold		86 755		
Wages		10 980		
Cost of Sales		97 735		
Gross Profit		37 705		
		£135 440		£135 440

PROFIT AND LOSS ACCOUNT
for year ending 31 December 19. .

	£		£
Wages	5 490	Gross Profit	37 705
General Expenses	6 540	Rent Received	850
Bad Debts	1 030		
Discount Allowed	875		38 555
Commission Paid	1 380	Net Loss	5 263
Carriage Outwards	2 362		
Salaries	21 627		
Interest on Loan	400		
Advertising	3 486		
Provision for Bad Debts	426		
Provision for Discounts	202		
	£43 818		£43 818

BALANCE SHEET
as at 31 December 19. .

		£	FIXED ASSETS			£
Capital		97 500	Goodwill		1 715	
Less Goodwill		1 715	*Less* Amount written off		1 715	
		95 785				—
Less Net Loss	5 263		Premises			50 000
and Drawings	13 375		Fixtures and Fittings			7 000
		18 638	Motor Vehicles			7 500
		77 147				64 500
LONG TERM LIABILITY			CURRENT ASSETS	£	£	
Loan		10 000	Closing Stock		11 850	
CURRENT LIABILITY			Debtors	8 520		
Creditors		3 775	*Less* Provision	426		
					8 094	
			and Discount Provision	202		
					7 892	
			Bank		6 050	
			Cash		630	
						26 422
		£90 922				£90 922

Chapter 23, Exercises set 23.1 – the Appropriation Account, page 319.

1. Share of Residue for each £6 375.
2. Share of Residue: £16 296 to Arthur; £10 864 to Brian.
3. Share of Residue: £16 460 to Sybrandt; £8 230 to Cornelis.

4. (a) Share of Residue: Nelson £11 480; Blake £5 740; Hardy
£5 740.
(b) Interest on capital recognizes the unequal contribution
made by the partners in financing the business, and
establishes that some reward shall be paid for this service
to the business before the final residue of the profits is
shared up.
5. See below:

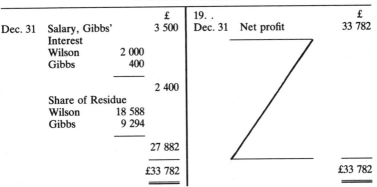

G. WILSON AND W. GIBBS
APPROPRIATION ACCOUNT

		£	19. .		£
Dec. 31	Salary, Gibbs'	3 500	Dec. 31	Net profit	33 782
	Interest				
	Wilson 2 000				
	Gibbs 400				
		2 400			
	Share of Residue				
	Wilson 18 588				
	Gibbs 9 294				
		27 882			
		£33 782			£33 782

Chapter 23, Exercises set 23.2 – Current Accounts of partners, page 324.

1. Balances on Current Accounts: Wilson £3 122 debit; Brown
£472 credit.
2. Balance on Current Account £2 940 credit.
3. Capital Accounts are unchanged at Hemp £60 000; Wool
£50 000; Cotton £40 000. Current Accounts: Hemp £3 692
credit; Wool £6 928 credit; Cotton £1 336 debit.
4. Current Account balance £9 144 credit.
5. Appropriation Account shares of residue David £12 318;
Peter £8 212. Current Account balances: David £2 168 credit;
Peter £5 722 credit.

Chapter 23, Exercises set 23.3 – the Final Accounts of partner-ships, page 326.

1. Net Profit = £26 590. Appropriation Account Residue:
Arthur £9 354; Brian £6 236. Current Account balances:
Arthur £1 414 Debit; Brian £1 543 debit. Balance Sheet totals
£81 158.

2.   Current Account balances: Bath £16 268 Credit; Wells £6 282 Credit; Balance Sheet totals £46 600.

3.   Current Account balances: Peele £10 399 Credit; Mellis £5 502 Credit; Balance Sheet totals £67 005.

4.   Gross profit £93 441, Net profit £53 240. Current Account balances (both credits): Haig £12 544; Grant £11 646. Balance Sheet totals £129 235.

5.   Gross profit £62 027; Net profit £27 891. Current Account balances: King £1 361.50 debit; Snagsby £3 253 Credit. Balance Sheet totals £47 187.

6.   Gross profit £43 623; Net profit £17 624. Current Accounts balances: Forsyth £7 131 Debit; Gordon £3 585 Debit; Balance Sheet totals £117 834.

7.   Books of Tree and Branch (see below).

	£		£
Opening Stock	21 670	Sales	131 165
Purchases	52 360	*Less* Returns	1 805
Less Returns Out	2 736	Net turnover	129 360
Net Purchases	49 624		
Total stock available	71 294		
Less Closing Stock	23 250		
Cost of stock sold	48 044		
Warehouse Wages	16 000		
Light and Heat	1 770		
Rates	750		
Cost of Sales	66 564		
Gross Profit	62 796		
	£129 360		£129 360

PROFIT AND LOSS ACCOUNT
for year ending 31 December 19. .

	£		£
Office Salaries	17 500	Gross Profit	62 796
Light and Heat	590	Discount Received	2 133
Rates	250	Bad debts provision	
Stationery	1 783	recovered	100
Sundry Expenses	2 320		
Postage and Telephone	1 680	Total profits	65 029
Insurance	1 077		
Discount Allowed	1 241		
Vehicle Expenses	4 932		
Depreciation:			
Fixtures	1 720		
Vehicles	3 600		
	5 320		
Total expenses	36 693		
Profit	28 336		
	£65 029		£65 029

APPROPRIATION ACCOUNT
for year ending 31 December 19. .

	£		£
Salary (Branch)	6 500	Net Profit	28 336
Interest on Capital			
Tree	4 000		
Branch	2 000		
	6 000		
Share of Residue			
Tree	11 877		
Branch	3 959		
	15 836		
	£28 336		£28 336

CURRENT ACCOUNTS
for year ending 31 December 19. .

	Tree £	Branch £		Tree £	Branch £
Drawings	8 750	6 250	Balance	2 500	4 500
Balance c/d	9 627	10 709	Salary		6 500
			Interest on Capital	4 000	2 000
			Share of Residue	11 877	3 959
	£18 377	16 959		£18 377	16 959
			Balance b/d	9 627	10 709

BALANCE SHEET
as at 31 December 19. .

CAPITAL	£	£	FIXED ASSETS	At Cost £	Less Depreciation to date £	Value £
Tree	50 000					
Branch	25 000		Freehold			
		75 000	Premises	42 500	—	42 500
			Fixtures &			
			Fittings	17 200	1 720	15 480
			Vehicles	18 000	3 600	14 400
CURRENT ASSETS				77 700	5 320	72 380
Tree	9 627					
Branch	10 709		CURRENT ASSETS		£	
		20 336	Stock		23 250	
			Debtors	2 600		
			Less Provision	260		
CURRENT LIABILITIES					2 340	
Creditors		7 006	Bank		3 206	
			Cash in Hand		701	
			Rates in Advance		240	
			Insurance in Advance		225	
					29 962	
		£102 342			£102 342	

Chapter 24, Exercises set 24.1 – Receipts and Payments Accounts, page 339.

1. Cash Balance £761.75.
2. Totals of Receipts and Payments Account £3 129.40.
3. Cash Balance £1 467.00.
4. See opposite.

NEW UNIVERSITY MOUNTAINEERING CLUB
RECEIPTS AND PAYMENTS ACCOUNT
for Summer Season 19. .

RECEIPTS	£	PAYMENTS	£
Student membership fees	432.50	Use of alpine huts, etc.	375.00
Grant from College	2 500.00	Camping fees	162.50
Collection for Alpine trip	893.75	Transport	632.50
Dance proceeds	192.50	Purchase of ropes, etc.	282.50
Annual dinner tickets	727.50	Guide books	12.75
		Refreshment expenses	284.00
		Dance expenses	91.25
		Dinner expenses	492.50
		Balance in hand c/d	2 413.25
	£4 746.25		£4 746.25

	£		
Balance in hand b/d	2 413.25		

Chapter 24, Exercises set 24.2 – Club Final Accounts, page 345.

1. Income and Expenditure Account totals £2 255; Surplus £805; Balance Sheet totals £1 232.50.
2. Income and Expenditure Account totals £3 275; Surplus £1 190; Balance Sheet totals read £1 700; Accumulated Fund total £1 190.
3. Income and Expenditure Account totals £2 915; Surplus £200; Balance Sheet totals £1 815.
4. Income and Expenditure Account totals £3 505 Surplus £389.75; Accumulated Fund total £3 417.25.
5. (a) See text.
   (b) Profit on Refreshments £173.50; Income and Expenditure Account totals £4 794; Surplus £4 186.75; Balance Sheet totals £12 420.75.
6. Income and Expenditure Account totals £42 680.00; Surplus £11 907.50; Balance Sheet totals £56 527.50.
7. Profit on Refreshments £497.50; Income and Expenditure Account totals £13 335; Surplus £1 355; Balance Sheet totals £24 595.
8. Amount of Subscription income £1 550.
9. (a) Trading Account totals £10 105; Profit on refreshments £2 495; (b) Receipts and Payments Account totals £14 910; Balance in Hand = £520; (c) Income and Expenditure Account totals £6 520; Surplus for year £95.
10. The Happy Venturer's Football Club:
    Calculation of the Accumulated Fund at the start of year:
    Accumulated Fund = Assets at start – liabilities
    (*Note*: In this case there were no liabilities)

	£
Cash in hand	100
Cash at bank	650
Stocks at start	1 550
Furniture & Fittings	2 800
Subscriptions due	100
Accumulated Fund	£5 200

RECEIPTS AND PAYMENTS A/C (CASH AND BANK)
for year ending 31 December 19. .

	Cash £	Bank £		Cash £	Bank £
Balances on			Wages (part timers)	2 000.00	
1 January	100.00	650.00	Wages (barman)	1 750.00	
Bank transfer	4 500.00		Postage etc.	375.00	
Dances and Socials		632.50	Rent		682.50
Subscriptions		2 450.00	Rates and		
Bar takings		14 252.50	Insurance		823.75
			Light and Heat		432.50
			Expenses (Dances &		
			Socials)		375.00
			Cash drawn		4 500.00
			Bar purchases		7 200.00
			Balances c/d	475.00	3 971.25
	£4 600.00	17 985.00		£4 600.00	17 985.00
	£	£			
Balances b/d	475.00	3 971.25			

TRADING ACCOUNT (BAR)
for year ending 31 December 19. .

	£		£
Opening Stock	1 550.00	Sales	14 252.50
Purchases	7 200.00		
Total stock available	8 750.00		
Less Closing stock	1 230.00		
Cost of stock sold	7 520.00		
Wages	1 750.00		
Cost of sales	9 270.00		
Profit on bar	4 982.50		
	£14 252.50		£14 252.50

TRADING ACCOUNT (DANCES & SOCIALS)
for year ending 31 December 19. .

	£		£
Expenses	375.00	Sales	632.50
Profit on dances etc.	257.50		
	£632.50		£632.50

INCOME AND EXPENDITURE ACCOUNT
for year ending 31 December 19. .

	£		£
Wages (part-timers)	2 000.00	Subscriptions	2 450.00
Postage	375.00	*Less* Previous year	100.00
Rent	682.50		
Rates & Insurance 823.75			2 350.00
Less amount in		*Add* Subs due	120.00
advance 70.00			
			2 470.00
	753.75	Profit on bar	4 982.50
Light and Heat	432.50	Profit on dances & socials	257.50
Depreciation	280.00		
		Total income	7 710.00
Total expenses	4 523.75		
Surplus for year	3 186.25		
	£7 710.00		£7 710.00

BALANCE SHEET
as at 31 December 19. .

	£		At Cost £	Less Depreciation £	Value £
ACCUMULATED FUND		FIXED ASSETS			
At Start	5 200.00	Fixtures &	2 800	280	2 520.00
Add surplus for year	3 186.25	Fittings			
	8 386.25	CURRENT ASSETS			
		Stock	1 230.00		
		Bank	3 971.25		
		Cash in hand	475.00		
		Subscriptions due	120.00		
		Insurance in			
		advance	70.00		
					5 866.25
	£8 386.25				£8 386.25

Chapter 25, Exercises set 25.1 – finding profits by the increased net worth method, page 356.

1. Profits for the year = £15 010.
2. Profits for the year = £17 328.50.
3. Profits for the quarter-year = £9 055.
4. Profits for the half-year = £31 750.
   Singleton cannot tell the turnover of his business, the gross profit he is making, or the expenses of the business under any particular heading.

5.   Profit for the year = £12 025.
6.   Profit for the year = £13 015.

Chapter 25, Exercises set 25.2 – producing a full set of Final Accounts from incomplete records, page 364.

---

1.   Opening Capital £30 079; Credit Sales for year £93 032; Credit Purchases £25 141; Gross Profit £84 604; Net Profit £66 955; Closing Capital £82 736; Balance Sheet totals £112 676.
2.   Opening Capital £76 950; Credit Sales for year £78 854; Credit Purchases £21 926; Gross Profit £46 052; Net Profit £28 604; Closing Capital £96 489; Balance Sheet totals £123 038.
3.   Opening Capital £25 458; Credit Sales for year £60 557; Credit Purchases £22 287; Gross Profit £36 390; Net Profit £12 181; Closing Capital £27 772; Balance Sheet totals £43 404.

Chapter 26, Exercises set 26.1 – Departmental Accounts, page 368.

---

1.   Gross profits: Dept. A £21 047.25; Dept. B £49 077.55; Total £70 124.80.
2.   Gross profits: Dept. A £68 709.20; Dept. B £34 069.05; Total £102 778.25. Net Profits: Dept. A £42 127.30; Dept. B £1 817.60. Total £43 944.90.
3.   (a) Gross profit: Junior £10 500 Senior: Gross loss £1 750. Total (net effect) £8 750.
        (b) Advice to Wellesley should be that his view of the 'Senior' activities should include a study of its profit potential so that either it moves into profit or it is closed down.
4.   Gross Profits: Groceries £62 135 Fruit £63 990. Total £126 125; Net Profit £61 010; Current Account balances £15 305 and £15 705; Balance Sheet totals £95 190.
5.   Gross Profit: Dept. A £33 842; Dept. B £22 803. Total £56 645. Net Profit: Dept. A £10 127; Dept. B £6 993. Total £17 120; Balance Sheet totals £90 375.

Chapter 27, Exercises set 27.1 – Manufacturing Accounts, page 383.

1. Prime Cost £132 108; Cost of Manufactured Goods £180 270; Gross profits £74 280.
2. Prime Cost £164 660; Cost of Manufactured Goods £233 394; Gross Profit £77 852.
3. Prime Costs £176 194.25; Manufacturing profit £20 716.00; Gross profit £63 480.00.
4. Break even point at 3 000 units; Costs at 7 000 units £84 000. Profits at 7 000 units £56 000.
5. Prime Costs £190 936.30; Manufacturing Profit £41 213.20; Gross Profit £100 419.30.
6. Break even point is at 5 000 units. Costs at 12 500 units £365 000. Profit at 12 500 units is £135 000.
7. Prime Costs £129 851.25; Manufacturing Loss £1 450.75; Gross profit £76 308.75.
8. Break-even point at 200 units. Revenue at 700 units £161 000.00; Profits £67 500. (Answers within £1 000 accepted.)
9. Prime Costs £177 325; Manufacturing profit £10 965; Gross profit £48 300.

Chapter 28, Exercises set 28.1 – Limited Company Accounts, page 400.

1. Balance on Appropriation Account £12 300; Balance Sheet total £121 600; Ordinary Shareholders' Interest in the Company £90 800.
2. Ordinary Shareholders' Interest £105 000; Net Value of Current Assets £55 250; Balance Sheet totals £125 000.
3. Balance on Appropriation Account £3 370; Ordinary Shareholders' Interest £136 870; Balance Sheet total £207 570.
4. Ordinary Shareholders' Interest £169 658; Balance Sheet totals £233 658.
5. Balance on Appropriation Account £14 131; Ordinary Shareholders' Interest in the Company £137 391; Balance Sheet totals £239 391.
6. Gross Profit £99 320; Net Profit £49 405 Balance Sheet totals £188 955; Ordinary Shareholders' Interest £176 955.
7. Gross Profit £141 055; Net Profit £80 386; Balance on Appropriation Account £5 781; Balance Sheet totals £198 781; Ordinary Shareholders' Interest £173 781.

Chapter 29, Exercises set 29.1 – Gross Profit Percentage, page 411.

1. (a) See text; (b) Gross Profit percentage = 33⅓%.
2. (a) See text.
    (b) Possible explanations are (i); A change in the mix of sales (more of the least profitable items being sold; (ii) Theft of money from the tills; (iii) Theft of stock; (iv) Breakages and other losses due to bad buying (such as decay of perishables); (v) Increased costs not being passed on to the customer in higher selling prices; (vi) Capital items wrongly included in purchases.
3. (a) Yes; (b) Yes; (c) No; (d) Yes – if the amounts taken in the second year were greater than the first year; (e) Yes (for the reasons see the text on page 408).
4. (a) Gross profit £118.350; Trading Account totals £218 000; (b) £218 000 turnover; (c) £118 350; (d) 54.3 per cent.

Chapter 29, Exercises set 29.2 – gross and net profit percentages, page 415.

1. Gross profit percentages: year 1 = 43.1%; year 2 = 44.8%. Net profit percentages: year 1 = 20.8%; year 2 = 28.0%. *Conclusions*: A very satisfactory position. The increased turnover resulted in a small increase in the gross profit percentage and a very satisfactory increase in the net profit percentage (the overhead expenses did not increase in line with turnover).
2. Stock valuation £10 000. Revenue Expenditure must be limited to £13 000.
3. Gross profit £24 920; Sales £49 840; Purchases £30 570.
4. Estimated results: Gross profit £63 000; Net profit £22 400.
5. Sales figure £107 000; Purchases figure £68 200.
6. (a) (i) Cost price of goods sold £250 000; (ii) Turnover £400 000; (iii) Gross profit on cost = 60 per cent; (iv) Gross profit on turnover = 37½ per cent; (v) Net profit on turnover = 12½ per cent.
    (b) Net profit for following year = £47 500.
7. Sheffield Gross profit percentage: 1st year = 25%; 2nd year = 25%. Sheffield Net profit percentage: 1st year = 16⅔%; 2nd year = 16⅔%.
    Manchester Gross profit percentage: 1st year = 33⅓%; 2nd year = 40%. Manchester Net profit percentage: 1st year = 14.7%; 2nd year = 21%.
8. Gross profit percentage: 1st year = 33%; 2nd year = 30% Net profit percentage: 1st year = 12%; 2nd year = 12½%.

9. (a) He is a debtor of W. Ames.
   (b) Ames has been making losses to the point where he has lost all his capital and will soon be out of business.
   (c) Rates are due from the previous period.
   (d) Packing Materials have been purchased in advance for next year.
   (e) Insurance has been paid in advance for next year.
   (f) Ames is overdrawn at the bank.
   (g) Advertising materials have been purchased for use in the coming year.

10. (a) R. Coombes is a creditor to whom Lord owes money.
    (b) T. Low has returned goods after payment for them and is temporarily not a debtor but a creditor.
    (c) As for 9(g) above. A stock of advertising brochures is in hand.
    (d) Rent is due to Lord's landlord for the previous period.
    (e) Lord is overdrawn at the bank.

Chapter 29, Exercises set 29.3 – rate of stock turnover, page 420.

1. Gross profit £25 000.
2. Net profit £19 500.
3. Net profit £37 500.
4. Net profit £18 000. At 5 times a year profit less by £5 000.
5. (a) Net profit £56 000; (b) Net profit £68 000. Conclusion: The higher the rate of stock turnover the more profit we make.
6. (a) Gross profit £27 000; (b) Expenses £14 040; (c) Net profit £12 960; (d) Estimated sales £143 640; (e) Estimated gross profit £30 240; (f) Estimated expenses £15 800; (g) Estimated net profit £14 400.
7. (a) Gross profit £42 000; (b) Net profit £26 250; (c) Expenses £15 750; (d) Estimated Sales £315 000; (e) Estimated gross profit £35 000; (f) Estimated expenses £15 750; (g) Estimated net profit £19 250.
8. Turnover   = £168 020.
    Cost of goods sold   = £127 680.
    Purchases   = £129 860.
    Rate of turnover of stock   = 16 times.
    Gross profit percentage   = 24%

Chapter 29, Exercises set 29.4 – Balance Sheet interpretation, page 429.

---

1. (a) Capital owned £76 250; (b) Capital employed £101 250; (c) Working Capital = £18 250; (d) Profit = 14.1 per cent of Capital invested.
2. (a) Capital owned £38 125; (b) Capital employed £58 125; (c) There is not really enough working capital: the working capital ratio is only just above 1.
3. (a) Balance Sheet totals £94 860. Capital £47 130.
    (i) Fixed assets = £54 200.
    (ii) See text – amount of working capital = £7 930.
    (iii) Just about solvent, but in a fairly illiquid situation.
4. Balance Sheet totals £51 625, Current Account balances: Grouse £16 930; Moor £9 960; Current assets £44 825; Fixed assets £6 800; Liquid assets £21 625; Current Liabilities £2 795; Working Capital £42 030.
5. Balance Sheet totals £75 825.
    (a) Hopeful obviously made a loss in the year and also overdrew £8 250 as drawings.
    (b) He is short of working capital.
    (c) However, the acid test ratio shows he is *desperately* short of liquid capital. He has only one quarter of the immediate funds he needs to pay his debts and is already overdrawn at the bank by £6 250.
6. Balance Sheet totals £20 975.
7. Current Assets £24 500; Working Capital £18 000; Effect on Working Capital – reduced by £1 500; Effect on Capital of Dee and Jaye – each increased by £500.
8. (a) See text.
    (b) (i) Increase.
        (ii) Increase.
        (iii) No effect.
        (iv) No effect.
        (v) Decrease.
9. (a) A Capital £28 450
        B Liabilities £20 550.
        C Assets £41 000.
        D Deficiency £12 000.
        E Liabilities £100 000.
    (b) (i) Fixed assets.
        (ii) Long-term liabilities.
        (iii) Current liabilities.
        (iv) Current assets.
    (c) Current assets and Current liabilities.

10. (a) Both.
    (b) Balance Sheet
    (c) Both.
    (d) Balance Sheet.
    (e) Balance Sheet.
    (f) Profit and Loss Account.
    (g) Balance Sheet.
11. (a) Increase of £275 (profit).
    (b) No change.
    (c) Decrease of £175 (loss).
    (d) Decrease of £250 (anticipated loss).
    (e) Decrease of £25 (loss).
12. (a) £19 250.
    (b) £19 000.
    (c) £18 875.
    (d) £18 700.
    (e) £18 500.
    (f) £18 000.
    (g) £17 500.
13. Cash balance £9 678.
14. (a) Cash deficit of £710.
    (b) I would advise him that he is going to be short of cash. He
        could:
        (i) Arrange a bank overdraft to cover him over the
            period or,
        (ii) Reduce the proposed capital expenditure to (say)
            half the present figure – postponing the balance until
            later.

Chapter 30, Exercises set 30.1 – simple Control Accounts, page 441.

1. Balance on Control Account £4 063 debit.
2. Balance on Control Account £9 870 credit; £135 debit.
3. (a) See text. (b) Balance on Control Account £205 534 debit.
4. (a) Balance on Control Account £31 327 debit.
   (b) (i) There could be a posting error to one or more of the
       debtors' accounts. (ii) The entries do not show any
       Journal Entries (e.g. bad debts). Have we forgotten to
       analyse the Journal for these entries? (iii) Have the
       figures used for the Control Account been correctly
       extracted from the records?

Chapter 30, Exercises set 30.2 – more difficult Control Accounts, page 444.

1. (a) The accounts of debtors.
   (b) See text.
   (c) It represents the total outstanding debts, and should agree with the total balances on the debtors' accounts in the Debtors' Ledger.
2. Balance on Control Account £23 445. This represents the total owed to sundry creditors at this date.
3. Balance on Sales Control Account £592 850; Balance on Purchases Control Account £154 502.
4. Balance on Control Account = £52 400. Therefore we conclude that no matter where the error on the Trial Balance may be it certainly is *not* in the Sales Ledger.
5. (a) Balance on Bought Ledger Control Account = £153 783; Balances on Sales Ledger Control Account = £24 862 Debit; £932 Credit.
   (b) We conclude there is a £10 error on the Purchases Ledger somewhere.

Chapter 31, Exercises set 31.1 – amalgamations, page 450.

1. Capital: Flower £50 000, Rose £35 000; Balance Sheet totals of new busines £104 050. Shares of residue of profit £6 940 each.
2. Capital: Whitehead £77 630, Poole £53 085; Balance Sheet totals of new business £133 705.
3. Capitals: Brown £35 500; Jones £80 000; Balance Sheet totals of new business £131 000.
4. Capitals: A. £132 135; B. £30 510; Balance Sheet totals of new business £185 120.

Chapter 32, Exercises set 32.1 – purchase of a business, page 457.

1. Goodwill £7 250; Balance Sheet totals £70 000.
2. Goodwill £4 500; Balance Sheet totals £37 854.
3. Amount due to vendor £25 968. (Rules in advance = £350.)
4. Goodwill £10 425; Balance Sheet totals £104 475.

Chapter 33, Exercises set 33.1 – accounting for Bills of Exchange, page 474.

1. Ledger entries are: (a) Debit Purchases Account £9 500, and credit Ship Supplies Ltd, £9 500. (b) After entering the bill payable in the Bills Payable Book, Ship Supplies Ltd are debited with the bill and Bills Payable Account is credited; £9 500 in each case. (c) On the due date debit Bills Payable Account and credit Bank Account; £9 500 in each case.
2. Ledger entries are similar to the entries for Question 1.
3. Ledger entries are similar to the entries for Question 1.
4. Ledger entries are: (a) Credit Sales Account £9 500 and debit R. Watson £9 500. (b) After recording the bill receivable in the Bills Receivable Book, R. Watson is credited with £9 500 and Bills Receivable Account is debited with £9 500. (c) On the due date the Bank Account is debited with the money received and Bills Receivable Account is credited.
5. Ledger entries are: (a) As in 4 above; (b) As in 4 above; (c) Debit Bank Account with the full amount £9 500 and credit Bills Receivable Account; (d) Credit Bank Account with the discount (£9 500 $\times$ $^{12}/_{100}$ $\times$ $^{60}/_{365}$ = £187.40) and debit Discount on Bills Account.
6. Ledger entries are: (a) As in 4 above; (b) As in 4 above; (c) Debit Navigational Components Ltd, with the discounted value of the bill (£9 306.88) and credit Bills Receivable Account. Calculation of discount:
   $$£9\ 500 \times {}^{14}/_{100} \times {}^{53}/_{365} = £193.12$$
   (d) Debit Discount on Bills Account £193.12 and credit Bills Receivable Account to clear the bill, which has now been received.
7. (a) See text. (b) Debit R. Maxwell Account £9 800 (restoring the debt to the debtor); Credit Bank Account £9 800.
8. (a) See text. (b) All we need is a Journal Entry, debiting Z Ltd, (restore the debt to the debtor) £4 800 and crediting Bank Account with the cheque for £4 800 (payable to R Ltd). When posted to the ledger the book-keeping entries are complete.

Chapter 34, Exercises set 34.1 – the concepts and principles of accounting, page 483.

1. (a) See text.
   (b) The problem is that it muddles up the two aspects of entity, the business entity and the personal identity of the proprietor.

2. (a) See text.
   (b) A is responsible to the Board, through whom he is a steward to the shareholders of the company, but the employees might also feel that he owed them a duty.
3. (a) See text.
   (b) She is entitled to assume that the concern will continue to operate for the foreseeable future in much the same way as it has been operating over the last year.
4. (a) See text. (b) Duality is still important because it alone provides a self-balancing system which gives confidence to all that the accounts have been properly prepared.
5. (a) See text. (b) No, they do not, because a firm of this type of name would be expected to have an 'efficient' fleet of long distance haulage vehicles, whereas nearly all the present value of the motor vehicles is in the 'executive car' fleet.
6. (a) See text. (b) The accountant should view the value of the damaged plant as the value to a disinterested outsider – viewed objectively – to establish its true value after the fire.
7. (a) See text. (b) It should be referred to in a special 'Note to the Accounts', giving the Board's reasons for changing the established arrangements.
8. The student should explain why prudence is necessary, and then illustrate it by (a) explaining FIFO, LIFO, and AVCO treatments of stock and (b) explaining about provision for bad debts and provision for discounts.
9. (a) See text. (b) The student should have dealt with payments in advance and payments in arrears at *both* ends of the financial year.
10. (a) See text. (b) (i) The problem is to price goods in such a way that we can replace the stock out of the proceeds of sale and still be left with a good profit margin. (b) (ii) When depreciating assets we need to build up a fund, to replace the assets at the new, inflated prices and not at the old 'historical cost' price.

Index